THE GEOGRAPHY OF OPPORTUNITY

JAMES A. JOHNSON METRO SERIES

JAMES A. JOHNSON METRO SERIES

The Metropolitan Policy Program at the Brookings Institution is integrating research and practical experience into a policy agenda for cities and metropolitan areas. By bringing fresh analyses and policy ideas to the public debate, the program hopes to inform key decisionmakers and civic leaders in ways that will spur meaningful change in our nation's communities.

As part of this effort, the James A. Johnson Metro Series aims to introduce new perspectives and policy thinking on current issues and attempts to lay the foundation for longer term policy reforms. The series examines traditional urban issues, such as neighborhood assets and central city competitiveness, as well as larger metropolitan concerns, such as regional growth, development, and employment patterns. The James A. Johnson Metro Series consists of concise studies and collections of essays designed to appeal to a broad audience. While these studies are formally reviewed, some will not be verified like other research publications. As with all publications, the judgments, conclusions, and recommendations presented in the studies are solely those of the authors and should not be attributed to the trustees, officers, or other staff members of the Institution.

Also available in this series:

On growth and development

Edgeless Cities: Exploring the Elusive Metropolis
Robert E. Lang

Growth and Convergence in Metropolitan America
Janet Rothenberg Pack

Growth Management and Affordable Housing
Anthony Downs, editor

Laws of the Landscape: How Policies Shape Cities in Europe and America
Pietro S. Nivola

Reflections on Regionalism
Bruce J. Katz, editor

Sunbelt/Frostbelt: Public Policies and Market Forces in Metropolitan Development
Janet Rothenberg Pack, editor

On transportation

Still Stuck in Traffic: Coping with Peak-Hour Traffic Congestion
Anthony Downs

Taking the High Road: A Metropolitan Agenda for Transportation Reform
Bruce Katz and Robert Puentes, editors

On trends

Redefining Urban and Suburban America: Evidence from Census 2000, vol. 1
Bruce Katz and Robert E. Lang, editors

Redefining Urban and Suburban America: Evidence from Census 2000, vol. 2
Alan Berube, Bruce Katz, and Robert E. Lang, editors

On wealth creation

Building Assets, Building Credit: Creating Wealth in Low-Income Communities
Nicolas P. Retsinas and Eric S. Belsky, editors

Low-Income Homeownership: Examining the Unexamined Goal
Nicolas P. Retsinas and Eric S. Belsky, editors

Savings for the Poor: The Hidden Benefits of Electronic Banking
Michael A. Stegman

On other metro issues

Evaluating Gun Policy: Effects on Crime and Violence
Jens Ludwig and Philip J. Cook, editors

THE GEOGRAPHY OF OPPORTUNITY

Race and Housing Choice in Metropolitan America

Xavier de Souza Briggs
Editor

BROOKINGS INSTITUTION PRESS
Washington, D.C.

Library of Congress Cataloging-in-Publication data

The geography of opportunity : race and housing choice in metropolitan America / Xavier de Souza Briggs, editor.
p. cm.
Summary: "A multidisciplinary examination of the social and economic changes resulting from increased diversity and their implications for economic opportunity and growth given persistent patterns of segregation by race and class, offering both public policy and private initiatives that would respond to those challenges"—Provided by publisher.
Includes bibliographical references and index.
ISBN-13: 978-0-8157-0873-5 (paper : alk. paper)
ISBN-10: 0-8157-0873-4 (paper : alk. paper)
1. Discrimination in housing—United States. 2. Residential mobility—United States. 3. Housing—United States. 4. Housing policy—United States. 5. Low-income housing—United States. 6. Metropolitan areas—United States. I. De Souza Briggs, Xavier N. II. Title.
HD7288.76.U5G46 2005
363.5'99'00973—dc22 2005009628

9 8 7 6 5 4 3 2 1

The paper used in this publication meets minimum requirements of the American National Standard for Information Sciences—Permanence of Paper for Printed Library Materials: ANSI Z39.48-1992.

Typeset in Adobe Garamond

Composition by Cynthia Stock
Silver Spring, Maryland

Printed by R. R. Donnelley
Harrisonburg, Virginia

In memory of

JOHN KAIN

Contents

Part Two—Housing Opportunity for Low-Income Families

Part Three—Metropolitan Development and Policy Coalitions

Part Four—Conclusions

Foreword

WILLIAM JULIUS WILSON

At the opening of the twenty-first century, and for the first time in America's history, non-Hispanic whites constitute a minority of the total population in the United States' hundred largest cities. The significant influx of Latinos and other immigrants to urban areas and the steady out-migration of whites have changed the complexion of cities and, in the words of Eric Schmitt, have fueled "a renaissance in some urban centers and forced civic leaders to confront wrenching decisions on how to cope with a new and fast-changing citizenry."[1]

As metropolises are undergoing ethnic change, economic and residential life in the urban United States features a relentless decentralization. Outer-edge suburbs have become the regions of population growth, employment growth, and wealth creation. Many of the older areas—central cities and inner-ring suburbs—are left behind, with growing concentrations of poverty, particularly minority poverty, and in the words of Bruce Katz, "without the fiscal capacity to grapple with the consequences: joblessness, family fragmentation, and failing schools."[2] Although the relative rate of suburbanization has slowed—between 1970 and 1980 more than 95 percent of metropolitan growth nationwide was in the suburbs, but by 1996 it had dipped to 77 percent—from 1989 to 1996 more than twice as many upper- and middle-income households (7.4 million) left cities for suburbs than moved from suburbs to cities (3.5 million).[3]

This metropolitanwide population shift is especially problematic for the older central cities of the East and Midwest. As David Rusk, the former mayor of Albuquerque, points out, because these cities were unable to expand territorially through city-county annexation or consolidation, they did not reap such benefits of suburban growth as the rise of industrial parks in new residential subdivisions, shopping malls, and offices.[4] Central city residents, especially those who are restricted in their housing choice, see their economic and social prospects severely restricted by the walls that separate the city and its suburbs.

Given the increase in racial and ethnic diversity, uneven metropolitan growth, and the divide between cities and suburbs, the *Geography of Opportunity* is an important and timely publication. Although the focus of this volume is on the geography of housing choice, the problems of housing opportunity, as reflected in persistent segregation by race and income and unequal patterns of metropolitan development, are considered within a broader framework that links the fortunes of cities and suburbs, and the solutions proposed span local jurisdictions. These regional solutions—commonly put forth in previous years—have here been rediscovered to address problems that American cities and suburbs have in common. There are three main reasons for this rediscovery, according to Bruce Katz: one, the recognition that metropolitan areas constitute the real competitive units in the new economy; two, the growing awareness that complex issues such as air quality and traffic congestion cross political boundaries and are immune to localized fixes; and three, the coexistence of persistent joblessness in the central cities and labor shortages in the suburbs. This rediscovery is especially important for those most adversely affected by the uneven geography of opportunity, whereby the location of housing restricts their access to the new economy and increases their exposure to problems such as air pollution and highway congestion.

Supporters of the idea of regional solutions have attempted to increase awareness, especially among suburbanites, that the outcomes of city and suburban cooperation will not benefit cities or city residents alone. Regionalists cite the growing evidence that cities and suburbs are economically interdependent. Examples of this evidence include the finding that the higher the ratio of city-to-suburb per capita income, the higher metropolitan employment and income growth and the greater the increase in housing values; and the finding that improvements in central city capital stock also increase suburban housing values, suggesting, as Paul Gottlieb puts it, "that suburban residents may have an incentive to increase contributions toward city infrastructure."[5]

Metropolitan regions compete for jobs in the global economy. In an era of low transportation and information costs, high mobility, and intense global competition, a metropolitan region is at a severe competitive disadvantage if it lacks a healthy urban core. In the global economy, firms choose among regions when determining where to locate. A major factor in this decision is the health of the central city. According to the U.S. Department of Housing and Urban Development (HUD), even firms that choose to locate in suburban areas will select among those surrounding vibrant central cities.

Metropolitan areas that will remain competitive—or become competitive—are those with an efficient transportation network to link corporate executives with other parts of the United States and with countries around the world, a well-trained workforce, a concentration of professional services, good schools, first-class hospitals, and a major university and research center. Many of these elements cannot come solely from suburban areas. They call for a viable central city.[6] In other words, the key to the health of a metropolitan region is city-suburban *integration.* To achieve such integration, it is important to address, and indeed provide part of the motivation to address, disparities in the geography of opportunity, through which many (usually people of color and of low income) are denied access to housing in the communities with the resources to facilitate social mobility.

The image of the metropolitan area is changing. Bruce Katz and Jennifer Bradley maintain that "so much of the unhappiness of the cities is also the unhappiness of the suburbs."[7] The familiar perception of a beleaguered urban core surrounded by prosperous suburbs is giving way to a new perception in which both urban and suburban communities suffer from too-rapid growth in outlying areas and slowed growth or even absolute decline in older, inner, areas. Observers who think about cities and suburbs as related, not antithetical, as comprising a single economic and social reality, share a vision of regionalism that represents, as Xavier de Souza Briggs puts it in this volume, "the political movement to address the linked fortunes of cities and suburbs by using regional, or jurisdiction-spanning, solutions."

The vision of regionalism also recognizes that, because the dichotomy between cities and suburbs is frequently drawn too sharply, we often overlook the new reality: namely, that today's suburbs are not an undifferentiated band of safe and prosperous white communities. Indeed, there are two kinds of suburb. The older, inner suburbs adjacent to the city feature a crumbling tax base, a growing concentration of poor children in the public schools, an eroding job market, population decline, crime, disinvestment, and deserted commercial districts. The residents of these suburbs are as much victims of the uneven geography of housing opportunity as are the residents of the inner city. On the other hand, the newer, or outer, suburbs are gaining economically. But according to HUD, they are also "straining under sprawling growth, that creates traffic congestion, overcrowded schools, loss of open spaces, and other sprawl-related problems and a lack of affordable housing." As Katz and Bradley put it, they are "choking on development, and in many cases the local governments cannot provide the services that residents need or demand."

According to these writers, the vision of regionalism foresees a policy agenda that changes the rules of the development game, pools metropolitan resources, gives people access to all areas in the metropolis, and reforms governance. Reforms put forward to achieve the objective of city-suburban cooperation range from proposals to create metropolitan governments to proposals to share the tax base across the metropolitan area, proposals for collaborative metropolitan planning, and proposals for regional authorities to solve common problems.

Among the problems shared by many metropolises is a weak public transit system. A commitment to address this problem through a form of city-suburban collaboration would benefit residents of both the city and the suburbs. Theoretically, everyone would benefit from mobility within the metropolitan area, but especially inner-city residents, whose lack of housing choice is reflected in long and demanding commutes to jobs. Allow me to elaborate.

An inadequate public transit system not only increases reliance on automobiles, it also makes it difficult for those without cars, particularly inner-city residents, to get to suburban jobs. As shown in this volume, racial and ethnic segregation, which restricts minority access to suburban housing, exacerbates the situation. As a result, African Americans and Hispanics bear the brunt of unemployment. For example, even with commutes in excess of one hour, welfare recipients in Boston can access only 14 percent of the entry-level jobs in the fast-growth areas in the metropolitan region. In the Atlanta metropolitan area, according to HUD, less than half of the entry-level jobs are located within a quarter mile of a public transit system.

Greatly exacerbating the problems related to the geography of opportunity is urban sprawl. It is generally recognized that public investment in core infrastructure improvements (roads, transit, sewers, utilities) is important for private investment. Indeed, private investment, according to Henry Richmond, relies heavily on core infrastructure maintenance and improvement.[8] But what is not generally perceived is that core infrastructure investments, in turn, are dependent on factors of density and distance for their initial feasibility and efficient operation. However, urban sprawl has made public investment in core infrastructure more costly and difficult. From 1970 to 1990, the urbanized area of American metropolitan regions expanded from eight to fifteen times as fast as population growth. As industrial and residential development spreads across an ever-broadening geographical area, more transportation costs and inefficiency are imposed on business, more urban minorities are further removed from access to jobs, and more pollution and destruction of natural resources occur.

Traffic congestion is a worsening problem, as sprawl raises the number and length of automobile trips. Even minor suburban roadways have become channels for thousands of commuters to and from new office complexes, factories, and shopping malls. According to Bruce Katz, urban road congestion increased by more than 22 percent between 1982 and 1994, and traffic congestion grew worse in forty-two major metropolitan areas between 1988 and 1994. In the fifty largest metropolitan areas, travel delays and added fuel consumption imposed excess costs of $51 billion in 1993, an increase of 6 percent from 1992. HUD reports that congested freeways are a national epidemic.

As traffic congestion increases, as farmlands and open space disappear, and as a sense of community vanishes, all families in a metropolitan area, not just those restricted to the inner city and inner suburbs, are affected.[9] Studies by Katz and by HUD reveal that an increasing number of businesses and households, both suburban and urban, recognize these costs and are interested in changing the policies that facilitate urban sprawl. Such recognition is aided by a vision of the metropolitan region as a single economic and social reality.

The vision of regionalism is especially important for those whose chances in life are limited by the uneven geography of opportunity. As is so clearly argued in this volume, proposals to address inequities in housing opportunities should be included in any discussion of regional policy. The thoughtful essays in this volume provide us with just the sort of material to inform such a discussion.

Notes

1. Eric Schmitt, "Whites in Minority in Largest Cities, the Census Shows," *New York Times,* April 30, 2001, p. A1.

2. Bruce Katz, "Beyond City Limits: The Emergence of a New Metropolitan Agenda," Brookings, April 1999, p. 1.

3. U.S. Department of Housing and Urban Development, *The State of Cities* (Government Printing Office, 1999).

4. David Rusk, *Cities without Suburbs* (Washington: Woodrow Wilson Center, 1993).

5. Paul D. Gottlieb, *The Effects of Poverty on Metropolitan Area Economic Performance* (Washington: National League of Cities, 1998), p. 24.

6. Derek Bok, "Cities and Suburbs," Aspen Institute Domestic Strategy Group, Washington, 1994.

7. Bruce Katz and Jennifer Bradley, "Divided We Sprawl," *Atlantic Monthly,* December 1999, pp. 26–33. Quotation is on p. 28.

8. Henry Richmond, "Program Design," American Land Institute, Portland, Ore., 1997.

9. There are also significant fiscal costs associated with urban sprawl. Spending on bridges, roads, sewers, and other public works escalates because of the high cost of extending existing networks and constructing new systems. HUD reports that in communities marked by sprawl, road costs in 1999 were 25–33 percent higher, utility costs 18–25 percent higher, and municipal and school district costs 3–11 percent higher than in sprawl-free communities.

Preface

As the nation changes, thanks to large-scale immigration and other demographic forces, sprawling growth at the local level, and a changing economy, ensuring equality of opportunity in America has become ever more challenging. Policymakers, activists, and researchers confront a host of puzzles about how the nation should adapt to the scope and scale of such change, particularly in the varied metropolitan regions where eight in ten Americans now live and work. Some of the most important puzzles link race and place to opportunity and well-being.

The project that led to this book was cosponsored by the Civil Rights Project at Harvard University, Brookings Institution's Metropolitan Policy Program, and Harvard's Joint Center for Housing Studies. With increased racial and ethnic diversity, persistent segregation by race and income, and uneven metropolitan development patterns as our primary concerns, in November 2001 we convened a symposium of researchers, practitioners, and policy officials in Washington to discuss a set of invited papers. The planning that followed that meeting led to the preparation of this book. For a sharper editorial focus, we solicited some new papers to fill important gaps in coverage—for example, on changes in the financial sector and the targeting of minority communities by predatory lenders and on the preferences Americans report regarding the racial make-up of their communities. Meanwhile, we benefited enormously from the wealth of demographic analyses published after the 2001 meeting, based largely on data from the 2000 census.

The contributors to this volume are economists, sociologists, urban planners, civil rights attorneys, political scientists, and policy advocates. Beyond the depth and breadth of their data, together these authors bring decades of experience in policy analysis and advocacy as well as a deep respect for the historical context of these issues in American public life. This book is our effort to help the nation face up to change in ways that expand opportunity, ensure equal rights, and extend hope to all.

Acknowledgments

Many generous souls made the possibility of this book a reality. In the spring of 2001, Christopher Edley and Gary Orfield, codirectors of the Civil Rights Project (CRP) at Harvard University, invited me to call for papers for a symposium to be held in November that year, and they offered unstinting encouragement at every stage that followed. At the CRP, Marilyn Byrne and Lori Kelley were the intrepid organizers who pulled our symposium together, contacted authors at multiple stages of revision, proofread drafts, and kept us calm.

The cosponsoring organizations, Harvard's Joint Center for Housing Studies and Brookings's Metropolitan Policy Program, supported this venture from the first. Directors Nicholas Retsinas (Harvard) and Bruce Katz (Brookings) recognized the importance of directly addressing issues of race, space, and opportunity as central to the future of housing and community change in America. I am deeply grateful to both.

Margery Austin Turner and the Urban Institute hosted our symposium, Housing Opportunity, Civil Rights, and the Regional Agenda, in Washington. I am grateful to her, to everyone who contributed a paper for that gathering, and to the dozens of other researchers, practitioners, government officials, and policy advocates who acted as discussants or otherwise helped develop the ideas.

The Rockefeller Foundation supported the symposium, as well as our ongoing efforts to use this book as a tool for public education and policy dialogue. At the foundation, Julia Lopez and Darren Walker championed our work and continue to push us forward.

Alan Altshuler and Langley Keyes, my colleagues at Harvard's Kennedy School and the Massachusetts Institute of Technology, respectively, read and generously commented on the drafts of my chapters, as did Ingrid Gould Ellen of New York University. Their advice was invaluable, and I am in their debt (even more than before). Other colleagues and friends—notably, David Ellwood, George Galster, Herb Gans, Sandy Jencks, Phil Thompson, and William Julius Wilson—contributed more indirectly, though no less critically, to my understanding of race, community, and inequality in America, and so these pages bear their imprint as well.

The year I spent as the Martin Luther King Jr. Visiting Fellow in the Department of Urban Studies and Planning at MIT, in 2002–03, contributed greatly to the progress of this volume, and to carry out the work in Dr. King's symbolic shadow was an honor I will always treasure. Department heads Bish Sanyal and Larry Vale supported me generously and later made it possible for me to make MIT a wonderful new home for my work.

The contributors to this volume endured my lengthy feedback—particularly about avoiding jargon and remembering the bigger picture, the public conversation in which housing opportunity is too often invisible or obscured—as well as the arduous process of making a broad subject focused without making it narrow. I appreciate their patience, their hard work, and their continued friendship.

Chris Kelaher, our acquisitions editor at Brookings, shepherded the project with the right mix of appreciation and skepticism at critical moments, and managing editor Janet Walker and copyeditor Diane Hammond helped us get the manuscript in shape with superb professionalism and attention to detail.

My family—Cynthia and Angela—put up with many weekends and late nights at the keyboard or on the phone. Thank you.

Finally, I thank Bill Apgar for awakening my interest in housing, Bob Crain for teaching me how to think systematically about segregation and its consequences, and people in the South Bronx, Rio de Janeiro, Cape Town, Mumbai, Salt Lake City, San Francisco, and many other urban places for letting me work alongside them, learning how to build community from the ground up. I am also grateful to my students and to the many community leaders, former colleagues at the U.S. Department of Housing and Urban Development, other dedicated public officials, activists, and educators whose work is an inspiration and whose vision is a guide.

THE GEOGRAPHY OF OPPORTUNITY

1

Introduction

XAVIER DE SOUZA BRIGGS

> Fundamental to the American Dream is somewhere to call home—a safe and welcoming "anchor place" where families are raised and memories are formed. Furthermore, housing must be viewed in the context of the community in which it is located. Improvements in housing need to be linked to improvements in schools, community safety, transportation and job access.
>
> —Report of the Bipartisan Millennial Housing Commission Appointed by the Congress of the United States (2002)

> "Community". . . means homogeneity of race, class and, especially, home values.
>
> —Mike Davis, *City of Quartz*

This is a book about closing the gap between the nation that we are becoming and the nation that we have, thus far, known how to be. By any measure, the United States is fast becoming the most racially and ethnically diverse society in history. During the 1990s, four of five new additions to the population—and two of three to the labor force—were people of color, and most big cities in America became "majority minority" for the first time in history. One-third of all population growth in the 1990s resulted from immigration—80 percent of it from Asia, Africa, Latin America, or the Caribbean.[1] And these trends are projected to continue in the decades ahead.

Nowhere are the opportunities and challenges posed by increased social diversity more significant than in metropolitan areas—the cities and suburbs where eight in ten Americans now live. As a nation, we have a long history of ambivalence toward diversity in our midst, and as Mike Davis underscores bluntly above, this ambivalence is not limited to foreign-born immigrants.

Together, these facts pose a distinctly metropolitan dilemma, and that dilemma is the focus of this book: How should America's cities and suburbs respond to dramatically increased racial and ethnic diversity given a history of inequality and the persistence of segregated communities? More specifically, how can we ensure opportunity and security for all given persistent patterns of segregation by race and class—patterns complicated by the unsustainable growth machine that we have come to know as "sprawl"? Compared with their counterparts in European and other wealthy regions, America's metropolitan areas are both very sprawling and very segregated by race and class, a dual pattern that creates what scholars have termed an uneven "geography of opportunity."[2] Understanding and changing that geography is crucial if America is to improve outcomes in education, employment, safety, health, and other vital areas over the next generation. I begin with a look at why this imperative is so invisible in the nation's public life.

The Missing Diversity Issue

Not all issues tied to social diversity receive equal billing in America. Affirmative action in education and the job market are understandably visible and controversial, given persistent racial inequality, a retrenchment in spending on social problems over the past three decades, and the nation's ambivalence about civil rights and race-based policy.[3] In the case of education, attention follows controversy and specific, high-stakes policy decisions. The high-profile Supreme Court decisions upholding certain minority preferences in university admissions brought renewed public inquiry and debate, as did the fiftieth anniversary of *Brown* v. *Board of Education* (1954), the landmark case that nullified official segregation by race in the nation's public schools. Whatever one's politics, attention is sorely needed—both to what diversity means in America, given our past and present, and to how the nation should respond to increased diversity and persistent racial inequality in ways that are consistent with its core values. Access to

1. Katz and Lang (2003).
2. Briggs (2003); Galster and Killen (1995); Ihlanfeldt (1999); Pastor (2001); Squires (2002).
3. Edley (1996).

jobs and educational opportunity is undeniably crucial, although specific policies to ensure fair and equitable access are often tricky to implement.[4]

Compare those high-profile challenges to a much less visible—and arguably more intractable—challenge, one inextricably linked to education and economic opportunity: the challenge to ensure that people of all backgrounds enjoy access to housing in communities that serve as steppingstones to opportunity, political influence, and broader social horizons rather than as isolated and isolating traps with second-class support systems.[5] This more invisible challenge defines the still-missing agenda for social equity in America, and it is not limited to an agenda for the inner-city "ghetto" neighborhoods that still absorb the media. A growing body of empirical evidence indicates that racial segregation is not merely correlated with unequal social and economic outcomes but also specifically contributes to worsening inequality in metropolitan areas, which drive the nation's and the world's economy.[6] Moreover, the evidence debunks a central myth in American public and private life—that members of racial and ethnic minority groups who gain higher skills and incomes eliminate any barriers to housing choice, escaping the narrow geography of opportunity that confronted so many of their parents. As Sheryll Cashin argues provocatively in her recent book *The Failures of Integration*, the challenge to make communities of opportunity widely accessible is no less urgent because some members of racial minority groups express "integration fatigue" or seek what Camille Charles describes, in chapter 3, as a racial comfort zone.[7]

As I outline below, two recent trends in American public life make it urgent to rethink these issues. First, the geography of race and class represents a crucial litmus test for the new "regionalism"—the political movement to address the linked fortunes of cities and suburbs with regional, or jurisdiction-spanning, solutions. Driven in part by growing concerns about the high social and economic costs of sprawl—the dominant pattern of U.S. metropolitan development—regionalism has gained considerable momentum since the early 1990s. Regionalism has variously emphasized economic competitiveness, environmental sustainability, social equity, and other issues, sometimes under the banner of "smart growth," or growth management, to curb sprawl.

The second major trend is the disappearance of housing policy as a public issue over the past two decades—that is, besides discussion of interest rates, taxation, and other economic policies that affect the housing costs and assets of mostly middle- and upper-income households. Housing is all but invisible as a

4. Clotfelter (2004); Guinier and Torres (2002).
5. Briggs (2004); Massey and Denton (1993).
6. Cutler and Glaeser (1997); Galster (1987).
7. Cashin (2004).

social policy issue, and this is particularly problematic in light of the nation's growing diversity and sharp economic inequality.

More *Pluribus*: Now What?

A flurry of reports and headlines, many of them based on 2000 census data, highlight important, ongoing changes in who we are as a nation and how we live. The reality of unprecedented racial and ethnic change, driven by immigration, is lost on few people in America. But too often the "So what?" and "Now what?" of that change receive only fleeting or sensationalized attention. The difficult tasks now are to understand what is driving the social and economic changes we will face as a far more diverse society, to examine the implications of those changes for economic opportunity and growth, to consider needed responses (public policy and private action) in light of the hard-won lessons of the past, and to build constituencies that will give those responses a chance.

To address those tasks, this project began with a dialogue among the Civil Rights Project at Harvard University, which focuses on bringing academic research to bear on public policy and practice on behalf of racial justice, and two collaborating institutions known for public policy research: the Brookings Institution's Metropolitan Policy Program (focused on the changing fortunes of cities and suburbs) and Harvard's Joint Center for Housing Studies (focused on housing markets). At the outset, we were struck by the dearth of well-developed research in several areas:

—The forces driving economic and racial segregation in housing patterns in increasingly diverse metropolitan areas.

—The role of growth management, a magnet for activism and reform, given the concerns about unhealthy sprawl, in shaping racial equity and housing opportunity.

—And the politics and effectiveness of efforts to reduce geographic barriers to racial justice and more equitable opportunity.

There is a large literature on the role of race in housing, to be sure, but rarely is the issue considered in the context of metropolitan politics and reform proposals. It is the multiple dimensions of this challenge—how to create access to communities of opportunity by expanding housing choices—that define the focus of this volume.

The volume addresses four main questions:

—What forces limit choice in housing and community location, defining an uneven geography of opportunity by race and class?

—Why is that uneven geography important? That is, what are its consequences for the social and economic prospects of people in America's cities and suburbs?

—What special barriers to housing opportunity confront low-income families, including the minority poor?

—What are the lessons, for politics and policy, of efforts made to expand housing choices and thereby *change* the geography of opportunity?

As noted above, the risks posed by the uneven geography of opportunity, not to mention the challenges associated with changing it, are all but invisible on the public agenda as well as in the nation's intellectual life. When social equity issues in housing receive attention at all, it is the affordability crisis, not the geography of exclusion, that attracts attention. In her best-selling *Nickel and Dimed*, for example, journalist Barbara Ehrenreich vividly captures the near impossibility of juggling dead-end jobs and high-cost, often unfit housing. The 2000 census indicates that some 28 million American families pay exorbitant costs for housing, according to federal standards of affordability. The cost gap widened sharply during the 1990s, as housing markets tightened in many cities and the stock of affordable housing continued its long-run disappearing act. Federal subsidies for low- and moderate-income families fell so sharply and abruptly following the second session of Congress in 1996 that journalist Jason DeParle labeled it "the year that housing died." America's faith that the private market, unaided by government, would meet all housing needs had evidently reached a new (and costly) pinnacle. As DeParle observed: "Housing problems are far more central to the lives of the poor than a number of issues—immunizations, school lunches—that have made recent headlines. The cost of shelter breaks the budgets of low-income Americans, crowds them into violent ghettos, far from good jobs and schools—or both."[8]

High costs are understandably more visible, but location, as DeParle hints and every realtor knows, helps define the real value of one's housing. What is more, race and location together make housing rather unique among public policy issues in America. Whereas most issues primarily engender debate about *who* (the policy target group), *what* (the design of public subsidy programs or regulation), and *how much* (public generosity relative to private obligation), housing is also, unavoidably, about *where*. To underscore this point, the important spatial dimensions of health and school access issues—primary care availability in low-income neighborhoods, school choice, and so forth—largely reflect segregated housing patterns.

Housing policymaking and the delivery of housing are fraught with territorial debates and the politics of place, since the attractiveness of places has, over the nation's history, been closely identified in the public mind with the race and

8. Jason DeParle, "The Slamming Door," *New York Times Magazine*, October 20, 1996, p. 52. See also Ehrenreich (2001). For census numbers, see Bipartisan Millennial Housing Commission (2002); Joint Center for Housing Studies (2003).

class traits of the people who live in those places.[9] The American dilemma related to increased racial and ethnic diversity therefore confronts a sobering legacy, and that dilemma has assumed a distinctively metropolitan character.

As John Goering notes in chapter 6 of this volume, in the late 1960s the U.S. government declared the racial and economic segregation of America's cities and suburbs an urgent national problem. On that challenge, it was thought, rested many of the country's hopes for closing gaps in education, jobs, health, safety, and other aspects of opportunity and well-being, as well as the gaps in understanding and trust that polarize our politics along class and race lines. As Ed Goetz and others note in chapter 11, by the early 1970s a number of states and localities pursued inclusionary and "fair share" housing policies, and some created options for overriding exclusionary land use decisions at the local level—"anti-snob zoning," for example.[10]

But after thirty years of modest experimenting with wider housing choice, it appears that the nation primarily lacks the will, not the way, to reduce persistent segregation by race and class. Outside of a handful of progressive, self-consciously integrated neighborhoods and small cities, racial segregation has, as a public concern, receded into memory, the stuff of civil rights lore and the integrationist aims of a bygone era. Those aims are familiar to many advocates and academics and certainly to a small and struggling "fair housing" field, but while opinion polls show greater tolerance of racial diversity in neighborhoods, the explicit aim of reducing segregation by race is not widely supported beyond that base of specialists.[11] For most Americans, in fact, the racial desegregation agenda is old news, because the problem, they believe, has long been solved: Fighting discrimination in the private housing market is thought to be government's only obligation, and as we will see, the public wrongly assumes that such discrimination is rare. Moreover, as I highlight in the next chapter, there have been significant declines in key measures of racial segregation. So perhaps, claim observers, the problem is resolving itself.

As for segregation by income level or social class, the prevailing public view is

9. Danielson (1976); Haar (1996); Jackson (2000).

10. For a concise overview of this history, and a review and update of fair share housing allocation, regional housing assessments, inclusionary zoning, and other policy and planning tools, see Meck, Retzlaff, and Schwab (2003).

11. In this chapter, I use *race* as shorthand to indicate identities defined, officially, by race and ethnicity. For example, *black* and *white* refer to members of those racial groups who do not identify as having Hispanic *ethnic* origins. *Hispanic,* meanwhile, is an ethnic group identifier inclusive of any race with which the members of that group identify. These distinctions are not canonical or universally accepted, as observers have noted for decades, and the creation of an official multiracial identification option in the 2000 census only adds to the complexity of distinguishing people in America on the basis of race. On trends in identity and self-identification over time, see Perlmann and Waters (2002); Bean and Stevens (2003); Alba and Nee (2003). On the history and politics of racial categories in the United States, including census practice, see Nobles (2000).

even more straightforward and less encumbered by a sense of public obligation: Surely people should be able to live wherever they can afford to live, among whomever they want? Segregation produces largely homogeneous communities, and certain kinds of homogeneity, as Mike Davis implies in the quotation above, are thought to provide a kind of insurance on property wealth, as well as the next generation's school and career prospects.

The shift away from inclusionary aims in the nation's mood and politics has been widely documented and discussed, as have the huge disparities produced by a generation of economic and social change in America.[12] Since the 1960s, on the whole, the picture has become starker: Cities lost jobs (and even in the 1990s gained fewer than the suburbs), poverty became significantly more concentrated geographically, and middle-class votes and political power likewise left the cities and older suburbs, where minorities remain disproportionately concentrated.[13] With the exception of a few measures, racial disparities in education, health, earnings, and wealth either persisted or widened in the 1980s and 1990s. In general, whites fared best, Asian Americans bifurcated into successful and unsuccessful subgroups, and median outcomes for blacks, Hispanics, and Native Americans were poorest.[14]

What is more, the stakes associated with geographic disparities by race rose considerably. Whether measured by median family income, poverty rate, unemployment, or other indicators, the gap between cities and suburbs widened dramatically in the post–World War II period, and the gaps *among* suburbs—particularly between affluent bedroom suburbs and mixed-income, more racially diverse suburban communities—have recently widened as well.[15] School failure is, if anything, more closely tied to segregation by race and class than it was thirty years ago, because millions of families with the best housing choices have exited diverse central cities for more homogeneous suburban school districts.[16] The mismatch between where many groups of job seekers live and where jobs are growing is greater than it was then, in part because of the increasingly decentralized pattern that economists call job sprawl. And newer threats—the crack cocaine epidemic, AIDS risk tied to intravenous drug use by addicts concentrated in high-poverty areas, and the long-run stressors, or "weathering," associated with living in high-risk, high-crime environments—reinforce the links among place of residence, physical and mental health, and life prospects. These links appear to be much sharper in the United States than in other wealthy nations, a fact that reflects this nation's sprawling local growth patterns, its history of race relations,

12. Rieder (1985); Weir (1998).

13. Jargowsky (1997); Dreier, Mollenkopf, and Swanstrom (2001); Massey and Denton (1993); Orfield (2002); Wilson (1987).

14. Blank (2001).

15. Ellen (1999); Ihlanfeldt (1999); Orfield (2002).

16. Clotfelter (2004; Frankenberg and Lee (2003).

the laissez-faire character of its local job markets, and the form and functions of its social safety net. Other inequities include environmental injustices, such as the disproportionate concentration of hazardous facilities, and their awful spillover effects, in low-income and minority communities.[17]

Although poverty became somewhat less concentrated in urban ghettos and racial minorities less city bound in the 1990s, it is not as though access to opportunity is now ensured for the nation's increasingly diverse population. Since tools for regulating land development at the local level were developed in the United States a century ago, diversity of race and class has been contained, ensuring that disadvantage is concentrated in particular places.[18] In the 1990s, as the population became more diverse, it was not the fact of containment that changed significantly but the shape of the "container," which morphed to include many at-risk suburbs, not just central cities. Because of the way communities develop physically in America—the way they sprawl and also tend to exclude lower-status people—the missing agenda for social equity turns out to hinge in part on a fledgling movement to create the safe, economically competitive, physically healthy, and environmentally sustainable development—"smarter" community growth—that would benefit people of all backgrounds.[19]

A key question is whether growth can be made more socially equitable as well. The movement for more sustainable patterns of community growth gained considerable momentum in the 1990s, but its success will depend to a great extent on the ability of leaders inside and outside government to recognize windows of opportunity, offer novel frames that change the face of divisive issues, and forge innovative coalitions.[20] Those political factors, in turn, will reflect how we think and talk about race, privilege, and opportunity in America.

Segregation Debates Old and New

Whereas advocacy and scholarship often emphasize the goal of stable racial integration at the neighborhood level,[21] the real priority is creating access for all, regardless of race and class, to communities of opportunity—whether neighborhoods or entire municipalities—with good schools, public services, and economic prospects. There are several reasons to redefine the challenge in this way. First, while it would be naïve to ignore the strong association, for a century now, between racial segregation (specifically) and economic inequality, in an increasingly diverse nation, racial integration per se is far too rough a proxy for real

17. See Ihlanfeldt and Sjoquist (1998); Ellen, Mijanovich, and Dillman (2001); Briggs (2003); Pastor (2001).

18. Jackson (2000).

19. Squires (2002).

20. Orfield (2002); Rusk (1999).

21. Galster (1990); Ellen (2000); Massey and Denton (1993).

access to opportunity. For more and more families in America, "making it" to the suburbs and a somewhat integrated neighborhood no longer ensures access to the schools, workplaces, valuable social networks, and other institutions that shape opportunity so powerfully.

Second, wider class segregation *within* racial groups over the past thirty years—what Robert Reich famously calls "the secession of the successful"—also makes racial integration a less and less reliable proxy for expanded opportunity.[22]

Third, neighborhood-level integration is often not a realistic hope, at least not in the short term, with rapid immigration and consumers' housing preferences pushing hard in the direction of ethnic enclaves. Add to that the reality that not all segregation is bad: Immigrant ethnic enclaves, for example, help millions of families find their footing and get ahead in America, while enclaves of native-born minorities can likewise be viable if public and private investment remain strong.

Fourth, as Camille Charles explores in chapter 3, support for racial integration per se is waning among minorities even as the attitudes reported by whites reflect greater tolerance.[23] But the desire for better schools, safer streets, and more economically viable communities remains strong and universal.

Fifth and finally, the scale of demographic change that the nation faces and the stakes involved in local decisions about how communities accommodate growth together suggest an opportunity to make social equity a part of the conversation about managing growth. Equity includes access to affordable housing regardless of race or ethnic background. While it is not clear that neighborhood racial integration is the most promising banner behind which to promote this goal, communities that exclude low- and moderate-income housing through various limits on development do tend to be less racially diverse, contributing to a segregated society.[24] These places have removed—or long neglected to build—entry points for a wide range of families.

Admittedly, the direct link between greater social equity—including racial equity—and more sustainable patterns of local development is easier to make in seminar than in the real world of politics and policymaking. Some advocates contend that denser, more transit-oriented patterns of metropolitan development, together with increased investment in cities and older suburbs, will attract whites to older areas and improve minorities' access to suburban jobs. But the growing interest in curbing sprawl has not thus far had a significant impact on the mechanisms that fragment metropolitan areas politically or segregate them

22. Reich (1992).

23. See also Bobo (2001).

24. The strongest link between local land use controls and racial diversity appears to work through rental housing: Over time, restricting rental development is strongly associated with having a smaller black and Hispanic population. See Pendall (2000); Pendall and others, chapter 10, this volume.

along race and class lines. Efforts to manage unplanned growth could actually make segregation worse, not better, as Rolf Pendall and his coauthors explain in chapter 10. And some aspects of decentralized or sprawling development appear to *benefit* people of color by enhancing access to low-cost housing—for example, entry-level homes where suburban land is cheap.[25] Also, sprawling, fast-growing "elastic" cities, most of them in the Sun Belt, do not reflect the entrenched patterns of segregation that mark former industrial cities in the Rust Belt. For the most part, places that had lower levels of segregation at the beginning of the 1990s saw the largest reductions in segregation over the decade.[26]

Careful observers and practitioners of "metropolitics" differ considerably over how to forge the coalitions needed to create the changes an equitable development agenda might require. Should cities and older suburbs organize at the state government level around their shared fiscal interests? Should advocates lead with race or consciously avoid traditional civil rights strategies and other race-based approaches? Should leaders build support for the common-fortunes principle known as regionalism, a powerful but rather abstract idea? Or should specific, linked problems be chosen—such as shortages of affordable housing, transportation inequities, and limited access to jobs—that a "big tent" of political interests might care about? This book will not resolve those important questions, but we hope to illuminate them in significant ways.

Plan and Perspective of the Book

At the core of this book is a concern for helping communities handle increased racial and ethnic diversity in ways that deliver on the promise of equal opportunity. Our focus is on the geography of housing choice—where people live in urban and suburban America, who their neighbors are, and how those patterns affect their opportunities in education, the job market, health, and other important domains. The authors have no single view on these challenges, emphasizing distinct tasks within the larger project of accommodating unprecedented diversity. What is more, they do not hold to any party line on how public policy should handle race, the legacy of the past, or the issue of defining and ensuring access to opportunity. Some contributors argue for universal policies to ensure that affordable housing can be found across a wider geography, overcoming long-standing barriers of race *and* class, while others stress the need for more targeted, group-specific strategies. But the contributors share a set of values and broad political perspectives that should be stated at the outset—that effective public policy must address the failures of the market to deliver meaningful choice regardless of race, that the nation bears a special responsibility for those

25. Glaeser and Kahn (2004).
26. Glaeser and Vigdor (2003).

who have faced historical disadvantages, and that tackling the uneven geography of opportunity is crucial to the future of the American experiment as a whole and, in particular, to the promise of equal opportunity.

The next chapter provides a critical look at what drives metropolitan growth patterns in America, at the changing geography of race and opportunity associated with those growth patterns, and at the social and economic consequences of that geography. I focus primarily on changes in racial segregation: The number of exclusively white communities has declined significantly in recent decades, for example, yet many integrating communities are in "at-risk" suburbs, with the crime, school failure, and other problems more typical of central cities. I then consider the best available evidence on the consequences of segregated housing patterns for access to good schools and job opportunities, noting the growing body of evidence on health impacts as well.

The chapters in part 1, "Housing Choice, Racial Attitudes, and Discrimination," consider the major forces that shape housing choice in America, including racial attitudes and avoidance patterns, discrimination in the housing market, and the shifting behavior of financial institutions. In chapter 3, Camille Charles shows how changing racial attitudes and neighborhood preferences help determine the make-up of the communities in which people of various backgrounds live. She offers compelling evidence that race per se, not merely race-related class prejudices, powerfully shape consumer views on which neighbors and neighborhoods are desirable. Moreover, there is a troubling hierarchy—a racial totem pole of preferred neighbors—that puts whites on top and blacks on the bottom of the preferences of both whites and minorities, including fast-growing immigrant groups. In chapter 4, Margery Austin Turner and Stephen L. Ross show how persistent patterns of racial discrimination—unequal terms of sale or rent, "steering" by real estate agents, and other tactics—shape the housing search for people of various racial backgrounds. The authors suggest ways that civil rights enforcement and education efforts should respond as discrimination becomes more subtle and thus more difficult to detect and punish. In chapter 5, William Apgar and Allegra Calder examine massive shifts in America's capital markets, including the rise of subprime and "predatory" mortgage lending, which heavily targets minority communities and threatens hard-won gains in minority homeownership and wealth creation. The authors outline what should be done to promote more equitable access to capital and to protect family assets, regardless of race.

Part 2, "Housing Opportunity for Low-Income Families": Programs meant to help low- and moderate-income families, many of them racial minorities, have too often exacerbated geographic barriers to opportunity, for example, by concentrating poor families in dangerous buildings and distressed neighborhoods. In chapter 6, John Goering, reviewing the history and scholarly evaluation of the federal Moving to Opportunity experiment, explores the promise of reforming such programs. He focuses in particular on what can be learned from efforts to deconcentrate poverty by helping families to leave ghetto neighborhoods. In chapter 7, James Rosenbaum, Stefanie DeLuca, and Tammy Tuck examine the social consequences of the most famous of these housing mobility programs—Chicago's court-ordered Gautreaux program, which helped thousands of very low-income, mostly black families leave high-poverty public housing for private apartments in the city and suburbs of Chicago. Focusing on Gautreaux's suburban movers and how they adapted to mostly white, middle-income communities, Rosenbaum and his coauthors suggest that movers' norms and capabilities can change dramatically in the context of a safer and more supportive community, notwithstanding the race and class differences between the in-movers and their suburban neighbors.

Susan Popkin and Mary Cunningham provide crucial evidence in chapter 8 on one of the most important shifts in U.S. housing policy in the past generation—the move to demolish much-maligned public housing projects. Focusing on Chicago, where all of the city's high-rise projects are being removed under an unprecedented transformation plan, Popkin and Cunningham warn of families that face homelessness, continued segregation by race and income, and other challenges when they leave the projects without adequate support. Addressing the intersection of law and program implementation, in chapter 9, veteran civil rights attorney Philip Tegeler examines the long-standing neglect of desegregation incentives in federal housing and community development programs and presents promising ideas for reform.

Part 3, "Metropolitan Development and Policy Coalitions": If the uneven geography of opportunity poses an essentially metropolitan dilemma in a changing nation, what key policy decisions and political forces will define the solutions? Since state and local land use policy, in particular, has so often been an instrument of exclusion, in chapter 10, Rolf Pendall, Arthur Nelson, Casey Dawkins, and Gerrit Knaap critically examine prospects for joining the goals of smarter growth, affordable housing, and racial equity. In chapter 11, Edward Goetz, Karen Chapple, and Barbara Lukermann discuss the rise and fall of an innovative commitment to creating a "fair share" of affordable housing throughout one major metropolitan area, the Twin Cities region. Because the region is often touted as a pacesetter in the movement for regional problem solving and because it became significantly more diverse, in terms of both race and income, in the 1980s and 1990s, the authors' findings are sobering: Fair share housing persists mainly in name, and the unraveling of this important public policy reflects the loss of both the financial and the political capital that metropolitan areas will need as they absorb much of the nation's increased diversity. Finally, in chapter 12, Mara Sidney analyzes the dual—and too often schizophrenic—agenda for expanding housing opportunity, showing how local advocates for fair housing (regardless of race) and affordable housing (for people with low or moderate income) either seize or miss opportunities to forge effective coalitions. She focuses on how state and local contexts affect the impact of federal policies on the issue framing public education, civil rights enforcement, and other strategies that housing advocates employ.

Part 4, "Conclusions": In chapter 13, Angela Glover Blackwell and Judith Bell, drawing on their experience at the leading edge of the movement for "equitable development," examine specific cases of applying that paradigm to state and local policymaking. Blackwell and Bell also outline a vision of leadership development that embraces and capitalizes on the nation's growing racial and ethnic diversity. In chapter 14, I conclude the book with an assessment of the politics of race and opportunity that define the housing issue and an outline of the range of public policies and private choices that will be needed to change the geography of opportunity. I emphasize the importance of distinguishing policies that *expand* one's housing choices from those that *protect* one's ability to exercise the choices available or that specifically *encourage* one to make better, more informed choices. I also highlight the folly of continuing more limited, piecemeal efforts, including a narrow approach to enforcing civil rights.

Rethinking Priorities

I argue above that the segregation of neighborhoods and entire jurisdictions by race and class is largely invisible, both on the public agenda and in the nation's intellectual life. To focus on the latter for a moment, in recent years some of the nation's most respected thinkers have urged a focus on the single issue (or two) that provides the greatest leverage to address increased economic inequality in the United States. Educational achievement is one such favorite.[27] Clearly, educational success is so important to earnings and wealth—and those so important to every other indicator of well-being—that the educational achievement gap dividing racial groups and income levels is a linchpin of inequality, one worthy of a much greater investment of energy and resources by our society. Moreover, there is nothing wrong with setting policy priorities, particularly when fiscal times are tough and citizens' faith in government and engagement in public affairs are at record lows. But the lack of attention to persistently high segregation is dangerous in at least two respects. First, it ignores the huge contribution that segregated living makes to inequality in education, employment, health, and other areas. Second, it presumes that gains in economic success will be mirrored in more integrated living patterns over time—a link for which the evidence is mixed at best. Addressing both points, the next chapter considers how our communities acquired their current shape and just how quickly and dramatically they are changing in demographic and spatial terms.

27. See for example Jencks and Phillips (1998).

References

Alba, Richard, and Victor Nee. 2003. *Remaking the American Mainstream.* Harvard University Press.

Bean, Frank D., and Gillian Stevens. 2003. *America's Newcomers and the Dynamics of Diversity.* New York: Russell Sage.

Bipartisan Millennial Housing Commission Appointed by the Congress of the United States. 2002. *Meeting Our Nation's Housing Challenges.* U.S. Government Printing Office.

Blank, Rebecca M. 2001. "An Overview of Trends in Social and Economic Well-Being, by Race." In *America Becoming: Racial Trends and Their Consequences,* vol. 1, edited by Neil J. Smelser, William Julius Wilson, and Faith Mitchell, pp. 21–39. Washington: National Academy Press.

Bobo, Lawrence. 2001. "Racial Attitudes and Relations at the Close of the Twentieth Century." In *America Becoming: Racial Trends and Their Consequences,* vol. 1, edited by Neil J. Smelser, William Julius Wilson, and Faith Mitchell, pp. 264–301. Washington: National Academy Press.

Briggs, Xavier de Souza. 2003. "Reshaping the Geography of Opportunity: Place Effects in Global Perspective." *Housing Studies* 18, no. 6: 915–36.

———. 2004. "Traps and Stepping Stones: Neighborhood Dynamics and Family Well-Being." Faculty Research Working Paper RWP04-015. Kennedy School of Government, Harvard University.

Cashin, Sheryll. 2004. *The Failures of Integration: How Race and Class are Undermining the American Dream.* New York: Public Affairs

Clotfelter, Charles T. 2004. *After Brown: The Ruse and Retreat of School Desegregation.* Princeton University Press.

Cutler, David, and Edward Glaeser. 1997. "Are Ghettos Good or Bad?" *Quarterly Journal of Economics* 112: 827–82.

Danielson, Michael. 1976. *The Politics of Exclusion.* Columbia University Press.

Davis, Mike. 1990. *City of Quartz: Excavating the Future in Los Angeles.* New York: Verso.

Dreier, Peter, John Mollenkopf, and Todd Swanstrom. 2001. *Place Matters: Metropolitics for the Twenty-First Century.* University Press of Kansas.

Edley, Christopher F., Jr. 1996. *Not All Black and White: Affirmative Action, Race, and American Values.* New York: Hill and Wang.

Ehrenreich, Barbara. 2001. *Nickel and Dimed: On (Not) Getting By in America.* New York: Henry Holt.

Ellen, Ingrid Gould. 1999. "Spatial Stratification within U.S. Metropolitan Areas." In *Governance and Opportunity in Metropolitan America,* edited by Alan Altshuler and others, pp. 192–212. Washington: National Academy Press.

———. 2000. *Sharing America's Neighborhoods: Prospects for Stable Racial Integration.* Harvard University Press.

Ellen, Ingrid Gould, Tod Mijanovich, and Keri-Nicole Dillman. 2001. "Neighborhood Effects on Health: Exploring the Links and Assessing the Evidence." *Journal of Urban Affairs* 23, nos. 3-4: 391–408.

Frankenberg, Erica, and Chungmei Lee. 2003. "Charter Schools and Race: A Lost Opportunity for Integrated Education." Civil Rights Project, Harvard University, July.

Galster, George C. 1987. "Residential Segregation and Interracial Economic Disparities: A Simultaneous-Equations Approach." *Journal of Urban Economics* 21: 22–44.

———. 1990. "Federal Fair Housing Policy: The Great Misapprehension." In *Building*

Foundations: Housing and Federal Policy, edited by Denise DiPasquale and Langley C. Keyes, pp. 137–56. University of Pennsylvania Press.

Galster, George C., and Sean P. Killen. 1995. "The Geography of Opportunity: A Reconnaissance and Conceptual Framework." *Housing Policy Debate* 6, no. 1: 7–43.

Glaeser, Edward L., and Matthew Kahn. 2004. "Sprawl and Urban Growth." In *Handbook of Regional and Urban Economics: Cities and Geography*, vol. 4, edited by J. V. Henderson and J. F. Thisse. New York: North-Holland.

Glaeser, Edward L., and Jacob Vigdor. 2003. "Racial Segregation: Promising News." In *Redefining Urban and Suburban America, Evidence from Census 2000,* vol. 1, edited by Bruce Katz and Robert E. Lang, pp. 211–34. Brookings.

Guinier, Lani, and Gerald Torres. 2002. *The Miner's Canary.* Harvard University Press.

Haar, Charles. 1996. *Suburbs under Siege: Race, Space, and Audacious Judges*. Princeton University Press.

Ihlanfeldt, Keith R. 1999. "The Geography of Economic and Social Opportunity in Metropolitan Areas." In *Governance and Opportunity in Metropolitan America,* edited by Alan Altshuler and others, pp. 213–52. Washington: National Academy Press.

Ihlanfeldt, Keith R., and David Sjoquist. 1998. "The Spatial Mismatch Hypothesis: A Review of Recent Studies and Their Implications for Welfare Reform." *Housing Policy Debate* 9, no. 4: 849–92.

Jackson, Kenneth. 2000. "Gentleman's Agreement: Discrimination in Metropolitan America." In *Reflections on Regionalism,* edited by Bruce Katz, pp. 185–217. Brookings.

Jargowsky, Paul. 1997. *Poverty and Place: Ghettos, Barrios, and the American City.* New York: Russell Sage.

Jencks, Christopher, and Meredith Philips, eds. 1998. *The Black-White Test Score Gap*. Brookings.

Joint Center for Housing Studies. 2003. "State of the Nation's Housing." Harvard University.

Katz, Bruce, and Robert E. Lang. 2003. "Introduction." In *Redefining Urban and Suburban America, Evidence from Census 2000,* vol. 1, edited by Bruce Katz and Robert E. Lang, pp. 1–13. Brookings.

Massey, Douglas S., and Nancy A. Denton. 1993. *American Apartheid: Segregation and the Making of the Underclass.* Harvard University Press.

Meck, Stuart, Rebecca Retzlaff, and James Schwab. 2003. *Regional Approaches to Affordable Housing.* Planning Advisory Service Report 513/514. Chicago: American Planning Association.

Nobles, Melissa. 2000. *Shades of Citizenship: Race and the Census in Modern Politics*. Stanford University Press.

Orfield, Myron. 2002. *American Metropolitics: The New Suburban Reality.* Brookings.

Pastor, Manuel, Jr. 2001. "Geography and Opportunity." In *America Becoming: Racial Trends and Their Consequences,* vol. 1, edited by Neil J. Smelser, William Julius Wilson, and Faith Mitchell, pp. 435–67. Washington: National Academy Press.

Pendall, Rolf. 2000. "Local Land-Use Regulation and the Chain of Exclusion." *Journal of the American Planning Association* 66: 125–42.

Perlmann, Joel, and Mary C. Waters, eds. 2002. *The New Race Question: How the Census Counts Multiracial Individuals.* New York: Russell Sage.

Reich, Robert B. 1992. *The Work of Nations: Preparing Ourselves for Twenty-First Century Capitalism.* New York: Vintage.

Rieder, Jonathan. 1985. *Canarsie: The Jews and Italians of Brooklyn against Liberalism.* Harvard University Press.

Rusk, David. 1999. *Inside Game/Outside Game: Winning Strategies for Saving Urban America.* Brookings.

Squires, Gregory D. 2002. "Urban Sprawl and the Uneven Development of Metropolitan America." In *Urban Sprawl: Causes, Consequences, and Policy Responses*, edited by Gregory D. Squires, pp. 1–22. Washington: Urban Institute.

Weir, Margaret, ed. 1998. *The Social Divide: Political Parties and the Future of Activist Government.* New York: Russell Sage.

Wilson, William Julius. 1987. *The Truly Disadvantaged: The Inner City, The Underclass, and Public Policy.* Chicago: University of Chicago Press.

2

More Pluribus, *Less* Unum? *The Changing Geography of Race and Opportunity*

XAVIER DE SOUZA BRIGGS

Location matters—for economic returns, quality of life, and many other reasons. But the value of a given location as a place to live, work, invest, or go to school can shift profoundly over time as communities grow and their makeup changes. This chapter takes a critical look at evidence on the key forces that drive metropolitan growth patterns in America; the changing geography of race and opportunity associated with those growth patterns; and the social and economic consequences of that geography, focusing on access to good schools and jobs. The chapter also outlines important evidence about the geography of crime and insecurity, poor health, and environmental hazards.

Growth and Its Discontents: America in Comparative Perspective

As noted in the introductory chapter, America's metropolitan areas are both very sprawling and very segregated by race and class, a pattern that is especially apparent when U.S. cities and suburbs are compared with those of Europe or other wealthy regions around the world.[1] As both liberal and conservative

1. Friedrichs, Galster, and Musterd (2003); Nivola (1999). Like the United States, a number of European nations are experiencing sharp increases in racial and ethnic diversity, thanks both to immigration and to comparatively low rates of natural increase among native ethnic groups. Sweden now has a larger foreign-born population than the United States has, and particular cities in the European Union—London, Malmö, Marseilles—face the opportunities and challenges of this

observers have shown, there was nothing "natural" or inevitable about these segregated outcomes. As much as individual housing preferences, deliberate policy decisions regarding transportation, education, housing finance, land use, and taxation and expenditure across all levels of government, and even those regarding energy policy, determine where people live, how much they depend on cars to move around, how much of their income must be spent on housing, and—to a striking degree—who their neighbors will be. Policy decisions also determine the benefits and costs that those housing and mobility patterns entail.[2] For its part, through mortgage insurance and other policies, the federal government directly encouraged segregation by race and class until roughly the middle of the twentieth century.[3] And as Philip Tegeler shows in chapter 9 of this volume, federal housing and community development programs have had segregating effects since then, in spite of affirmative policies meant to desegregate communities. Add direct and indirect effects through policies that shape land use, real estate practices, and lending (all discussed in this volume), and the local development game is hardly the textbook example of a free market. Rather, it is a competitive, unevenly regulated, and subsidized regime.

The 1990s brought more of the century-old urban development pattern known as sprawl as well as increased decentralization and specialization in local government. During the 1990s land consumption in metropolitan areas proceeded at twice the rate of population growth, and even metropolitan areas that lost population, such as Buffalo and Pittsburgh, continued to develop at the fringe.[4] Contrary to the popular perception that sprawl is king in western cities, the West is home to some of the densest metropolitan areas in America, and many of them became denser over the 1980s and 1990s, while metro areas in the South sprawled rapidly to accommodate high population growth and, in the Northeast and Midwest, sprawled at remarkably high rates in spite of their slow population growth rates.[5] Overall, population density per acre of land has steadily decreased for metropolitan areas, as households demand larger housing, rely increasingly on cars to meet their transportation needs, and continue to migrate toward warmer and less dense areas of the country. The social costs and benefits of sprawl are widely debated, and divergent trends—having more cars

new diversity at much higher percentages. In Europe, increased diversity and some nativist backlash in the political arena contribute to interest in "social exclusion," as Europe strengthens its regional identity and relaxes certain border controls. In general, segregation patterns in immigrant gateway cities in Europe parallel the segration patterns for Asians and Hispanics in the United States.

2. Danielson (1976); Massey and Denton (1993); Altshuler and others (1999); Nivola (1999); Ellen (2000); Savitch (2002); Glaeser and Kahn (2004); Wilson and Hammer (2001).

3. Massey and Denton (1993).

4. U.S. Department of Housing and Urban Development (2000).

5. Fulton and others (2001).

on the road but also stricter pollution emissions standards, for example—make for confusing net patterns over time.[6]

From the standpoint of race and housing choice, sprawling new growth creates exit options from older, built-up areas—but more often for white households and middle- and upper-income minorities than for other groups. One way Americans separate themselves from urban problems is by leaving them behind and creating new local governments as suburban communities develop. Paralleling the trend in sprawl, the number of municipal governments increased by 15 percent between 1952 and 2002, and excluding school districts, the number of special-purpose governments—for managing water resources, public hospitals, cemeteries, fire services, metropolitan transportation, and other functions—roughly tripled during the period.[7] While the incorporation of new cities and towns within larger metropolitan areas means greater autonomy and choice for residents of those places, metropolitan areas with higher levels of government fragmentation (more jurisdictions) per capita also exhibit higher levels of economic inequality between cities and suburbs.[8]

As Rolf Pendall and his coauthors remind us in their chapter on growth management and racial equity (chapter 10), growth is inevitable, but the form it takes—inclusionary or exclusionary—is not. Consider these projections: Over the next twenty-five years, the nation will lose about 15 million housing units and gain about 30 million households. This means that the country will need to create about 45 million housing units somewhere—or about 37 percent as many as the number of total units in the nation's housing stock at the end of the first quarter of 2004—to accommodate a larger and more diverse population.[9] Patterns of new development—currently dominated by the sprawl model—are therefore enormously important.

Mobility matters too, of course. About half (49 percent) of the nation's population moved between 1995 and 2000, continuing a migration rate that has changed little in the past few decades.[10] These moves have affected investments

6. For an in-depth review of sprawl's causes and social and environmental consequences, as well as long-run scenarios for population growth in America under alternative approaches to managing growth, see Burchell and others (2002). Detailed and widely read progressive commentaries include Moe and Wilkie (1997); Benfield, Raimi, and Chen (1999); and Squires (2002). For conservative critique and response, most of it founded on public choice theory in economics, see Glaeser and Kahn (2004), Staley (1999, 2000), and discussion in Henig (2002).

7. U.S. Census Bureau (2002).

8. Ellen (1999).

9. Nelson (2003); U.S. Department of Housing and Urban Development (2004). Based on analyses of the American Housing Survey, conducted by the Census Bureau and funded by the U.S. Department of Housing and Urban Development, the nation loses about 0.6 percent of its housing stock annually. Meanwhile, projections for continued population growth and household size are based on trends in births, deaths, household formation, and immigration (Joint Center for Housing Studies 2003).

10. Schacter, Franklin, and Perry (2003).

in both newer and older communities, as well as community makeup. Whites and the middle class continued a net migration out of cities in the 1990s, citing two primary reasons for leaving: crime and poor school quality. As sociologist Camille Charles notes in chapter 3, white Americans strongly associate these problems with increased minority presence in a community, particularly with the presence of blacks.

It is increasingly clear that how the United States handles increased racial and ethnic diversity will, for better or worse, be linked in the decades ahead to how it handles sprawl and other symptoms of uneven metropolitan development. On this score, there is a growing chorus of regionalists—those who advocate metropolitan responses to challenges that cross local government boundaries, including those associated with rapid sprawl: traffic congestion, concentrated poverty, overcrowded schools, "zoning for dollars," and others.[11]

Regionalism, which first appeared in the 1920s and enjoyed some prominence in the 1960s and 1970s, is not a single, coherent school of thought on urban policy but a set of hopes for wiser local development patterns and more rational governance to meet regionwide needs.[12] Regionalists emphasize, variously, that the benefits of planning, governing, and investing resources across jurisdictional boundaries include enhanced fiscal efficiency, economic competitiveness, environmental sustainability, and social equity.[13] But recent renewed hopes for more cooperation between cities and suburbs—in particular, for more regional planning and investment to address what David Rusk, the noted urban analyst and former mayor, terms the "sprawl machine"—confront several powerful and closely linked barriers to change.[14] More optimistically, the barriers might be thought of as defining the key litmus test of the new regionalism. The first barrier is a very strong preference for local decisionmaking (home rule) in American politics—in survey after survey, it seems, the more local, the better.[15] Second is the dominant American lifestyle, which favors a car-bound and sprawling suburban model of consumption (instead of more compact, transit-oriented living), along with local fiscal autonomy, low taxes, and a limited local obligation to meet the needs of the disadvantaged. And third—the focus here—is the geography of race and class.

11. Zoning for dollars, also known as fiscal zoning, is the establishment and use of local zoning regulations to favor real estate development that generates high property tax revenue and comparatively low municipal service costs (including public education costs). This practice often favors new retail stores, for example, over new housing development. Fiscal zoning is particularly effective at excluding modestly priced, multifamily housing, a key predictor of a community's economic and racial diversity over time. See Pendall and co-authors, chapter 10, this volume; Fischel (2001).

12. On the history of regionalism, see Fishman (2002); Henig (2002).

13. Henig (2002); Orfield (2002); Pastor and others (2000); Rusk (1999).

14. See Rusk (1999).

15. Danielson (1976); Fischel (2001).

As thoughtful observers of the new regionalism point out, social equity has been and will continue to be the most problematic plank in the platform.[16] For example, antisprawl, "smart growth" advocacy across the nation has not, thus far, included strong or steady supporters of affordable and inclusionary housing.[17] Yes, Americans of all races are working together more than ever before, as workplace statistics confirm,[18] but can they share communities? Can they live together, and educate their young people together, across persistent social divides? This question is a test of the new regionalism's political strength as well as its potential to improve lives and communities. The race and class segregation of American communities will help shape regionalism and determine its impact. Conversely, barriers to regional progress and smarter growth patterns will also be critical barriers to racial justice and social equity.

People and Places: Changing Demography and Settlement Patterns

As newspaper headlines, Census Bureau reports, and scholarly research document, the sharp growth in racial and ethnic diversity in recent years has been driven not only by immigration—the second great wave in the nation's history, which began with immigration reform in 1965, is also the first to be dominated by non-European immigrants—but also by a sharp decrease in the birth rate for non-Hispanic whites over the past generation. Eleven million immigrants came to this country in the 1990s, contributing to one-third of all population growth over that period, and more than 80 percent of those came from Africa, Asia, or Latin America and the Caribbean. Their growth fueled by immigration and higher-than-average birth rates, Hispanic Americans recently became the nation's largest minority (up from 22.4 million to 38.7 million between 1990 and 2002), overtaking blacks (36.6 million). Meanwhile, the 72 percent increase in Asians and Pacific Islanders (up from 7.4 million to nearly 12.7 million) was the largest in percentage terms.[19] About 3.5 million persons identify

16. Henig (2002); Jackson (2000).

17. Downs (2004).

18. Estlund (2003).

19. Suro and Singer (2003); U.S. Census Bureau (2001, 2003). The 2000 census brought a significant, and widely contested, change in the way data on racial-ethnic identity were collected, and these changes carry over for the population estimates through July 1, 2002 (reported in this chapter), that represent current indicators of growing racial and ethnic diversity. For the first time, respondents were allowed to check more than one race—an option chosen by more than 6.8 million Americans (2.4 percent of the population). But as before, the racial identity question was separated from an ethnic identity question about having "Spanish, Hispanic, or Latino origin," which the federal government defines as "a person of Cuban, Mexican, Puerto Rican, Central or South American, or other Spanish culture, regardless of race." Together, the two questions generate no fewer than 126 possible identity combinations, meaning that racial-ethnic data from the year 2000 are not directly comparable with those of earlier censuses (Katz and Lang 2003). Population growth rates cited in this chapter, like most now reported by researchers and the media, now reflect

themselves as Native Americans, a figure that also has increased in recent decades, because of both higher-than-average fertility rates and growth in ethnic pride among the nation's First Peoples. But these conventional racial statistics obscure a changing, and some say blurring, color line: About 7 million persons in America now identify themselves as multiracial, and one in four marriages involving either Hispanics or Asians crosses group lines.[20]

Over the 1990s, most central cities in America became "majority minority" for the first time in history, and one-quarter of the central cities that saw growth—a key concern for every mayor, economic development director, and business roundtable participant in the land—would actually have shrunk if not for growth in their Hispanic populations.[21] While almost half of the nation's immigrants arrive in the New York, Chicago, and Los Angeles metropolitan areas, the fastest rates of increase—the most rapidly felt local changes—are found in emerging gateways, such as Atlanta, Raleigh, Las Vegas, and Nashville.[22]

Ninety-five percent of the nation's foreign-born population lives in metropolitan areas, and while U.S. history has cast central cities in the role of primary immigrant gateway, just over half of the foreign-born population is now living in the suburbs. The majority of both Asians and Hispanics now live in suburban areas. In some metropolitan areas, in fact, the suburbs are the first stop for immigrant workers and families, not a destination attained over generations.[23]

Housing Segregation and Mobility Patterns, by Race and Income

Analysts generally track residential segregation by race in two ways: by measuring how unevenly racial groups are distributed in a given metropolitan area and by measuring how much an "average" member of each group is exposed to other groups at the neighborhood level (neighborhoods are typically defined as census tracts that contain, on average, a few thousand households). The two measures can lead to different impressions of how segregated a place is. Consider a hypothetical metropolitan area with only whites and blacks. The area may have a small black population that is very evenly distributed across neighborhoods, but because there are so few members of the group to "go around," the average white person will live in a neighborhood with very few blacks, while the reverse

"race alone or in combination" responses for Hispanics and the four major non-Hispanic groups (Asian, black, Native American, white). For example, "Asians" includes those who selected only that racial category and those who selected it in combination with another racial category, such as white, but not the small number who selected Asian plus Hispanic origin (as some Filipinos do). This means that although almost 98 percent of census 2000 respondents chose only one racial category, the total of the alone-or-in-combination responses exceeds (by 2.6 percent) the total population of the United States.

20. Lindsay and Singer (2003).

21. Berube (2003).

22. Suro and Singer (2003).

23. Frey (2003).

will be true for the average black: He or she will have mostly white neighbors. This hypothetical metropolitan area would have an encouragingly low "unevenness" score but would also show very low average across-group "exposure" for whites and very high exposure for blacks.[24]

By these indexes, the latest census provides a very mixed picture of segregation levels and trends in the United States at the turn of the twenty-first century. On one hand, as measured by unevenness of distribution, segregation rates in the most highly segregated metropolitan areas—the rates of black segregation from whites, most of all in older cities of the Northeast and Midwest—continued to fall. This continues a three-decade-long trend and represents a national drop in black–nonblack segregation to its lowest point since 1920.[25] In general, neighborhoods that integrate black and white households became much more numerous, as well as more stable, in the 1980s than they were in the 1970s.[26] Over three-fourths (76.3 percent) of tracts integrated by 1980 remained so by 1990, while 16.6 percent of those tracts became majority black and 7 percent predominantly white. White losses in mixed neighborhoods were three times greater in the 1970s than in the 1980s. Where black-white neighborhood integration is concerned, economist Ingrid Gould Ellen finds that the primary correlates of racial stability are a neighborhood's history of past stability (stability is self-perpetuating, to some degree); its distance from a metropolitan area's main area of minority concentration (integrated neighborhoods that are more distant are more racially stable); its percentage of rental housing (among whites, renters are the most likely to integrate); a secure set of amenities (amenities help attract and retain a variety of households); and the black presence in the metropolitan area as a whole (holding other factors equal, racially integrated neighborhoods are more stable in the West, for example, where blacks constitute a smaller share of metropolitan populations).[27] Many integrated neighborhoods continued to be mixed in the 1990s, and the continued decline of black-white segregation during the 1990s appears to have come primarily from the partial integration of neighborhoods that were once exclusively white.[28]

24. For a discussion of segregation measures and their merits, see Massey (2001); Massey, White, and Phua (1996).

25. Glaeser and Vigdor (2003).

26. Ellen (2000, pp.12-19) defines a racially integrated neighborhood as a census tract in which blacks make up between 10 and 50 percent of the population. She then studies the non-Hispanic white shares of population of those tracts at the beginning and end of each decade. Analysts understand stability to include identifiable equilibrium points, at which the number of persons of a given racial group who are added to a neighborhood (either through birth or in-migration) is about equal to the number of persons of that group who are lost (either through death or out-migration). A perfectly stable racial mix would require a rare pattern indeed: complete equilibrium across all racial groups present in the neighborhood.

27. Ellen (2000); Nyden, Maly, and Lukehart (1997).

28. Rawlings, Harris, and Turner (2004).

Table 2-1. *Indexes of Dissimilarity, 330 U.S. Metropolitan Areas, 2000*[a]

Index	*White-black*	*White-Hispanic*	*White-Asian*
Maximum index	84.7	75.4	58.8
Median index	52.3	38.2	35.2
Minimum index	20.2	11.6	14.5
(Standard deviation)	(13.7)	(12.1)	(7.9)
Change in median index, 1990–2000	–6.2	–4.6	–11.8

Source: Author's calculations using Lewis Mumford Center, University at Albany, census data file.

a. Dissimilarity measures unevenness in two population distributions (whites versus blacks, say), on a 100-point scale. The index indicates the percentage of either group that would need to move in order to make the composition of each neighborhood (census tract) match that of the metropolitan area as a whole. Higher scores thus reflect greater unevenness (higher segregation). On measures of segregation, see Massey, White, and Phua (1996). The White House Office of Management and Budget designates census geography, with updates common in areas undergoing significant demographic transition. For 2000, 331 metropolitan areas were designated; segregation measures could not be calculated for all due to missing data.

At the same time, black-white segregation rates remain distressingly high in absolute terms, particularly in the Rust Belt cities of the Northeast and Midwest. As sociologist John Logan described the decline, "It's at a rate that my grandchildren, when *they* die, will still not be living in an integrated society."[29] Not only is the national median rate of segregation from whites higher for blacks than for other minority groups, but the black-white rates range upward to extremes that Hispanics and Asians do not experience in any metropolitan area (table 2-1).

The rate of decline in black-white segregation has been especially slow in a number of large and highly segregated metropolitan areas, such as Detroit, Milwaukee, New York, and Chicago. Logan notes that during the 1980s and 1990s these areas showed some of the highest rates of concentrated minority poverty in the nation. For blacks and for some Hispanic subgroups, extreme racial isolation is a marker for extreme social and economic distress. From the standpoint of integrating neighborhoods, in the 1990s both the lowest levels of residential segregation by race and the most encouraging improvements were in the West and South, in metropolitan areas than tended to be small or medium-sized and growing quickly and in which blacks constituted a modest share of the population.[30]

In terms of exposure, the average white person in U.S. cities and suburbs lives in a neighborhood that is overwhelmingly white (about 84 percent) and thus offers little exposure to other racial or ethnic groups. That typical neighborhood for a white person is just 7.1 percent black, 6.2 percent Asian, and 3.2 percent

29. National Public Radio, "Segregation in the Cities," *Talk of the Nation,* May 10, 2001; Logan (2003).

30. Glaeser and Vigdor (2003).

Table 2-2. *Average Neighborhood Racial Composition, 331 U.S. Metropolitan Areas, 2000*[a]
Percent

Race	*White*	*Black*	*Asian*	*Hispanic*
Hispanic	3.2	9.4	11.7	42.1
Asian	6.2	2.6	19.3	4.2
Black	7.1	54.8	9.7	13.0
White	83.5	33.2	59.3	40.7

Source: See table 2-1.
a. Exposure (p^*) measures the composition of the average census tract of members of a given racial or ethnic group.

Hispanic (table 2-2). Notwithstanding the number of very racially isolated and poor ghettos and typically more mixed-income immigrant ethnic enclaves, Asians, Hispanics, and blacks are, on average, much more exposed to other racial-ethnic groups than are whites. But over the 1980s and 1990s, high rates of immigration combined with concentrated settlement patterns to decrease the rate of Asian and Hispanic exposure to whites (figure 2-1). In part, this reflects a clustering that is typical for newly arrived immigrants, especially those whose first language is not English. Immigrants arrive faster than they can "diffuse" (spread out) across the housing market; moreover, ethnic enclaves offer assistance to new arrivals, from help in finding housing to securing a job and child care, obtaining familiar food, and celebrating religious and cultural traditions. A century ago, Italians, Irish, and other groups showed a similar pattern of heavy immigration followed by residential and commercial clustering and therefore increased segregation. But immigrant ethnic enclaves can also be constraining, in that they limit contact with native English speakers, who tend to have higher incomes, greater educational attainment, and valuable social networks. The threshold question for any society committed to equal opportunity is whether wider housing choices exist for people who *want* to exercise them.

Over time, members of the two large, fast-growing immigrant groups, Asian and Hispanic American, move to the suburbs and take residence in more racially diverse neighborhoods. This is particularly true of the higher-skilled, middle-income members of those groups.[31] But even middle-income immigrants are relatively isolated from white neighborhoods—a pattern that is more pronounced for blacks—and some of the fastest growth in immigrant and black suburbanization is occurring in at-risk suburbs, which feature school failure, weak fiscal capacity, and other problems long associated with vulnerable cities.[32]

31. Zhou (2001); Alba and Nee (2003)
32. Orfield (2002).

Figure 2-1. *Minority-to-White Neighborhood Exposure in Average Tract, 325 U.S. Metropolitan Areas, 1980, 1990, and 2000*[a]

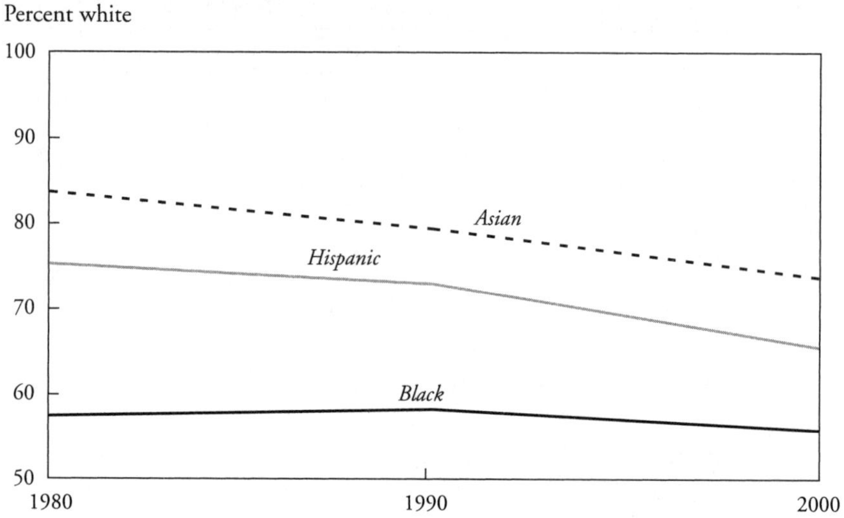

Source: See table 2-1.
a. On the exposure measure, see note for table 2-2.

What is more, as suburbs became more racially and ethnically diverse in the 1990s, minority segregation in the suburbs increased. And in suburbs, just as in central cities, blacks are the group most segregated from whites.

It is a commonplace in America to assume that, since housing discrimination has been illegal since 1968, segregation by race merely reflects differences in income among racial and ethnic groups: Differences in where people live must simply reflect differences in what they can afford. Yet nationally the average black family earning more than $60,000 a year lives in a neighborhood with a higher poverty rate and lower educational attainment than the average white family earning less than $30,000.[33] Two chapters in this volume detail the latest evidence on why this commonplace assumption—that income determines housing location—is so incomplete (chapter 3, on racial attitudes and neighborhood preferences; and chapter 4, on current patterns of housing discrimination, in which testing agents of different races are matched on income and other traits).

In the housing market, we all make choices that are shaped in powerful ways by the choices of others. Their choices have a significant impact on the kinds of communities in which we can live. For example, blacks and other minorities with sufficient income can, barring discrimination, move into a racially integrated community, but they cannot ensure that the community will remain integrated.

33. Logan, Oakley, and Stowell (2003).

White avoidance of more racially diverse neighborhoods is a powerful factor in destabilizing integrated communities and prevents same-race communities from becoming stably integrated. Analyses focusing on neighborhood change over time and trajectories of individual households across neighborhoods over time both corroborate this pattern.[34]

On the other hand, geographers William Clark and Sarah Blue find that for blacks, Hispanics, and Asians living in metropolitan areas with a high percentage of foreign-born residents (gateway communities) higher education and, to a lesser extent, higher income are associated with higher rates of residential integration with whites.[35] These researchers stress that effects of class vary considerably by racial group and metropolitan area. Immigration and domestic migration patterns are obviously factors, because they shift the racial and economic profile of people who are in a given local (metropolitan) market for housing.

There are racial differences in income, of course, and so segregation by race does owe, albeit in modest measure, to differences in buying power. How segregated is the United States, then, by those differences? Using census data from 1950 to 2000, sociologists Douglas Massey and Mary Fischer find that income segregation declined at the regional and state levels but increased within metropolitan areas—that is, at the level of neighborhoods and local jurisdictions—over the past half-century.[36] What this means is that income is more evenly distributed across states and major regions—a pattern, argue the researchers, that reflects growth in affluence in the South as well as increased poverty in the Northeast and Midwest over a long period of economic restructuring, immigration, and significant internal migration across states. On the other hand, within any given metropolitan area, people of different incomes were less likely to share the same neighborhoods in the year 2000 than in 1970 or 1950. The trend is not limited to one racial group: For example, using the top and bottom fifths of the income distribution to describe rich and poor, respectively, Massey and Fisher find that segregation of the rich from the poor increased 34 percent among whites and 27 percent among blacks between 1970 and the 2000.

Most of this increase appears to be associated with the economic dislocations of the 1970s and 1980s. In most regions of the country, as several studies have shown, the concentration of poverty in metropolitan areas actually declined somewhat in the 1990s.[37] That is in part because some poor families gained

34. Ellen (2000); Quillian (2002). In his seminal analysis of segregative dynamics in housing markets, Schelling (1971) found that even small differences in the neighborhood preferences of various racial groups can lead to large and persistent rates of segregation. Avoidance, or "self-steering" away from particular neighborhoods, captures a significant component of this dynamic.

35. Clark and Blue (2004). Neighborhood integration with whites, as well as "suburban attainment," have long been used by analysts of race and immigration as indexes of minority group assimilation or progress over time. Alba and Nee (2003); Zhou (2001).

36. Massey and Fischer (2003).

37. Jargowsky (2003); Kingsley and Pettit (2003).

income and in part because of migration patterns (higher-income households gentrifying urban neighborhoods; lower-income households moving out). Geographically concentrated poverty shifted away from in-demand urban neighborhoods and toward older suburbs, particularly in the nation's hundred largest metropolitan areas. There, between 1980 and 2000, the number of suburban census tracts with poverty rates of 30 percent or higher grew 89 percent, and the number of poor residents more than doubled.

Overall, Massey and Fischer indicate, income segregation has not decreased appreciably from its 1990 high. That is, even if the trend toward greater economic division did not get worse over the past decade, it did not reverse. One reason is that income inequality—which continued to increase in the 1990s, even though rising incomes at last lifted those on the bottom[38]—touches all racial groups in America. The sharp increase in residential segregation by income in America over the past thirty years thus reflects an expanded class divide within each racial group as well as a greater tendency for people with different financial resources, social contacts, political habits, and educational access to live apart.[39]

Whether in cities or suburbs, low-income, minority, and female-headed families are more likely than other families to live in poor neighborhoods at a given point in time.[40] But as noted above, housing mobility is relatively high in America. One-third of all renter households move every year, and about half of the households in the country (renters and owners together) move every five years. In addition, neighborhoods can change dramatically "around" someone who has not moved. So what kinds of neighborhoods are the various types of family exposed to over time? The limited empirical evidence on this question is sobering: When the long-run patterns of a representative national sample of black and white households are compared, race trumps both income and female-headed family structure as a predictor of the type of neighborhood to which families are exposed. Using the Panel Study of Income Dynamics for the

38. Burtless and Jencks (2003).

39. As Dickens (2003) and Levy (2003) note (in comments on the Massey-Fischer study), trend analyses that rely on summary measures of income segregation inevitably mask not only the details of social contact and their actual impact on human lives but also the local drivers of observed patterns. Poor people may have little contact with nonpoor neighbors, those with contact may or may not benefit in ways we expect, and so on. Social researchers analyze many of these issues under the rubric of *neighborhood effects* and suggest a variety of ways that people at different income levels might affect each other, for better or worse, when they share neighborhoods. See Xavier de Souza Briggs, "Traps and Stepping Stones: Neighborhood Dynamics and Family Well-Being," (www.papers.ssrn.com [October 23, 2004]); Ellen and Turner (2003); Jencks and Mayer (1990); Leventhal and Brooks-Gunn (2000). Moreover, we might want society to respond differently to choices by middle-income people of color—say, to leave poorer neighborhoods—as opposed to changes in income levels for people (of any racial background) residing in a given place. Though very different, both types of change can produce higher income segregation.

40. Jargowsky (1997).

1979–90 period, sociologist Lincoln Quillian analyzed the probability that a family living in a poor neighborhood one year would be in a given type of neighborhood a year later (a nonpoor neighborhood, the same poor neighborhood, or a different poor neighborhood).[41] He also analyzed moves into poor neighborhoods from nonpoor ones and long-run patterns of "recurrence" (falling back into poor neighborhoods in repeated cycles over time after a family once managed to live in a nonpoor neighborhood). These shifts can occur because a family has moved, because the neighborhood has changed around the family, or for both reasons, so the probabilities capture effects of various structural advantages that some types of family enjoy.

Quillian finds that most blacks but only 10 percent of whites will live in a poor neighborhood at some point in a decade and that little of the difference is accounted for by racial differences in poverty rate or family structure. For example, when blacks in female-headed households with income below the poverty line were compared with whites in comparable households, 57 percent of blacks but only 27 percent of whites spent at least half of a ten-year span in a poor neighborhood. By this measure, even blacks in *male*-headed households with income *above* the poverty line face more risk (39 percent) than whites in female-headed, poor households—and far more than whites in comparable households (3 percent). Blacks leave poor neighborhoods often, but they fall back into such neighborhoods much more often than whites, leading Quillian to conclude, "For African-Americans, the most difficult part of escape from a poor neighborhood is not moving out but staying out."[42] It is not yet clear whether the sharp racial differences in neighborhood exposure changed in the 1990s or whether white-Hispanic and white-Asian differences are nearly as large as white-black ones.

School Opportunity: The Fall and Rise of Racial Segregation

For many people of color and for some white people too, moving to the suburbs and even attaining middle-income status do not equate to "making it" anymore—not if some middle- and upper-income families are increasingly able to seclude themselves from others. Perhaps the most important consequence is the geographic concentration of school failure. As noted in the introductory chapter,

41. Quillian (2003).

42. Quillian (2003, p. 237). In a related study (see note 39), I used simulation techniques to estimate potential effects of shifting transition probabilities (for example through housing policy and other tools), including escape (from poor areas to nonpoor ones), moving over (from poor area to poor area), and falling back (from nonpoor areas to poor ones). I find that even massive improvements in the riskiest transitions—doubling the odds of escape and halving those of moving over and falling back—would leave some households exposed to poor neighborhoods for significant periods over the long run. As such, in the conclusion to this volume, I outline the importance of helping families to buffer themselves from risk and connect to opportunities *wherever* they happen to be living.

housing integration, whether by race or class, is at best a proxy for access to opportunity or upward mobility in America. Access to good schooling, on the other hand, is a much more direct measure of an individual's prospects. Americans generally like to think of education as the great equalizer. Surely, even if wealth and income will always be somewhat unequal and the more affluent will always be able to afford somewhat better homes and neighborhoods, schools will reward anyone, of any generation, who strives. Few issues in public life, and certainly in domestic social policy, are more hotly debated than educational quality.[43] But the trend in this debate, at least over the past twenty years, has been to pay much more attention to what resources schools have, particularly in terms of teacher quality, teacher expectations of students, and physical facilities, than to the race and class makeup of the student body, which reflect segregated housing patterns. This lopsided focus is particularly worrisome in light of recent reforms stressing accountability and wider parental choice in education.

Why does enrollment composition matter? In 1966 the landmark federal study *Equality of Educational Opportunity*, led by sociologist James Coleman, indicated that differences in school resources explained only a modest portion of differences in school achievement (as measured by test scores), for both white and minority students. On the other hand, differences in enrollment—racial composition, parents' educational background, at-home resources—explained far more. Show me the neighborhoods where most of the kids have encyclopedias at home and plans to go the college, said Coleman—today one looks for Internet access and plans for a professional career as well—and I will show you the high-scoring schools. Subsequent and more technically advanced studies yield similar results, as have studies of the long-run effects of careful desegregation experiments, which indicate particularly powerful effects on low-income minority students who attend desegregated schools with white peers.[44] Compared with counterparts schooled in segregated minority schools, the desegregated students were not only more likely to attend college and have higher earnings, they had more racially diverse social networks as adults and were more comfortable navigating racially diverse environments throughout their lives.

This compelling and varied research evidence suggests that it is important not only to improve the contributions that schools and parents make to a child's achievement wherever the child happens to be enrolled but also to look for ways to teach disadvantaged children together with relatively advantaged peers. In public education, that has generally meant desegregating schools, since local school enrollment tracks the segregation of neighborhoods and municipalities by income and race. In an era of public school choice, it also means taking steps to further integration as school enrollments shift and new school options appear.

43. Jencks and Phillips (1998).

44. Coleman (1966). For a review of the studies, see Clotfelter (2004); Crain and Wells (1994).

In real estate, on the other hand, the effects of the segregated patterns that Coleman discovered two generations ago point to the marketing advantages of homogeneously affluent school districts, most of them racially homogeneous as well. Real estate agents are among the first to snap up reports of school test scores and college entry. Higher-scoring school districts fetch higher housing prices (other factors being equal), and economists find that changes in test scores register in housing prices too, underscoring the importance of school achievement to many homebuyers.[45] In these high-performing schools districts, even buyers without children—buyers who, in effect, pay higher property taxes to support schools that they do not use—benefit financially from the favorable impact of good schools on housing prices.

As a policy objective, school desegregation since the landmark *Brown* v. Board of Education ruling, in 1954, has faced stiff competition from other cherished public priorities—preserving local decisionmaking in public education, respecting the primacy of parental choice, and specifically avoiding "forced" busing, which often is unpopular with minority groups and whites alike—as well as from the private interests that those priorities protect, including property wealth.[46] For these and other reasons, school desegregation has received less and less support from the courts, which have released many local school districts from court-supervised desegregation efforts.[47]

An earlier Supreme Court decision to block compulsory metropolitan desegregation programs, the 1974 *Milliken* decision, ensured the perpetuation of race and class barriers in education that are directly produced by segregated housing patterns. These barriers to equal opportunity at the elementary and secondary levels are all the more striking in the wake of the Supreme Court's 2003 *Grutter* rulings on undergraduate and law school admissions to the University of Michigan, which hold that diversity is a benefit to students of all races and, more controversially, that it is a compelling enough benefit to warrant a systematic approach to "affirmative" admission of minority students to mostly white institutions of higher learning.[48] For now, the courts have decided that institutions of higher learning can continue to swim upstream against the

45. Kane, Staiger, and Samms (2003). These researchers add that housing values (in the Charlotte-Mecklenburg school district) did not respond quickly to changes in test scores and hypothesize that this may be because parents understand that scores fluctuate from year to year—are "noisy," in the terms that analysts use—or because parents are more interested in the socioeconomic make-up of the schools than the test scores (alone) in a given year. Interestingly, given the lack of attention to school siting and neighborhood segregation in many public school choice debates, Kane, Staiger, and Samms also find that parents place a high value on school proximity, holding other factors equal. For a critical review of the evidence on housing choice, housing prices, and school segregation, see Clotfelter (2004).

46. Clotfelter (2004).

47. Orfield and Eaton (1996).

48. *Grutter* v. *Bollinger* (2003a, 2003b).

massive educational inequality by race to which segregation contributes in primary and secondary schools.

Today, almost 40 percent of public school students are minority, roughly double the share in the 1960s. This fact—along with the protection (through *Milliken)* of suburbs against metropolitanwide desegregation—has produced an increase in elementary and secondary school segregation by race as well as class. Hispanic students are the most segregated, by ethnicity, income, and even language.[49] Asians are the most integrated group, and their college graduation rate, which is almost double the national average, is four times that of Latinos. After steady decline from the 1950s through the 1980s, black segregation in schools has increased to levels not seen in thirty years. A growing share of black and Hispanic students, particularly in the big-city school systems, attend schools that are virtually all nonwhite, characterized by high student poverty rates, limited school resources, less experienced and credentialed teachers, less educated parents, high student turnover, overcrowded and disorderly classrooms, and a host of health and other problems.

These patterns are not limited to central cities. They reflect patterns of racial and economic change in many older suburbs and satellite cities as well, and those patterns in turn reflect avoidance by middle-class housing consumers of neighborhoods and school districts perceived to be shifting toward minority poverty.[50] Indeed, economist Charles Clotfelter finds that between-district segregation now explains a much larger share of overall segregation in metropolitan areas than was previously the case. In the most segregated metropolitan areas, between-district segregation represented less than 4 percent of all segregation in 1970, compared with an astonishing 84 percent in the year 2000. Between-district racial segregation is a greater problem in large metropolitan areas than in smaller ones, which offer fewer separate districts into which families may sort themselves. Such segregation—perhaps the most direct measure of the uneven geography of race and opportunity—is also much larger than segregation between public and private schools. Summarizing the long-run effects of countervailing court decisions—*Brown* and then *Milliken*—Clotfelter concludes, "Whites who wanted to cushion or avoid the effects of [desegregating] actions had several means of doing so. The principal one was to seek out whiter school districts."[51]

49. Frankenberg, Lee, and Orfield (2003).

50. Ellen (2000). Orfield (2002) offers the particularly striking example of Matteson, Illinois, a suburb of Chicago that underwent significant economic and racial change in the 1980s and 1990s. Black families that moved into Matteson—pioneers, in that they were integrating a formerly all-white community—actually arrived with higher incomes and higher student test scores, on average, than those of their white neighbors. Yet perceptions that racial change spelled certain school decline and a threat to property values set in motion a self-fulfilling prophecy. Matteson has resegregated considerably, this time losing much of its white, middle-class population and income diversity as well.

51. Clotfelter (2004, p. 67).

What do persistent patterns of racial segregation imply in an age of school choice? When parents are dissatisfied with their assigned public schools, they can move into a new school district, send their children to private schools (religious or nonreligious), teach their children at home, or—more and more, thanks to the federal No Child Left Behind act of 2002—make use of a growing number of public school options, including magnet and voucher programs and semiautonomous but publicly funded charter schools. The share of student enrollment in assigned public schools has decreased steadily, from 80 percent to 76 percent between 1993 and 1999 alone, a change explained almost entirely by the increase, from 11 percent to 14 percent, in the share of students attending "chosen" public schools.[52] These alternatives are increasingly important arbiters of segregation (or integration) in education.

This is not just a reflection of the interest in choice shown by government and reform advocates. Choice options are particularly popular with low-income and minority families, which have perhaps the greatest stake in the improvement of public education. But the evidence thus far indicates that without mechanisms to improve the information and transportation options available to all families and without the aim of racial integration, choice is compounding the problem of school segregation. According to a study by the Civil Rights Project at Harvard University, ten years after the founding of the charter school movement in America, 70 percent of black charter school students attended highly segregated schools (with 90 percent or higher minority enrollments), compared to just 34 percent of black public school students, a significant difference, since fully one-third of all charter school students are black. Hispanic students make up just under 20 percent of both charter and public school enrollments, and their segregation rates are similar for both types of schools (42 percent of charter school students and 37 percent of public school students are in highly segregated schools). As the authors note, "The justification for segregated schools as places of opportunity is basically a 'separate but equal' justification, an argument that there is something about the schools that can overcome the normal pattern of educational inequality that afflicts these schools."[53] But while studies show that parents in such chosen schools are generally more satisfied and more actively involved with their children's schools[54]—not a bad thing by any means—there is not yet any systematic research to show that charter schools actually perform better than assigned public schools. Moreover, many charter schools are founded by groups that wish to target specific populations, including racial groups. Political scientist Gary Orfield, a long-time analyst of segregation trends, reminds us that a variety of earlier choice experiments in racially integrated schools produced white flight. "Those experiences," says Orfield,

52. Bielick and Chapman (2003).
53. Frankenberg and Lee (2003, p. 53).
54. Bielick and Chapman (2003).

"were apparently unknown or overlooked by designers and supporters of many charter school policies."[55]

This assessment of how and where America is schooling its young people is not a defense of centralized decisionmaking or of big, impersonal schools. There is evidence that certain kinds of flexibility in the classroom and in the organization of schools *can* improve learning, and studies of charter schools as a group inevitably lump together a wide array of approaches, making broad statements about performance unreliable. But segregation in public schools is steadily growing in ways that threaten the social and economic prospects of black and Hispanic students most of all, and charter schools and other choice options appear, if anything, to be exacerbating segregation. In schools as in housing, and in cities as well as in increasingly diverse suburbs, the objective of integration frequently conflicts with other objectives. As reports by the Civil Rights Project detail, the movement toward choice in education appears to present an opportunity—thus far untapped—to promote *inclusive* choice through expanded options and information, along with flexibility and innovation.

Geographic Access to Jobs

Much like the Coleman report, which stoked interest in the composition of public school enrollments, a classic economic analysis of the late 1960s has spurred considerable interest in the spatial mismatch between local job and housing locations. John Kain's influential study of racial differences in employment and metropolitan employment decentralization ("job sprawl") sounded an early warning of the massive restructuring of the U.S. economy that would later devastate minority and less skilled workers, as well as the neighborhoods in which they were concentrated.[56] Decentralization accompanied the erosion of an economy defined by heavily unionized, high-wage, blue-collar factory jobs concentrated in central cities.[57] Deindustrialization (the emergence of a service economy driven by small to medium-sized firms rather than big factories) and sprawling physical development patterns (including the establishment of new job centers, or "edge cities," in suburban areas) both have contributed to the jobs-housing mismatch. By the mid-1990s, about 70 percent of all jobs in the manufacturing, retailing, and wholesaling sectors, which tend to have many entry-level positions, were in the suburbs, and suburban job growth and business expansion continued to outstrip that in cities throughout the decade.[58]

The jobs-housing mismatch disproportionately affects black and Hispanic households, as well as certain low-income Asian refugee groups, because these groups tend to live farther away from areas of job growth than other groups.

55. Frankenberg, Lee, and Orfield (2003, preface).
56. Kain (1968).
57. Bluestone and Harrison (1982); Wilson (1987).
58. Kasarda (1995); U.S. Department of Housing and Urban Development (2000).

The mismatch also affects job-hunting low-wage workers and welfare recipients regardless of race. To a significant degree, the link to job outcomes appears to be a function of unequal access to transportation by race: Many suburban jobs are inaccessible by public transportation, and car ownership rates are much lower for blacks and Hispanics than for whites and for low-income people than for higher-income people. But the mismatch also affects job outcomes through less direct factors, such as weaker social networks for transferring job information and endorsements and the stigma associated with living in a low-income, predominantly minority neighborhood.[59] Besides creating barriers to employment, the mismatch between housing and job locations means long commutes in many directions (for workers of all racial groups) and hellish traffic congestion in many metropolitan areas—both classic symptoms of sprawl.[60]

Underscoring the importance of housing choice in economic outcomes, economists Steven Raphael and Michael Stoll find that, during the 1990s, blacks' overall proximity to jobs improved somewhat (about 13 percent), largely because of black residential mobility within metropolitan areas—that is, because people, not jobs, moved. Still, blacks on average remain more physically isolated from jobs than members of any other racial group. Overall proximity to jobs did not change significantly for whites, Hispanics, or Asians during the 1990s. Raphael and Stoll find that metropolitan areas with higher levels of residential segregation by race also show larger jobs-housing mismatches by race. In a related study, the researchers find that efforts to raise minority car-ownership rates to match those of whites, for example through ownership assistance (car voucher) programs that have a positive track record, could eliminate as much as 45 percent of the black-white differential and 17 percent of the Hispanic-white differential in geographic access to outlying jobs.[61]

Summary

The segregation of metropolitan areas by race and class shifted somewhat in the 1990s, bringing the risks long associated with inner cities into older suburbs as the latter became more racially and economically diverse. Poverty concentration declined in central cities, but the long-run trend, between 1970 and 2000, was one of wider class divide: Segregation by income increased sharply for both blacks and whites. New evidence on household mobility and neighborhood

59. Ihlanfeldt and Sjoquist (1998). Tilly and others (2001) label the stigma "space as a signal." The pattern was first identified by Kirschenman and Neckerman (1991) in a survey of Chicago-area firms.

60. Putnam (2000); Squires (2002).

61. Raphael and Stoll (2000, 2002). A number of states have car-ownership programs targeting welfare recipients, to aid in the transition to work and help meet other life needs, such as access to child care and family supports (Goldberg 2001).

change over time shows that blacks are much more likely than whites to get trapped in poor neighborhoods for long periods of time and to fall back into them repeatedly even after they manage to leave. While much more research is needed, particularly on patterns of Asians and Hispanics, these tendencies lead to major racial differences in long-run exposure to particular types of neighborhood—those rich either in resources or in risk factors.

School segregation increased in the 1990s. Between-district segregation became the dominant component of racial segregation in education, underscoring the effect of unequal housing choice on educational inequality; and a growing share of the nation's children left assigned public schools for charter schools and other chosen alternatives. Minorities making those choices were more likely to attend segregated schools than were their counterparts in assigned public schools.

Access to the sprawling "geography of jobs" likewise tracked housing choices. Minorities faced more spatial barriers, and blacks on average were the group most isolated from areas of job growth, though housing mobility reduced that isolation somewhat in the 1990s. Beyond the education and employment patterns specified here, a growing body of evidence suggests that housing segregation contributes to persistent racial disparities in exposure to crime and violence, physical and mental health status and health-related behaviors (disease, trauma, and other stressors, poor diet and exercise habits), and a variety of environmental health hazards, including pollution.[62]

On the positive side, many minorities, including a growing number of immigrants, showed substantial housing mobility, and if performance improves in the schools with the lowest achievement scores, in time the movement for school accountability and choice could mitigate the high educational costs of living in segregated minority neighborhoods. But many minority families that moved to the suburbs in the 1990s, even if they became homeowners, did not escape the pattern that contains poverty, school failure, and job isolation in particular geographic areas. The "container" may no longer follow city limits, but it still contains (separates).

There is no reason to think that trends over the 1990s are anomalies or transient patterns that might reverse themselves. In the decade ahead, for example, the Census Bureau projects that fully two-thirds of all new household growth in America will come from racial and ethnic minority groups, both native and foreign born.[63] In this context, persistent inequalities by race—in the geography of residence, in access to quality schools and jobs and to safe and healthy neighborhoods, and in incomes—do not bode well for the society. True, none of these factors fully determines economic security, health, political influence, or

62. Ellen, Mijanovich, and Dillman (2001); Pastor (2001).
63. Joint Center for Housing Studies (2003).

other essentials of well-being, and the most important litmus test for any society is probably not equality of resources among groups at any point in time but fair and just access to opportunity and rewards *over* time—that is, whether groups are able to move up and whether they believe that they can do so. Still, these trends suggest reason for serious concern as the nation becomes more diverse and continues its attachment to sprawling, segregated growth at the local level. The uneven geography of opportunity—and in particular the limits on housing choice that are tied to race and income—are perhaps more important than ever before.

References

Alba, Richard, and Victor Nee. 2003. *Remaking the American Mainstream*. Harvard University Press.

Altshuler, Alan, and others. 1999. "Governance and Opportunity in Metropolitan America." In *Governance and Opportunity in Metropolitan America*, edited by Alan Altshuler and others, pt. 1. Washington: National Academy Press.

Benfield, F. Kaid, Matthew Raimi, and Donald Chen. 1999. *Once There Were Greenfields: How Urban Sprawl Is Undermining America's Environment, Economy, and Social Fabric.* Washington: Natural Resources Defense Council.

Berube, Alan. 2003. "Racial and Ethnic Change in the Nation's Largest Cities." In *Redefining Urban and Suburban America: Evidence from Census 2000,* vol. 1, edited by Bruce Katz and Robert E. Lang, pp. 137–54. Brookings.

Bielick, Stacey, and Christopher Chapman. 2003. *Trends in the Use of School Choice, 1993–1999.* Statistical Analysis Report 2003-031. National Center for Education Statistics, U.S. Department of Education.

Bluestone, Barry, and Bennett Harrison. 1982. *The De-Industrialization of America.* New York: Basic Books.

Burchell, Robert W., and others. 2002. *Costs of Sprawl—2000.* Transportation Research Board of the National Research Council. Washington: National Academy Press.

Burtless, Gary, and Christopher Jencks. 2003. "American Inequality and Its Consequences." In *Agenda for the Nation*, edited by Henry J. Aaron, James M. Lindsay, and Pietro S. Nivola, pp. 61–108. Brookings.

Clark, William A. V., and Sarah A. Blue. 2004. "Race, Class, and Segregation Patterns in U.S. Immigrant Gateway Cities." *Urban Affairs Review* 39, no. 6: 667–88.

Clotfelter, Charles T. 2004. *After Brown: The Ruse and Retreat of School Desegregation.* Princeton University Press.

Coleman, James. 1966. *Equality of Educational Opportunity.* U.S. Government Printing Office.

Crain, Robert L., and Amy S. Wells. 1994. "Perpetuation Theory and the Long-Term Effects of School Desegregation." *Review of Educational Research* 64, no. 4: 531–53.

Danielson, Michael. 1976. *The Politics of Exclusion.* Columbia University Press.

Dickens, William. 2003. "Comment on Massey and Fischer." *Brookings-Wharton Papers on Urban Affairs 2003:* 1–30

Downs, Anthony. 2004. "Growth Management, Smart Growth, and Affordable Housing." In *Growth Management and Affordable Housing: Do They Conflict?* edited by Anthony Downs, pp. 264–74. Brookings.

Ellen, Ingrid Gould. 1999. "Spatial Stratification within U.S. Metropolitan Areas." In *Governance and Opportunity in Metropolitan America*, edited by Alan Altshuler and others, pp. 192–212. Washington: National Academy Press.

———. 2000. *Sharing America's Neighborhoods: Prospects for Stable Racial Integration.* Harvard University Press.

Ellen, Ingrid Gould, Tod Mijanovich, and Keri-Nicole Dillman. 2001. "Neighborhood Effects on Health: Exploring the Links and Assessing the Evidence." *Journal of Urban Affairs* 23, nos. 3-4: 391–408.

Ellen, Ingrid Gould, and Margery Austin Turner. 2003. "Do Neighborhoods Matter, and Why?" In *Choosing a Better Life? Evaluating the Moving to Opportunity Social Experiment*, edited by John Goering and Judith Feins, pp. 313–38. Washington: Urban Institute.

Estlund, Cynthia. 2003. *Working Together: How Workplace Bonds Strengthen a Diverse Democracy.* Oxford University Press.

Fischel, William A. 2001. *The Homevoter Hypothesis: How Home Values Influence Local Government Taxation, School Finance, and Land Use Policies.* Harvard University Press.

Fishman, Robert. 2002. "The Death and Life of American Regional Planning." In *Reflections on Regionalism*, edited by Bruce Katz, pp. 107–23. Brookings.

Frankenberg, Erica, and Chungmei Lee. 2003. "Charter Schools and Race: A Lost Opportunity for Integrated Education." Civil Rights Project, Harvard University, July.

Frankenberg, Erica, Chungmei Lee, and Gary Orfield. 2003. "A Multiracial Society with Segregated Schools: Are We Losing the Dream?" Civil Rights Project, Harvard University, January.

Frey, William. 2003. "Melting Pot Suburbs: A Study of Suburban Diversity." In *Redefining Urban and Suburban America: Evidence from Census 2000,* vol. 1, edited by Bruce Katz and Robert E. Lang, pp. 155–80. Brookings.

Friedrichs, Jürgen, George Galster, and Sako Musterd. 2003. "Neighborhood Effects on Social Opportunities: The European and American Research and Policy Context." *Housing Studies* 18, no. 6: 797–806.

Fulton, William, and others. 2001. "Who Sprawls Most? How Growth Patterns Differ Across the U.S." Metropolitan Policy Program, Brookings, July.

Glaeser, Edward L., and Matthew Kahn. 2004. "Sprawl and Urban Growth." In *Handbook of Regional and Urban Economics: Cities and Geography*, vol. 4, edited by J. V. Henderson and J. F. Thisse. New York: North-Holland.

Glaeser, Edward L., and Jacob Vigdor. 2003. "Racial Segregation: Promising News." In *Redefining Urban and Suburban America: Evidence from Census 2000,* vol. 1, edited by Bruce Katz and Robert E. Lang, pp. 211–34. Brookings.

Goldberg, Heidi. 2001. *State and County Supported Car Ownership Programs Can Help Low-Income Families Secure and Keep Jobs.* Washington: Center on Budget and Policy Priorities.

Grutter v. Bollinger. 2003a. 71 U.S.L.W. 4498.

———. 2003b. 71 U.S.L.W. 4480.

Henig, Jeffrey. 2002. "Equity and the Future Politics of Growth." In *Urban Sprawl: Causes, Consequences, and Policy Responses*, edited by Gregory D. Squires, pp. 325–50. Washington: Urban Institute.

Ihlanfeldt, Keith R., and David Sjoquist. 1998. "The Spatial Mismatch Hypothesis: A Review of Recent Studies and Their Implications for Welfare Reform." *Housing Policy Debate* 9, no. 4: 849–92.

Jackson, Kenneth. 2000. "Gentleman's Agreement: Discrimination in Metropolitan America." In *Reflections on Regionalism*, edited by Bruce Katz, pp. 185–217. Brookings.

Jargowsky, Paul. 1997. *Poverty and Place: Ghettos, Barrios, and the American City.* New York: Russell Sage.

———. 2003. "Stunning Progress, Hidden Problems: The Dramatic Decline of Concentrated Poverty in the 1990s." Metropolitan Policy Program, Brookings, May.

Jencks, Christopher, and Susan E. Mayer. 1990. "The Social Consequences of Growing up in a Poor Neighborhood." In *Inner-City Poverty in the United States,* edited by Lawrence E. Lynn and Michael G. H. McGeary. Washington: National Academy Press.

Jencks, Christopher, and Meredith Phillips. 1998. "The Black-White Test Score Gap: An Introduction." In *The Black-White Test Score Gap,* edited by Christopher Jencks and Meredith Phillips, pp. 1–53. Brookings.

Joint Center for Housing Studies. 2003. *State of the Nation's Housing.* Harvard University.

Kain, John. 1968. "Housing Desegregation, Negro Employment, and Metropolitan Decentralization." *Quarterly Journal of Economics* 32, no. 2: 175–97.

Kane, Thomas J., Douglas O. Staiger, and Gavin Samms. 2003. "School Accountability Ratings and Housing Values." *Brookings-Wharton Papers on Urban Affairs 2003*: 83–138.

Kasarda, John. 1995. "Industrial Restructuring and the Changing Location of Jobs." In *State of the Union: America in the 1990s,* vol. 1, *Economic Trends,* edited by Reynolds Farley, pp. 215–68. New York: Russell Sage.

Katz, Bruce, and Robert E. Lang. 2003. "Introduction." In *Redefining Urban and Suburban America, Evidence from Census 2000,* vol. 1, edited by Bruce Katz and Robert E. Lang, pp. 1–13. Brookings.

Kingsley, G. Thomas, and Kathryn Pettit. 2003. "Concentrated Poverty: A Change in Course." National Neighborhood Indicators Project, Urban Institute, May.

Kirschenman, Joleen, and Kathryn M. Neckerman. 1991. "'We'd Love to Hire Them But . . .': The Meaning of Race for Employers." In *The Urban Underclass,* edited by Christopher Jencks and Paul E. Peterson, pp. 203–32. Brookings.

Leventhal, Tama, and Jeanne Brooks-Gunn. 2000. "The Neighborhoods They Live In: The Effects of Neighborhood Residence on Child and Adolescent Outcomes." *Psychological Bulletin* 126, no. 2: 309–37.

Levy, Frank. 2003. "Comment on Massey and Fischer." *Brookings-Wharton Papers on Urban Affairs 2003*: 1–30.

Lindsay, James M., and Audrey Singer. 2003. "Changing Faces: Immigrants and Diversity in the Twenty-First Century." In *Agenda for the Nation,* edited by Henry J. Aaron, James M. Lindsay, and Pietro S. Nivola, pp. 217–60. Brookings.

Logan, John. 2003. "Ethnic Diversity Grows, Neighborhood Integration Lags." In *Redefining Urban and Suburban America: Evidence from Census 2000,* vol. 1, edited by Bruce Katz and Robert E. Lang, pp. 235–56. Brookings.

Logan, John, Deirdre Oakley, and Jacob Stowell. 2003. "Segregation in Neighborhoods and Schools: Impacts on Minority Children in the Boston Region." Metro Boston Equity Initiative of the Civil Rights Project, Harvard University, September.

Massey, Douglas S. 2001. "Residential Segregation and Neighborhood Conditions." In *America Becoming: Racial Trends and Their Consequences,* vol. 1, edited by Neil J. Smelser, William Julius Wilson, and Faith Mitchell, pp. 391–434. Washington: National Academy Press.

Massey, Douglas S., and Nancy A. Denton. 1993. *American Apartheid: Segregation and the Making of the Underclass.* Harvard University Press.

Massey, Douglas S., and Mary Fischer. 2003. "The Geography of Inequality in the United States, 1950–2000." *Brookings-Wharton Papers on Urban Affairs 2003*: 1–30.

Massey, Douglas S., Michael J. White, and Voon Chin Phua. 1996. "The Dimensions of Segregation Revisited." *Sociological Methods and Research* 25, no. 2: 172–206.

Moe, Richard, and Carter Wilkie. 1997. *Changing Places: Rebuilding Community in the Age of Sprawl.* New York: Henry Holt.

Nelson, Arthur. 2003. "Top Ten State and Local Strategies to Increase Affordable Housing Supply." Fannie Mae Foundation. *Housing Facts and Findings* 5, no. 1: 1, 4–7.

Nivola, Pietro S. 1999. *Laws of the Landscape: How Policies Shape Cities in Europe and America.* Brookings.

Nyden, Philip, Michael Maly, and John Lukehart. 1997. "The Emergence of Stable, Racially and Ethnically Diverse Urban Communities: A Case Study of Nine U.S. Cities." *Housing Policy Debate* 8, no. 2: 491–534.

Orfield, Gary, and Susan E. Eaton. 1996. *Dismantling Desegregation: The Quiet Reversal of Brown v. Board of Education.* New York: New Press.

Orfield, Myron. 2002. *American Metropolitics: The New Suburban Reality.* Brookings.

Pastor, Manuel, Jr. 2001. "Geography and Opportunity." In *America Becoming: Racial Trends and Their Consequences,* vol. 1, edited by Neil J. Smelser, William Julius Wilson, and Faith Mitchell, pp. 435–67. Washington: National Academy Press.

Pastor, Manuel, Jr., and others. 2000. *Regions that Work: How Cities and Suburbs Can Grow Together.* University of Minnesota Press.

Putnam, Robert. 2000. *Bowling Alone: The Collapse and Revival of Community in America.* New York: Simon and Schuster.

Quillian, Lincoln. 2002. "Why Is Black-White Residential Segregation So Persistent? Evidence on Three Theories from Migration Data." *Social Science Research* 31: 197–229.

———. 2003. "How Long Are Exposures to Poor Neighborhoods? The Long-Term Dynamics of Entry and Exit from Poor Neighborhoods." *Population Research and Policy Review* 22: 221–49.

Raphael, Steven, and Michael A. Stoll. 2000. "Can Boosting Minority Car-Ownership Rates Narrow Inter-Racial Employment Gaps?" Working paper. Joint Center for Poverty Research, Northwestern University.

———. 2002. "Modest Progress: The Narrowing Spatial Mismatch between Blacks and Jobs in the 1990s." Metropolitan Policy Program, Brookings, December.

Rawlings, Lynette, Laura Harris, and Margery Austin Turner, with Sandra Padilla. 2004. *Race and Residence: Prospects for Stable Racial Integration.* Policy Brief 3. Metropolitan Housing and Communities Center, Urban Institute, March.

Rusk, David. 1999. *Inside Game/Outside Game: Winning Strategies for Saving Urban America.* Brookings.

Savitch, H. V. 2002. "Encourage, then Cope: Washington and the Sprawl Machine." In *Urban Sprawl: Causes, Consequences, and Policy Responses,* edited by Gregory D. Squires, pp. 141–64. Washington: Urban Institute.

Schacter, Jason P., Rachel S. Franklin, and Marc J. Perry. 2003. *Migration and Geographic Mobility in Metropolitan and Nonmetropolitan America: 1995 to 2000.* CENSR-9. Census Bureau.

Schelling, Thomas C. 1971. "Dynamic Models of Segregation." *Journal of Mathematical Sociology* 1: 143–86.

Squires, Gregory D. 2002. "Urban Sprawl and the Uneven Development of Metropolitan America." In *Urban Sprawl: Causes, Consequences, and Policy Responses,* edited by Gregory D. Squires, pp. 1–22. Washington: Urban Institute.

Staley, Samuel. 1999. "The Sprawling of America: In Defense of the Dynamic City." Policy Study 236. Reason Public Policy Institute, Los Angeles, February.

———. 2000. "The Vanishing Farmland Myth and the Smart Growth Agenda." Policy Brief 12. Reason Public Policy Institute, Los Angeles, January.

Suro, Roberto, and Audrey Singer. 2003. "Changing Patterns of Latino Growth in Metropolitan America." In *Redefining Urban and Suburban America: Evidence from Census 2000,* vol. 1, edited by Bruce Katz and Robert E. Lang, pp. 181–210. Brookings.

Tilly, Chris, and others. 2001. "Space as a Signal: How Employers Perceive Neighborhoods in Four Metropolitan Labor Markets." In *Urban Inequality: Evidence from Four Cities,* edited by Alice O'Connor, Chris Tilly, and Lawrence D. Bobo, pp. 304–39. New York: Russell Sage.

U.S. Census Bureau. 2001. *Overview of Race and Hispanic Origin.* Census 2000 brief. U.S. Government Printing Office.

———. 2002. *2002 Census of Governments,* vol. 1, no. 1, *Government Organization.* GC02(1)-1. U.S. Government Printing Office.

———. 2003. *National Population Estimates to July 1, 2002 (Tables).* U.S. Government Printing Office.

U.S. Department of Housing and Urban Development. 2000. *The State of the Cities 2000.* U.S. Government Printing Office.

———. 2004. *U.S. Housing Market Conditions: First Quarter 2004.* U.S. Government Printing Office.

Wilson, Franklin D., and Roger B. Hammer. 2001. "Ethnic Residential Segregation and Its Consequences." In *Urban Inequality: Evidence from Four Cities,* edited by Alice O'Connor, Chris Tilly, and Lawrence D. Bobo, pp. 272–303. New York: Russell Sage.

Wilson, William Julius. 1987. *The Truly Disadvantaged: The Inner City, the Underclass, and Public Policy.* University of Chicago Press.

Zhou, Min. 2001. "Contemporary Immigration and the Dynamics of Race and Ethnicity." In *America Becoming: Racial Trends and Their Consequences,* vol. 1, edited by Neil J. Smelser, William Julius Wilson, and Faith Mitchell, pp. 200–40. Washington: National Academy Press.

PART I

Housing Choice, Racial Attitudes, and Discrimination

3

Can We Live Together? Racial Preferences and Neighborhood Outcomes

CAMILLE ZUBRINSKY CHARLES

The geography of America's metropolitan regions is clearly color coded. But the ways in which distinctive racial attitudes and neighborhood preferences shape racial patterns in housing—and through them the geography of opportunity—are not widely understood. For most Americans, the complexities become at least somewhat clear when they think about their own housing needs and neighborhood choices—about the ways in which they go about choosing where, how, and around whom they wish to live.

For example, when my husband and I moved to Philadelphia seven years ago, we were confronted with having to find a place to live in a city with which we were almost completely unfamiliar. Instinctively, we set about grilling our new friends and soon-to-be colleagues and reading everything we could find about the metropolitan area's neighborhoods and its housing market—a crash course in Philadelphia real estate. We did what most people do: We gathered as much information as we could and, within a set of constraints and preferences, found a house that fit our needs as well as possible. Some of the constraints and preferences, however, were more obvious and easily negotiated than others. Clearly, our most basic and fundamental constraint was economic. I was an assistant professor and my husband a full-time student and research assistant. We were selling a home but had not owned it long enough to do more than break even, so there was no equity for "buying up."

Beyond our economic constraints (which, incidentally, still allowed us to move into a larger home located in a better neighborhood than the one we left behind), we had preferences that were clearly a function of our stage in life. We were planning to have children, so we needed more room than we had needed before; our families live on the West Coast, so we knew that we would need extra room for out-of-town guests as well. We wanted to have access to local recreational facilities (a dog park would be nice, in addition to the standard fare with a children's playground) and a neighborhood that was safe enough—and close enough—that I could walk to and from the university, even at night. We paid attention to neighborhood school quality but, significantly, decided that our options were such that this did not have to be a primary concern (we could either move or opt for private school when the time came). We wanted a fireplace, a large kitchen, and a yard. These constraints and preferences, some about the housing unit and others about location (neighborhood), were similar to those of most (fairly) young, upwardly mobile, recently married couples planning to have both kids and careers.

But less typically, my husband and I also knew that the neighborhood we settled in and built our new life in had to be racially integrated. Plainly put, we both valued diversity, but we also wanted to live among a substantial number of "people like us" (our co-ethnics). I cannot say exactly what we meant by "substantial," since we never talked about it directly. As it turns out, though, a range of locations that we considered offered a composition that was acceptably "substantial." This standard was roughly the same for both of us; we knew it when we saw it—and when we did not. Beyond our basic economic constraints, it turns out that this was among the most important of our preferences. Without this mutually understood, but otherwise unspoken, level of co-ethnic representation, *together* with meaningful integration with "people not like us" (out-groups), even our "dream house" in an otherwise perfect neighborhood was not likely to be an option.

The issue of neighborhood racial composition is a concern for most people in America, whether or not they are willing to say so openly and whether or not they are even consciously aware of it. For my husband and me, it was conscious, possibly because I study racial attitudes and residential segregation for a living and possibly because we are professionally successful people of color who often find ourselves in the minority in a variety of settings—particularly in the workplace and at school, where we spend the majority of our days. The fact is that our concerns about the racial composition of our neighborhood are inexorably tied to our racial group membership. My husband and I are African American. According to survey data, if we were white (or Hispanic or Asian), our preferences would likely be different. We would still prefer a neighborhood with more than token numbers of same-race residents, but exactly what that meant—and equally important, *which* out-groups were acceptable other-race neighbors—

would vary in predictable ways. This chapter is about those differences and how they shape our communities.

Many public discussions of racial attitudes tend to center on what white people think. But the housing choices made by all groups are a function, in part, of racial attitudes and preferences. For example, many nonwhites believe that the presence of a "critical mass" of co-ethnics offers both the comfort of familiarity and a buffer against potential hostility. A racially integrated neighborhood signals to nonwhite potential residents that people like them are valued and welcome there, especially if the neighborhood has a strong showing of inhabitants of the same race as the potential residents. Similarly, areas that are overwhelmingly white—or largely devoid of co-ethnics—often are perceived as hostile and unwelcoming. At the same time, however, racial prejudice also plays a role in nonwhites' preferences, even though they express concern about racial hostility directed at them. Whites also prefer a meaningful co-ethnic presence. In fact, this preference is stronger among whites than any of the nonwhite groups. It appears, however, that the preferences of whites are more directly shaped by active racial prejudice. These preferences are not just reports made to survey researchers; careful economic analysis of whites' neighborhood outcomes indicates that racial preferences have a significant effect on the racial makeup of whites' neighborhoods once income, life stage, and a variety of other factors are held constant.[1]

Thus racial attitudes and intergroup relations, which are critical aspects of neighborhood outcomes, are often downplayed or neglected in efforts intended to improve housing options, increase neighborhood residential integration, or reduce inequality more generally. As America is transformed demographically and as the shape of its sprawling metropolitan communities continues to evolve, understanding these attitudes and preferences is crucial. Segregation contributes powerfully to social and economic inequality, fragmented politics, and intergroup relations, in which different racial and ethnic groups continue to see the worst in each other.[2] This chapter begins with a review of recent trends in racial attitudes, paying particular attention to attitudes related to neighborhood racial composition and neighborhood preferences. This is followed by an analysis of both patterns of preferences among whites, blacks, Hispanics, and Asians and the primary forces driving those preferences, using newly available survey data from four of the nation's largest metropolitan areas: Atlanta, Boston, Detroit, and Los Angeles. The chapter ends with a consideration of the implications of racial attitudes and preferences for efforts to reshape the geography of race and reduce racial inequality.

1. Ihlanfeldt and Scafidi (2004).
2. Du Bois (1990).

Trends in Racial Attitudes: A Mix of Progress and Stagnation

The sociologist Larry Bobo, in an overview of trends in American racial attitudes and relations, concludes that "the glass is half full or the glass is half empty, depending on what one chooses to emphasize." The good news is that the second half of the twentieth century was a period of "steady and sweeping movement toward general endorsement of the principles of racial equality and integration."[3] While blacks have a long history of endorsing racial equality and integration, that has not been the case for a substantial portion of the white population.[4] By the early 1970s, however, the vast majority of whites endorsed equal access to employment and the integration of public transportation.

The shift in white attitudes toward school integration was slower, but analyses of trends in racial attitudes show that by the mid-1990s, whites almost universally endorsed this principle as well. Yet despite improvement, whites still showed less support for equality of access to housing and even less support for interracial marriage; indeed, the greatest evidence of increased acceptance of racial equality and integration is found in the most public or impersonal societal arenas.[5] Overall, however, Bobo characterizes these trends as sweeping and robust, illustrative of a positive shift "in fundamental norms with regard to race."[6] Combined with other noteworthy improvements—the increasing size and relative security of the black middle class, the increasing presence of blacks and other minorities in positions of political and corporate power, and small but meaningful declines in residential segregation—it is clear that Gunnar Myrdal's "American dilemma" is closer to being resolved than ever before.[7]

Unfortunately, others support a more pessimistic interpretation. These trends highlight persisting socioeconomic inequity by race and, just as troubling, vastly different perceptions of its root causes. Patterns of persisting inequality are well known. Blacks and Hispanics complete fewer years of school and are concentrated in lower-status jobs than whites, and they earn less income and accumulate less wealth.[8] There is also substantial evidence of systematic racial discrimination against blacks—in the labor and housing markets and in interpersonal relations—irrespective of their social class.[9]

3. Bobo (2001, pp. 294, 269).

4. Because social scientists have only recently attempted to study the racial attitudes of Latinos and Asians, we know very little regarding trends in racial attitudes for these groups. Thus most of this discussion is centered on the racial attitudes of whites and blacks. When possible, however, I include what is known about Asian and Hispanic attitudes.

5. Bobo (2001); Schuman and others (1997).

6. Bobo (2001, p. 273).

7. Myrdal (1972).

8. Farley (1996); Oliver and Shapiro (1995).

9. Bertrand and Mullainathan (2004); Bobo and Suh (2000); Feagin and Sikes (1994); Feagin and Vera (1995); Kirschenman and Neckerman (1991); Waldinger and Bailey (1991); Yinger (1995). Newer research suggests that Hispanics and Asians also face racial discrimination in the housing market. See for example Turner and others (2002); Turner and Ross, chapter 4, this volume.

Although the proportion of whites with uniformly negative stereotypes of minorities has declined substantially, antiminority stereotypes remain common among whites. The vast majority of whites—between 54 and 78 percent, depending on the trait in question—still express some negative stereotypes of blacks and Hispanics; for nearly a quarter of whites, these are firmly negative views. A much lower percentage of whites (between 10 and 40 percent, again, depending on the trait) stereotype Asians negatively.[10] The expression of negative racial stereotypes has also changed. Now it is likely to be more qualified and less categorical than in previous eras, more rooted in cultural and volitional explanations than in beliefs about biological inferiority. Moreover, whites are not alone in the tendency to stereotype; evidence suggests that although the story is more complicated, minority groups also hold negative stereotypes, both of whites and of each other.[11]

In addition to patterns of racial stereotyping and perhaps in part because of persisting racial stereotypes, whites and nonwhites continue to hold decidedly different opinions about both the prevalence of racial discrimination and the causes of racial inequality. Whites acknowledge some discrimination but tend to minimize its present-day importance, suggesting that it is largely the domain of "a few bad apples." Moreover, if blacks and other minority groups cannot get ahead, whites are inclined to perceive it as a consequence of their own lack of motivation or other cultural deficiencies. Specifically, only 20 to 25 percent of whites believe that blacks and Hispanics face "a lot" of discrimination in the areas of employment, and even fewer—less than 10 percent—believe that this is true for Asians.[12]

Blacks, Hispanics, and to a much smaller degree Asians, on the other hand, report that racial discrimination is systemic, pervasive, and as a consequence deeply implicated in persisting racial inequality. Fully 70 percent of blacks and 60 percent of Hispanics but less than 10 percent of Asians believe that to be the case regarding structural barriers facing their own group.[13] Thus if African Americans and Hispanics are inadequately prepared for college admission relative to whites and Asians (for example, by having lower college entrance exam scores and taking fewer advanced placement courses), whites are more inclined to believe that it is primarily because these groups lack motivation or do not value education. On the other hand, blacks, Hispanics, and, again to a far lesser extent, Asians are more inclined to invoke explanations rooted in structural barriers, that is, the persistence of racial discrimination in society or a lack of opportunity for a good education.

10. Bobo (2001); Charles (2000a, 2001); Smith (1990); Sniderman and Carmines (1997).

11. Bobo (2001); Bobo and Massagli (2002); Charles (2000a, 2001).

12. Bobo (2001, pp. 281–82).

13. Bobo (2001); Bobo and Suh (2000); Zubrinsky and Bobo (1996). All groups believe that Asians face very little racial discrimination, including Asians themselves. Blacks and Hispanics also tend to downplay the structural barriers facing the other group.

Naturally, persisting antiminority stereotypes and clear-cut differences in opinions about racial discrimination and inequality have had an impact on political attitudes—particularly support for progressive social policies. Research by James Kluegel and Elliot Smith indicates that the more whites' explanations for inequality are rooted in cultural or volitional deficiencies rather than structural barriers, the less likely they are to support government intervention. Again, however, there is variation in support according to the type of integration involved: whites' support for intervention is highest regarding the most public, impersonal domains (for example, access to public accommodations and transportation) and lowest regarding efforts to integrate more personal domains, such as neighborhoods and public schools. By the early 1970s, for example, nearly all whites believed that public transportation should be integrated and believed in equal employment opportunities; by the mid-1990s, 96 percent of whites favored school integration. As recently as 1988, however, only about half of whites expressed support for a law barring racial discrimination in the sale or rental of housing, and in 1990, 20 percent of whites opposed interracial marriage (Bobo 2001; Schuman and others 1997).[14]

Similarly, support for affirmative action among whites depends on the type of policy proposed, with those intended to increase the human capital attributes of disadvantaged groups garnering more support than those to extend preferential treatment.[15] Blacks express greater support for a variety of affirmative action policies, either because they represent a way to compensate for past discrimination or because they are perceived as an important strategy for combating ongoing discrimination.[16] Policies that involve quotas are unpopular among both whites and blacks.[17]

On the whole, whites' attitudes toward the implementation of policies to ensure equality of treatment show no clear positive trend and in many instances contradict the shift toward embracing racial equality and integration in principle.[18] This is evidenced by whites' continued opposition to many race-based social policies (for example, affirmative action) as well as those with implicit racial elements (for example, powder versus crack cocaine sentencing and welfare reform).[19]

14. See Kluegel and Smith (1982); Schuman and Bobo (1988). It should be noted that antiminority animus is not the only source of opposition to government involvement in effecting positive racial change.

15. Bobo and Kluegel (1993); Bobo and Smith (1994); Kluegel and Smith (1982); Lipset and Schneider (1978); Schuman and others (1997).

16. Schuman and others (1997).

17. Bobo and Kluegel (1993); Kluegel and Smith (1982); Steeh and Krysan (1996).

18. Bobo (2001); Schuman and others (1997).

19. Bobo and Kluegel (1993); Gilens (1995, 1996); Hurwitz and Peffley (1997); Peffley, Hurwitz, and Sniderman (1997).

A final troubling trend in racial attitudes is particularly relevant to discussions of housing opportunity, housing choice, and increasing residential integration. Despite some improvement, there are substantial differences in both the meaning and preferred levels of racial integration across racial categories. For many whites, a racially integrated neighborhood is one that is majority white. Whites are willing to live with a small number of blacks (and slightly more Hispanics and Asians); however, they prefer predominantly same-race neighborhoods. Blacks, Hispanics, and Asians, on the other hand, all prefer substantially more racial integration and are more comfortable as a numerical minority. But each minority group has a preference for a greater number of co-ethnic (nonwhite) neighbors than most whites could tolerate in their own neighborhood—suggesting that racial change in neighborhoods might inevitably lead to "tipping" toward a majority race makeup rather than a stable mix. That is one reason that careful observers focus on the question of how stable neighborhood integration is in America, not just how extensive it is.[20] Also telling is the fact that neighborhood racial composition preferences reveal a racial hierarchy in which whites are always the most preferred out-group and blacks are unequivocally the least preferred.[21]

There is good reason to believe that the "bad news" trends detailed above are a driving force in neighborhood racial composition preferences. A growing body of research points to the direct effects of negative racial stereotypes on preferences for integration. As expected, the more negatively a particular racial group is perceived, the less desirable its members are perceived as potential neighbors, and that is especially true for whites. Whites' perceptions of neighborhood desirability are also influenced by racial composition. As the number of minorities in a neighborhood increases, it becomes increasingly undesirable to whites, particularly if the minority residents are black or Hispanic. This is true even when neighborhoods are, as Ingrid Ellen puts it, structurally strong (that is, safe, largely owner occupied, and middle class or affluent). For minority group members, neighborhood desirability is tied to their perceptions of racial tolerance; understandably, those communities perceived by minorities as hostile toward people like themselves are less desirable than those perceived as welcoming. As a result, minority group members tend to find integrated (mixed) neighborhoods more attractive and to view overwhelmingly white neighborhoods with suspicion or trepidation.[22] From this vantage point, it is encouraging that, according to census data, the number of exclusively white neighborhoods dropped significantly, both in central cities and suburbs, during the 1990s.[23]

20. See, for example, Ellen (2000); Rawlings and others (2004).

21. Bobo (2001); Bobo and Zubrinsky (1996); Charles (2000a, 2001); Farley, Schuman, and others (1978, 1994); Farley, Steeh, and others (1993).

22. See Ellen (2000). Also see Charles (2001); Farley, Steeh, and others (1993); Krysan and Farley (2002); Zubrinsky and Bobo (1996).

23. Rawlings and others (2004).

More generally, persistent adherence to negative racial stereotypes—particularly but not exclusively among whites—and often severely divergent views on racial issues contribute to interracial interactions "rife with the potential for missteps, misunderstanding, and insult" and a fair amount of mistrust.[24] This sense of interracial awkwardness no doubt factors into people's preferences about where to live and who lives around them and into how they search for housing. On a variety of fronts, then, the attitudes and preferences of a variety of racial and ethnic groups are critically important to developing effective strategies for expanding housing opportunities and choices as well as reducing racial inequality in America.

The Multicity Study of Urban Inequality

Until fairly recently, knowledge of attitudes toward racial residential integration was limited in one or more of the following ways:[25]

—Studies considered only whites and blacks in an increasingly multiracial society.[26]

—Data from a single metropolitan area might not be generalizable to other areas or to the nation as a whole.[27]

—Studies relied on awkward or limited measures of preferences.[28]

The most well-respected and widely cited study of preferences, however, is limited not only because it considers only Detroit-area whites and blacks but also because it is nearly thirty years old. In the classic study "Chocolate City, Vanilla Suburbs," the sociologist Reynolds Farley and colleagues introduced an innovative visual "show card" method of measuring attitudes toward racial integration. Results revealed substantial white resistance to even minimal levels of residential integration with blacks; conversely, the majority of Detroit-area blacks preferred a neighborhood that was half black and half white.[29] When asked to explain their selection, two-thirds of blacks stressed the importance of racial harmony. These findings have influenced important general assessments of the social and economic status of African Americans by Derek Bok and by Gerald Jaynes and Robin Williams, as well as two major treatises on the process

24. Bobo (2001, p. 279).

25. Typical limitations include questions about a single threshold of integration (such as half out-group) rather than a range of questions or survey methods (like a phone survey) that offer respondents no visual cues.

26. Farley, Shuman, and others (1994); Farley, Steeh, and others (1993); Krysan (2002); Krysan and Farley (2002); Timberlake (2000).

27. Bobo and Zubrinsky (1996); Charles (2000a, 2000b); Farley, Schuman, and others (1994); Farley, Steeh, and others (1993); Timberlake (2000); Zubrinsky and Bobo (1996).

28. Bobo and Zubrinsky (1996); Clark (1992).

29. Farley, Schuman, and others (1978, p. 328).

of residential segregation (Douglas Massey and Nancy Denton) and restricted housing opportunity (John Yinger).[30]

The 1992–94 Multi-City Study of Urban Inequality (MCSUI) addresses each of these limitations. The MCSUI is a large (8,916 respondents), multifaceted survey research project that was designed to examine cross-cutting explanations for racial inequality broadly defined and provide fresh data from a major metropolitan area from each region of the country—Atlanta, Boston, Detroit, and Los Angeles. These metropolitan areas have a variety of racial mixes—ranging from mainly white-black (Atlanta and Detroit) to the epitome of multiethnicity (Los Angeles)—and their own histories of economic and political development, race relations, and segregation.[31] Similarly, each area's more recent neighborhood context, pattern of racial residential segregation, experience of economic restructuring, and response to racial-ethnic tensions or immigration make these data unique in their capacity to address the wide range of factors related to housing.

A specific aim of the MCSUI was to replicate the methodology developed for the Detroit area survey for each metropolitan area, providing for the first time a fully multiracial examination of neighborhood racial composition preferences across metropolitan areas. Together, the data facilitate examination of changes in the neighborhood racial composition preferences of whites and blacks since the 1970s; the neighborhood racial composition preferences of Hispanics and Asians—two rapidly growing, internally diverse groups—providing baseline information and allowing comparison with whites and blacks; and ways in which racial attitudes shape preferences for neighborhood racial integration for these groups. In short, the MCSUI offers what are arguably the best, most up-to-date data on neighborhood racial composition preferences and racial attitudes.

30. Bok (1996, p. 182); Jaynes and Williams (1989, pp. 141–44); Massey and Denton (1993); Yinger (1995).

31. The MCSUI is a face-to-face household survey of adults twenty-one years of age or older. The primary sampling unit for the survey is the census tract stratified by racial-ethnic composition and the percentage of the population with incomes below the poverty line. Stata Press's survey data commands were employed for all statistical procedures to correct for the multistage cluster sampling method (Stata Press 1999, 321–33). Respondents identified as one of the following: non-Hispanic white (2,935), African American or black (3,167), Hispanic (1,695), or Asian (overwhelmingly of Korean, Japanese, or Chinese descent: 1,090), for a total of 8,887 respondents. In addition to generating over samples of blacks (Los Angeles and Boston), Hispanics (Boston), and Asians (Los Angeles), efforts were made to fully capture the views, opinions, and experiences of immigrants. To accomplish this, the English-language version of the survey was also translated into Spanish, Korean, Mandarin, and Cantonese. Those respondents who either did not speak English or preferred to conduct the interview in one of these other languages were interviewed using the appropriate foreign language survey. Unadjusted response rates range from 68 percent (Los Angeles) to 78 percent (Detroit). For further details, see Inter-University Consortium for Political and Social Research (2000).

Preferred Neighborhood Racial Composition

In the Detroit area survey, white respondents were asked about their comfort with and willingness to enter neighborhoods with varying degrees of integration with blacks. Black respondents received a similar questionnaire in which they rated neighborhoods of varying racial composition (ranging from entirely black to entirely white) from most to least attractive and indicated their willingness to enter each of the neighborhoods. The scenarios represented realistic assumptions about the residential experiences and options of both groups of respondents. The original experiment was expanded in Los Angeles and Boston to include Hispanics and Asians, both as respondents and as potential neighbors. Hispanic and Asian respondents completed questionnaires similar to the one originally used for black respondents.[32] Neighborhood cards similar to those used in the original show card experiment are presented in figure 3-1. The neighborhood racial composition preferences of whites, blacks, Hispanics, and Asians are detailed below.

Whites' Preferences

To gauge the preferences of whites, respondents were shown five cards similar to those in the top row of figure 3-1. Consistent with the original Farley-Schuman experiment, each card depicts fifteen houses with varying degrees of integration with a single target group, either black, Hispanic, or Asian; the respondent's home is identified by an X in the middle of each card. The experiment begins with respondents being asked to imagine that they live in an all-white neighborhood; they are then shown the second card and asked how comfortable they would feel in a neighborhood with a single nonwhite household. Respondents expressing some level of comfort (either "very" or "somewhat comfortable") are asked about increasingly integrated neighborhoods until they either indicate discomfort or reach the final card: a neighborhood that is majority minority (see card 5 in the white respondent scenario, figure 3-1).

This first line of questioning is intended to capture respondents' comfort with racial change and tests the "white flight" hypothesis, a long-standing explanation for residential segregation that posits that uncomfortable levels of racial integration motivate whites to leave their existing neighborhoods for new ones. However, a full understanding of the importance of neighborhood racial composition in residential decisionmaking also requires consideration of whites'

32. Using a split-ballot technique, one-third of each respondent racial category in Los Angeles (whites, blacks, Hispanics, and Asians) and Boston (whites, blacks, and Hispanics) was randomly assigned to one of three out-groups (for example, one-third of Hispanics completed the Hispanic-white experiment, one-third completed a Hispanic-black experiment, and the remaining one-third of Hispanics considered integration with Asians). For details, see Charles (2001); Zubrinsky and Bobo (1996).

Figure 3-1. *Neighborhood Show Cards for White and Black Respondents*[a]

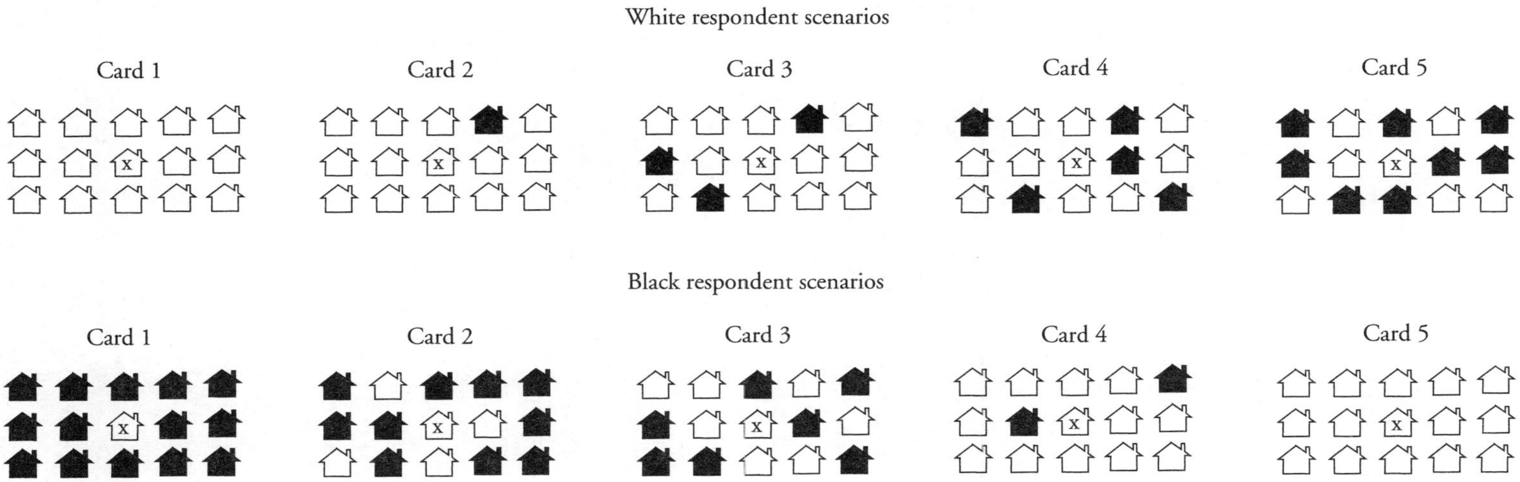

Source: Inter-University Consortium for Political and Social Research (2000).

a. White houses represent white neighbors, and black houses, black neighbors. In later figures, dark grey indicates Hispanic neighbors, and light grey, Asian neighbors. X marks the respondent's house.

willingness to *move into* racially integrated areas once they have decided to move. To capture this side of the decisionmaking process, the second line of questioning asks white respondents whether they would consider moving into any of the neighborhoods shown on the cards.[33] Results from these experiments are summarized in figure 3-2, according to target group.

The reassuring news is that, relative to the 1970s, whites expressed greater comfort with higher levels of integration where they already lived and were more willing to move into racially integrated areas. Indeed, a sizable majority (between 60 and about 85 percent) of whites was comfortable in a neighborhood that was one-third nonwhite, yet a ranking of out-groups by race is evident: White respondents were most comfortable with Asians and least comfortable with blacks, and comfort declined as the number of out-group neighbors increased. When presented with the majority-minority neighborhood, moreover, whites' comfort levels declined dramatically. This is most clear in relation to black neighbors, where whites' comfort level dipped below 40 percent, a decline of more than 20 percent from the immediately preceding scenario—the largest decline in the table. In fact, declines in white comfort from one card to the next were typically the largest when whites were considering integration with blacks.

The second panel in figure 3-2 details whites' willingness to enter each of the neighborhoods. The two panels are similar except that, compared to their expressed comfort with integration (first panel), declines in whites' willingness to enter integrated neighborhoods begins earlier and their willingness to enter is never as high as their comfort with neighborhood racial change. For example, while 60 percent of whites were comfortable with a neighborhood that was one-third black, only 45 percent were willing to move into the same neighborhood. And tolerance of a majority-minority neighborhood was roughly 10 percent lower when whites contemplated the purchase of a new residence than when they considered racial change in their current neighborhood. Still, just over half of whites said that they would move into a neighborhood that is majority Asian. Clearly, whites' tolerance for residential integration is conditioned by the race of their potential neighbors, with Asians topping the hierarchy, Hispanics in the middle, and blacks on the bottom.

Blacks' Preferences

A slightly different experiment tests the neighborhood racial composition preferences of blacks. Instead of being asked about comfort levels in a neighborhood

33. Specifically, white respondents were asked, "Suppose you have been looking for a house and have found a nice one you can afford. This house could be located in several different types of neighborhoods, as shown on these cards. Would you consider moving into any of these neighborhoods?" The split ballot used for the previous experiment continues to apply here: Whites previously indicating comfort with increasing numbers of black neighbors, for example, are then asked to consider moving into neighborhoods with varying degrees of integration with blacks.

Figure 3-2. *White Responses to Cards 2–5*[a]

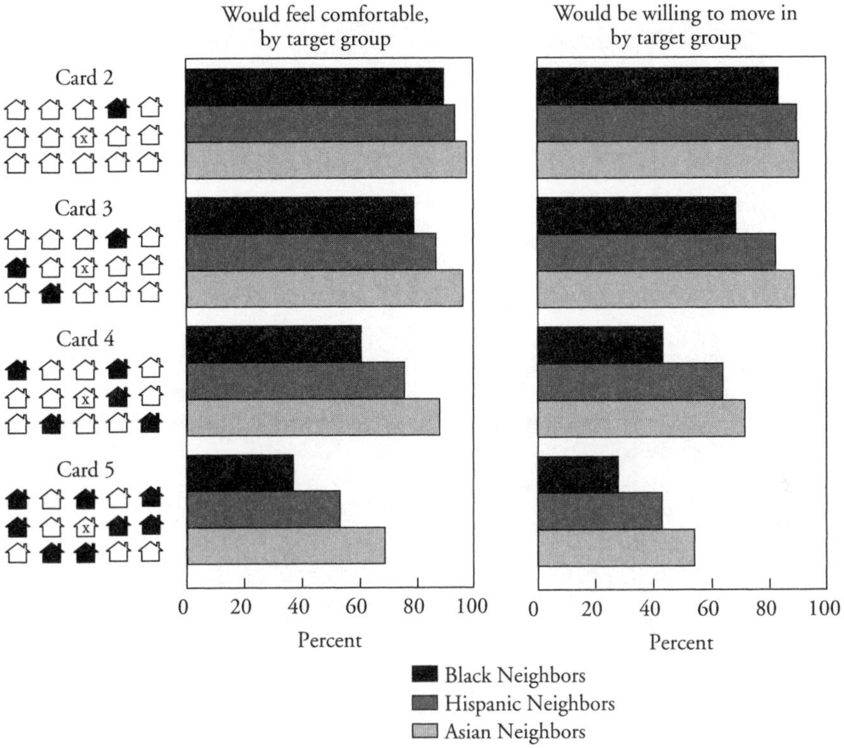

Source: See figure 3-1.
a. For houses and for bars in graph, white is for white neighbors, black is for black neighbors, dark gray is for Hispanic neighbors, light gray is for Asian neighbors.
$p < .001$

undergoing racial transition, blacks were asked to imagine that they had been searching for a house and found a nice one that they could afford (see figure 3-3). The affordability constraint is intended to exclude economic considerations, making the decision one based entirely on racial composition. Blacks were told that this house could be located in several types of neighborhood and shown five cards similar to those in the bottom row of figure 3-1. These five neighborhood cards differed from the white respondents' cards, ranging from an all-black neighborhood to one entirely white, Hispanic, or Asian, except for the black respondent's home in the middle.[34] In the first part of the experiment, respondents were instructed to arrange the neighborhoods from most to least attractive. In the second part of the experiment, they were asked whether there were

34. As was the case for whites, black respondents were randomly assigned to one of the three target groups.

Figure 3-3. *Black Responses to Cards 1–5*[a]

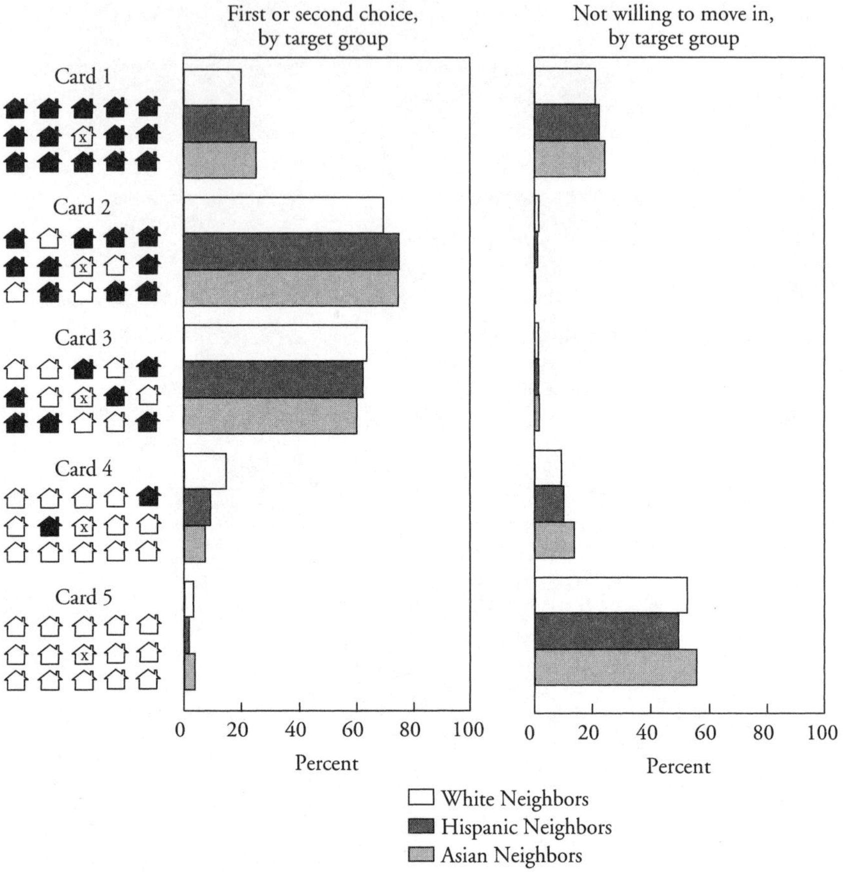

Source: See figure 3-1.
a. See figure 3-2, note a.
$p < .001$ for attractiveness; $p < .05$ for unwilling to move cards 1, 2, and 5; $p < .01$ for card 4; ns for card 3.

any neighborhoods that they would simply refuse to move into. As with the follow-up question asked of white respondents, the second question is intended to assess the willingness of black respondents to actually enter a neighborhood rather than simply reveal what is or is not attractive to them.

Blacks appeared to want both a sizable co-ethnic presence and substantial racial integration. The two most popular neighborhoods across target groups were cards 2 and 3 (the former is about 27 percent out-group and the latter most closely approximates a 50-50 split). Still, the race of potential neighbors mattered when blacks were asked to compare integrated scenarios to all-black ones. Blacks were least likely to find the all-black alternative most attractive when prospective integration was with whites, followed by Hispanics, and then Asians. That pattern persisted as the number of out-group members increased: A neighborhood with only two other black households was twice as appealing when the rest were white compared to when the rest were Asian; the same neighborhood with potential Hispanic households was in the middle. Irrespective of target-group race, however, fewer than 5 percent of blacks rated the single-black-on-the-block alternative as the most attractive.

In direct correspondence with these patterns of neighborhood attractiveness, the neighborhood that blacks were least willing to move into was the one that was otherwise devoid of other blacks (right-hand panel, figure 3-3). Roughly 60 percent of respondents were unwilling to enter such a neighborhood, irrespective of the race of potential neighbors. A substantial minority of blacks was also unwilling to enter an entirely same-race neighborhood. Patterns of neighborhood attractiveness and willingness to enter areas with varying degrees of racial integration were consistent with blacks' historical desire for substantial integration. However, there is a growing preference among blacks for neighborhoods that are majority same-race, contrary to previously more distinct preferences for 50-50 neighborhoods. This shift is consistent with blacks' perceptions of persisting prejudice and discrimination and dwindling faith in the likelihood of racial equality.[35] It may also explain why as many blacks found the all-black neighborhood most attractive as said they were unwilling to move into such a neighborhood. And although it was not as clear-cut as for whites, there was a ranking of out-groups, at least in terms of the top position: Blacks appeared most comfortable being a numerical minority when their prospective neighbors were white.

Hispanics' Preferences

The measure of Hispanics' neighborhood racial composition preferences is based on the same set of questions used for blacks (though Hispanics were sampled in only two of the four MCSUI metropolitan areas, Boston and Los Angeles). Target-group race was especially important for Hispanics: When potential neighbors were black, the most attractive neighborhoods were the two least integrated alternatives. Ninety-one percent of Hispanics chose the neighborhood with four black households as their first or second choice; fully 60 percent said that the entirely same-race neighborhood was most attractive, compared with 40 percent when potential neighbors were Asian and only 20 percent when they were white (see figure 3-4).

Alternatively, when potential neighbors were white, the neighborhood closest to 50-50 was the first or second choice of most Hispanics; the slightly less integrated alternative (card 2) came in a close second. Similarly, neighborhoods that were, except for themselves, all white or all Asian were about five times more

35. Bobo (2001); Cose (1993); Feagin and Sikes (1994); Hochschild (1995).

Figure 3-4. *Hispanic Responses to Cards 1–5*[a]

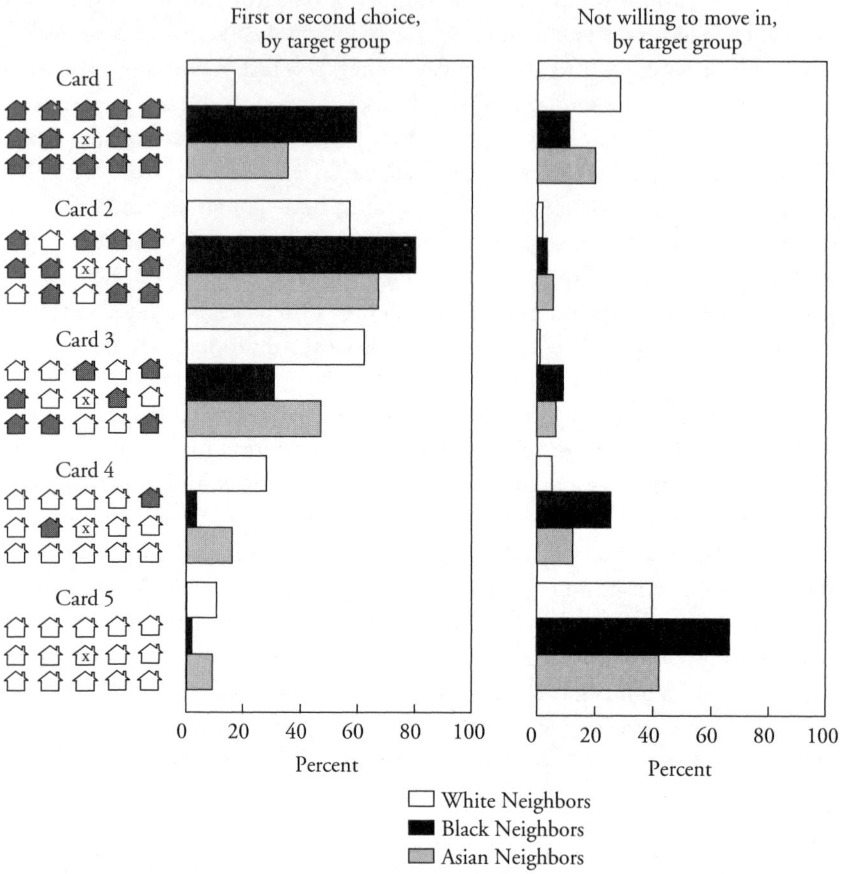

Source: See figure 3-1.
a. See figure 3-2, note a.
$p < .001$.

likely to be found attractive than were (except for themselves) all-black neighborhoods. Analogous to the black preference for some co-ethnic presence in the neighborhood, the notion of living in an area that was not otherwise white and in which the respondent was the only Hispanic household, or one of only two, was especially unappealing.

The pattern of Hispanic reluctance to move into various neighborhoods is also similar to that found among black respondents: As the number of co-ethnic neighbors declined, Hispanics were increasingly unwilling to move into a neighborhood. Again, that was most true when potential neighbors were black and least so when they were white. To some extent, then, Hispanics shared with blacks a desire for both a sizable co-ethnic presence along with fairly substantial neighborhood racial integration; and as with both whites and blacks, the relative strength of those preferences depended on whom they were integrating with. There was a clear racial hierarchy of preferred neighbors, with whites at the top and blacks on the bottom. Finally, Hispanics were more likely than blacks to rank the all-their-own-race neighborhood most attractive. Research suggests that this may reflect high rates of immigrant status, the language barriers that many Hispanic immigrants face, and the greater reliance of Hispanics than blacks on ethnic cultural institutions.[36]

Asians' Preferences

Consistent with the design of the original show card experiment, Asian respondents—Chinese, Japanese, and Koreans in Los Angeles only—ranked five neighborhood cards (see the bottom of figure 3-1) with varying degrees of integration with whites, blacks, or Hispanics from most to least attractive and then indicated which, if any, they were unwilling to move into (figure 3-5).

In broad terms, Asians shared with both blacks and Hispanics the desire for both meaningful integration and a strong co-ethnic presence. Notably, though, Asians' preferences were more similar to those of blacks and Hispanics on some dimensions and more consistent with the preferences of whites on other dimensions. Like those of all other groups, Asian' preferences depended on the race of potential neighbors in ways that reflected a clear racial hierarchy: As with blacks and Hispanics, for instance, a neighborhood made up of entirely their own race was least attractive to Asians when the alternative was integration with whites; as with Hispanics and whites, the entirely same-race scenario was most attractive when integration meant living in close proximity to blacks. The magnitude of these differences is striking: only 17 percent of Asians chose the all-same-race neighborhood in the Asian-white scenario, compared with more than 55 percent in the Asian-Hispanic scenario and an astonishing 75 percent in the Asian-black scenario. Also like blacks and Hispanics, virtually all Asians selected card 2 (nearly 66 percent same-race) as most attractive when the target group was another nonwhite group. When potential neighbors were white, however, the approximately 50-50 neighborhood (card 3) was the first or second choice of four-fifths of Asian respondents.

Summary

Compared with actual levels of neighborhood segregation by race in America, the preferences outlined above suggest substantial openness to residential integration

36. Research suggests important differences by immigrant status and acculturation. The foreign-born, particularly those with five years or fewer in the United States and those with limited English proficiency, prefer substantially more same-race neighbors compared to their native-born and long-term-immigrant counterparts and also compared to those who communicate effectively in English (Charles 2003). This is a strong basis for ethnic enclaving.

Figure 3-5. *Asian Responses to Cards 1–5*[a]

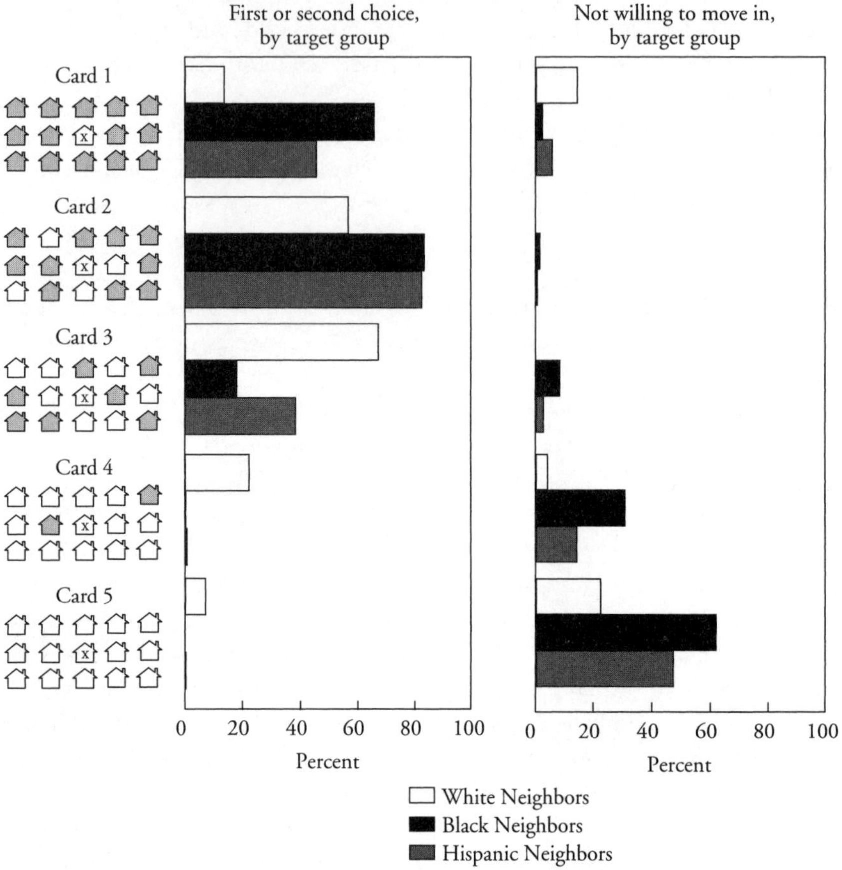

Source: See figure 3-1.
a. See figure 3-2, note a.
$p < .001$.

on the part of all four major racial and ethnic groups.[37] MCSUI respondents did not give unreflective prointegration responses, however. It is immediately apparent that members of each racial group reacted differently to each potential out-group neighbor. Indeed, the clear-cut racial ranking of out-groups as potential neighbors—and the consensus across groups regarding the top (whites) and bottom (blacks) positions of the hierarchy—provides a sobering counterpoint to the overall openness to integration.

37. To some extent this may reflect socially desirable response bias for many respondents, especially whites, reluctant to object to interracial neighborhood contact. It is difficult to conclude, however, that the patterns reflect serious bias of this kind, nor do they represent a sharp disjuncture with actual aggregate-level residential patterns.

Moreover, general awareness of a widely shared perception of blacks as the least desirable neighbors could be more consequential for individual housing choices and location than a deeply held personal aversion. To wit, blacks may be discouraged by the potential for negative reactions from a small number of hostile whites (who are not necessarily easy to distinguish from their less intolerant counterparts) from moving into predominantly white neighborhoods. That could explain the slight decline in blacks' preferences for half-white, half-black neighborhoods and in their willingness to enter previously all-white areas. At a minimum, the racial hierarchy of preferences closely mirrors actual residential segregation by race.[38] Could it be, though, that asking about race taps class-based stereotypes or other confounding factors? Precisely *how* does race matter when people choose where, and among whom, to reside?

What Drives Neighborhood Preferences? Rethinking Racial Stereotypes and Prejudice

As I acknowledged at the outset, a variety of factors shape residential decision-making: cost and affordability, the quality of the housing stock or preferences for particular amenities, proximity to work or other important destinations, the quality of public schools, and stage of life, to name the major considerations.[39] Aggregate residential outcomes therefore can result from any of several individual-level processes. For understanding patterns of racial residential preferences, however, three hypotheses are typically considered. In the first, class is the real driver and race merely a correlate: Real or perceived differences in socioeconomic status that correlate highly with racial-ethnic affiliation contribute to "racial" residential preferences. The second hypothesis emphasizes self-segregation, arguing that all social groups tend to be ethnocentric, that is, they prefer to associate and interact with their own. The third hypothesis asserts that more active out-group avoidance or domination is at the root of neighborhood racial composition preferences. The discussion below briefly elaborates on each of these schools of thought, summarizing relevant MCSUI findings.

Real and Perceived Differences in Socioeconomic Status

The first hypothesis posits that neighborhood racial composition preferences are primarily the result of real or perceived group differences in socioeconomic status indicators—income, occupation, and associated differences in lifestyle (see Mary Jackman and Robert Jackman on class identities as involving lifestyle considerations). Specifically, it is the collection of undesirable social class characteristics sometimes associated with blacks (and increasingly Hispanics) and the

38. See also Bobo and Zubrinsky (1996).
39. Ellen (2000); Galster (1988).

neighborhoods where they are concentrated—not race per se—that identifies members of those groups as undesirable neighbors. These differences are so influential both within and across groups that "except for the genuinely poor, all people . . . are willing to pay, and pay substantially, to avoid class integration."[40] The racial proxy of W. A. V. Clark and David Harris and the race-based neighborhood stereotyping hypotheses of Ingrid Ellen are recent examples of this long-standing hypothesis.[41] Clark, in his 1988 article, highlights several social class characteristics that increase opposition to black neighbors, many of which are increasingly applicable to Hispanics as well: In addition to huge differences in wealth, black households are more likely to have a female head, unemployed adult members, and more residents per household. Taking things a step further, Harris, in his 2001 article, argues that these perceptions also leave blacks averse to having too many black neighbors.

However, despite its common-sense appeal—and the important fact that the correlation between race and class status does complicate interracial perceptions—there is little evidence to support this hypothesis. Analysis of MCSUI data comparing actual housing expenditures across racial groups (separating owners and renters) shows a great deal of overlap, suggesting that many blacks, Hispanics, and Asians can indeed afford to live in "desirable" neighborhoods, despite the very real income differences among these groups. Just over 40 percent of both white and black MCSUI respondents reported mortgage payments between $400 and $1,000 a month, along with nearly one-third of Hispanics; the majority of Asian homeowners spent well over $1,000 a month (57.4 percent spent between $1,000 and $2,000 a month). The pattern was similar for renters, and the patterns held both within and across the four cities.[42] Moreover, minority group members had accurate perceptions of their own financial capabilities, recognizing that a significant portion of their group can afford to live in "desirable" suburban areas. Finally, MCSUI analyses reveal little or no association between perceiving a group to be economically disadvantaged and preferring integration with that group.[43] Analyzing the same data to understand the

40. Leven and others (1976, pp. 202–03); Jackman and Jackman (1983).

41. Clark (1986, 1988); Harris (1999, 2001); Ellen (2000).

42. It also appears unlikely that inaccurate knowledge of housing costs account for racial group differences in housing outcomes or preferences. All groups possess fairly accurate knowledge of housing prices in the metropolitan areas where they live; and when information is inaccurate, all groups are similarly in error. Several other studies show that affordability and other race-neutral economic factors (for example, job location) account for no more than a small portion of black-white residential segregation (Alba and Logan 1993; Charles 2000b; Farley, Steeh, and others 1993; Galster 1988; Zubrinsky and Bobo 1996). Socioeconomic disadvantage is a factor for Hispanics and Asians; however, this is primarily a function of the continuous flow of new immigrants. With the accumulation of time in the United States and generational shifts from foreign-born to native, these groups are able to improve their residential outcomes (see, for example, Alba and Logan 1993; Massey and Denton 1993).

43. Charles (2000a, 2000b, 2001).

impact of whites' preferences (net of other factors) on the actual racial makeup of whites' neighborhoods, the economists Keith Ihlanfeldt and Benjamin Scafidi likewise find no evidence to support the notion that whites stereotype black neighborhoods, which are typically poorer and weaker in structural socioeconomic terms, rather than blacks per se, as Ingrid Ellen suggests (Ihlanfeldt and Scafidi acknowledge that that possibility remains unresolved). Notably, the study controlled not only for personal traits associated with a willingness to integrate—younger and more educated whites were more willing, for example—but also for respondents' experience of racial integration in the workplace and neighborhood. Ihlanfeldt and Scafidi emphasize that "altering whites' neighborhood preferences in favor of integration has dramatic effects on the racial composition of their neighborhoods," and they show that workplace and neighborhood contact with blacks positively shift whites' preferences.[44]

On the whole, it does not appear that minorities' search for housing is constrained primarily by cost or by issues associated with cost. Likewise, the perception of various minority groups as economically disadvantaged plays at best only a minimal role in shaping neighborhood racial composition preferences, which are highly predictive of the racial makeup of white neighborhoods.

Mutually Expressed Ethnocentrism

According to the second hypothesis, all racial groups naturally exhibit "strong desires for own-race combinations in the ethnicity of neighborhoods."[45] This view maintains that the preference for same-race neighbors is driven by positive feelings about one's own group, not by anti-out-group animus and, moreover, that the preferred racial composition of a neighborhood is just one of many characteristics taken into consideration in the search for housing.[46] Feelings of in-group attachment are said to act simultaneously with group differences in socioeconomic status to explain aggregate patterns; residential segregation simply reflects the mutually ethnocentric social preferences of consumers.[47]

The main problem with this hypothesis is its loose construction of "own-group preference." For example, despite Clark's claim of "strong similarities in own-race preferences" across racial groups, he finds that whites express the strongest preference for having a majority of same-race neighbors, with almost no whites expressing interest in living in a neighborhood that is less than half

44. Ihlanfeldt and Scafidi (2004); Ellen (2000). To control for the endogeneity of location choice, Ihlanfeldt and Scafidi use a simultaneous equation model. Quotation is from Ihlanfeldt and Scafidi, p. 355.

45. Clark (1992, p. 451).

46. A stronger version of this hypothesis singles out blacks, suggesting that current residential patterns simply reflect a black preference for self-segregation. See Patterson (1997); Thernstrom and Thernstrom (1997).

47. Clark (1986, pp. 108–09).

white.[48] Moreover, consistent with the pattern of preferences found in the MCSUI data, in Clark's survey, whites, Hispanics, and Asians *all* expressed the strongest desire for same-race neighbors when the target out-group was blacks.

The bivariate patterns of preferences detailed earlier support this hypothesis to some extent. But those patterns also suggest that in-group attachment is secondary to the race of potential neighbors: If ethnocentrism were the primary factor shaping preferences, expressions of comfort, attractiveness, and willingness to enter would be far more similar across target-group categories. Multivariate analysis of MCSUI data also suggests that ethnocentrism plays *some* role in shaping neighborhood racial composition preferences, but its role is always small and inconsistent, even when predicting preferences for same-race neighbors.[49]

Detailed analyses of qualitative MCSUI data further substantiate this conclusion, providing virtually no support for the ethnocentrism hypothesis among blacks. Variants of ethnocentrism were common among white respondents, but careful examination reveals that large fractions also expressed negative stereotypes of blacks, especially when potential neighbors were black. When potential neighbors were Hispanic or Asian, whites were more inclined to express concern about cultural differences, mainly in terms of language differences. In the end, the majority of whites articulated their objections to residential integration by invoking negative racial stereotypes.[50]

Emphasizing a "natural" ethnocentrism minimizes the extent to which the preferences of one group constrain those of others' and distracts attention from persisting structural inequalities. If the preference for same-race neighbors were similar across groups—and accompanied by the experience of equal quality of life across groups—it might be persuasive to view in-group preferences as neutral and efforts to alter residential choices and outcomes as futile. That is not the case, and to proceed as though it were seems to be both shortsighted and ill fated.

Racial Prejudice

There are two variants of the prejudice hypothesis with respect to attitudes toward neighborhood racial integration. The first is in line with traditional prejudice, and in contrast to the mutually expressed ethnocentrism hypothesis, it stresses out-group hostility as the driving force in attitudes about interracial contact in neighborhoods.[51] The expected influence of traditional prejudice on neighborhood racial composition preferences is straightforward: Negative racial

48. Clark (1992, pp. 463–64)

49. Charles (2000a); Timberlake (2000).

50. Farley, Schuman, and others (1994); Krysan (2002); Krysan and Farley (2002).

51. Allport (1954); Katz (1991); Pettigrew (1982). Typically, prejudice is defined as an irrational antipathy (against minority groups and their members) that is heavily imbued with negative affect and negative stereotypes that make the views of prejudiced individuals unreceptive to reason and new information (Jackman 1994).

stereotypes should be strongly associated with objections to residential integration. The second variant of the prejudice hypothesis is rooted in Herbert Blumer's theory of race prejudice as a sense of group position. Rather than placing simple anti-out-group sentiment at the core of prejudice, Blumer asserts that prejudice involves a specific group status or relative group position. The group position hypothesis suggests that neither mere in-group preference nor simple out-group hostility is sufficient to give prejudice social force. Instead, what matters is the magnitude or degree of difference that in-group members have socially learned to expect and maintain relative to members of specific out-groups.[52] Accordingly, the greater the affective differentiation from members of an out-group—with differentiation understood to be an indicator of a preferred superior group position—the greater the resistance to sharing neighborhoods with that group.

Both variants argue that individuals' residential decisionmaking process is influenced by their attitudes about an out-group. The trends in racial attitudes outlined previously point to the plausibility of the prejudice hypothesis, particularly those regarding persisting adherence to negative racial stereotypes, especially among whites but among other groups as well; perceptions of social distance across racial lines, especially of the distance between blacks and other groups; and whites' beliefs regarding the sources of racial inequality. Patterns of neighborhood racial composition preferences also support the prejudice hypotheses, particularly the group-position variant. In particular, patterns of neighborhood racial composition preferences reveal a clear racial hierarchy of out-groups as potential neighbors mirroring the relatively clear-cut racial order found in contemporary American society more generally. Historically and currently, in economic and other aspects of status, whites are the dominant American social group, while blacks are on the bottom.[53] For all minority groups, economic and social advancement is associated with greater proximity and similarity to white Americans. For whites, on the other hand, integration with any other group—but especially with blacks—brings the threat of loss of relative status.

Both more conclusive and more convincing, however, is evidence from multivariate analyses of MCSUI data that examine the relative influence of real and perceived differences in social class, ethnocentrism, and racial prejudice on neighborhood racial composition preferences. After controlling for a variety of sociodemographic characteristics, the racial hierarchy of preferences identified in bivariate results persists.[54] While offering strong empirical support for the prejudice hypothesis, however, the Farley-Schuman show card experiment is limited to the extent that respondents consider integration with only one out-group. To

52. Blumer (1958); Bobo (1988, 1999); Quillian (1996).

53. See Gans (1999); Jankowski (1995); Jaynes and Williams (1989); Massey and Denton (1993); Oliver and Shapiro (1995).

54. Zubrinsky and Bobo (1996).

understand preferences in multiracial contexts such as Los Angeles, the Farley-Schuman methodology was extended to include asking respondents to consider residential integration with several out-groups simultaneously and to create their "ideal" multiethnic neighborhood.[55] Patterns of preferences based on this experiment reveal decidedly more aversion to integration than was previously thought.

All groups tended to specify substantially integrated neighborhoods while at the same time preferring one wherein own-race representation exceeded that of any out-group. And while all groups preferred neighborhoods dominated by co-ethnics, that preference was strongest among whites (51 percent) and weakest among blacks (41 percent). Whites also were most likely to prefer entirely own-race neighborhoods: 11 percent—a rate more than one and a half times that of Hispanics (7 percent) and Asians (7 percent) and almost four times that of blacks (3 percent). Once again blacks were always the least preferred out-group neighbors, evidenced in the high rates of complete exclusion of this group from the preferred multiethnic neighborhoods of others. More than one-fifth of whites expressed integration preferences that excluded blacks entirely, as did nearly one-third of Hispanics and a striking 41 percent of Asians. Interestingly, foreign-born Asians and Hispanics were more likely than their native-born counterparts to exclude black neighbors—a pattern that may reflect racial tensions between long-time black residents in Los Angeles and immigrant newcomers, such as Korean business owners operating in predominantly black neighborhoods.[56]

Despite their status as least-preferred neighbors, blacks appeared least resistant to integration. Blacks had the lowest average percentage of same-race neighbors—indicating substantially more comfort with being the numerical minority in an integrated neighborhood—and were significantly less likely to create all-same-race neighborhoods. Finally, blacks, Hispanics, and Asians all preferred integration with whites to integration with other-race minorities.

For a first-cut examination of the influence of racial stereotypes on neighborhood racial composition preferences, Table 3-1 presents summary measures of preferences for various out-group and same-race neighbors, controlling for racial stereotypes. Respondents rated all four racial groups on a series of stereotype traits: intelligence, preference for welfare dependence, difficulty to get along with socially, tendency to discriminate against other groups, and involvement in drugs and gangs.[57] Positive stereotypes are those in which respondents either perceived no difference between members of their own group and a target group or perceived a target group favorably relative to their own group. Unfavorable

55. See Charles (2000a).

56. Johnson, Oliver, and Farrell (1992).

57. The racial stereotyping measure used here is a "difference" score that captures both variants of the prejudice hypothesis. Ratings (difference scores) range from –6 (favorable out-group perception relative to respondents' own group) to +6 (unfavorable out-group perception relative to respondents' own group), with a score of 0 indicating no perceived difference between groups. A

Table 3-1. *Summary Statistics, Multiethnic Neighborhood Show Card Experiment, by Respondent and Target-Group Race and Racial Stereotypes, Los Angeles*[a]

Percent

	Whites (N = *863)*			*Blacks* (N = *1,118)*			*Hispanics* (N = *988)*			*Asians* (N = *1,056)*		
Target race	*Positive stereotypes*	*Negative stereotypes*	p	*Positive stereotypes*	*Negative stereotypes*	p	*Positive stereotypes*	*Negative stereotypes*	p	*Positive stereotypes*	*Negative stereotypes*	p
White neighbors												
Mean	. . .	. . .		22.38	19.93	*	26.50	24.92		32.93	29.05	
None[b]	. . .	. . .		7.47	14.22	*	12.23	13.32		4.35	9.55	**
N				633	485		669	319		159	897	
Black neighbors												
Mean	20.31	13.69	***	. . .	. . .		15.22	12.31	*	13.25	10.01	
None[b]	6.65	23.69	***	. . .	. . .		22.44	33.73	*	30.11	41.35	
N	137	726					181	807		41	1015	
Hispanic neighbors												
Mean	20.96	14.21	***	20.96	14.21	***	. . .	. . .		20.00	18.98	
None[b]	6.50	22.41	***	9.17	11.93		. . .	. . .		21.80	27.70	
N	167	696		448	670					35	1021	
Asian neighbors												
Mean	18.69	13.47	***	18.69	13.47	***	15.86	15.79		. . .	. . .	
None[b]	12.23	25.67	***	11.58	23.86	**	22.45	23.67		. . .	. . .	
N	457	406		594	524		695	293				
Same-race neighbors												
Mean	39.02	52.82	***	38.59	42.70	*	41.41	47.59	**	41.81	44.47	
All same	3.62	12.12	***	1.92	3.40		6.61	6.48		2.18	7.16	*
N	154	709		502	616		440	548		38	1018	

Source: Inter-University Consortium for Political and Social Research (2000).

a. Racial stereotypes are measured using a difference score similar to that used by Charles (2000a). It is scaled from –6 to +6. High (positive) scores indicate unfavorable measures of out-groups relative to one's own group; low (negative) scores reflect favorable ratings of out-groups relative to one's own group; a score of zero indicates no perceived difference. Positive stereotypes are any in which respondents report favorable or neutral perceptions of out-groups relative to their own group (–6 to 0); negative stereotypes are any in which respondents rate out-groups unfavorably relative to their own group (greater than 0). For same-race target group, stereotypes are for all relevant out-groups.

b. Percent of respondents who completely excluded the target group.

*$p < .05$; **$p < .01$; ***$p < .001$.

perceptions of an out-group relative to their own group are characterized as negative. When considering preferences for same-race neighbors, racial stereotype scores are the combined average for all out-groups (for example, for whites, out-group racial stereotypes are the difference scores for blacks, Hispanics, and Asians).

Patterns for white respondents provide striking evidence supporting the prejudice hypotheses: Whether one considers integration with particular out-groups or same-race preferences, racial stereotypes matter. When whites hold negative racial stereotypes, their preferences for integration with those groups decline significantly and preferences for same-race neighbors increase. Consistent with trends in racial attitudes, whites are most likely to view blacks and Hispanics in negative terms and much less likely to hold negative views of Asians. For the relatively small number of whites with neutral or positive stereotypes of out-groups, the ideal multiethnic neighborhood is less than 40 percent same-race, more than 10 percentage points lower than the percentage preferred by the majority of whites, who hold negative stereotypes of other groups. Note, too, that whites with negative racial stereotypes are more than three times as likely to exclude blacks and Hispanics, and just over twice as likely to exclude Asians, as their counterparts with neutral or favorable perceptions of these groups.

Racial stereotypes are substantially less powerful and less consistent predictors of preferences among nonwhites, especially Hispanics and Asians. Still, for blacks, negative stereotyping is clearly associated with objections to neighborhood racial integration, particularly with whites and Asians. Among Hispanics, preference for black neighbors is significantly influenced by racial stereotypes, in the anticipated direction. For Asians, that is true only when potential neighbors are white, but this may reflect a lack of variation in Asians' adherence to antiblack and anti-Hispanic stereotypes. Asian stereotypes of blacks and Hispanics are overwhelmingly negative, with less than fifty of 1,056 Asians responding favorably with regard to those groups. Negative out-group stereotypes also significantly increase nonwhites' preferences for same-race neighbors. For whites, these patterns offer strong support for the prejudice-as-group-position hypothesis, while the patterns for other racial groups support both the traditional prejudice hypothesis (in that they suggest tense interminority group relations and hostility) and the prejudice-as-group-position hypothesis (in that upward mobility is associated with greater proximity to whites, irrespective of what these groups might think of them).

---

split-ballot format was employed for the stereotyping questions to test the importance of particular race-gender combinations. One-third of each respondent group category was asked to rate the four racial groups on each of the traits; one-third rated racial group males; and the remaining one-third rated racial group females. Respondents were randomly assigned to one of these categories, making it possible to generalize to the entire sample category. A comparison of stereotypes by experimental ballot finds no overall gender effect on the stereotyping scales; hence the final stereotype difference score is constructed from pooled ballots.

Table 3-2. *Correlations, Race-Related Attitudes and Perceptions*[a] *and Multi-Ethnic Neighborhood Racial Composition Preferences, Los Angeles Subsample of the 1992-94 Multi-City Study of Urban Inequality*

Target group race	*Whites*	*Blacks*	*Hispanics*	*Asians*
White neighbors				
Stereotype Difference Score	. . .	–.139*	–.125*	–.044
Perceived SES Difference Score	. . .	.140*	.043	.039
In-Group Attachment	. . .	–.075	–.108*	.070
Black neighbors				
Stereotype Difference Score	–.310***	. . .	–.200***	–.240**
Perceived SES Difference Score	–.063	. . .	.037	–.221**
In-Group Attachment	–.001	. . .	–.033	.019
Hispanic neighbors				
Stereotype Difference Score	–.320***	–.110*	. . .	–.232**
Perceived SES Difference Score	–.040	.021	. . .	–.157
In-Group Attachment	–.076	.029	. . .	–.051
Asian neighbors				
Stereotype Difference Score	–.287***	–.130*	–.046	. . .
Perceived SES Difference Score	–.050	.091	–.003	. . .
In-Group Attachment	–.022	–.013	–.030	. . .
Same-race neighbors				
Stereotype Difference Score	.302***	.175**	.160***	.057
Perceived SES Difference Score	.071	–.073	–.108**	.063
In-Group Attachment	.003	.096	.140**	–.015
N	863	1,118	988	1,056

Source: See table 3-1.

a. Figures are Pearson correlations with preferences for the corresponding group as neighbors. The stereotype and SES difference scores are scaled from –6 to +6. High (positive) scores indicate unfavorable ratings of out-groups relative to one's own group; low (negative) scores indicate favorable ratings of out-groups; 0 indicates no perceived difference. In instances in which the target group is the same race as the respondents, measures of perceived social class difference and racial stereotypes are combined for all out-groups (for example, for Hispanic respondents, these measures reflect perceptions of/attitudes about whites, blacks, and Asians).

*$p < .05$; **$p < .01$; ***$p < .001$.

Correlations between neighborhood racial composition preferences and measures of each of these race-related attitudes and perceptions, presented in table 3-2, further emphasize the primary importance of racial stereotyping, both in absolute terms and relative to either perceived social class differences or ethnocentrism. Multivariate analyses corroborate these patterns.[58] The measure of perceived difference in socioeconomic status is similar to the stereotype

58. Farley, Schuman, and others (1994); Charles (2000a); Timberlake (2000); Zubrinsky and Bobo (1996).

difference score, and in-group attachment is based on a group's sense of common fate: the extent to which members believe that what happens to their group happens to them.[59]

These and other data clearly point to racial stereotypes as the race-related attitude or perception that is most influential in forming neighborhood racial composition preferences. As stereotypes of out-groups become increasingly unfavorable or negative, preferences for those groups as neighbors decline and preferences for same-race neighbors increase. Again, that is especially true for whites, for whom racial stereotypes are the only significant predictor of preferences for both out-group and same-race neighbors. The relationship between racial stereotyping and preferences is generally weaker and less consistent among nonwhites, but it is always in the expected direction. Stereotypes are most highly correlated with nonwhites' preferences when the target group is black or Hispanic, again consistent with the trends in racial attitudes detailed previously and also with both variants of the prejudice hypothesis. Evidence that either the perceived-class-difference hypothesis or the ethnocentrism hypothesis is influential in individuals' residential decisionmaking is marginal at best. However, the type of racial prejudice that matters—traditional prejudice or prejudice as a sense of group position—depends very much on the race of the respondent.

Conclusions

The goals of this chapter are, first, to reveal patterns of neighborhood racial composition preferences and the forces that drive them and, second, to situate those preferences within the broader context of American race relations. The good news for the future of public policy related to housing opportunity, housing choice, and inequality is that whites are increasingly willing to live in close proximity to racial minorities and that a sizable number of blacks, Hispanics, and Asians are still willing to live in predominantly white areas. To capitalize on that willingness, however, policymakers must be aware of the way that race shapes both people's day-to-day interactions and their overall worldview.

The bad news, both for public policy and the nation, is that most whites still prefer predominantly or overwhelmingly white neighborhoods, while most nonwhites prefer more coethnic (nonwhite) neighbors than whites would be willing to tolerate in their neighborhoods. Most whites, including many who are willing to share residential neighborhoods with racial minorities, still adhere to negative stereotypes. Conversely, most blacks, Hispanics, and Asians have a keen sense of their subordinate position relative to that of whites and of whites' negative

59. Research suggests that feelings of common fate are important aspects of both African American and Asian American group identities (Dawson 1994, 1999; Espiritu 1992; Gurin, Hatchett, and Jackson 1989; Tate 1993; Tuan 1999), and that assumptions of common fate influence in-group favoritism (Tajfel 1982).

stereotypes of them, and that often leaves them suspicious of overwhelmingly white areas—a sort of "better safe than sorry" outlook.

Across racial groups, patterns of neighborhood racial composition preferences reveal a clear and consistent racial ranking of out-groups as potential neighbors. Whites are always the most preferred out-group neighbors, but they are also the group most likely to prefer entirely same-race neighborhoods or only limited contact with nonwhites, especially blacks. Blacks are always the least preferred out-group neighbors, while being the most open to substantial integration with all other groups and the least likely to prefer entirely same-race neighborhoods. Asians and Hispanics fall between those extremes. To varying degrees, all groups express preferences for both meaningful integration and a strong coethnic presence—comfort, if not safety, in numbers—yet preference for a strong coethnic presence appears to depend on the race of potential neighbors and to be strongest when potential neighbors are black.

Available evidence indicates that active, present-day racial prejudice plays a particularly important role in driving preferences. For all groups, the effect of racial stereotyping is always stronger and more consistent than that of perceived social class differences or in-group attachment. And although the evidence supports both variants of racial prejudice, it is particularly convincing with respect to the sense-of-group-position hypothesis. That is especially true for whites, the group at the top of the hierarchy: Maintaining their advantages and privileges requires a certain amount of social distance from nonwhites—particularly blacks and Hispanics, who occupy the lowest positions on the totem pole. More than token integration with these groups signals an unwelcome change in status relationships. Indeed, the racial pecking order is so widely understood that Hispanics and Asians—many of them unassimilated immigrants—mirror (and arguably exaggerate) it in their own preferences for integration.

Conversely, with whites clearly occupying the most privileged position in American society, nonwhites have traditionally associated upward social mobility with proximity to them, and many nonwhites who hold negative stereotypes of whites are nonetheless interested in having them as neighbors.[60] At the same time, minority-group members tend to rate as less desirable those communities they perceive as hostile, and they often perceive overwhelmingly white communities in this way. Nonwhites' beliefs about discrimination and hostility, combined with a suspicion that whites do not think as they do, may cause some minority homeseekers to limit their housing search to areas where they feel welcome or to not search at all.[61] Thus rather than reflecting ethnocentrism, a neighborhood's racial makeup acts as a signal for minority homeseekers. Those areas with substantial coethnic representation are viewed as welcoming, while

60. Jankowski (1995); Jaynes and Williams (1989); Massey and Denton (1993).
61. Yinger (1995); Charles (2001).

those with very few or no coethnic residents evoke concerns about hostility, isolation, and discomfort.[62] For all groups, preferences for same-race neighbors have more to do with aversion to others than with group solidarity.

These clearly racial concerns cut across class lines. Indeed, studies of the attitudes and experiences of middle-class blacks suggest that, paradoxically, this subset of blacks may be most pessimistic about the future of race relations, most likely to believe that whites have negative attitudes toward them, and increasingly less interested in living in predominantly white neighborhoods.[63] Thus the most upwardly mobile blacks may be among the most suspicious of whites and the least interested in sharing neighborhoods with them. For this group, affordability is not nearly the obstacle that whites' racial prejudice is, an obstacle due in no small measure to the fact that most whites—irrespective of their own social class—adhere to negative racial stereotypes, deny the persistence of pervasive racial prejudice and discrimination, and are quite likely to oppose race-based social policies.

Whites' racial prejudice—and minority responses to it—pose a more obvious but equally difficult challenge for improving the housing options of the poor, including those who receive housing assistance through rental vouchers, public housing, or other programs. For many, the obvious material benefits clearly outweigh concerns about day-to-day experiences of prejudice and discrimination (see James Rosenbaum, Stefanie DeLuca, and Tammy Tuck, chapter 7, this volume; Susan Popkin and Mary Cunningham, chapter 8, this volume). For a nontrivial few, however, fears of isolation and hostility will prevail. Some participants will return to the ghetto, and others will opt out of programs entirely when confronted with the prospect of moving into a potentially hostile environment.[64] Though they are not at the bottom of the status hierarchy, Asians and Hispanics are also subordinate groups grappling with similar racial issues. As knowledge of Asian and Hispanic racial attitudes increases, a similar paradox may emerge within these groups as well.

Today, in the early twenty-first century, race still matters, and it matters over and above social class. But the key to building public support for new policy is understanding how and why race matters. White objections to race-based social policy point to the need for well-crafted, universal housing policies that can gain broad public support but that also target certain groups so as to address issues tied to race and racial disadvantage. Potentially useful strategies for encouraging whites and nonwhites to share neighborhoods come from studies documenting the characteristics of stable integrated neighborhoods. Residents of these communities often work together on community betterment projects (for example,

62. Meyer (2000).
63. Feagin and Sikes (1994); Hochschild (1995); Sigelman and Tuch (1997).
64. Rubinowitz and Rosenbaum (2000).

building playground equipment for a park or working to have street lights installed) or general community-building efforts that bring people of various racial backgrounds together to work toward a common goal. Such activities, particularly when they become part of the larger neighborhood culture, can fundamentally alter attitudes on both sides of the racial divide by highlighting what residents have in common, helping to build trust, and potentially reducing stereotypes.[65]

Another common strategy emphasizes mounting aggressive public relations campaigns that sing the praises of particular communities. Some of these may stress the value added by diversity, while others may highlight desirable neighborhood amenities, services, and community events that make the target area generally attractive; those that do both might ultimately be the most successful.[66] Aggressive marketing strategies seem particularly beneficial when neighborhoods can be advertised as among "the best" in a particular metropolitan area. Positive marketing might also help to attract blacks, Hispanics, and Asians to overwhelmingly white communities by signaling, beyond an openness to diversity, an active interest in creating stable, friendly, and racially diverse communities.

Active, diligent enforcement of antidiscrimination laws is also both appropriate and necessary. That, however, is likely to be a far more difficult and potentially less rewarding task. Beyond the burden-of-proof and subtle-discrimination problems, there is a gulf of misunderstanding separating whites and minorities.[67] For example, where blacks may see racism whites may see an isolated incident or a misinterpretation of events and argue that blacks are overreacting. In response, blacks may become increasingly distrustful of a system that is supposed to protect them, pessimistic about the future of race relations, and less inclined to incur the psychological costs associated with filing a complaint.

To give teeth to antidiscrimination enforcement, what is needed, as George Galster and Erin Godfrey note, is "a new enforcement strategy that builds the capacity of local, state, and federal civil rights agencies to conduct widespread, ongoing audit studies" as a credible deterrent to discrimination.[68] Tests could be of randomly selected real estate agencies and of those suspected of discrimination; those agencies found to consistently treat all clients fairly could be publicly rewarded, while those shown to discriminate could be sanctioned, both publicly and financially. In the lending market, where audit studies are more difficult, regular analysis of Home Mortgage Disclosure Act data could chart the practices of lenders. Such strategies have the potential to create meaningful deterrents.

65. Allport (1954); Ihlanfeldt and Scafidi (2004); Nyden and others (1998).

66. Ellen (2000).

67. See Briggs, chapter 14, this volume; Galster and Godfrey (2003); Turner and others (2002); Yinger (1995).

68. Galster and Godfrey (2003, p. 24).

Furthermore, with regular monitoring, published records of documented systematic discrimination could help to alter whites' beliefs about inequality and discrimination and could be used by victims as evidence in complaints. Together, these benefits could help move Americans toward better racial understanding because whites would have the "proof" of what happens to blacks in the housing market (see Turner and Ross, chapter 4, this volume).

Without such efforts, and given the disheartening state of race relations more generally, it seems unlikely that Americans will learn to live together more extensively and constructively in the near future. It has been argued that America's increasing racial and ethnic diversity might serve as a buffer for blacks, creating opportunities for residential mobility and contact with whites. Yet Hispanics and Asians are at least as likely to hold negative stereotypes of blacks as whites are, and they are more likely to object to the prospect of sharing neighborhoods with blacks. Furthermore, while whites hold negative stereotypes of both Hispanics and Asians, they tend to be less severe than their stereotypes of blacks. Whites are likely to view blacks as culturally deficient while perceiving largely immigrant Hispanic and Asian populations as culturally different. Similarly, stereotypes of immigrants working hard and uncomplainingly at menial jobs may further fuel antiblack sentiment, fostering the belief that blacks "push too hard" or "are always looking for a handout." Hence, rather than operating as a source of greater options and acceptance for blacks, increasing racial diversity may simply add to the climate of resistance to blacks as neighbors and further complicate efforts to achieve either greater racial understanding or better housing options within the uneven geography of opportunity.

References

Alba, Richard D., and John R. Logan. 1993. "Minority Proximity to Whites in Suburbs: An Individual-Level Analysis of Segregation." *American Journal of Sociology* 98, no. 6: 1388–427.

Allport, Gordon W. 1954. *The Nature of Prejudice.* New York: Doubleday Anchor.

Bertrand, Marianne, and Sendhil Mullainathan. 2004. "Are Emily and Greg More Employable than Lakisha and Jamal? A Field Experiment on Labor Market Discrimination." *American Economic Review* 94, no. 4: 991.

Blumer, Herbert. 1958. "Race Prejudice as a Sense of Group Position." *Pacific Sociological Review* 1: 3–7.

Bobo, Lawrence. 1988. "Group Conflict, Prejudice, and the Paradox of Contemporary Racial Attitudes." In *Eliminating Racism: Profiles in Controversy,* edited by Phyllis A. Katz and Dalmas A. Taylor, pp. 85–116. New York: Plenum Press.

———. 1999. "Prejudice as Group Position: Micro-Foundations of a Sociological Approach to Racism and Race Relations." *Journal of Social Issues* 55: 445–72.

———. 2001. "Racial Attitudes and Relations at the Close of the Twentieth Century." In *America Becoming: Racial Trends and Their Consequences,* edited by N. Smelser, W. J. Wilson, and F. Mitchell, pp. 262–99. Washington: National Academy Press.

Bobo, Lawrence, and James R. Kluegel. 1993. "Opposition to Race Targeting: Self-Interest, Stratification Ideology, or Racial Attitudes?" *American Sociological Review* 58: 443–64.

Bobo, Lawrence, and Michael P. Massagli. 2002. "Stereotypes and Urban Inequality." In *Urban Inequality: Evidence from Four Cities*, edited by Alice O'Connor, Chris Tilly, and Lawrence D. Bobo, pp. 89–162. New York: Russell Sage.

Bobo, Lawrence, and Ryan A. Smith. 1994. "Anti-Poverty Policy, Affirmative Action, and Racial Attitudes." In *Confronting Poverty: Prescriptions For Change*, edited by Sheldon H. Danziger, Gary D. Sandefur, and Daniel H. Weinberg, pp. 365–95. Harvard University Press.

Bobo, Lawrence, and Susan Suh. 2000. "Surveying Racial Discrimination: Analyses from a Multiethnic Labor Market." In *Prismatic Metropolis: Inequality in Los Angeles*, edited by Lawrence D. Bobo and others, pp. 523–60. New York: Russell Sage.

Bobo, Lawrence, and Camille L. Zubrinsky. 1996. "Attitudes on Residential Integration: Perceived Status Differences, Mere In-Group Preference, or Racial Prejudice?" *Social Forces* 74: 883–909.

Bok, Derek. 1996. *The State of the Nation: Government and the Quest for a Better Society*. Harvard University Press.

Charles, Camille Zubrinsky. 2000a. "Neighborhood Racial-Composition Preferences: Evidence from a Multiethnic Metropolis." *Social Problems* 47, no. 3: 370–407.

———. 2000b. "Residential Segregation in Los Angeles." In *Prismatic Metropolis: Inequality in Los Angeles*, edited by Lawrence D. Bobo and others, pp. 167–219. New York: Russell Sage.

———. 2001. "Processes of Racial Residential Segregation." In *Urban Inequality: Evidence from Four Cities*, edited by Alice O'Connor, Chris Tilly, and Lawrence D. Bobo, pp. 217–71. New York: Russell Sage.

———. 2003. "Comfort Zones: Immigration, Acculturation, and the Neighborhood Racial Composition Preferences of Latinos and Asians." Department of Sociology, University of Pennsylvania.

Clark, W. A. V. 1986. "Residential Segregation in American Cities: A Review and Interpretation." *Population Research and Policy Review* 5: 95–127.

———. 1988. "Understanding Residential Segregation in American Cities: Interpreting the Evidence, a Reply to Galster." *Population Research and Policy Review* 7: 113–21.

———. 1992. "Residential Preferences and Residential Choices in a Multiethnic Context." *Demography* 29: 451–66.

Cose, Ellis. 1993. *The Rage of a Privileged Class*. New York: HarperCollins.

Dawson, Michael C. 1994. *Behind the Mule: Race and Class in African American Politics*. Princeton University Press.

———. 1999. "'Dis Beat Disrupts': Rap, Ideology, and Black Political Attitudes." In *The Cultural Territories of Race: Black and White Boundaries*, edited by Michele Lamont, pp. 318–42. University of Chicago Press and Russell Sage Foundation.

Du Bois, W. E. B. 1990 (1903). *The Souls of Black Folk: Essays and Sketches*. New York: Vintage.

Ellen, Ingrid Gould. 2000. *Sharing America's Neighborhoods: The Prospects for Stable Racial Integration*. Harvard University Press.

Espiritu, Yen Le. 1992. *Asian American Pan-Ethnicity: Bridging Institutions and Identities*. Temple University Press.

Farley, Reynolds. 1996. *The New American Reality: How We Are, How We Got There, Where We Are Going*. New York: Russell Sage.

Farley, Reynolds, Howard Schuman, and others. 1978. "'Chocolate City, Vanilla Suburbs': Will the Trend toward Racially Separate Communities Continue?" *Social Science Research* 7: 319–44.

———. 1994. "Stereotypes and Segregation: Neighborhoods in the Detroit Area." *American Journal of Sociology* 100: 750–80.

Farley, Reynolds, Charlotte Steeh, and others. 1993. "Continued Racial Residential Segregation in Detroit: 'Chocolate City, Vanilla Suburbs' Revisited." *Journal of Housing Research* 41: 1–38.

Feagin, Joe R., and Melvin P. Sikes. 1994. *Living with Racism: The Black Middle Class Experience.* Boston: Beacon.

Feagin, Joe R., and Hernán Vera. 1995. *White Racism: The Basics.* New York: Routledge.

Galster, George C. 1988. "Residential Segregation in American Cities: A Contrary Review." *Population Research Policy Review* 7: 93–112.

Galster, George C., and Erin Godfrey. 2003. "By Words and Deeds: Racial Steering by Real Estate Agents in the U.S. in 2000." Population Studies Center, University of Michigan. Paper prepared for the Urban Affairs Association annual meeting, Cleveland, March.

Gans, Herbert J. 1999. "The Possibility of a New Racial Hierarchy in the Twenty-First Century United States." In *The Cultural Territories of Race: Black and White Boundaries,* edited by Michele Lamont, pp. 371–90. University of Chicago Press and Russell Sage Foundation.

Gilens, Martin. 1995. "Racial Attitudes and Opposition to Welfare." *Journal of Politics* 57: 994–1014.

———. 1996. "Race Coding and White Opposition to Welfare." *American Political Science Review* 90: 593–604.

Gurin, Patricia, Shirley Hatchett, and James S. Jackson. 1989. *Hope and Independence: Blacks' Response to Electoral and Party Politics.* New York: Russell Sage.

Harris, David R. 1999. "'Property Values Drop When Blacks Move in, Because . . .': Racial and Socioeconomic Determinants of Neighborhood Desirability." *American Sociological Review* 64 (June): 461–79.

———. 2001. "Why Are Whites and Blacks Averse to Black Neighbors?" *Social Science Research* 30, no. 1: 100–16.

Hochschild, Jennifer. 1995. *Facing up to the American Dream: Race, Class, and the Soul of the Nation.* Princeton University Press.

Hurwitz, Jon, and Mark Peffley. 1997. "Public Perceptions of Race and Crime: The Role of Racial Stereotypes." *American Journal of Political Science* 41: 375–401.

Ihlanfeldt, Keith R., and Benjamin Scafidi. 2004. "Whites' Neighborhood Racial Preferences and Neighborhood Racial Composition in the United States: Evidence from the Multi-City Study of Inequality." *Housing Studies* 19, no. 3: 325–59.

Inter-University Consortium for Political and Social Research. 2000. *1992–1994 Multi-City Study of Urban Inequality.* 3d version. Institute of Social Research, University of Michigan.

Jackman, Mary R. 1994. *The Velvet Glove: Paternalism and Conflict in Gender, Class, and Race Relations.* University of California Press.

Jackman, Mary R., and Robert W. Jackman. 1983. *Class Awareness in the United States.* University of California Press.

Jankowski, Martin Sanchez. 1995. "The Rising Significance of Status in U.S. Race Relations." In *The Bubbling Cauldron: Race, Ethnicity, and the Urban Crisis,* edited by Michael Peter Smith and Joe R. Feagin, pp. 77–98. University of Minnesota Press.

Jaynes, Gerald David, and Robin M. Williams Jr. 1989. *A Common Destiny: Blacks in American Society.* Washington: National Academy Press.

Johnson, James H., Jr., Melvin L. Oliver, and Walter C. Farrell. 1992. "The Los Angeles Rebellion: A Retrospective View." *Economic Development Quarterly* 6, no. 4: 356–72.

Katz, Irwin. 1991. "Gordon Allport's *The Nature of Prejudice.*" *Political Psychology* 12: 125–57.

Kirschenman, Joleen, and Kathryn M. Neckerman. 1991. "'We'd Love to Hire Them, but . . .': The Meaning of Race for Employers." In *The Urban Underclass*, edited by Christopher Jencks and Paul E. Peterson, pp. 203–32. Brookings.

Kluegel, James, and Elliot Smith. 1982. "Whites' Beliefs about Blacks' Opportunity." *American Sociological Review* 47: 518–32.

Krysan, Maria. 2002. "Whites Who Say They'd Flee: Who Are They, and Why Would They Leave?" *Demography* 39, no. 4: 675–96.

Krysan, Maria, and Reynolds Farley. 2002. "The Residential Preferences of Blacks: Do They Explain Persistent Segregation?" *Social Forces* 80: 937–80.

Leven, Charles L., and others. 1976. *Neighborhood Change: Lessons in the Dynamics of Urban Decay*. Cambridge: Ballinger.

Lipset, Seymour, and William Schneider. 1978. "The Bakke Case: How Would It Be Decided at the Bar of Public Opinion?" *Public Opinion* 1: 38–44.

Massey, Douglas S., and Nancy A. Denton. 1993. *American Apartheid: Segregation and the Making of the Underclass*. Harvard University Press.

Meyer, Stephen Grant. 2000. *As Long as They Don't Live Next Door: Segregation and Racial Conflict in American Neighborhoods*. Lanham, Md.: Rowman and Littlefield.

Myrdal, Gunnar. 1972 (1944). *An American Dilemma: The Negro Problem and Modern Democracy*. New York: Random House.

Nyden, Philip, and others. 1998. "Neighborhood Racial and Ethnic Diversity in U.S. Cities." *Cityscape* 4, no. 2: 1–17.

Oliver, Melvin L., and Thomas M. Shapiro. 1995. *Black Wealth/White Wealth: A New Perspective on Racial Inequality*. New York: Routledge.

Patterson, Orlando. 1997. *The Ordeal of Integration: Progress and Resentment in America's Racial Crisis*. Washington: Civitas.

Peffley, Mark, Jon Hurwitz, and Paul M. Sniderman. 1997. "Racial Stereotypes and Whites' Political Views of Blacks in the Context of Welfare and Crime." *American Journal of Political Science* 41: 30–60.

Pettigrew, Thomas F. 1982. "Prejudice." In *Dimensions of Ethnicity: Prejudice*, edited by S. Thernstrom, A. Orlov, and O. Handlin, pp. 1–29. Cambridge: Belknap.

Rawlings, Lynette, and others. 2004. "Race and Residence: Prospects for Stable Racial Integration." Policy Brief 3. Metropolitan Housing and Communities Center, Urban Institute, March.

Quillian, Lincoln. 1996. "Group Threat and Regional Change in Attitudes toward African Americans." *American Journal of Sociology* 102: 816–60.

Rubinowitz, Leonard S., and James E. Rosenbaum. 2000. *Crossing the Class and Color Lines: From Public Housing to White Suburbia*. University of Chicago Press.

Schuman, Howard, and Lawrence Bobo. 1988. "Survey-Based Experiments on White Racial Attitudes toward Residential Integration." *American Journal of Sociology* 94: 273–99.

Schuman, Howard, and others. 1997. *Racial Attitudes in America: Trends and Interpretations*. 2d ed. Harvard University Press.

Sigelman, Lee, and Steven A. Tuch. 1997. "Metastereotypes: Blacks' Perceptions of Whites' Stereotypes of Blacks." *Public Opinion Quarterly* 61: 87–101.

Smith, Tom W. 1990. "Ethnic Images." General Social Survey Technical Report 19. National Opinion Research Center, University of Chicago.

Sniderman, Paul M., and Edward G. Carmines. 1997. *Reaching beyond Race*. Harvard University Press.

Steeh, Charlotte, and Maria Krysan. 1996. "The Polls-Trends: Affirmative Action and the Public." *Public Opinion Quarterly* 60: 128–58.

Tajfel, Henri. 1982. "Social Psychology of Inter-Group Relations." *Annual Review of Psychology* 33: 1–39.

Tate, Katherine. 1993. *From Protest to Politics: The New Black Voters in American Elections*. Harvard University Press.

Thernstrom, Stephan, and Abigail Thernstrom. 1997. *America in Black and White: One Nation, Indivisible*. New York: Simon and Schuster.

Timberlake, Jeffrey M. 2000. "Still Life in Black and White: Effects of Racial and Class Attitudes on Prospects for Residential Integration in Atlanta." *Sociological Inquiry* 70, no. 4: 420–45.

Tuan, Mia. 1999. *Forever Foreigners or Honorary Whites? The Asian Ethnic Experience Today*. Rutgers University Press.

Turner, Margery Austin, and others. 2002. "Discrimination in Metropolitan Housing Markets: National Results from Phase I HDS 2000." U.S. Department of Housing and Urban Development.

Waldinger, Roger, and Tom Bailey. 1991. "The Continuing Significance of Race: Racial Conflict and Racial Discrimination in Construction." *Politics and Society* 19: 291–323.

Yinger, John. 1995. *Closed Doors, Opportunities Lost: The Continuing Cost of Housing Discrimination*. New York: Russell Sage.

Zubrinsky, Camille L., and Lawrence Bobo. 1996. "Prismatic Metropolis: Race and Residential Segregation in the City of Angels." *Social Science Research* 25: 335–74.

4

How Racial Discrimination Affects the Search for Housing

MARGERY AUSTIN TURNER AND STEPHEN L. ROSS

Paul and his wife, both African American, were looking to buy their first home in the suburbs of Washington. They saw an advertisement in the Sunday newspaper's classified section for a house that looked promising at a price they could afford, and Paul called to make an appointment with the real estate agent. When he met with the agent, she was warm and encouraging, telling him not only about the house he had seen advertised but also about another that she had on the market in the same price range. Since she had a little time that afternoon, the agent suggested that she and Paul drive out to inspect the house she recommended. It was less expensive than the one advertised in the newspaper, and the agent emphasized its affordability as a selling point, saying, "It's a real bargain." Paul noticed that the neighborhood was racially mixed, and some of the apartment buildings on the neighboring block were a bit run down. After he had walked through the house, he told the agent that he would talk things over with his wife and call her back.

Later that week, the same real estate agent met with another young husband, Steve, who called about the same advertisement. Steve and his wife were white, with the same level of income and savings as Paul and his wife. Although the agent was very busy when Steve arrived, she gave him information about two other houses as well as the one advertised and arranged to drive out to inspect all three with Steve the next day. One of the houses they visited was the same one she had shown Paul, while the other two (including the advertised home) were close to the top of Steve's price range and in a more affluent neighborhood. All the people Steve saw as they drove around that neighborhood were white. The agent encouraged Steve to think seriously about the higher-priced homes, remarking, "It may be a bit of a stretch now, but you'll see much more appreciation over the years, and you don't need to have any concerns about the schools in this area." When they returned to her office, she gave Steve a package of information about financing options that would make the higher-priced homes affordable, as well as the card of a mortgage broker that she recommended. She promised to keep her eye out for other houses that might be right for Steve and his wife and said that she would stay in touch with them.[1]

In 1968 Congress passed the Fair Housing Act, outlawing discrimination in housing on the basis or race and ethnicity. But more than three decades later, minority homeseekers still cannot count on getting the same information and assistance that comparable whites receive when they visit real estate or rental offices to inquire about homes advertised in the local newspaper. Direct comparison of the experiences of minority and white homeseekers shows that—like Paul and his wife—African Americans and Hispanics are likely to be told about fewer available homes and apartments than comparable whites; to be steered to neighborhoods with larger minority populations and lower house values; and to be given less assistance with the complexities of mortgage financing. Asians, Pacific Islanders, and Native Americans also face significant levels of discrimination when they search for housing.

The frequency of discrimination against African Americans and Hispanics has declined over the last decade, and it is rare today for a real estate or rental agent to blatantly "slam the door" on a black or Hispanic customer.[2] In fact, minority homeseekers may not even be aware that they have been discriminated against since they are generally treated courteously and told about at least one available house or apartment. And as discussed by Xavier de Souza Briggs in chapter 2 in this volume, factors other than outright discrimination—particularly white avoidance of mixed or minority neighborhoods—play a critical role in sustaining residential segregation and inequality. Nonetheless, the housing discrimination that persists in the United States today still creates serious barriers to free and full housing choice. When an African American or Hispanic homeseeker like Paul is denied information about available houses or apartments, his search for housing becomes longer and more expensive, even though

1. This scenario is typical of differences in treatment documented in the Housing Discrimination Study conducted under the auspices of the U.S. Department of Housing and Urban Development in 2000.

2. Evidence is not available on trends in levels of discrimination against Asians–Pacific Islanders and Native Americans, because (as discussed further below) only one rigorous study has measured discrimination against these two groups.

he may not realize it. When he is steered away from predominantly white neighborhoods, patterns of racial and ethnic segregation in both housing and education are perpetuated, and his chances of accumulating wealth from his housing investment are undermined. And when he is denied advice and information about mortgage financing, his chances of obtaining favorable loan terms or buying the most house he can afford may be compromised.[3]

Most Americans know that housing discrimination based on race or ethnicity is illegal and agree that it is wrong. African Americans have made substantial economic and educational gains relative to whites, and both African Americans and Hispanics have increased their presence in the owner-occupied housing market.[4] And as discussed by Camille Charles (chapter 3, this volume), white people's attitudes toward African Americans and Hispanics and their expressed willingness to live in integrated communities have improved quite dramatically over the last several decades. Nonetheless, high levels of inequality in housing outcomes and segregation in urban and suburban neighborhoods persist. People's evolving racial attitudes and willingness to live in integrated communities do not tell us enough about the extent to which minority homeseekers still encounter discrimination in the housing marketplace. Only direct observation of their experiences with real estate and rental agents can provide that information.

During the summer and fall of 2000 and 2001, local nonprofit organizations in twenty major metropolitan areas nationwide conducted more than 4,600 paired tests, directly comparing the treatment that African Americans and Hispanics received to the treatment that whites received when they visited real estate or rental offices to inquire about available housing. This study, which was sponsored by the U.S. Department of Housing and Urban Development and conducted by the Urban Institute, provides the most complete and current information available about the persistence of housing discrimination against African American and Hispanic homeseekers in large urban areas of the United States and about the progress made in combating discrimination during the 1990s. Subsequent phases of the study produced the first national estimates of discrimination against Asians and Pacific Islanders, as well as (for three states) the first rigorous estimates of discrimination against Native Americans searching for housing outside of native lands.

Paired Testing: A Tool for Enforcement and Learning

Paired testing is a powerful tool for observing discrimination in action. In a paired test, two individuals—one white and the other minority—pose as equally

3. Oliver and Shapiro (1997); Yinger (1995).
4. Abravanel and Cunningham (2001); Blank (2001); Masnick (2003).

qualified homeseekers and separately visit a real estate or rental agent to ask about available houses or apartments. Both testers are carefully trained to present themselves as credible customers, making the same inquiries, expressing the same preferences, and offering the same financial qualifications. From the perspective of the real estate or rental agent, the only difference between the two customers is their race or ethnicity; they should therefore receive the same information and assistance. Systematic differences in treatment—as when the minority customer is told that an apartment is no longer available when the white is told that he or she can move in the following month—provide direct evidence of discrimination on the basis of race or ethnicity.

This methodology originated as a tool to enforce fair housing laws by detecting and documenting individual instances of discrimination. It often provides powerful evidence, easily understandable by juries and the general public, of individual instances in which minorities are denied equal access to housing. Since the late 1970s, paired testing has also been used to rigorously measure the prevalence of discrimination across the housing market as a whole.[5] When a large number of consistent and comparable tests are conducted for a representative sample of real estate and rental agents, the tests directly measure patterns of adverse treatment based on a homeseeker's race or ethnicity. By its very design, paired testing controls for differences in the qualifications of white and minority homeseekers. And because both testers in each pair visit the same office and make the same requests, it controls for possible differences in search strategies. Finally, when paired testing directly documents unequal treatment of equally qualified customers, it has tremendous narrative power.[6]

In 2000 the U.S. Department of Housing and Urban Development (HUD) launched the third national paired-testing study to measure patterns of racial and ethnic discrimination in urban housing markets nationwide (shortened here to HDS 2000). Its predecessors, the 1977 Housing Market Practices Study and the 1989 housing discrimination study, found significant levels of racial and ethnic discrimination in both rental and sales markets of urban areas nationwide.[7]

5. Fix and Struyk (1992).

6. This testing methodology has been extended from housing to employment, automobile sales, taxi service, home insurance, and mortgage lending (see Fix and Turner 1998). A report from a workshop convened by the National Research Council confirms the potential of this methodology and discusses ways in which it can be strengthened (National Research Council 2002).

7. Wienk and others (1979); Turner, Struyk, and Yinger (1991). HDS 2000 involved three phases of paired testing in all, in forty-six metropolitan areas, producing not only rigorous measures of change in adverse treatment against blacks and Hispanics nationwide but also site-specific estimates of adverse treatment for major metropolitan areas, estimates of adverse treatment for smaller metropolitan areas and adjoining rural communities, and new measures of adverse treatment against Asians and Native Americans. In this chapter, we focus on the national findings for African Americans and Hispanics, not only because they represent the nation's two largest minority groups but also because they are the only groups for which rigorous information on discrimination

Evidence from the 1979 study helped build support for the 1988 Fair Housing Act amendments, which significantly strengthened federal enforcement powers. Although the 1989 study was not designed to yield precise estimates of changes in discrimination, it found no evidence that overall levels of adverse treatment against African Americans had declined since 1977. These findings were used to help justify higher levels of funding for fair housing outreach, education, and enforcement during much of the 1990s.

HDS 2000 was designed to rigorously assess the extent of progress in the fight against housing discrimination. The results presented here, which focus on discrimination against African Americans and Hispanics, are based on a nationally representative sample of twenty-two large metropolitan areas. Each house or apartment tested was identified through an advertisement for housing available for sale or rent, randomly selected from major metropolitan newspapers. One white and one minority tester were assigned to each house or apartment sampled and given the same level of income, assets, and debt, making them equally qualified to buy or rent the advertised unit.

Because measuring change in the incidence of discrimination against African Americans and Hispanics was a high priority, HDS 2000 replicated most of the basic testing protocols implemented in the 1989 study. This strategy is not without some risks. The real estate industry had undergone considerable change over the intervening decade, due to industry consolidation, increased emphasis on agent licensing, and expansion of fair housing legislation.[8] If typical patterns of housing search have changed over the intervening years or if new forms of discrimination have evolved among housing providers, an invariant set of testing protocols may mismeasure a changing phenomenon, potentially understating the magnitude of discrimination. On the other hand, if measurement protocols are redefined with every decade, it is impossible to determine whether the incidence of discrimination (consistently defined) is rising or falling.[9]

Housing Discrimination in 2000

HDS 2000 offers a wealth of new information and analysis about discrimination in rental and sales markets and yields five fundamental findings about housing discrimination in metropolitan America today:

---

trends is available. See Turner and Ross (2003a, 2003b) for a complete discussion of findings for Asians and Pacific Islanders and Native Americans, including challenges involved in conducting rigorous paired tests for these groups.

8. Anderson, Lewis, and Springer (2000); Mathias and Morris (1999).

9. See Turner and others (2002) for a more complete discussion of the HDS 2000 methodology, including sampling design, testing protocols, measurement procedures, and tests of statistical significance.

—African Americans and Hispanics still face significant discrimination in housing.

—Discrimination against African American renters and homebuyers and against Hispanic homebuyers has generally declined since 1989.

—Housing discrimination is a nationwide phenomenon.

—Geographic steering represents an increasingly important form of discrimination.

—Analysis of variations suggests possible causes of discrimination.

Each of these findings has important implications for understanding the role of discrimination in perpetuating residential segregation and inequality and for ongoing efforts to combat housing discrimination through education, outreach, and enforcement.

African Americans and Hispanics Still Face Significant Discrimination

In both rental and sales markets of metropolitan areas nationwide, black and Hispanic homeseekers experienced significant levels of adverse treatment relative to comparable white homeseekers (see figure 4-1). Specifically, whites were consistently favored over their black or Hispanic partners in 17 to 23 percent of tests.[10] In other words, in roughly one of five visits to a real estate or rental agent, black and Hispanic customers were denied some of the information and assistance that comparable white customers received as a matter of course. Whites were more likely to find out about available houses and apartments, more likely to be given the opportunity to inspect these units, more likely to be offered favorable financial terms, more likely to be steered toward homes for sale in predominantly white neighborhoods, and more likely to receive assistance and encouragement in their housing search.

Discrimination takes different forms in the rental and sales markets (see table 4-1).[11] For both African American and Hispanic renters, the most prevalent forms of discrimination are denial of information about available houses or apartments and denial of opportunities to inspect units. African American homebuyers may find out about as many available homes as comparable whites, but they still experience significant discrimination when it comes to inspecting the homes. In addition, they are likely to be steered away from predominantly white and affluent neighborhoods and to receive inferior assistance with financing and other aspects of the homebuying transaction. In contrast, Hispanic

10. Our "best estimate" of discrimination is the gross measure for the overall consistency composite, which reflects the extent to which whites were consistently favored over their minority partners. The pattern of results is the same using alternative measures, including the gross hierarchical composite and the net hierarchical composite. See Turner and others (2002).

11. Table 4-1 reports both gross estimates of the incidence of white-favored treatment and net measures of the extent to which white-favored treatment exceeds minority-favored treatment. Although both measures are important, we generally focus on the net measure to identify forms of treatment in which whites are systematically favored over their minority partners.

Figure 4-1. *Levels of Housing Discrimination, Black and Hispanic Renters and Buyers*[a]

Percent

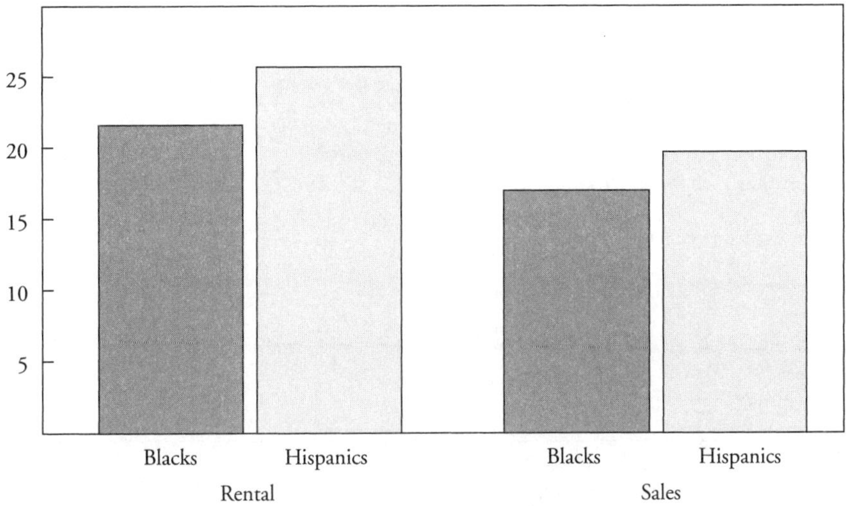

Source: Turner and others (2002).
a. Percentages reflect the share of tests in which the white tester was consistently favored.

homebuyers appear to face statistically significant levels of discrimination only with respect to geographic steering and financing assistance.

Thus African Americans and Hispanics may have to visit more agents to find out about the same number of homes or apartments, and they may never be told about some of the options available to whites. They may give up on some desirable units because they were not offered an opportunity to inspect them. They may have to pay more in rent or fees, and they may face more hurdles in figuring out how to apply for a mortgage loan. Lack of agent assistance may discourage some minorities from continuing their housing search altogether. Clearly, fair housing efforts should focus on all aspects of the housing transaction, not just on whether housing units are made available to minority customers. The denial of opportunities to inspect available houses and apartments represents an important form of discrimination against black and Hispanic renters and black homebuyers. The primary source of adverse treatment facing Hispanic homebuyers is the lack of real estate agents' assistance with mortgage financing.

Although the results presented here provide convincing evidence that discrimination persists in metropolitan rental and sales markets, they do not necessarily represent all segments of the housing market. Like previous national paired testing studies, HDS 2000 is limited in its coverage of urban housing markets and the experience of minority homeseekers. The sample of real estate

Table 4-1. *Forms of Housing Discrimination, Black and Hispanic Renters and Buyers*[a]
Percent

Form of discrimination	*Black*		*Hispanic*	
	Gross upper bound	*Net lower bound*	*Gross upper bound*	*Net lower bound*
Rental treatment				
Housing availability	32.0	4.6	34.4	12.4
Opportunities to inspect housing	26.5	7.2	25.8	8.0
Housing costs	21.5	. . .	23.0	4.4
Agent encouragement	36.3	. . .	35.9	. . .
Sales treatment				
Housing availability	46.2	. . .	47.2	. . .
Opportunities to inspect housing	41.7	5.7	38.5	. . .
Geographic steering	11.8	3.9	14.8	4.3
Assistance with financing	33.9	5.0	38.2	13.4
Agent encouragement	37.5	5.9	34.7	. . .

Source: Turner and others (2002).
a. All reported measures are statistically significant at a 90 percent confidence level or higher.

and rental agents to be tested was drawn from newspaper advertisements, and the economic characteristics of testing teams were matched to the characteristics of the advertised units. Not all housing units for sale or rent are advertised in major metropolitan newspapers, not all real estate and rental agents use newspaper advertising to attract customers, and not all homeseekers rely on newspaper advertisements in their housing search. Therefore, results presented here do not necessarily reflect the experience of the typical minority homeseeker but rather that of homeseekers qualified to rent or buy the average housing unit advertised in a major metropolitan newspaper.

Preliminary research on housing search strategies indicate that most minority homeseekers—like most whites—use newspaper advertisements as at least one source of information about available housing, and they visit with real estate or rental agents to find out more about potential homes.[12] However, more research is needed to understand whether and how search strategies of minority homeseekers differ from those of whites and how the housing search process may be influenced by anticipated or perceived discrimination. For example, if minority homeseekers expect discrimination from real estate agents whose offices are located in predominantly white neighborhoods, they may avoid these agents altogether, potentially limiting the number of available homes about which they can learn and effectively restricting themselves to racially mixed or minority neighborhoods. Alternatively, if minorities are unaware of the discrimination

12. Newburger (1995); Turner and Wienk (1993).

they experience because they receive at least some information from the agents they visit, they may have to invest considerably more time in their housing search to find the kind of homes they want, or they may revise their expectations about what they can find because of the incomplete information they receive.

It is also essential to recognize that the results presented here do not encompass all phases of the housing market transaction. HDS 2000, like most paired testing studies, focuses on the initial, in-person encounter between a homeseeker and a rental or sales agent. But minorities may experience discrimination before this encounter can even occur if they are unable to make an appointment to meet with the real estate or rental agent. A growing body of exploratory research suggests that most Americans can identify a person's race or ethnicity over the telephone with a fairly high degree of accuracy.[13] If that is the case, some real estate and rental agents may use telephone screening to avoid minority customers altogether. Although testers in HDS 2000 made appointment calls and sometimes had difficulty making appointments, a test was not considered for analysis until both partners had visited the real estate or rental office in person. Future research should explore the reliability and effectiveness of measuring discrimination on the basis of telephone calls.

Additional incidents of adverse treatment may also occur later in the housing transaction, when a renter submits an application or negotiates lease terms or when a homebuyer makes an offer on a particular unit or applies for mortgage financing. It is difficult to extend paired testing into these stages of the transaction because credit checks are likely to be conducted and because it may be illegal to sign an application with false information. Some local fair housing organizations have recruited and trained testers who use their actual rather than assigned characteristics. It is then possible to permit a credit check, although it may still be risky to allow testers to sign and submit applications. Moreover, although using testers' actual characteristics may be feasible for a small number of enforcement tests, it is difficult to see how sufficient numbers of testers could be recruited to make this approach feasible for a large-scale research effort.

Discrimination against African American Renters and Homebuyers and against Hispanic Homebuyers Has Generally Declined since 1989

As discussed earlier, HDS 2000 was designed explicitly to rigorously measure changes in levels and patterns of differential treatment since the last national paired testing study. Table 4-2 presents measures of change in discrimination from 1989 to 2000.[14] These results demonstrate that the nation has made

13. Massey and Lundy (1998).

14. Note that these are not exactly the same measures as reported in 1989; HDS 2000 refined and strengthened measures to produce more rigorous estimates of differential treatment. Moreover, the HDS 2000 sample of sites does not include all of the metropolitan areas covered by the 1989 estimates, and the 1989 weights that are used for the analysis presented here were adjusted to ensure comparability between the estimated 1989 and 2000 incidences of adverse treatment.

Table 4-2. *Change in Housing Discrimination, 1989–2000*[a]
Change in percent

	Black		*Hispanic*	
Form of discrimination	*Gross upper bound*	*Net lower bound*	*Gross upper bound*	*Net lower bound*
Rental treatment				
Housing availability	–14.0	–8.8	–7.0	. . .
Opportunities to inspect housing	–9.4	–6.5	–9.9	. . .
Housing costs	–5.1	–8.1	. . .	. . .
Agent encouragement	. . .	. . .	–7.3	–9.0
Overall	–4.8	–8.7	. . .	. . .
Sales treatment				
Housing availability	. . .	–13.3	5.0	–10.5
Opportunities to inspect housing	16.1	. . .	8.0	–14.7
Geographic steering	7.5	5.9	7.4	. . .
Assistance with financing	. . .	. . .	5.3	13.1
Agent encouragement	–4.1	–6.1	–7.6	–14.5
Overall	–12.0	–8.2	–7.1	. . .

Source: Turner and others (2002).
a. All reported measures are statistically significant at a 90 percent confidence level or higher.

progress in combating housing market discrimination, achieving significant reductions for black renters and for both black and Hispanic homebuyers.

The precise pattern of change in discrimination varies with tenure (that is, whether the homeseeker is a renter or a buyer) and with customers' race or ethnicity. For African American renters, the incidence of discrimination (that is, systematic white-favored treatment) declined significantly overall and for most categories of treatment. Declines in the lower-bound net estimates of discrimination are also statistically significant for three of four categories of treatment and for the overall composite measure. Taken together, these findings reflect a consistent pattern of decline across multiple forms of discrimination against African American renters. It appears that changing attitudes, education, and enforcement have combined to reduce—though not eliminate—the barriers that black renters face when they search for housing in metropolitan housing markets.

The picture is less encouraging for Hispanic renters. Again, the gross incidence of adverse treatment declined significantly for three categories of treatment (availability, inspections, and agent encouragement). But none of the overall indicators changed significantly between 1989 and 2000. And the lower-bound net measure of discrimination declined significantly only in the area of agent encouragement. Thus we cannot conclude that discrimination against Hispanic renters has declined. In metropolitan rental markets, discrimination against Hispanics now appears to be more prevalent than discrimination against African Americans, according to both gross and net measures.

The persistence of discrimination against Hispanic renters may reflect landlord prejudice against Hispanics, which may have been heightened by the dramatic growth of the Hispanic population in many parts of the United States and the continuing socioeconomic gap between Hispanics and non-Hispanic whites. In addition, the study's results reinforce concerns that the Hispanic community may not be well served by the current enforcement system or process for allocating federal outreach and enforcement dollars.[15] They suggest an urgent need for HUD and local fair housing organizations to reach out more aggressively to Hispanics and to community organizations that serve them to provide information about their fair housing rights, about how to detect possible discrimination, and about what to do about it. In addition, outreach and education efforts that target rental housing providers should stress the fact that discrimination against Hispanics is illegal under the federal Fair Housing Act. It is important to note here that all of the Hispanic testers involved in HDS 2000 were fluent English speakers. Some had accents, and all were identifiably Hispanic, but they were not limited in their ability to speak or understand English. Recent immigrants with limited English proficiency may face additional discrimination, and different outreach and education strategies may be required to effectively address their needs.

For both black and Hispanic homebuyers the gross incidence of adverse treatment actually increased between 1989 and 2000 for several categories of treatment. In other words, the share of tests in which whites were favored over their minority counterparts rose. However, the lower-bound net estimates of systematic discrimination dropped significantly for most forms of treatment. This somewhat puzzling result occurred because the incidence of minority-favored treatment increased more than the incidence of white-favored treatment. In other words, differential treatment is even more likely today than it was a decade ago, but it is less likely to consistently favor whites over minorities. This change may reflect systematic efforts by some real estate agents to favor minority customers; it may reflect an increase in mixed treatment, where whites are favored in some ways while minorities are favored in others; or it may reflect, at least in part, an increase in random differential treatment that has nothing to do with race or ethnicity.[16]

The 1990s saw a dramatic expansion in the market for homeownership for all groups. Between 1989 and 1998, homeownership rates for whites rose from

15. Yzaguirre, Arce, and Kamasaki (1999).

16. The biggest measurable source of nonsystematic differences in treatment was meeting with different rental or sales agents. When both testers met with the same agent, the gross incidence of differential treatment (both white-favored and minority-favored) was lower. The net measure, however, stayed about the same. Between 1989 and 2000, the share of sales tests in which both partners met with the same agent declined from about 50 percent to only 25 percent. This probably explains some of the increase in both white-favored and minority-favored treatment for sales tests.

67 to 69 percent; for African Americans, from 38 to 43 percent; and for Hispanics, from 39 to 43 percent. These increases were due in part to a sustained economic boom and low interest rates and also to changes in the mortgage market that reduced down payment requirements and increased the availability of credit to households with a blemished credit history, and to federal initiatives designed to expand homeownership.[17] These trends plus the improving economic circumstances of African Americans and the growing Hispanic population combined to give minorities a larger share of the owner-occupied housing market. Whites represented 85 percent of owner-occupied households in 1995 but only 56 percent of the increase in owner occupancy between 1995 and 2000. In contrast, African Americans and Hispanics represent 17 and 27 percent of the increase in homeownership, respectively.[18]

Although the evidence from HDS 2000 suggests that systematic discrimination against African American and Hispanic homebuyers has declined, the persistently high levels of gross differential treatment are troubling. They reflect the need for even greater educational and enforcement efforts to promote equal treatment of all qualified customers. In addition, more research is needed to explore the circumstances in which minority-favored treatment occurs and to understand how it relates to continuing patterns of white-favored treatment. Moreover, despite the overall decline in discrimination against minority homebuyers, there is strong evidence that some forms of discrimination in the sales market are on the rise. Specifically, Hispanic homebuyers appear to face an increasing incidence of discrimination with respect to financing assistance, which may limit their ability to effectively negotiate the mortgage market and achieve homeownership. And as discussed further below, geographic steering on the basis of race has increased significantly since 1989. Steering disadvantages both minority and white homeseekers, limiting their neighborhood options and perpetuating residential segregation. Education and enforcement efforts should focus on these subtle but increasingly prevalent forms of discrimination.

The fact that some forms of discrimination are on the rise despite the decline in overall levels raises the possibility that housing discrimination may take different forms today than a decade ago. Some fair housing advocates suggest that in fact discrimination may not be falling at all but shifting to forms of treatment or stages of the transaction that are not captured by the HDS testing protocols. This possibility poses a significant challenge for the design of future national testing studies; if they replicate the HDS 2000 methodology, they may miss important new forms of discrimination, but if they implement a methodology designed to capture new forms of discrimination, they may be unable to rigorously estimate the extent of change over time.

17. See Bostic and Surette (2001); Apgar and Calder, chapter 5, this volume.
18. Masnick (2003).

Housing Discrimination Is a Nationwide Problem

One of the innovations of HDS 2000 was to conduct sufficient numbers of tests at each sample site to produce estimates of differential treatment for individual metropolitan areas. In the 1989 study samples large enough to report metropolitan-level estimates were produced in only five in-depth sites. But in HDS 2000, approximately seventy paired tests were conducted for each tenure category (rental or sales) and each racial or ethnic minority in each of the metropolitan areas in the national sample. Therefore all of the indicators of differential treatment reported at the national level are also reported for each metropolitan area in which testing was conducted. However, the statistical precision of the metropolitan-level estimates is not as great as that of the national estimates, so these results need to be interpreted with some caution.

Although patterns of differential treatment vary across metropolitan areas, overall levels of treatment favoring whites are generally not significantly different from the national average. African American renters appear to face the highest levels of consistent adverse treatment in Atlanta and the lowest levels in Chicago and Detroit. Consistent adverse treatment of African American homebuyers is significantly higher than the national average in Austin and Birmingham, while black homeowners face relatively low levels of consistent adverse treatment in Atlanta and Macon. Results for Hispanic renters are significantly different from national results only in Denver, which exhibits below-average levels of consistent adverse treatment. On the sales side, Hispanics in Austin and New York face relatively high levels of consistent adverse treatment, while Pueblo, Colorado, and Tucson, Arizona, exhibit relatively low levels. Multivariate analysis, which tested for differences across metropolitan areas while controlling for other factors, finds no evidence of systematic variation in net estimates of discrimination.

These results suggest that discrimination against African American and Hispanic homeseekers remains a problem in large metropolitan areas nationwide—that no region of the country or group of metropolitan areas is immune. Nonetheless, evidence of local variations in treatment may provide useful information for designing education and enforcement methods. For example, in some metropolitan areas, minorities are highly likely to be denied information about available housing units, while in others, geographic steering or unequal assistance with financing play a bigger role. Local fair housing organizations and state and local governments can and should use information about patterns of discrimination in their metropolitan area to identify the most appropriate targets for their education, enforcement, and outreach efforts. To illustrate, in a metropolitan area with high levels of geographic steering, local fair housing organizations might develop specialized training sessions for real estate agents. In a metropolitan area with a growing Hispanic population and high levels of discrimination against Hispanics, and city government might provide organizations serving immigrant communities with the funds for Spanish-language materials and for bilingual assistance in filing fair housing complaints.

Geographic Steering Represents an Increasingly Important Form of Discrimination

Geographic steering constitutes a serious form of discrimination that limits the housing and neighborhood choices available to both minority and white homebuyers, and it may help perpetuate patterns of residential segregation. White and minority homebuyers may both be treated courteously, shown a wide variety of housing options, and offered plenty of advice and encouragement. But if whites are systematically shown houses in more predominantly white neighborhoods, while minorities are steered to mixed or minority neighborhoods, they may never find out about opportunities for greater residential integration. As discussed earlier, HDS 2000 finds that the incidence of steering since 1989 increased significantly, even though other measures of systematic discrimination declined.

In the 1990s the number of African Americans and Hispanics in the homeownership market substantially increased, and the number of racially mixed and minority suburban neighborhoods increased as well. The greater willingness on the part of real estate agents to provide these homebuyers with information on housing may in part derive from the greater number of mixed and minority neighborhoods in which housing units might be available. In turn, the increase in the number of such neighborhoods is associated with the increased ability of real estate agents to engage in racial steering.

In addition to the basic steering indicators reported for both 1989 and 2000, HDS 2000 developed an expanded analysis of geographic steering to include information steering, segregation steering, and class steering. All three forms of geographic steering can occur through the use of three techniques—recommendations, inspections, and editorializing.[19] *Information steering* means that whites get information about a wide diversity of neighborhoods while minorities are limited to just a few. It occurs when whites are told about or shown homes in a larger number of neighborhoods, but it can also occur when real estate agents simply talk about the advantages and disadvantages of more neighborhoods. *Segregation steering* means that whites are encouraged to consider more predominantly white neighborhoods than their black or Hispanic counterparts, through the location of homes recommended or shown or through positive and negative comments about particular neighborhoods. *Class steering* means that whites are encouraged to consider more affluent neighborhoods than comparable blacks or

19. This analysis was conducted at three geographic levels: census tract, place, and school district. Census tract results are presented here.

Hispanics. Again, this can occur when whites are recommended or shown homes in more affluent neighborhoods, or when they are told positive things about these neighborhoods.

All three forms of steering occur at significant levels when black and white homeseekers are involved (see table 4-3). African American homebuyers are told about fewer neighborhoods overall; are recommended, shown, and told about homes in less predominantly white neighborhoods; and hear favorable things about less affluent neighborhoods. Black-white segregation and class steering occur more often when the advertised home or the agent's office are located in neighborhoods with a high percentage of whites. A roughly comparable incidence of segregation steering also occurs in tests involving Hispanics (and non-Hispanic white counterparts), though the other types of steering appear less prevalent. Segregation and class steering of Hispanics are manifested more strongly when the advertised home is located in predominantly non-Hispanic white neighborhoods, though variations related to agent office location are less clear.

These findings clearly indicate that geographic steering warrants increased attention in education and outreach efforts. Historically, many local testing organizations have focused their efforts primarily on rental testing; conducting rigorous tests of discrimination by sales agents is considerably more demanding for both testers and their supervisors. Moreover, to obtain credible evidence of

Table 4-3. *Housing Discrimination through Geographic Steering, Black and Hispanic Homeseekers*[a]

Percent

	Black		*Hispanic*	
Form of geographic steering	*Gross upper bound*	*Net lower bound*	*Gross upper bound*	*Net lower bound*
Information steering				
Homes recommended	14.1	. . .	15.4	. . .
Homes inspected	10.0	. . .	9.9	. . .
Commentary	38.5	15.0	35.0	. . .
Segregation steering				
Homes recommended	16.5	3.8	17.1	. . .
Homes inspected	12.1	3.8	15.0	5.0
Commentary	37.1	13.7	35.1	6.2
Class steering				
Homes recommended	6.9	. . .	7.0	. . .
Homes inspected	5.2	. . .	5.1	. . .
Commentary	34.9	11.5	30.7	. . .

Source: Turner and others (2002).

a. All reported measures are statistically significant at a 90 percent confidence level or higher.

geographic steering, testers need to avoid giving sales agents cues about where they want to live and may need to visit multiple homes and record any comments made about the surrounding neighborhoods. Education and outreach efforts may also be needed to train real estate agents about the risks and implications of geographic steering and to sensitize both minority and white homebuyers to the fact that they may not be learning about all the housing opportunities that they might like to consider.

While minority homeseekers are generally thought of as the primary victims of housing discrimination, geographic steering also victimizes whites, by denying them information about housing opportunities in racially mixed or minority neighborhoods. White homebuyers who are interested in living in an integrated community need to be aware of the discriminatory barriers that might stand in their way. In addition, white homebuyers who are steered away from minority neighborhoods should be encouraged to file formal complaints with a local fair housing organization, with their local or state fair housing agency, or with HUD. HDS 2000 finds that white homeseekers, not minorities, are likely to hear explicit comments on the race or ethnicity of a neighborhood. So whites are more likely to be aware that steering has occurred and thus are in a better position to complain about it.

Analysis of Variations Suggests Possible Causes of Discrimination

To craft effective remedies for housing market discrimination, it can be helpful to understand the factors that cause real estate and rental agents to treat minority customers less favorably than comparable whites. In addition to producing national and metropolitan estimates of discrimination, HDS 2000 looked for patterns of variation in discrimination based on location, timing, tester characteristics, agent or agency characteristics, and neighborhood characteristics. This analysis tests three basic hypotheses about the causes of discrimination, assessing the extent to which it appears to stem from agent prejudice, from efforts by agents to protect their business with prejudiced white customers, or from agents' stereotypes about what minority and white customers want or can afford.[20]

Many forms of discrimination clearly vary with housing agent characteristics. For every type of test, at least some evidence is found that older agents discriminate more than younger agents. Both prejudice and professional experience tend to increase with age, so this result could be interpreted in either of two ways. One possibility is that older agents retain prejudiced attitudes that generally are declining in America and that younger agents, who are less prejudiced, continue to practice less discrimination as they mature. Alternatively, higher levels of discrimination among older agents may mean that their years of experience have led them to make stereotyped assumptions about what white

20. Yinger (1995).

and minority customers want and can afford. For example, an agent with many years of experience may have concluded that few white customers want to buy homes in racially mixed neighborhoods and that therefore it is a waste of time to recommend or show homes in such neighborhoods to whites. This explanation would suggest that younger agents are likely to discriminate more over time as they accumulate experience.

Some evidence is found that female agents discriminate more than male agents, possibly suggesting that women are less comfortable than men with interacting with minorities. In addition, discrimination is higher when testers encounter more staff at the same agency than their minority partners. This result suggests that discrimination may be more likely to occur in larger agencies that have a wider variety of homes to offer customers and can essentially tailor their services to what they believe to be the different capabilities or needs of white and minority homeseekers.

Some results support the view that agent prejudice is a key cause of discrimination. Specifically, Hispanic agents discriminate less against Hispanic renters than do white agents and less against black female homebuyers than against black male homebuyers. A few results also support the view that housing agents discriminate on the basis of their perceptions of black and Hispanic preferences, to avoid spending time on transactions that are unlikely to be consummated.[21] In particular, some forms of discrimination against Hispanics in the rental market are lower in largely Hispanic neighborhoods, and some forms of discrimination against black homebuyers are lower in largely black neighborhoods. Finally, one result supports the view that agents discriminate to avoid racial or ethnic tipping (that is, reaching the proportion of minorities at which a neighborhood is no longer considered attractive by whites), which would undermine all the personal contacts they have developed in the white community. To be specific, discrimination against blacks in the sales market declines with the average value of housing in the advertised unit's neighborhood.

Although analysis of the variations in discrimination offers some insight into the causes of discrimination, paired testing is probably not the most effective research method for exploring this issue further. Attitudinal surveys of real estate and rental agents, or ethnographic research that observes and explores the culture and incentives of these businesses, may offer much greater insight on factors that encourage or discourage discrimination. This kind of research could be useful in designing outreach and education efforts for real estate and rental agents and agencies. For example, it might suggest a training session to address

21. This behavior represents a form of statistical discrimination, in which agents make assumptions about the preferences and resources of individual minority customers based upon information about minorities as a group. Ondrich, Ross, and Yinger (2003) provide a careful discussion of statistical discrimination in housing markets and find strong evidence that it occurs, using data from the 1989 study.

particular stereotypes or particular business incentives that firms should consider modifying.

Conclusion

Paired testing has proven to be a powerful tool for directly observing differences in the treatment that minority and white homeseekers experience when they inquire about the availability of advertised housing units. HUD has been a leader among federal agencies in the measurement of racial and ethnic discrimination, sponsoring major national paired-testing studies at roughly ten-year intervals since the late 1970s to monitor the nation's progress in combating housing discrimination and to assess the effectiveness of fair housing enforcement. The latest study (HDS 2000) provides sobering evidence that blacks and Hispanics still face significant levels of discrimination in both rental and sales markets in metropolitan areas nationwide. But it also indicates that discrimination is declining for both black and Hispanic homebuyers and for black renters, offering grounds for optimism that outreach, education, and enforcement efforts are making a dent in this national problem.

The results summarized in this chapter provide strong support for continued efforts at the federal, state, and local level to educate renters and homebuyers about their fair housing rights, to reach out to make sure that victims of discrimination get help, to train real estate and rental agents to treat all their customers fairly, to investigate instances of suspected discrimination, and to vigorously enforce fair housing laws. Since the housing study of 1989, federal enforcement of the fair housing law has been strengthened and federal spending on fair housing enforcement and education was expanded. If measurable progress in combating discrimination had not been seen, one would have had to question the efficacy of these policy tools.

However, the unacceptably high levels of discrimination that persist suggest ways in which fair housing efforts can be strengthened. Our results argue for greater outreach to Hispanic homeseekers, particularly renters, the only group for whom discrimination has not declined over the decade. And while overall levels of discrimination against minority homebuyers are falling, we see disturbing evidence of increases in geographic steering and unequal assistance with mortgage financing. Both of these forms of discrimination are subtle and difficult to detect, but they can have a profound impact on homebuyers' free access to the full range of housing available.

In the ongoing fight against housing discrimination, paired testing is certain to play a critical role, both in enforcement and in measurement and monitoring. But because housing market conditions and practices are likely to evolve over time, testing methods need to adapt in order to capture emerging forms of discrimination. New approaches should include rigorously analyzing adverse treatment based on telephone communications, sampling the full range of housing available for sale or rent (not just units advertised), and extending the testing process into later stages of the housing transaction. In addition, related research using methods other than paired testing is needed to better understand the strategies and information sources that minorities use to search for housing, the impact of discrimination on those strategies, the role that persistent discrimination plays in perpetuating residential segregation and housing inequities, and the factors that contribute to unequal treatment by real estate and rental housing agents.

References

Abravanel, Martin, and Mary Cunningham. 2002. *What Do We Know?* U.S. Department of Housing and Urban Development.

Anderson, Randy, Danielle Lewis, and Thomas M. Springer. 2000. "Operating Efficiencies in Real Estate: A Critical Review of the Literature." *Journal of Real Estate Literature* 8: 3–16.

Blank, Rebecca M. 2001. "Trends in Social and Economic Well-Being, by Race." In *American Becoming: Racial Trends and Their Consequences,* edited by N. Smelser, W. Wilson, and F. Mitchell, pp. 21–39. Washington: National Academy Press.

Bostic, Raphael W., and Brian J. Surette. 2001. "Have the Doors Opened Wider? Trends in Homeownership Rates by Race and Income." *Journal of Real Estate Finance and Economics* 23, no. 3: 411–34.

Fix, Michael, and Raymond J. Struyk. 1992. *Clear and Convincing Evidence: Testing for Discrimination in America.* Washington: Urban Institute.

Fix, Michael, and Margery Austin Turner. 1998. *A National Report Card on Discrimination in America.* Washington: Urban Institute.

Masnick, George S. 2003. "The New Demographics of Housing." *Housing Policy Debate* 13: 275–322.

Massey, Douglas S., and Garvey Lundy. 1998. "Use of Black English and Racial Discrimination in Urban Housing Markets." Population Studies Center, University of Pennsylvania.

Mathias, Charles, and Marion Morris. 1999. "Fair Housing Legislation: Not an Easy Row to Hoe." *Cityscape: A Journal of Policy Development and Research* 4, no. 3: 21–34.

National Research Council. 2002. *Measuring Housing Discrimination in a National Study: Report of a Workshop.* Washington: National Academy Press.

Newburger, Harriet. 1995. "Sources of Difference in Information Used by Black and White Housing Seekers: An Exploratory Analysis." *Urban Studies* 32, no. 3: 445–70.

Oliver, Melvin L., and Thomas M. Shapiro. 1997. *Black Wealth/White Wealth: A New Perspective on Racial Inequality.* New York: Routledge.

Ondrich, Jan, Stephen Ross, and John Yinger. 2003. "Now You See It, Now You Don't: Why Do Real Estate Agents Withhold Available Houses from Black Customers?" *Review of Economics and Statistics* 85: 854-73.

Turner, Margery, and Stephen Ross. 2003a. *Discrimination in Metropolitan Housing Markets: Phase 2—Asians and Pacific Islanders.* U.S. Department of Housing and Urban Development.

———. 2003b. *Discrimination in Metropolitan Housing Markets: Phase 3—Native Americans.* U.S. Department of Housing and Urban Development.

Turner, Margery, Raymond Struyk, and John Yinger. 1991. *Housing Discrimination Study: Synthesis.* U.S. Department of Housing and Urban Development.

Turner, Margery, and Ron Wienk. 1993. "The Persistence of Segregation in Urban Areas: Contributing Causes." In *Housing Markets and Residential Mobility,* edited by T. Kingsley and M. Turner, pp. 198–218. Washington: Urban Institute.

Turner, Margery, and others. 2002. *Discrimination in Metropolitan Housing Markets: National Results from Phase I of HDS 2000.* U.S. Department of Housing and Urban Development.

Wienk, Ron, and others. 1979. *Measuring Racial Discrimination in Housing Markets: The Housing Market Practices Study.* U.S. Department of Housing and Urban Development.

Yinger, John. 1995. *Closed Doors, Opportunities Lost: The Continuing Costs of Housing Discrimination.* New York: Russell Sage.

Yzaguirre, Raul, Laura Arce, and Charles Kamasaki. 1999. "The Fair Housing Act: A Latino Perspective." *Cityscape: A Journal of Policy Development and Research* 4, no. 3: 161–70.

5

The Dual Mortgage Market: The Persistence of Discrimination in Mortgage Lending

WILLIAM APGAR AND ALLEGRA CALDER

Efforts to promote equal access to mortgage capital by racial and ethnic minorities have historically been a key component of the civil rights agenda in the United States. From the struggle to enact fair housing and fair lending legislation in the 1960s to the community-based advocacy that prompted Congress to pass the Home Mortgage Disclosure Act (HMDA) and the Community Reinvestment Act in the 1970s, housing and civil rights advocates have pursued a common goal of eradicating racial discrimination in home mortgage lending. Today, the fight continues as housing advocates seek to expand regulatory and legislative action to halt predatory lending practices that burden many minorities with mortgages they cannot afford and often do not need.[1]

Successful efforts to promote fair lending must take into account the changing nature of discriminatory practices in the marketplace. In the immediate post–World War II period, racial discrimination in mortgage lending was easy to spot. From government-sponsored racial covenants in the Federal Housing Administration (FHA) guidelines to the redlining practices of private mortgage

1. As commonly described in existing literature, predatory lending may involve mortgage bankers, brokers, realtors, appraisers, home improvement contractors, or others involved directly or indirectly in mortgage lending. Predatory practices include outright deception and fraud and also efforts to manipulate the borrower through aggressive sales tactics or to exploit their lack of understanding about loan terms. For further discussion see U.S. Department of Housing and Urban Development and U.S. Department of Treasury (2000, hereafter HUD/Treasury 2000).

lenders and financial institutions, minorities were denied access to home mortgages in ways that severely limited their ability to purchase a home.

Today, mortgage lending discrimination is more subtle. Even though mortgage loans are now readily available in low-income minority communities, by employing high-pressure sales practices and deceptive tactics, some mortgage brokers push minority borrowers into higher-cost subprime mortgages that are not well suited to their needs and can lead to financial problems down the road. Consequently, more than three decades after the enactment of national fair lending legislation, minority consumers continue to have less-than-equal access to loans at the best price and on the best terms that their credit history, income, and other individual financial considerations merit.

The shifting nature of mortgage market discrimination comes in the midst of an explosion of mortgage lending to both lower-income and minority households and communities. Supported by a strong economy, favorable interest rates, and innovations in mortgage finance, the share of home purchase loans going to lower-income households and households living in lower-income communities increased steadily, from 31 percent in 1993 to 35 percent in 2001.[2] Over the same period, home purchase lending to Hispanic borrowers increased by 159 percent and to African American borrowers by 93 percent, while lending to whites grew by just 29 percent. As thousands of credit-impaired and often lower-income families purchased a home, the homeownership rate rose to a record high.

Unfortunately, the growth of lower-income lending and expanded outreach to minority consumers is linked to a dual mortgage delivery system, in which these borrowers are served with a different mix of products and by different types of lenders than commonly serve higher-income markets. Typically, products that target lower-income and credit-impaired borrowers have higher interest rates and less favorable terms than the conventional prime loans that serve the mainstream market. In addition, many of the alternative mortgage providers that have emerged fall outside of the existing federal regulatory framework, which remains largely focused on encouraging deposit-taking banking organizations to provide mortgage capital to low-income and minority communities.

Many households have benefited from these innovative mortgage products; however, they pose serious challenges for some borrowers. High-cost lenders disproportionately target minority, especially African American, borrowers and communities, resulting in a noticeable lack of prime loans among even the highest-income minority borrowers. In 2001 prime loans accounted for only 70.8 percent of home refinancing for African Americans with incomes in excess of 120 percent of area median income living in predominantly African American

2. Lower-income borrowers are defined as having incomes below 80 percent of area median income in 1990; lower-income neighborhoods have an income of less than 80 percent of area median income in 1990.

high-income neighborhoods.[3] In contrast, the figure is 83.1 percent for lower-income white borrowers living in predominantly white lower-income communities.[4] This, in part, reflects the fact that minorities have lower credit scores, on average, than whites. But there is concern that some high-cost lenders actively seek out minority applicants who may be vulnerable to deceptive, high-pressure marketing tactics due to their limited mortgage product options and limited knowledge of the mortgage system.

The increase in high-cost, inappropriate, or predatory mortgage loans in lower-income and minority neighborhoods raises serious public policy questions. Many families with overpriced loans quickly discover that they are unable to make current mortgage payments, which may result in foreclosure. Indeed, high-cost lending in the 1990s appears to be linked to a troubling rise in foreclosures, threatening not only to undo low-income homeownership gains but also to destabilize the already weak neighborhoods where these loans are concentrated. Clearly, an enhanced understanding of mortgage market dynamics is needed to design an appropriate policy response to predatory lending practices, to assist borrowers trapped in high-cost mortgages, and to minimize the harm resulting from high levels of foreclosures.

This chapter discusses the trends that are reshaping the mortgage banking industry and assesses the consequences of current mortgage lending patterns for lower-income and minority borrowers and communities. A summary of the available evidence suggests that although legitimate risk factors play a significant role in the allocation of mortgage credit, borrower race and neighborhood racial composition still appear to be significantly linked to access to prime loans. While the current structure of the mortgage market may efficiently serve affluent and financially savvy borrowers, the growing presence of some unscrupulous mortgage brokers in the marketplace increases the vulnerability of inexperienced borrowers, who often lack the ability to shop effectively in today's complex mortgage market and frequently end up paying too much for mortgage credit. In extreme cases, the current broker compensation structure actually reinforces the incentive for unscrupulous mortgage brokers to employ deceptive or even predatory practices, saddling poorer households with mortgage debt well in excess of their ability to repay.

The Changing Structure of the Mortgage Banking Industry

The mortgage industry of today bears little relationship to the mortgage industry of even the 1990s. The advent of automated underwriting, credit scoring,

3. A predominantly African American neighborhood is a census tract in which African Americans constitute at least 50 percent of the population. A high-income neighborhood has an income of more than 120 percent of the average median income as of 1990.

4. A predominantly white neighborhood is a census tracts in which the population is 90 percent white.

and risk-based pricing as well as the growing importance of mortgage brokers, national mortgage banking organizations, and expanded secondary mortgage markets have produced what some label a revolution in mortgage finance. This section summarizes these trends and assesses their implications for mortgage markets.

The declining importance of bank deposits as a funding source for mortgages has largely driven the structural shifts within the industry. Historically, deposit-taking institutions such as thrift institutions and commercial banks originated the bulk of mortgages. In 1980 nearly half of all mortgages were originated by thousands of thrifts, while commercial banks originated another 22 percent.[5] Throughout the 1980s, many deposit-taking institutions held the loans they originated. Although mortgage insurance was an important element for FHA and other government-backed loans, the private mortgage insurance industry was still in its infancy. Moreover, mortgage underwriting standards and documents varied considerably from one institution to the next. As a result, third-party investors were reluctant to purchase mortgages that lacked standardized terms, mortgage insurance, and other features designed to reduce risk.

Since the 1980s that system has changed. The availability first of FHA insurance and then of private market insurance helped to extend the reach of the mortgage market to low-income and low-wealth borrowers. The Community Reinvestment Act, passed by Congress in 1977, also encouraged banks and their affiliates to turn their attention to previously underserved markets. Though these efforts substantially expanded access to capital, they also served to segment the market into distinct mortgage delivery channels, with one offering products targeting low-income and largely minority borrowers, while another targets the mainstream market.

The secondary market also developed and matured over that period. Even as late as 1990 less than half of all mortgages were securitized and sold on the secondary market—a figure bolstered by the fact that at that point Ginnie Mae was securitizing virtually 100 percent of all FHA loans.[6] Today, nearly 70 percent of all home mortgages are securitized and sold on the secondary market, due in large part to the growing presence in the marketplace of Fannie Mae and Freddie Mac, both government-sponsored enterprises. The ability to package and sell loans in the secondary market reduced the need to hold deposits (or other sources of cash) to fund mortgage loans. Fannie Mae and Freddie Mac, along with private mortgage conduits, standardized loan contracts and thus streamlined and rationalized mortgage markets, helping to foster an increasingly efficient mortgage delivery system.[7]

5. U.S. Department of Housing and Urban Development (1997).

6. Inside Mortgage Finance (2003). Three federal institutions secure home mortgages: Ginnie Mae (Government National Mortgage Association), Fannie Mae (Federal National Mortgage Association), and Freddie Mac (Federal Home Loan Mortgage Corporation).

7. Renieri (1996).

Most state-level restrictions on *intra*state banking were relaxed or removed in the 1980s; *inter*state banking became a reality at the federal level in the 1990s.[8] Banks could now expand beyond boundaries that had been in place since the Great Depression, and larger organizations increased the scale and scope of their operations through mergers and acquisitions. Lacking the economies of scale needed to compete in an increasingly automated business, many smaller banks and thrift institutions abandoned their mortgage origination activities entirely. Mortgage lending became dominated by a handful of financial services giants, making consolidation one of the most striking features of industry change. By 1990 the top twenty-five originators accounted for 28.4 percent of an industry total of less than $500 billion in home mortgages. In 2003 these lenders accounted for 76.6 percent of the $3.7 trillion in loans originated that year.[9]

Loans are originated through one of three channels: retail, correspondent, or broker. Retail activity is most akin to traditional lending, wherein lenders reach out to potential customers, take mortgage applications, and underwrite and fund loans for those who meet their underwriting standards. Many retail lenders conduct business from branch operations. Increasingly, however, the marketing and even the closing of loans is being done by telephone or on the Internet. Once funded, a retail loan may be held in a portfolio by the lender or packaged and sold on the secondary market. Correspondent lenders typically are smaller mortgage banks, thrifts, or community banks that operate much like retail lenders in that they take applications and underwrite and fund mortgages. Although loans are funded in the name of the correspondent, they are later sold to a wholesale lender under prearranged pricing and loan delivery terms and in compliance with established underwriting standards. Brokers, by contrast, do not fund loans; they simply identify potential customers, process the paperwork, and submit the loan application to a wholesale lender, which underwrites and funds the mortgage.

In the 1980s retail lending dominated the industry. Since then—and particularly over the past ten years—wholesale activity, which includes both correspondent lenders and brokers, has grown rapidly. Concurrent with this trend has been an increase in the number of firms engaged in these activities. For example, in 2002 there were as many as 44,000 firms (with some 240,000 employees) engaged in mortgage brokerage and correspondent lending activities, up markedly from the 7,000 firms operating in 1987.[10] In 2003 retail lending accounted for 41.3 percent of origination volume, while brokers accounted for 27.9 percent and correspondent lenders for 30.8 percent.[11]

8. For a more complete discussion of trends in federal regulation of the banking and mortgage banking industries see Joint Center for Housing Studies (2002, section 2).

9. Inside Mortgage Finance (2004).

10. Wholesale Access Mortgage Research and Consulting, "Mortgage Brokers 2002," August 13, 2003, Columbia, Md.

11. Authors' calculations from Inside Mortgage Finance (2004).

Brokers do not work on behalf of the borrower or the wholesale lender or investor who funds the loan. Instead they receive compensation from the borrower in the form of origination fees and points, and often they receive an origination fee from the mortgage banker at the time that the loan is funded. A mortgage delivery system wherein brokers are compensated for making loans but have no long-term interest in loan performance is subject to what economists call "principal agent risk." A broker (the agent) has little or no incentive to worry about whether the information presented in the mortgage application is accurate as long as the information gathered is sufficient to cause the mortgage banker (the principal) to fund the loan, triggering payment of the broker's fees (which is not to suggest that all mortgage brokers mislead borrowers; many work hard on behalf of borrowers to match them with the best product). Without a long-term interest in the performance of the loan, brokers are immune from the potential adverse consequences of both failing to match the borrower with the best available mortgage and failing to provide accurate data to underwrite the loan. Both affect the odds that the loan will default, which can have devastating consequences for the borrower.

Econometric studies demonstrate that borrowers with similar characteristics can and do receive different pricing depending on the process or channel through which they receive their loan. Building on a study by Michael LaCour-Little and Gregory Chun that confirms that broker-originated loans are likely to prepay faster, a study by William Alexander and others shows that these loans are also more likely to default than loans originated through a retail channel, even after controlling for credit and ability-to-pay factors. The authors argue that because of growing capital market awareness of the "principal agent risk" associated with broker-originated loans, borrowers who receive funding through the broker channel are charged a premium over apparently similar borrowers who receive their loans through retail channels. This is a result of the need to compensate lenders for the higher default and prepayment risk associated with these broker-originated loans.[12]

The Rise in Lending to Minorities and Minority Communities

The increase in lending to lower-income borrowers over the 1990s was propelled by strong gains in lending to minorities, although increases in the number of HMDA loan records that do not report the race of the borrower makes precise tracking of trends difficult.[13] Minorities represent less than one-fifth of

12. LaCour-Little and Chun (1999); Alexander and others (2002).

13. From 1993 to 2001, the number of loans without a designation of race increased from 63,382 to 458,818 for purchase loans and from 188,621 to 1.06 million for home refinance loans. In 2001 borrower race was missing for some 12.1 percent for all home purchase loans and 18.6 percent of all home refinance loans.

Table 5-1. *Mortgage Lending, by Neighborhood Income and Racial Composition, 1993 and 2001*

Neighborhood type, by income and racial composition[a]	*Home purchase loans per census tract (number)* 1993	2001	*Lenders per census tract (number)* 1993	2001	*Top 25 lenders per census tract (number)* 1993	2001	*Loans by top 25 lenders (percent)* 1993	2001
Less than 80 percent area median income								
Predominantly white	32.6	52.2	11.9	19.7	2.9	7.4	25.4	46.8
Predominantly minority	15.7	30.3	8.4	15.1	2.4	5.9	32.3	49.7
Between 80 and 120 percent area median income								
Predominantly white	60.9	90.1	19.4	28.5	4.9	10.4	26.2	47.8
Predominantly minority	42.0	72.5	17.9	26.2	5.0	9.8	33.3	51.7
More than 120 percent area medium income								
Predominantly white	90.8	117.3	26	32.2	7	12.1	30.0	51.3
Predominantly minority	64.9	106.5	21.8	28.5	5.6	10.3	32.8	54.9

Source: Joint Center for Housing Studies using enhanced HMDA database.

a. Predominantly white neighborhoods have less than 10 percent minority population; predominantly minority neighborhoods have more than 50 percent minority population.

all homeowners, but they account for 34 percent of the increase in home purchase lending between 1990 and 2001 and for nearly 40 percent of the increase in the number of homeowners.

Data in table 5-1 confirm the transformation of the mortgage lending landscape in minority communities across the country over the period 1993 to 2001. While there remains a clear tendency for lenders (including the top twenty-five lenders) to serve customers in higher-income and largely white neighborhoods, the growth in the number of lenders serving lower-income and minority neighborhoods is nevertheless encouraging. From 1993 to 2001, the loans made to buyers in predominantly minority, lower-income neighborhoods almost doubled, as did the number of lenders and number of top twenty-five lenders active in these areas. Moreover, in 2001 the top twenty-five lenders account for close to half of all loans made in these neighborhoods.

Nevertheless, a gap persists between homeownership rates for minorities and those for whites. In 2003 the African American homeownership rate stood at 48.4 percent, the Hispanic rate at 47.4, and the rate for other minorities at 56.5 percent—all considerably below the 75.1 percent rate for whites. While the rates reflect differences in household income, wealth, age, and family composition among the various racial and ethnic groups, those factors do not entirely account for the gap.[14]

New technologies, such as automated underwriting and credit scoring systems, have enabled lenders to better evaluate and price risk. Therefore they can offer mortgages with lower down payment requirements to low-income or low-wealth but creditworthy borrowers and make higher-priced loans to borrowers with less-than-perfect credit histories.[15] Although these subprime loans tend to be higher cost and less flexible than prime loans, they often are the only choice for borrowers with less-than-perfect credit histories.

From 1993 to 2001, there was an eightfold increase in the number of home purchase loans reported by lenders specializing in subprime lending.[16] Although variation in the definition of what constitutes a subprime mortgage hinders precise measurement, according to one widely used mortgage industry source the volume of subprime loan originations increased from $35 billion in 1994 to $332 billion in 2003.[17] As a percentage of all mortgage originations, subprime loans increased from less than 5 percent in 1994 to more than 13 percent in 2000, before falling back slightly by 2003 due to a boom in prime mortgage refinancing.

By 2001 subprime lenders accounted for more than 6 percent of all home purchase lending, up from just 1 percent in 1993. For lower-income households living in lower-income communities, the subprime share topped 10 percent. For the same population, subprime refinancing loans accounted for a striking 27 percent of home refinance loans, a more than fourfold increase in market share over the period 1993–2001. For low-income African Americans living in lower-income communities, the subprime share of home purchase loans was 18 percent and 42 percent for refinancing loans.

Loans for manufactured homes also grew notably during the 1990s, along with sales of these homes. Almost half of all manufactured homes are sited on rented land and financed with personal, as opposed to real estate, loans. As a result, many manufactured home loans include rates that are from 2 to 5 percentage points higher than those on conventional prime real estate loans.[18] Government-backed loans, particularly those insured by the FHA, also have somewhat higher interest rates. Over the 1993–2001 period government-backed

14. Yinger (1998).

15. For a more complete discussion of the factors influencing the growth of mortgage lending in the 1990s, see Joint Center for Housing Studies (2004).

16. Although HMDA data do not label the loan type directly, HUD supplies a list of each lender's specialization in prime, subprime, or manufactured home lending. For a brief description of the HUD methodology, see Scheessele (2002).

17. Inside Mortgage Finance (2004).

18. Vermeer and Louie (1996); Collins, Carliner, and Crowe (2002).

Figure 5-1. *Share of Growth in Home Purchase Lending, by Lender Type, 1993–2001*[a]

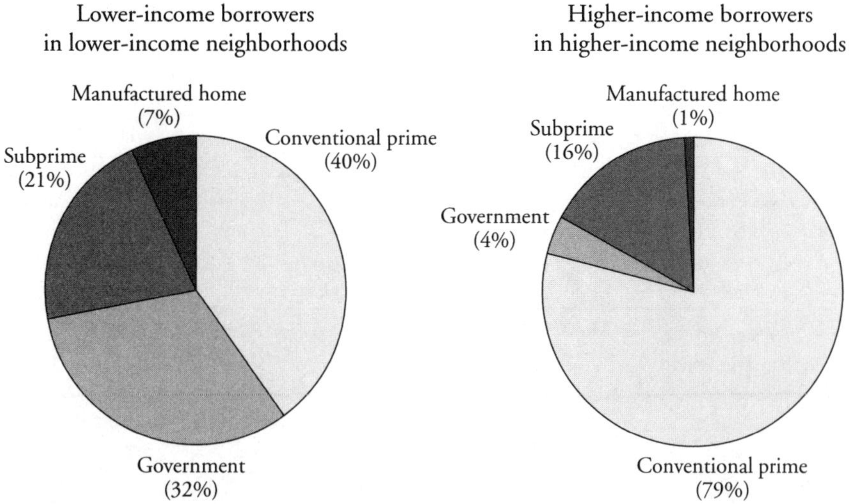

Source: Joint Center for Housing Studies (2002).

a. Lower-income borrowers have income of less than 80 percent of area median in that year; lower-income neighborhoods have income of less than 80 percent of area median in 1990. Higher-income borrowers have income of at least 80 percent of area median that year; higher-income neighborhoods have at least 80 percent of area median in 1990.

loans accounted for between 10 and 14 percent of all home purchase loans.[19] Collectively, these alternative loan products were a major contributor to the overall growth of home lending. Over the 1993–2001 period, government-backed, subprime, and manufactured home lending accounted for nearly one-third of the 1.4 million increase in the number of home purchase loans. Prime loans to lower-income borrowers in lower-income neighborhoods, on the other hand, account for only about 40 percent of all growth in home purchase lending (see figure 5-1). This contrasts significantly with prime loans to higher-income borrowers in higher-income neighborhoods, which accounted for almost 80 percent of all home purchase lending growth over the period.

There is a pronounced gap between the ability of minorities and that of whites to secure prime mortgages. In 2001 prime conventional lenders accounted for nearly three-quarters of all home purchase lending to whites but less than 50 percent of lending to Hispanics and only 40 percent of lending to African Americans. While there are noticeable income differences, on average, between borrowers of different races and ethnicities, the racial gap in prime

19. Government-backed loans may also be guaranteed by the U.S. Department of Agriculture's Rural Housing Service or the Veteran's Administration.

Table 5-2. *Prime Loans as Share of All Loans, by Neighborhood Characteristics, 2001*
Percent

Level of home price appreciation, growth in household income, and mortgage denial rates	Less than 80 percent area median income: Predominantly white	Less than 80 percent area median income: Predominantly African American	Between 80 and 120 percent area median income: Predominantly white	Between 80 and 120 percent area median income: Predominantly African American	More than 120 percent area median income: Predominantly white	More than 120 percent area median income: Predominantly African American
Rise in housing value						
Less than 10 percent	64.2	35.8	69.7	42.3	84.2	61.5
10–25 percent	60.1	29.0	68.8	37.3	85.7	59.9
25–50 percent	58.2	28.9	66.3	36.0	85.3	59.8
50–75 percent	60.9	32.1	69.0	38.5	86.9	63.2
More than 75 percent	60.7	32.6	69.5	42.4	87.4	65.9
Rise in household income						
Less than 10 percent	58.6	33.1	65.9	41.5	82.7	57.7
10–25 percent	58.5	29.6	65.4	36.9	83.6	57.2
25–50 percent	60.4	30.5	68.3	38.0	85.6	61.5
50–75 percent	61.2	31.4	69.8	39.0	87.3	64.8
More than 75 percent	64.3	36.7	72.1	46.5	88.7	69.8
Mortgage denial rates						
Less than 5 percent	77.6	44.5	81.6	52.1	92.6	79.1
5–14 percent	65.2	33.6	71.8	41.7	87.9	67.9
15–25 percent	54.1	31.1	61.9	37.7	81.3	58.2
26–30 percent	48.6	28.5	56.3	33.8	77.5	51.7
More than 30 percent	43.6	28.9	52.8	36.8	75.4	52.7

(Column group heading: *Neighborhood type, by income and racial composition*[a])

Source: Joint Center for Housing Studies, based on enhanced HMDA database.

a. Predominantly white neighborhoods have less than 10 percent minority population; predominantly African American neighborhoods are more than 50 percent African American.

lending persists even after controlling for borrower income. Indeed, a white borrower with an income of less than 80 percent of area median has about the same likelihood of obtaining a prime mortgage as an African American borrower with an income in excess of 120 percent of area median (see table 5-2).

There also appears to be a gap between the shares of prime loans made in neighborhoods of different racial and ethnic compositions, independent of the race of the borrower (see table 5-3). For example, prime lending accounts for 70 percent of all home purchase lending but only 57 percent of home purchase

Table 5-3. *Prime Loans as Share of All Loans, by Neighborhood Characteristics and Income and Race of Borrower, 2001*
Percent

	Lower-income borrower[b]				*Higher-income borrower*[b]			
Neighborhood type by racial composition and income[a]	*White*	*African American*	*Hispanic*	*Asian or other*	*White*	*African American*	*Hispanic*	*Asian or other*
Predominantly white								
Lower income	54.9	29.1	42.0	51.2	85.1	67.8	75.0	80.3
Higher income	65.4	36.3	48.4	65.3	89.4	73.5	81.6	89.0
Predominantly African American								
Lower income	54.5	31.8	44.5	48.3	85.9	59.5	64.3	72.4
Higher income	48.0	27.7	39.0	48.4	81.1	55.0	56.8	68.4
Predominantly Hispanic								
Lower income	52.7	32.1	40.4	61.0	79.1	48.2	56.4	74.0
Higher income	48.3	32.0	42.6	56.3	73.4	51.1	65.5	69.7

Source: Joint Center for Housing Studies, based on enhanced HMDA database.

a. Predominantly white neighborhoods have less than 10 percent minority population; predominantly African American neighborhoods are more than 50 percent African American; predominantly Hispanic neighborhoods are more than 50 percent Hispanic.

b. Lower-income borrower has less than 80 percent of area median income; higher-income borrower has more than 120 percent of area median income.

lending in lower-income census tracts. For lower-income census tracts in which African Americans account for more than 50 percent of total households, the prime share for African American borrowers falls to 27.7 percent.

Observed differences in the prime loan share of total lending by race and income cannot be taken as proof of discriminatory practices in mortgage markets. At a minimum, the simple results presented here do not control for many of the objective factors that lenders use to determine whether a particular individual qualifies for a particular type of loan. Such discrepancies, however, support advocates' claims that the rise of alternative mortgage products has resulted in a new and subtler form of discrimination based on race and ethnicity that has a disparate, and largely unfavorable, impact on minority borrowers and communities.

The Dual Mortgage Market: Risk or Race?

Discrimination in housing and mortgage markets is more subtle today than when entire neighborhoods were redlined and not only mortgage brokers and real estate agents but also government programs such as the FHA refused to serve minorities looking for homes in largely white neighborhoods. Nonetheless, there can be no doubt that it persists.[20] Documenting the extent and impact of ongoing mortgage lending discrimination, however, has proven more difficult than proving its existence. Efforts to isolate the impact of race on the spatial pattern of mortgage lending are hindered by the lack of publicly available data on the credit characteristics of individual mortgage applicants.

Although credit quality data are widely used to underwrite and price loans, the mortgage industry claims that the data are proprietary. Whatever one thinks about the merits of this claim, historically the industry's failure to make the data available has enabled the mortgage industry to refute studies that find evidence of discriminatory practices. Arguing that on average African Americans and other minorities have more problematic credit histories, industry apologists frequently dismiss findings of disparate treatment as simply the failure to distinguish "risk from race."[21]

Researchers and advocates have analyzed HMDA data to document both the rise in subprime lending and the corresponding absence of prime lending in lower-income and minority neighborhoods. Though there are undoubtedly different risks associated with lending to individuals living in different neighborhoods, the racial disparity is substantial. For example, subprime refinancing loans are three times more likely to be made in low-income than in upper-income neighborhoods and five times more likely to be made in predominantly African American than in white neighborhoods.[22] In a comprehensive review of neighborhood lending patterns in Chicago in the late 1990s, Daniel Immergluck and Marti Wiles observe that conventional lenders served higher-income white areas while FHA and subprime lending was concentrated in lower-income and minority communities. Characterizing this as a "dual mortgage market," they note that the racial disparities were too great to be explained by differences in the credit quality of the borrowers and argue that the patterns resulted instead from the failure of "mainstream lenders" to seek out creditworthy borrowers in lower-income and minority communities.[23]

The HUD-Treasury 2000 report similarly concludes that a lack of competition from prime lenders enabled subprime lenders to gain a growing share of mortgage lending activity in lower-income and minority communities. In addition, the report notes that upper-income African American borrowers were

20. See, for example, U.S. Department of Housing and Urban Development (2002a), which documents persistent discrimination in both the rental and sales markets of large metropolitan areas. The study notes, however, that the incidence of discriminatory practices did generally decline over the decade of the 1990s.

21. The phrase "risk or race" was coined by Bradford (2002).

22. U.S. Department of Housing and Urban Development and U.S. Department of Treasury (2000).

23. Immergluck and Wiles (1999).

twice as likely as lower-income white borrowers to hold subprime refinancing loans. When Calvin Bradford examines subprime lending patterns in 331 metropolitan areas (using HMDA data and data from the 2000 census), he finds that African Americans and Hispanics are disproportionately represented in the subprime refinancing market and that the disparity appears to grow as income increases. Moreover, he points out that racial disparities in lending exist in all regions and in cities of all sizes. Indeed, the study suggests that some of the biggest disparities exist in the nation's smallest metropolitan areas.[24]

None of the studies mentioned above had information on the credit characteristics of borrowers, and they were forced to acknowledge that some unknown part of the disparity in lending patterns undoubtedly resulted from differences in borrower- and property-related risk factors. To address that question, several studies have gone to considerable lengths to more fully evaluate the "risk or race" question. To estimate the probability that an individual borrower selected a conventional prime, subprime, or FHA insured mortgage, Anthony Pennington-Cross and his colleagues analyze a database of home purchase loans that combines HMDA data with data from FHA administrative files, a sample of real estate transactions, and borrower credit quality.[25] While the study confirms that borrower income, debt, and credit history and neighborhood factors significantly influenced the pattern of mortgage lending, race and ethnicity still appear to be key to explaining why African Americans, Native Americans, and Hispanics are less likely than whites to have access to lower-cost, prime home purchase loans.

Similarly, Paul Calem and colleagues examine spatial variation in subprime lending across census tracts in Chicago and Philadelphia. In addition to detailed borrower data, this study incorporates a variety of tract-level measures drawn from the 2000 census, such as income, education, and race-ethnicity. Of note is the use of tract-level risk measures, including the share of properties in foreclosure as well as the share of individuals within the tract with low (or no) credit ratings (the information was obtained from a major national credit bureau). While the authors concede that more could be done to control for individual borrower risk, they conclude that race, both at the neighborhood and borrower levels, remains a strong factor in explaining the distribution of subprime lending. In particular, they found that "even after inclusion of the full set of explanatory variables, in both cities there is a strong geographic concentration of subprime lending in neighborhoods where there is a large population of African American homeowners."[26] They conclude that African American borrowers,

24. Bradford (2002).

25. Pennington-Cross, Yezer, and Nichols (2000).

26. Paul Calem, Kevin Gillen, and Susan Wachter, "The Neighborhood Distribution of Subprime Mortgage Lending" (//realestate.wharton.upenn.educ/papers.php). Calem, Gillen, and Wachter (2002, p. 14).

regardless of where they live, have a higher likelihood of obtaining a subprime loan than a prime loan and that race of the borrower matters as well as race of the neighborhood.

Marsha Courchane and colleagues go a step further, combining detailed loan and borrower information, including credit scores, with survey research on borrower characteristics and attitudes to examine whether borrowers are "inappropriately" channeled into the subprime market. They confirm that whether borrowers obtain subprime or prime mortgages depends in large measure on risk-related mortgage underwriting variables. They also find that including measures of the borrowers' market knowledge, search behavior, and choices available contribute significantly to explaining borrowers' outcomes. This implies that credit risk alone may not fully explain why borrowers end up in the subprime market. Rather, the study supports the alternative view that the current mortgage delivery system is inefficient, since households with similar economic, demographic, and credit risk characteristics do not pay the same price for mortgage credit.[27]

In an effort to isolate the effects of race on access to mortgage lending in Los Angeles and Chicago, HUD conducted a pilot study that applied the paired-testing methodology widely used to test for discrimination in the home purchase and rental markets.[28] The pair, consisting of one white and one minority tester with similar income, credit quality, and other attributes commonly used in originating and risk weighting mortgages, visited randomly selected lenders. The study concludes that in both cities African American and Hispanic homebuyers face a significant risk of receiving less favorable treatment than whites when they visit mortgage lending institutions to inquire about financing options. The study notes that unfavorable treatment early in the home purchase process may cause some borrowers to limit their housing search to homes that cost less than they can actually afford, may prevent them from choosing the most favorable loan products, and may cause some to abandon the search entirely.

Research by the Joint Center for Housing Studies also addresses the "risk or race" question.[29] As part of this effort, the center created numerous measures of risk related to lending in various neighborhood settings, including a tract-level measure of household income growth and home price appreciation. In addition, the study included a measure of credit quality, defined as the share of home

27. Courchane, Surette and Zorn (2004),

28. U.S. Department of Housing and Urban Development (2002b).

29. Joint Center for Housing Studies (2004). Because it is difficult to assess spatial and racial patterns in mortgage lending with simple descriptive statistics, the Joint Center estimated a series of multivariate equations to predict the probability that households in 2001 obtained a prime conventional mortgage. Information on borrower characteristics and neighborhood characteristics are included as explanatory variables. In addition, the equations include lender variables, such as lender size and the number of lenders active in the neighborhood.

mortgage applications in each census tract that were denied over the 1995–99 period. As shown in table 5-3, a racial lending gap persists in a variety of neighborhood settings. Even in areas with income growth and home price appreciation in excess of 75 percent over the decade, the share of higher-income African Americans gaining access to conventional prime loans trailed that of white borrowers by 20 percentage points. And in areas with historically the lowest mortgage denial rates—and arguably containing households with the highest average credit quality—the share of higher-income African Americans obtaining prime mortgages still trails that of whites.

The econometric analysis confirms that many factors contribute to the disproportionately low share of conventional loans going to African American and Hispanic borrowers and to all borrowers living in African American and Hispanic neighborhoods. As in most previous studies on the topic, the analysis—even after controlling for neighborhood and borrower characteristics, including several measures of risk—confirms that race remains a factor.

The Adverse Consequences of the Dual Market Structure

The relatively low share of conventional prime loans made to lower-income and minority borrowers raises questions about whether all borrowers receive credit on the most favorable pricing and terms for which they qualify. Even small increases in the interest rate of a loan can affect a borrower's ability to make monthly payments and cover basic living expenses. In addition, default and foreclosure rates are higher on subprime, government-backed, and manufactured home loans than on prime conventional loans. And the incidence of abusive lending practices appears to be higher in the subprime industry. Clearly, there are many adverse consequences related to the inability to access prime conventional mortgages, both for borrowers and the neighborhoods in which they live.

Higher Costs

The harm done to a particular borrower who qualifies for—yet fails to secure—a prime loan depends on the loan type and credit characteristics of the individual borrower. The HUD-Treasury report estimates that more than half of all subprime loans originating between July and September 1999 had interest rates in excess of 10.5 percent, well above rates for prime loans over the same period, which ranged from 7 to 8 percent. Clearly, the cost of not obtaining a prime loan can be substantial. Indeed, data for 1999 suggest that 17 percent of subprime borrowers paid more than 4 percentage points above prime rates.[30]

In addition to higher interest rates, subprime loans typically include higher fees to compensate the lender for the higher default and prepayment risk

30. Mortgage Information Corporation (1999) (now Loan Performance).

involved. Through hearings in five cities, the HUD-Treasury report found many instances "of fees that far exceeded what would be expected or justified based on economic grounds, and fees that were 'packed' into the loan amount without the borrower's understanding" (p. 2). The report also notes the all-too-common practice of making loans without regard to the borrower's ability to repay. In these instances, high front-end fees—often rolled into the mortgage and paid out of equity claimed by the lender during the foreclosure process—are sufficient to compensate the lender even in situations where the probability is very high that the borrower will default on the loan.

Abusive Practices

While mortgage lending to credit-impaired borrowers has expanded their access to credit, it has also exposed them to numerous abuses, such as predatory lending. While mortgage lending is regulated by state and federal authorities, none of the existing statutes and regulations governing mortgage transactions clearly defines predatory lending. As commonly described in the literature, predatory lending may involve mortgage bankers and brokers, real estate agents, appraisers, home improvement contractors, or others involved directly or indirectly in mortgage lending. Predatory practices include outright deception and fraud, along with efforts to manipulate borrowers through aggressive sales tactics or to exploit their lack of understanding of loan terms. Even though predatory lending can and does occur in the prime market, competition among lenders, greater standardization and simplicity of mortgage products, and better access of borrowers to financial information ordinarily deter it. Unfortunately, competition in the subprime market may be rendered less effective by the disproportionate presence of mortgage brokers. In 2003 some 47.6 percent of all subprime originations flowed through a mortgage broker, compared with only 28.1 percent for prime mortgages.[31]

In an extensive review of the policy issues, Kathleen Engel and Patricia McCoy identify three distinct mortgage markets: the prime market, the "legitimate" subprime market, and the predatory market. They argue that predatory lenders tend to target borrowers who are disconnected from credit markets and therefore lack information about the best available products or who are subject to lingering mortgage market discrimination. Engel and McCoy document numerous predatory practices that serve to strip borrowers' home equity, burden borrowers with higher interest rates and fees, or disregard borrowers' ability to repay, thereby setting them up for foreclosure. In the most egregious examples, unscrupulous real estate agents, mortgage brokers, appraisers, and lenders dupe unsuspecting borrowers into purchasing a home at an inflated price or with significant undisclosed conditions requiring repair. These practices harm borrowers

31. Inside Mortgage Finance (2004).

and their communities, and they also impose costs on mortgage investors and insurers.[32]

Mortgage loans are priced in the secondary market on the basis of assumptions about the underlying market value of the asset. By reducing true equity in the home (the market value less the amount of the mortgage), an inflated appraisal makes it difficult for a borrower to sell the home and repay the mortgage in a time of distress. That in turn increases the likelihood that the mortgage will go into default and also increases the magnitude of losses incurred by the mortgage insurer and investors during the foreclosure process.

Foreclosures

Foreclosures are on the rise in many of the nation's most vulnerable neighborhoods, particularly those with substantial concentrations of minority households. The increase appears to stem from the growing presence of subprime lending in these communities and in particular from the extension of loans to borrowers with limited capacity to repay or at rates that are well above the market rate. Employing the best available data on loan performance, Amy Cutts and Robert Van Order estimate that as of June 2002 the serious delinquency rate for conventional prime loans was 0.55 percent.[33] In contrast, subprime loans had a serious delinquency rate of 10.44 percent, nearly twenty times higher. Further, the more risky subprime loans examined by Cutts and Van Order (labeled in the study as "C" or "CC" loans) had rates as high as 21 percent. Serious delinquency rates with these loans were more than twice those of FHA-insured mortgages (4.45 percent), the source of many foreclosure problems in prior years. Subprime loans are now the most default-prone mortgage segment of the home loan market.

A report on foreclosure activity by Mark Duda and William Apgar documents the negative impact that rising foreclosures have on low-income and low-wealth minority communities. Citing more than ten foreclosure studies in particular metropolitan areas, the report concludes that, although economic factors obviously play a role, the studies paint a remarkably consistent picture of rising foreclosures even in a period of strong economic growth, led in large measure by the relatively high incidence of foreclosure among subprime loans in lower-income and minority neighborhoods.[34]

The tendency for foreclosures to cluster in low-income, low-wealth, minority neighborhoods is a common finding of the existing literature. A HUD study of Baltimore notes that the number of foreclosures between 1995 and 1999 increased from 1,900 to more than 5,000 and that the increase was particularly

32. Engel and McCoy (2002).

33. Cutts and Van Order (2003). The term *serious delinquency* is applied to loans that are already in foreclosure or with payments that are ninety days or more late.

34. Duda and Apgar (2004b); Gruenstein and Herbert (2000a, 2000b).

pronounced in African American areas. More than one-quarter of the subprime loans in foreclosure in the first three months of 2000 were less than a year old, and more than half were less than two years old. The fact that so many loans were in foreclosure less than two years after origination suggests that many borrowers may not have had the capacity to repay the loan at the time that it was made. A study of foreclosures in the city and county of Los Angeles also finds them highly concentrated in the most distressed areas. For the three-year period from April 2001 to April 2004, some 45 percent of all Los Angeles area foreclosures were in census tracts with a population that was at least 80 percent minority, with a median income falling into the two lowest-income quintiles. Indeed, more than one-quarter of the foreclosures in the region were disproportionately clustered in just eighty-six census tracts whose minority population share was greater than 80 percent and whose median income was in the lowest-income quintile.[35]

High default and foreclosure rates have led many analysts to question whether the recent increase in low-income homeownership—built in part on the rapid growth of subprime lending—is sustainable or even desirable. Foreclosures can and do have a devastating impact on individual families, which lose their homes and are left with damaged credit records. This not only undermines their ability to secure a home loan in the future but also raises the cost of borrowing for other purposes, such as purchasing a car to get to work. In distressed neighborhoods, foreclosed properties can remain vacant for prolonged periods of time, depressing property values and becoming a magnet for crime. By discouraging families or new businesses from moving into a neighborhood, high foreclosure rates contribute to neighborhood instability and stigmatization.

Why the Dual Mortgage Market Persists

Thousands of mortgage banking operations compete to offer loan products to millions of potential borrowers. Indeed, by several measures the market is more competitive today than two decades ago. Though many smaller thrifts and savings institutions have shut down their mortgage lending operations, they have been replaced by well-capitalized financial services giants with access to low-cost mortgage funds through an increasingly sophisticated secondary mortgage market. Aided by the outreach efforts of thousands of mortgage brokers and correspondent lenders, these giants have reached every corner of the market, including lower-income and minority communities.

Yet despite substantial competition on the supply side of the marketplace, a dual market persists. In part this reflects the failure of the regulatory system to adapt to the sweeping changes that have transformed the mortgage banking

35. U.S. Department of Housing and Urban Development (2000); Duda and Apgar (2004a).

industry. But it also reflects the limited ability of consumers to shop for the best products available in the marketplace and thereby to protect themselves from predatory or overpriced mortgages. If borrowers are aware of prevailing mortgage rates and terms, competitive pressure will force individual brokers and correspondents to offer the best products available or lose business. But because mortgages are complex and consumers lack basic information about mortgage pricing and how to interpret what information is available, this competitive market check may be missing.

Moreover, structural factors that reinforce the tendency for the dual mortgage market to misprice mortgage capital arise from the growing importance of mortgage brokers and correspondent lenders in the market. The market incentives of brokers and loan correspondents are different from those of retail lending operations. Subject to whatever regulatory constraints operate effectively in the market, a broker has incentives to charge the highest combination of fees and mortgage interest rates the market will bear.

What is perhaps most striking is the way homeowners search (or in many instances do not search) for the best loan available. A study by Kellie Kim-Sung and Sharon Hermanson supports the idea that refinancing loans are frequently "sold, not sought," in that they result from extensive and often unsolicited outreach by brokers to homeowners who are not actively in the market for a loan.[36] The authors find that 56 percent of borrowers with broker-originated loans report that the broker initiated contact with them, while only 24 percent of borrowers with lender-originated loans report that the lender initiated contact. A higher share of broker-originated loans go to African American borrowers (64 percent) than to white borrowers (38 percent), and broker-originated loans are also more common among borrowers who are divorced or female. It is not surprising that a larger share of borrowers with broker-originated loans (70 percent, compared with 52 percent for lender-originated loans) "counted on lenders or brokers to find the best mortgage," since the borrowers did not initiate the search for the refinance loan. Unfortunately, their trust is often misplaced. Borrowers with broker-originated loans are more likely to pay points (25 percent, compared with 15 percent for lender-originated loans) and more likely to have a loan with a prepayment penalty (26 percent, compared with 12 percent for lender-originated loans).

These findings imply that some brokers actively work to identify borrowers who lack the experience to correctly evaluate mortgage terms and prices. Survey data suggest that for a variety of reasons—including historical mistrust of banks—lower-income and minority individuals are least likely to comparison shop for mortgage credit. Moreover, lacking basic information about mortgage terms and rates, they are more likely to succumb to "push marketing" tactics.

36. Kim-Sung and Hermanson (2003).

Whatever the case may be, it is disturbing that more than three decades after the enactment of fair lending legislation, fundamental disparities between minorities' and whites' access to mortgage capital remain.

Historically, fair housing and fair lending advocates have focused on pressuring lenders to expand access to mortgage credit, through tools such as Community Reinvestment Act reviews and fair lending audits and litigation. While there is some potential for a market-based correction, as long as brokers continue to have incentives to overcharge borrowers or present misleading information, the task of ensuring fair pricing in the marketplace falls to regulators and to consumers themselves. Unfortunately, the current regulatory setup is not well structured to address the problems associated with mispriced mortgage credit. Indeed, while there should be more aggressive enforcement of laws and regulations governing deceptive marketing practices or failure to accurately disclose loan terms to the borrower before closing, there is limited recourse for a borrower who simply overpays. Consumer protection regulations generally focus on ensuring that the loan information provided by the mortgage broker to the borrower is "fair and accurate," that the appraised value of the home is a fair representation of current market value, and that the terms and cost of the loan are provided in advance of closing for the borrower to review.

Although the Federal Trade Commission prohibits false advertising by brokers, following the doctrine of "Let the buyer beware," it does not require a broker to offer the best price available in the market. Yet clearly many borrowers are not up to the challenge of protecting their own interests. As previously discussed, many consumers do not adequately shop for mortgages, instead relying on brokers to provide them with information. Further, many consumers falsely believe that approval of their mortgage application is validation that they can handle the mortgage payment. Nothing could be further from the truth. At the time of closing, each of the parties to the loan transaction (except the borrower) is fully aware of the probability that the loan will move to default and foreclosure. Lacking this knowledge, many borrowers willingly enter into a transaction that may impose serious financial and emotional costs on themselves and their neighbors.

The mortgage market falls short of the competitive ideal, wherein buyers and sellers have ready access to information about product terms and pricing. Simple economics suggests that markets work best when consumers make informed choices. However, in the language of economics, there exists an "asymmetry of information" between buyers and sellers, particularly with respect to the price of mortgage credit. Mortgage industry professionals participate in numerous transactions over the course of weeks and months and have ready access to information on fees, rates, and terms comprised by the overall pricing of mortgage credit in the marketplace. In contrast, consumers only occasionally search for a loan to purchase or refinance a home and hence begin shopping with limited prior experience and equally limited access to the information needed to make an educated choice. Given the complexity and number of mortgage products, even the most sophisticated borrower may find it difficult to evaluate the details of a mortgage. Yet if borrowers have financial or legal advisers to guide them, they may have access to better mortgage information; at a minimum, higher-income and higher-wealth borrowers have more extensive financial resources to draw upon and hence have greater capacity to bear any excessive costs and avoid default.

Consumers could spend more time and money to better educate themselves about the price, terms, and features of alternative mortgage products, but from the perspective of the efficient use of societal resources, it makes little sense for individual consumers to devote considerable resources to ferret out information that could be readily provided by mortgage brokers and originators. Rather, it makes more sense to consider mortgage pricing information as a public good and to recognize that there is a role for government to provide the pricing information needed to support the efficient operation of the mortgage market.

While improved disclosure of the terms of a particular loan offered to a consumer would help, as would continued consumer education, these steps are not sufficient to achieve the desired results due to the complexity of the mortgage lending process. Federal regulators operating under applicable fair lending and fair trade authorities must expand their efforts to ensure that consumers obtain the pricing information needed to make informed choices. This could take the form of a national registry of best available mortgage products or other efforts to assist local government and community-based organizations to help families better understand the pricing and payment structure of mortgage products as they relate to borrower income, credit score, and ability to meet down payment and closing cost requirements.

Such readily available information—equivalent to the "blue books" or consumer reports that have successfully guided shoppers for automobiles and other consumer durables—would help consumers to find the best available deal and better protect them from the adverse consequences of aggressive and often deceptive marketing practices. Working to enable borrowers or their trusted advisers to be better shoppers and to resist "too good to be true" marketing promises would go a long way to reduce the incidence of predatory lending and also stem the increase in foreclosures that inevitably follows in the wake of such practices.

Conclusion

Since the 1980s the mortgage market in the United States has evolved into one of the most efficient and effective capital markets in the world. Through the securitization of mortgages and the emergence of new large-scale organizations that take full advantage of economies of scale in the origination, underwriting, and servicing of mortgages, the majority of borrowers have access to a plentiful supply of mortgage capital, at rates that rival those of the best and most financially secure corporate borrowers in the market.

Unfortunately, because of the dual mortgage market structure, not all borrowers, particularly not all lower-income and minority borrowers, have access to the best mortgages and best terms for which they qualify. In addition to better enforcement of existing consumer protection regulations, there needs to be a concerted effort to help lower-income and minority borrowers navigate the intricacies of the mortgage transaction. In particular, while general mortgage counseling may help, potential borrowers must have access to the type of loan-specific and trusted advice that currently is available to higher-income borrowers—advice that enables them to evaluate any current loan offer against the best terms available in the market.

Although it is more subtle than the neighborhood redlining of the past, the dual market structure of the current mortgage industry nevertheless still denies lower-income minorities equal access to prime mortgages. By pushing higher-cost and more default-prone subprime mortgages, the dual market steals scare resources from some of the nation's most vulnerable residents and works to further destabilize some of the nation's most distressed neighborhoods. Though tremendous progress has been made, ensuring equal access to mortgage credit must remain a prominent component of today's civil rights agenda.

References

Alexander, William P., and others. 2002. "Some Loans Are More Equal than Others: Third-Party Originations and Defaults in the Subprime Mortgage Industry." *Real Estate Economics* 30, no. 4: 667–97.

Bradford, Calvin. 2002. *Risk or Race? Racial Disparities and the Subprime Refinance Market.* Washington: Center for Community Change.

Calem, Paul, Kevin Gillen, and Susan Wachter. 2002. "The Neighborhood Distribution of Sub-prime Mortgage Lending." Working paper 404. Zell/Laurie Real Estate Center at Wharton, University of Pennsylvania.

Collins, Michael, Michael Carliner, and David Crowe. 2002. "Examining Supply-Side Constraints to Low-Income Homeownership." In *Low Income Homeownership: Examining the Unexamined Goal,* edited by Nicolas P. Retsinas and Eric Belsky, pp. 175–99. Brookings.

Courchane, Marsha J., Brian J. Surette, and Peter M. Zorn. 2004. "Subprime Borrowers: Mortgage Transitions and Outcomes." *Journal of Real Estate Finance and Economics* 29, no. 4: 365–92.

Cutts, Amy Crews, and Robert Van Order. 2003. *On the Economics of Subprime Lending.* Washington: Federal Home Loan Mortgage Corporation.

Duda, Mark, and William Apgar. 2004a. *Mortgage Foreclosure Trends in Los Angeles: Patterns and Policy Issues.* Los Angeles Neighborhood Housing Service. Washington: Neighborhood Reinvestment Corporation.

———. 2004b. *Preserving Homeownership: Community Development Implications of the New Mortgage Market.* Neighborhood Housing Services of Chicago. Washington: Neighborhood Reinvestment Corporation.

Engel, Kathleen C., and Patricia A. McCoy. 2002. "A Tale of Three Markets: The Law and Economics of Predatory Lending." *Texas Law Review* 80, no. 6: 1257–381.

Gruenstein, Debbie, and Chris Herbert. 2000a. *Analyzing Trends in Subprime Originations and Foreclosures: A Case Study of the Atlanta Metro Area.* Cambridge, Mass.: Abt Associates.

———. 2000b. *Analyzing Trends in Subprime Originations and Foreclosures: A Case Study of the Boston Metro Area.* Cambridge, Mass.: Abt Associates.

Immergluck, Daniel, and Marti Wiles. 1999. *Two Steps Back: The Dual Mortgage Market, Predatory Lending, and the Undoing of Community Development.* Chicago: Woodstock Institute.

Inside Mortgage Finance. 2003. *The 2003 Mortgage Market Statistical Annual.* Bethesda, Md.

———. 2004. *The 2004 Mortgage Market Statistical Annual.* Bethesda, Md.

Joint Center for Housing Studies. 2002. *The 25th Anniversary of the Community Reinvestment Act: Access to Capital in an Evolving Financial Services System.* Report prepared for the Ford Foundation. Harvard University.

———. 2004. *Credit, Capital and Communities: The Implications of the Changing Mortgage Banking Industry for Community Based Organization.* Report prepared for the Ford Foundation. Harvard University.

Kim-Sung, Kellie K., and Sharon Hermanson. 2003. "Experience of Older Refinance Mortgage Loan Borrowers: Broker- and Lender-Originated Loans." *AARP Public Policy Institute, Data Digest*, January.

LaCour-Little, Michael, and Gregory Chun. 1999. "Third-Party Originators and Mortgage Prepayment Risk: An Agency Problem?" *Journal of Real Estate Research* 17, no. 1–2: 55–70.

Mortgage Information Corporation. 1999. *Market Pulse.* Third quarter. San Francisco.

Pennington-Cross, Anthony, Anthony Yezer, and Joseph Nichols. 2000. *Credit Risk and Mortgage Lending: Who Uses Subprime and Why?* Washington: Research Institute for Housing America.

Renieri, Lewis S. 1996. "The Origins of Securitization, Sources of Its Growth, and Its Future Potential." In *A Primer on Securitization,* edited by Leon T. Kendall and Michael J. Fishman, pp. 79–91. MIT Press.

Scheessele, Randall M. 2002. *1998 HMDA Highlights.* Housing Finance Working Paper 9. Office of Policy Development and Research, U.S. Department of Housing and Urban Development.

U.S. Department of Housing and Urban Development. 1997. *Survey of Mortgage Lending Activity.*

———. 2000. *Unequal Burden in Baltimore: Income and Racial Disparities in Subprime Lending.*

———. 2002a. *Discrimination in Urban Housing Markets: National Results from Phase I HDS 2000.*

———. 2002b. *All Other Things Being Equal: A Paired Testing Study of Mortgage Lending Institutions.*

U.S. Department of Housing and Urban Development and U.S. Department of Treasury. 2000. *Curbing Predatory Home Lending: A Joint Report.*

Vermeer, Kimberly, and Josephine Louie. 1996. "The Future of Manufactured Housing." Joint Center for Housing Studies, Harvard University.

Yinger, John. 1998. "Evidence on Discrimination in Consumer Markets." *Journal of Economic Perspectives* 12: 23–40.

PART II

Housing Opportunity for Low-Income Families

6

Expanding Housing Choice and Integrating Neighborhoods: The MTO Experiment

JOHN GOERING

Ghettos often are not popular—with either those living in them or those looking in from outside—and neither, typically, are the boldest measures for transforming ghettos. It is anything but news to say that few people in America seem to want or welcome the poor in their neighborhoods, particularly if the poor also belong to a racial or ethnic minority. The integration of social classes, mixing the poor with the more affluent (and often the minority poor with more affluent whites), has been politically suspect, if not lethal, for decades. As a result, taking the path of least resistance, the U.S. Department of Housing and Urban Development (HUD) has undertaken little or no proactive racial or class integration programs since the inception of federal housing policies roughly seventy years ago. Indeed, some find that intensifying urban economic inequality, together with entrenched patterns of economic and racial isolation in many metropolitan areas, has created even more trenchant structural obstacles to providing credibly "integrated housing."[1]

Despite such pessimism, recent analyses of 2000 census data suggest that patterns of racial and economic isolation that have appeared intractable for decades have undergone change. The 1990s brought reductions in both the

1. See Abrams (1955); Lemann (1991); Bonastia (2000); Gramlich, Laren, and Sealand (1992); Massey, Gross, and Shibuya (1994); Glaeser, Kahn, and Rappaport (2000); Farley, Danziger, and Holzer (2000); Dreier, Mollenkopf, and Swanstrom (2001); Aspen Institute (2002).

racial isolation of blacks and the concentration of poor households in inner cities.[2] It is, of course, difficult to pinpoint the reasons for this shift toward greater desegregation and deconcentration. It is most likely the result of a mix of housing market, demographic, and sociological transformations that have enabled more families to live less isolated lives. It is also probable that the modest number of legal and policy initiatives has helped to marginally increase racial and class integration in American cities.[3] The Section 8 (rental housing subsidy) program, initiated during the Nixon administration, might well have been partially instrumental.

The purpose of this chapter is to review and assess what is known about the root sources and early effects of the largest, most research-oriented federal effort to promote economic deconcentration in a select number of American cities: the Moving to Opportunity for Fair Housing Demonstration (MTO), authorized by Congress in 1993. The demonstration has, to date, allocated roughly $80 million in federal and philanthropic funds to help answer three questions:

—Can federal housing programs effectively promote the dispersal or deconcentration of low-income families, many of them racial minorities, across the neighborhoods of America's metropolitan areas?

—What short- and longer-term effects—positive or negative—might this demonstration have on the lives of those who volunteer to participate?

—Can we judge at this point whether it is possible for MTO, a small demonstration project in five metropolitan areas, to become a permanent national program? That is, is it possible to mount a federal effort that promotes the dispersal of much larger numbers of families?

Let me immediately address the latter question, since uncertainty on this point might discourage some readers from continuing. No, it is not in my judgment feasible to have the federal government immediately launch a major effort to disperse poor public housing families. However, I do argue that the possibility is closer to becoming politically and programmatically feasible than at any point over the past several decades. Moreover, giving residents the option of moving away from public housing ghettos is an essential requirement for constructing a long-term, equitable, and effective national housing policy.

To explicate this "on the one hand but not the other" answer, I begin with an overview of the intellectual sources of the MTO demonstration. Following this, I examine the community opposition to the program that briefly arose in Baltimore in 1994. A direct effect of that opposition was to cut the MTO demonstration in half, truncating it to a single year's congressional funding as opposed to two years. Understanding such NIMBY (not-in-my-backyard) reactions helps us appreciate what can go wrong when the federal government attempts to do

2. Iceland, Weinberg, and Steinmetz (2002); Jargowsky (2003).
3. Nyden and others (1998); Ellen (2000).

too many complex social and political tasks concurrently and without adequate public involvement.

While a full social science assessment of the behavioral effects of MTO is beyond the scope of this chapter, I also provide highlights of its impacts because they form the basis of the countervailing argument—that some readily achievable benefits can emerge from allowing families to move out of ghettos. This empirical conclusion converts into the argument that such options are feasible and, for some public housing families, a necessary component of equitable housing policies.[4] I conclude with a discussion of MTO's prospects as a full-scale program.

The Policy Foundations of MTO

The MTO demonstration program has three broad policy and political foundations, each of which has been influential in shaping the parameters of the demonstration. Each in turn also reflects the historical dynamics of regional economic and racial prerogatives, including the systemic rejection of poor and minority families.[5] The first foundation is the uneven history of efforts by the federal government to reduce the concentration of poor families in the inner cities, including inner-city public housing. The racial desegregation of public housing is a separate but overlapping foundation, while the modest social experiments to test the edges of innovation in housing policy constitutes the third foundation.

Reducing the Concentration of Poor Families in Inner Cities

Central to the issue of the isolation of housing for the poor is the fact that although public housing for families began as a temporary, if racially segregated, safe haven for the working poor, it relatively quickly became a long-term home for poor, mainly minority households.[6] Tenants of public housing interviewed more than forty years ago recognized that public housing projects lacked stable families and were places where "all manner of antisocial behavior runs rampant, a bad environment for bringing up children, a receptacle for the very lowest elements of society."[7] By the late 1960s, most public housing developments for families in the larger cities had become racially and economically segregated. Congress soon halted virtually all funding for similar projects.[8]

For nearly forty years, studies and commissions have warned about such concentrations of poverty and have looked for tools to undo them. A 1966 White

4. Goering and Feins (2003).

5. Jackson (2000).

6. Hirsch (1983); Massey and Denton (1993); Hays (1995); Goering, Kamely, and Richardson (1997).

7. Hartman (1963, p. 286).

8. Bickford and Massey (1991, pp. 1011–36); Newman and Schnare (1997).

House conference warned of the perils of overconcentrations of the poor: "The slums and ghettos have grown larger, overcrowding has intensified, and the alienation of the ghetto dweller has become a national crisis. Too, often public housing and urban renewal have aggravated rather than ameliorated the degree of segregation and congestion."[9] Another presidential task force, the Kerner Commission, issued in 1968 a now epic caution about racial and spatial isolation.[10] The report supported policies that would simultaneously fund both "ghetto enrichment" and "policies that will encourage Negro movement out of central city areas." The report recognized that it was essential for U.S. policymakers to work to enrich but not "embalm" the ghetto while offering those who wished it the choice to leave.[11] "The idea," Thomas Pettigrew pointed out more than three decades ago, "is simply to provide an honest choice between separation and integration." In his view, the long-term goal is "the transformation of these ghettos from racial prisons to ethnic areas freely chosen or not chosen."[12] The policy dyad—promoting inner-city development coupled with dispersal programs—appears beguilingly simple. It has, however, proven to be treacherously difficult and costly to implement.

In the 1970s, for example, George Romney, then the secretary of HUD, began a fledgling effort to generate a small number of integrated, scattered-site housing projects at the same time that HUD continued building traditional public housing developments for families and the elderly. Opposition to his integration efforts quickly emerged from both affected local communities and the White House, ending HUD's first effort to use its resources and rules proactively to promote housing integration. At the same time federal courts attempted to order HUD to establish requirements aimed at deconcentrating new developments, most notably through the Shannon decision.[13]

During the Carter administration, a number of task forces were established within HUD to learn how to create more housing opportunities. One, on assisted housing mobility, recommended the goal of promoting mobility and deconcentration. The administration's efforts were aimed at promoting regionwide mobility away from inner cities by making use of the new Section 8 tenant-based housing program.[14] Robert Embry, a HUD assistant secretary in charge of community development at the time, led this new regional housing mobility program, which was soon initiated in a small number of communities. However, it quickly encountered an unanticipated obstacle—resistance from members of

9. Quoted in Pettigrew (1971, p. 21).

10. U.S. National Advisory Commission (1968, p. 22).

11. Moynihan (1971).

12. Pettigrew (1971, p. 323).

13. 436 F.2d 809 (3d Cir 1970). For more on the Shannon decision, see Tegeler, chapter 9, this volume. For more on HUD's early efforts, see Lemann (1991); Bonastia (2000).

14. See Vernarelli (1986). The section 8 program, which initially included certificates and vouchers, has been renamed the housing choice voucher program.

the minority community. This effort to promote alternatives to racial and economic concentration foundered because advocates for the minority poor believed that the government intended to forcibly displace the poor so that inner cities could be more efficiently rebuilt and gentrified to house the white middle class.[15] The absence of any major funding efforts to rebuild housing within the central city to offset the "losses" from the mobility program was a fatal policy flaw. Relations between HUD and minority community advocates became so conflict ridden that Embry says he had received death threats.[16] Funding for the program was stopped but continued to operate using extant funding. When the Reagan administration arrived in 1981, however, it promptly terminated the program as inappropriate "social engineering."[17]

This deconcentration initiative left no research or public data imprint that could serve as a vehicle for understanding whom it served, how well it worked, its costs, and whether participating families experienced any significant benefits. For nearly the next twenty years, neither policymakers at HUD nor those in Congress promoted research or demonstrations on either racial or economic deconcentration. This inaction, coupled with a shift in the demand for public housing, produced dramatic changes in the occupancy of public housing projects. By the late 1990s, they were solidly minority: 47 percent black and 19 percent Hispanic. Looking only at public housing located in "ghetto poor" communities (conventionally defined as those in which 40 percent or more residents have income below the federal poverty line), nearly 90 percent of resident families were black or Hispanic, and on average more than half of their neighbors (55 percent) were poor.[18] The public housing population was among the poorest in the country, with only one-fifth earning any income from wages. While the average median American household in the late 1990s was earning nearly $50,000, public housing families living in high-poverty areas (as of 1998) averaged only $9,000 a year. Increasingly, applicants on the waiting lists for public housing were heavily minority.

The well-documented migration of middle-income whites and blacks to the suburbs of most metropolitan centers only aggravated segregation by race and class in metropolitan areas. Such separation is a major driver of both dispersal efforts and NIMBY resistance to them. Segregation has also appeared in the more middle-income, suburban minority communities that emerged during the 1990s.[19]

Beginning in the early 1990s, the twin goals of revitalizing the inner cities and offering residents the option of moving out of public housing became

15. Calmore (1979); De Bernardo (1979).
16. Personal communication, August 23, 2000.
17. Goering (1986).
18. Lief and Goering (1987); Hirsch (1983).
19. Dreier, Mollenkopf, and Swanstrom (2001); Patillo-McCoy (1999).

viable, if modest and experimental, parts of federal housing policy for the first time.[20] Congress created programs aimed at doing two things concurrently: rebuilding poor, inner-city public housing neighborhoods and implementing a small number of initiatives to promote residential mobility out of "the projects."

In 1993 Congress created both the MTO demonstration and the Hope VI program, the latter to demolish the most troubled public housing projects and replace them with rebuilt mixed-income communities. The Hope VI program targeted roughly 100,000 of the worst public housing units for demolition. Severely blighted public housing developments were to be replaced with more mixed-income communities to which a modest number of former tenants would be eligible to return. However, those rebuilding efforts encountered problems in regenerating communities. Some are still plagued by crime, gangs, drugs, and tenants who resist efforts to relocate them from their former homes.[21] Whether the outcomes of Hope VI will result in a net advantage or disadvantage for the minority poor is yet to be determined, although the Bush administration had as of 2004 recommended termination of the program.[22]

What occurred by the mid-1990s, however, was that inner-city residents of a small number of the worst public housing projects in the nation had the choice of either moving out, through a one-year demonstration project, or remaining in the hope of getting a newly modernized apartment in a mixed-income development. In both cases, HUD was promoting income mixing on a scale not seen and not possible for decades before. However, neither HUD nor local housing authorities anticipated the potential for negative interaction between the two program options.

Addressing the Racial Segregation of Public Housing

The increasing racial isolation of black and Hispanic families in public housing that began in the 1940s made both HUD and local public housing agencies vulnerable to claims of illegal segregation.[23] Following the enactment of fair housing laws in the 1960s, a number of plaintiffs sued local and federal housing agencies for illegally segregating residents and blocking options for more integrated living. The second of MTO's three policy foundations emerged through the efforts of plaintiffs and the federal courts, which almost uniformly agreed that HUD and local public housing agencies illegally and often unconstitutionally denied minority poor families the choice to live in less segregated communities. They also typically ordered the authorities to repair the damage by reducing

20. Schill (1992); Williams and Sander (1993); Polikoff (1995); Henry Cisneros, "Regionalism: The New Geography of Opportunity" (www.huduser.org, March 1995).

21. Popkin and others (2000b, pp. 181–90).

22. Goetz (2000); Dimond (2000, p. 260); Venkatesh (2002); Popkin and Cunningham, chapter 8, this volume.

23. Edsall and Edsall (1992); Hays (1995, pp. 233–62); Vernarelli (1986).

racial segregation of public housing residents. Nevertheless, such lawsuits often could do little to achieve the goal of reducing racial segregation within the old stock of public housing units.[24] Bureaucratic resistance within HUD and the local public housing agencies added to the obstacles to deconcentrate minorities, even when the agencies were ordered to by federal courts.

Some desegregation cases have, however, had success in promoting housing mobility.[25] Remedial court orders often offered project tenants the chance to move out of their segregated communities through court-established programs. Beginning with the initiation of the Section 8 program in 1974, plaintiffs typically included tenant-based housing as a critical component of desegregation remedies. It was well-timed research on the effects of one of these court-ordered remedies—the Gautreaux case in Chicago—that contributed fundamentally to the political and policy foundations for MTO.

Among the major housing segregation lawsuits was one brought in Chicago that, after years of litigation, required HUD and the Chicago Housing Authority to remedy the segregation that they had imposed on project residents by providing a housing mobility option throughout the Chicago region for about 7,100 black families.[26] Starting in the late 1970s, HUD made annual allocations of Section 8 tenant-based assistance to the Gautreaux program. Black applicants for, or residents of, segregated projects were offered the opportunity to move into racially mixed areas through the use of Section 8 assistance. Roughly three-quarters of all the families were required to move to predominantly white, usually suburban areas, while about one-quarter were allowed to move to city neighborhoods with 30 percent or more black residents.[27]

The components of Gautreaux relief were, however, a necessary but not a sufficient basis for building MTO. Social science research on the impact of this program on families' lives provided critically useful evidence that the families that moved experienced positive social and educational effects. Research by James Rosenbaum and colleagues offered evidence that there were improvements in the educational performance of children exposed to better performing, less-segregated neighborhoods over a period of seven to ten years after families moved into racially integrated communities. The children were less likely to drop out of school and more likely to take college-track classes than their peers in the comparison group, who had moved to poorer, relatively segregated parts of Chicago.[28]

24. Briggs, Darden, and Aidala (1999); Vale (2000); Goering (1986); Popkin and others (2000b); Popkin and others (2003, p. 194); Polikoff (no date).

25. Polikoff (1995).

26. Davis (1993); Rubinowitz and Rosenbaum (2000).

27. Rubinowitz and Rosenbaum (2000); Rosenbaum, DeLuca, and Tuck, chapter 7, this volume.

28. Rosenbaum (1992); Rubinowitz and Rosenbaum (2000); Popkin and others (2000a)

The policy message from the Gautreaux research seems clear: Changes not observed in any other domestic urban policy initiative had occurred in the lives of poor children apparently because they had moved to less economically and racially isolated neighborhoods. The contrasts between the achievements of families that moved to largely white, suburban communities and those who stayed in inner-city, largely black neighborhoods were impressive—to the press, to policymakers, and quite soon after to Congress.

In designing MTO, the judicially required race-conscious objectives of Gautreaux were replaced with poverty criteria, so that MTO would be enacted as an economic desegregation initiative, in no small part because "race-conscious policies and racial integration aims have lost considerable support in recent decades."[29] Congress quickly funded MTO, and the new HUD secretary, Henry Cisneros, moved aggressively to implement the demonstration project in five selected cities.

Undertaking Social Experimentation

The third policy foundation of MTO is the use of randomized social experiments to evaluate the effects of housing policy.[30] In the history of federal housing policy, there have been relatively few major demonstrations designed to study the impacts of federally subsidized rental assistance on the deconcentration of families in public housing. In the early 1970s, the Experimental Housing Allowance program helped establish the programmatic and research basis for the Section 8 tenant assistance or certificate program.[31] Two decades would pass before Congress agreed to initiate a second major Section 8 experiment, MTO, which aimed at devising a method for managing and then examining the behavioral impacts of the dispersal of public housing families in multiple metropolitan housing markets.

To ensure the utility of its research and policy conclusions, MTO was designed as a social experiment. The design was required to counteract the vitiating effects of personal selection, or selection bias, in the design of most prior research, including Gautreaux. If policymakers cannot distinguish the effects of a demonstration from those of the personal motivations and enthusiasms of its participants, they cannot be certain that the program, by itself, is effective. MTO's random assignment procedure cured the problem of selection bias and established it as a prime source for experimental evidence on the effects of neighborhood context on the choices, attitudes, and behavior of low-income families that move from projects.[32] At the heart of MTO is the requirement to move from a community with high poverty to one with far less—from an area

29. Briggs (2003, p. 201); but see Roisman (2001).
30. Galster (1996); Shroder (2000).
31. Winnick (1995); Hays (1995); Galster (1996).
32. Mayer and Jencks (1989); Jencks and Mayer (1990).

where 40 percent or more of residents are poor to one where 90 percent or more are *not* poor.

Community Opposition to MTO

MTO's design resulted from a combination of legislative decisions as well as a number of critical design choices recommended by policy experts and researchers. MTO was initially planned as a two-year effort to assist up to 5,000 families, but it soon became a one-year demonstration that assisted at total of roughly 285 families in each of five cities. Before enrollment of families into MTO could begin in the Baltimore area, however, the project encountered community opposition that led to termination of its second and final year of funding.

Trouble in Essex

The first signs of political trouble for MTO came in the early spring of 1994, when residents who lived in the eastern section of Baltimore County expressed concern that the MTO demonstration there appeared to be a "secret." No one in the county, they said, had been informed about the demonstration, and they were worried that Baltimore County had been targeted as a new home for people from the city's worst public housing projects. The announcement of the planned demolition of Baltimore public housing projects under the Hope VI program appeared to suburban residents as a harbinger of thousands, rather than a mere hundred, of MTO moves.

Such concerns and fears were shaped by the political, social, and geographic gulf that separated the city from the county of Baltimore. The city is surrounded on three sides by the county, and over the previous three decades many city residents had fled to the county when, in their minds, the racial and economic makeup of the city changed for the worse. The city of Baltimore was, indeed, one of the poorest MTO sites.[33] "Wholesale, low-income blacks were moved into public housing units, straining the system with extreme social problems. . . . Failing buildings and inadequate city services went hand in hand with ineffective schools, alcoholism, traffic in drugs, unwanted pregnancies, and a high rate of juvenile delinquency."[34] By the late 1970s, Baltimore had become two cities: a black inner city and a white outer city and suburban area. By the late 1990s, as Baltimore city shrank in size and became more heavily black, the suburban county grew into a generally more prosperous, white community.

By the mid-1980s, parts of Baltimore County—most notably the towns of Essex and Dundalk—began to experience many of the troubles previously thought to occur only in cities. Topping the list was the decline in the number

33. McDougall (1993); Hirsch (2000, pp. 410–13).
34. McDougall (1993, p. 56).

of industrial jobs, a concomitant increase in unemployment, and a growing sense of vulnerability to racial change.[35]

Organizing Community Opposition

After the official HUD announcement of an agreement with the housing authority of the city of Baltimore to administer the MTO demonstration, a new community group was formed, the Eastern Political Association, which actively opposed MTO. Members of the association believed that virtually all of the city's public housing was going to be demolished under the Hope VI program and the residents of the projects moved to their area through the MTO program. "Many residents see MTO as the first step in a government plan to tear down the city's housing projects and move the residents to eastern Baltimore County."[36]

HUD and Baltimore city housing officials attempted to address the rumors and ill feeling by participating in a large community meeting in Baltimore County. Nothing, however, that HUD officials could say helped stem residents' anger and fears. Because fall 1994 was an election year, there were numerous additional public forums in which to capitalize on community opposition to MTO and HUD. Almost all those campaigning at the federal, state, or local level in the Baltimore County area expressed negative opinions about MTO.[37] U.S. senator Barbara Mikulski, of Maryland, quickly learned from the angry citizens of Baltimore County and from their local U.S. representative about their opposition to MTO, which included the argument that their suburbs were already struggling from the loss of local employment and that there simply were no jobs or real opportunities there for MTO families. As a result of this turmoil, HUD was told to "kill MTO."[38] Senator Mikulski commented at the time that "the program has been bungled by the city administration and by the group that was supposed to administer it. . . . There has not been enough consultation with the community out there. That has exacerbated discontent to the point that it would be only a hollow opportunity for the poor people in the program."[39]

The opposition in Baltimore County was a setback for the administration's efforts to promote more regional mobility within the Section 8 program. HUD had garnered no reserves of political good will, nor did it have a track record that could dispel fears that it would mishandle any further housing integration

35. Newman (1995, pp. 83–84); Lucas (1997).

36. Larry Carson and Pat Gilbert, "Plan to Relocate Families from Inner City Fuels Fears," *Baltimore Sun,* July 31, 1994, p. B1.

37. Michael Olesker, "Playing on Fears: DePazzo Exploits Stereotype of Poor," *Baltimore Sun,* September 6, 1994, p. B1.

38. Ann Mariano, "Hill Panel Halts Plan to Move Poor Families," *Washington Post,* September 3, 1994, p. E1.

39. Ed Brandt, "Relocation Program Won't Grow: New Money Halted in Housing Plan for Inner City Families," *Baltimore Sun,* September 10, 1994, p. B1.

schemes. As a result, in spring 1995 the *New York Times* could publish MTO's ostensible obituary under the headline "Housing Voucher Test in Maryland Is Scuttled by a Political Firestorm."[40] HUD allowed MTO to appear to die while leaving in place the first full year of funding for the demonstration. MTO demonstration and research activities continued despite the reduced size of the program. None of the other MTO sites experienced any comparable community or political opposition, in part because of their differing ecological, community, and political dynamics.[41] MTO at the end of the enrollment period included its full complement of roughly 1,600 families.

Analyzing Community Opposition

Any assessment of the role for MTO in future housing policy and program options requires some assessment of the sources of responsibility or "blame" for the outburst of community opposition to MTO. Planners and policymakers could probably have been less naïve about the likely intensity and potential impact of suburban opposition to the program in Baltimore and more proactive in dealing with it. For at least four decades social scientists have cautioned that any threat to a person's social status, coupled with the feeling of being trapped, "tends to produce panic."[42] Possibly more coalition building to enlist community support for the effort might also have helped. It is also possible that that opposition might have been mollified if federal and local officials had more carefully explained the purposes and limits of both MTO and Hope VI earlier on in the implementation process.

But given the long history of opposition to most of HUD's prior attempts at deconcentration, officials may well have wasted their time.[43] While each of the jurisdictions surrounding the city of Baltimore could have been more fully briefed by HUD and city public housing officials about the distinctions between MTO and Hope VI, the handful of families involved in MTO at the time (roughly 140) suggested that such a tiny project needed less rather than more bureaucratic and political involvement. It is also easy to speculate that had local officials and candidates for office not used anti-MTO rhetoric for their own purposes they might have helped build and sustain some support for

40. Karen De Witt, "Housing Voucher Test in Maryland Is Scuttled by a Political Firestorm," *New York Times,* March 28, 1995, p. B10.

41. Charles, chapter 3, this volume, states that participants moving from ghetto neighborhoods into predominantly white, economically stable areas suffered discomfort and discrimination in their new neighborhoods. Although Rubinowitz and Rosenbaum (2000) report that some unmeasured level of this occurred with Gautreaux, it did not occur to any substantial reported degree with MTO in part because many families moved into low-poverty communities with substantial minority populations (Goering and Feins 2003).

42. Williams (1964, p. 387).

43. Galster and others (2003); James Hogan, "Scattered Site Housing: Characteristics and Consequences" (www.huduser.org/publications/pubasst/scatter.html).

MTO. Expediency and local politics are, however, so inextricably and even necessarily interwoven that candidates for office might be excused for seeing the panic as an inescapable factor in their own political future. Their actions were as much a result as a cause of their community's biases and fears.

Local residents and their community spokespersons each espoused negative class and racial stereotypes that formed the heart of their opposition to MTO. As in many communities, there were no articulated reserves of community tolerance or social capital to offset such politically manipulated fears (see Camille Charles, chapter 3, this volume). HUD had no other demonstrated successes with housing integration to support its argument that substantially more good than harm would be done.[44] There is also some evidence from the Baltimore area that whites' fears about the negative effects of subsidized housing were not unfounded.[45] For at least the Baltimore suburbs, not all protest was unfounded racial hysteria.

However, both social scientists and politicians have for decades found ample reasons to explain—or explain away—such examples of ecologically rooted white privilege. It is easy to find a rationale in which no individual actor or agency is responsible for the maldistribution of opportunities, resources, and choices by class and race. While pointing the finger of blame in any single direction may be inappropriate, pointing to multiple sources is an exercise in political, if not social science, futility.

Growing a Bigger MTO

MTO's operations demonstrate that it is possible for HUD and local public housing authorities to successfully operate an economic and racial desegregation program using Section 8 rental assistance in metropolitan housing markets. Preliminary research on MTO's effects on families also demonstrates that statistically significant beneficial changes have occurred in families' lives within five years of their participation in MTO. Neighborhood context and content mattered, and significant neighborhood effects occurred most notably in the lives of children. Initial research has found improvements in mental and physical health and positive labor effects in two localities.[46]

44. Sleeper (2003, pp. 96–97). Also see Charles, chapter 3, this volume. Kenneth Jackson reminds us that it was government housing programs, especially FHA and VA, that created for many (mostly white) families the previously unavailable opportunity to purchase a new home in a new suburb. FHA, he points out, "helped turn the building industry against the minority and inner-city housing market, and its policies supported the income and racial segregation of the suburbs" (Jackson 1985, p. 205). Many residents of the eastern Baltimore County suburbs were beneficiaries of such policies, whose effects have lingered long after official de jure segregation was abolished from federal programs.

45. Research by Galster, Tatian, and Smith (1999) finds that concentrations of section 8 housing that exceed a certain threshold can adversely affect neighborhood property values. See also Galster, Quercia, and Cortes (2000); Guhathakurta and Mushkatel (2002); Briggs (2003).

46. Goering and Feins (2003).

A wide range of often quite major behavioral changes in family members appear, at this middle stage, to be attributable to the MTO demonstration. What sensible policy observations can be reached about MTO given the impressive, if provisional, nature of such evidence? Is there enough evidence to warrant proposing a broader, more permanent program modeled after MTO for use by local housing agencies? The Bipartisan Millennial Housing Commission, for example, argued that MTO research "demonstrates that relocating families to better neighborhoods can improve educational, mental health, and behavioral outcomes."[47]

While some may find the results unpersuasive or feel that not enough is known about how MTO could best be made a national policy option while avoiding community backlash, an equally plausible response to the positive results would be to adapt the MTO model to create a national program allowing local public housing agencies to link intensive housing counseling to a geographically limited voucher. While the complexity of such choices must be acknowledged,[48] if the news of positive effects on children suggests that MTO should become a national policy option, what might bringing MTO to scale be like?

When asked what it might be like to "bring MTO to scale," Phillip Thompson argues that it could not become a general, large-scale program, at least not in the New York area. "Given the fierce resistance to even modest public housing development in nearby Yonkers," he argues, "the notion that significant portions of the NYCHA [the New York City Housing Authority] population could be integrated into Long Island and Westchester is fanciful. Political problems aside, HUD's entire $70 million national MTO budget would have only a minor impact on deconcentrating public housing in New York City."[49]

What Thompson misunderstands in estimating "scale" is that any future MTO extension would involve only a modest number of families annually. Going to scale would mean providing all families that have children and live in high-poverty public or assisted project-based housing the option of receiving a voucher—and counseling—to help them move to a low-poverty neighborhood. Following MTO's legislative design, it would not require families to move, since MTO envisions assisting only families that wish to move. There are approximately 200,000 families with children living in high-poverty project-based housing nationwide that could be given the option to move.[50] MTO's experi-

47. Bipartisan Millennial Housing Commission (2002, p. 11).

48. Briggs (2003).

49. Thompson (1999, p. 126). Full-scale would not imply a Fiss-like (Fiss 2000) program aimed at offering all residents of high-poverty communities the option to move out. I concur with Hochschild's (2003, p. 69) reaction to the Fiss proposal that "what ghetto residents really deserve is the right either to move or to stay in a community worth staying in."

50. This is based on an analysis of 1998 "Picture of Subsidized Housing" data, which show that approximately 520,000 units of public housing and section 8 project-based assisted units are located in census tracts greater than 40 percent poverty (//webstore.huduser.org). Of those, approximately 40 percent of the units are occupied by households with one or more children under the age of eighteen.

ence suggests that approximately 25 percent of those families would likely volunteer or take advantage of the opportunity to move. Of that number, if lease-up rates (number of leases that have been signed) remained comparable, roughly half (or 48 percent) would in fact move. Going to scale, therefore, could theoretically involve 24,000 families nationwide that actually move from public housing in high-poverty neighborhoods to privately owned rental housing in low-poverty neighborhoods.

Moreover, there would likely be a staggered allocation of vouchers just as occurred in the Gautreaux program. To allocate the total number over ten years, 2,400 families a year would be apportioned among the relevant jurisdictions. Assuming that roughly sixty of these jurisdictions of a total of more than 3,000 would be targeted, that would result in an annual allocation of roughly forty vouchers for each jurisdiction over a ten-year period. Shortening or lengthening the period or increasing the number of jurisdictions involved could reduce the burden on any individual site. At such a modest size, an MTO extension would likely have only a limited deconcentration effect in any one city but would not be likely to lead to a massive concentration of poor families in any one neighborhood or city, if the program is administered with care.

Nonetheless, political opposition has been a frequent obstacle to HUD efforts to promote either economic or racial mobility, and it would likely reappear at the time of legislative consideration of an MTO extension. As Hugh Heclo reminds us, "Dealing in any realistic way with this socioeconomic catastrophe [poverty] is going to be costly and will demand a long-term commitment to people whom many Americans would not want as neighbors. This is the dirty little secret buried in the shelves of social science poverty studies."[51]

If legislators do consider adopting another larger-scale program modeled after MTO, some preliminary policy suggestions would apply. How might a successor to MTO be extended to other cities or expanded to a somewhat larger scale?

—Implement the program more carefully and involve the public. Among the lessons from the 1994 opposition to MTO is that by giving better notice to the affected communities and by moving at a slower pace, opposition might well have been lessened if not altogether mollified. The explicit and up-front exclusion of areas that did not have 10 percent or less poverty should have been announced and publicized more clearly, since a nontrivial number of protestors came from areas that were not eligible sites for relocation of MTO families.

—Fully explain the design and implementation of the program. HUD, local public housing agencies, and nonprofits could do a better job of explaining potential links between any MTO-like housing mobility program and any large-scale public housing demolition program (such as HOPE VI) if both programs are statutorily reconsidered. Regionwide consultations are necessary rather than

51. Heclo (1994, p. 422).

optional. But should tenant relocation programs tied to Hope VI be massive or badly administered, that appears likely to mean that MTO-like options cannot be implemented concurrently.

—Recognize that restricted voucher programs will work only for some families. Among the issues affecting any future expansion of MTO is evidence that the MTO option is not suited for everyone. It will attract families with specific characteristics and levels of motivation, and it is that motivation that appears important to effective leasing-up of units in lower-poverty areas. Agencies could also do a better job of explaining the mobility option's demonstrated benefits and motivating families to make use of it.[52]

—Evaluate community resistance to HUD's program initiatives to better understand its sources, timing, and virulence. Such research might enable policymakers to better measure, anticipate, and manage such concerns. It appears likely that community resistance varies enough across communities to indicate that no cookie-cutter solutions should be attempted.[53]

—Counseling helps. Housing counseling appears to have measurable benefits in promoting lease-ups in low-poverty areas.[54] There are also some limits to what it can accomplish in influencing participants' housing search patterns and locality choices. Overcoming ingrained patterns of evaluating housing and neighborhood choices—within racially fragmented markets—entails some measure of risk for families and requires considerable skill for housing counselors. Counseling should include potential Section 8 landlords.

—Recognize restrictions and the meaning of opportunity. Allowing relocation only to low-poverty areas may have some associated risks. It will be important, for example, to understand what levels of neighborhood "affluence" might best determine the selection of receiving neighborhoods, while also working to ensure that large numbers of Section 8 families are not allowed into "fragile" areas. Concomitantly, "10 percent poor" should not remain the sole definition of what an area of opportunity includes. Labor market and school performance characteristics should be among the variables used to select neighborhoods in future expansions of MTO.[55]

A program like MTO is also certainly not right for every city. Massive deconcentration will certainly not succeed under present conditions or for the foreseeable future, but modest levels of deconcentration can occur if there is sufficient political will in the locality and if it is coupled with empirical documentation of the benefits to families that move and the absence of harm to receiving communities. MTO offers the first systematic research opportunity in decades to reply

52. See Goering and Feins (2003); Popkin and others (2000a); Blumstein (2000); John Fountain, "Violence Is Down, but Some Areas Still Suffer," *New York Times*, January 11, 2001.

53. Downs (1973); Hirsch (1983); Rieder (1985); Bonastia (2000); Galster and others (2003).

54. Finkel and Buron (2001).

55. O'Regan and Quigley (1999); Devine and others (2003).

to critics who assume that only the worst can emerge from a HUD dispersal program. Just as important, it offers families living in federal slums the chance to move to opportunities and to develop a personal "capability set" that reflects society's better tendencies.[56]

Conclusion

Moving to Opportunity is the first multisite experimental demonstration project to promote housing integration, mostly by income but also to a more modest extent by race, and to study its social and economic effects. It is also HUD's first nonjudicially driven desegregation initiative in roughly thirty years. It represents a nearly fifteen-year research commitment to gather experimental evidence on the effects of living in and leaving public housing projects for better-off communities.

Community residents and elected officials as well as researchers now have fairly persuasive, if provisional, evidence that poor families benefit from leaving behind crime-ridden slums. Deconcentrating the poor is both feasible and beneficial for participating families. Ongoing research will help to find a more definitive answer to the core question posed for MTO: Can families' lives be significantly improved by simply offering them the choice to move out? It is essential, of course, to recall that the political commitment to authorize and fund federal agencies like HUD to conduct program-based research on the effectiveness of poverty reduction and racial desegregation programs has been fragile and episodic. While MTO appears to be a relevant housing choice for additional families and public housing authorities, there is not yet evidence that it is a model for program implementation on a permanent, larger scale.[57] MTO managed to find low-poverty rental housing for roughly 140 families in each of five cities, hardly testing the limits of the substantial, progressive increases in program scale that would be needed to learn how to manage larger numbers of families, receiving neighborhoods, and cities.

But until implementation of the MTO and HOPE VI programs, HUD had made no attempts to simultaneously promote economic and racial mixing on any scale. Indeed, it is still accurate to restate Thomas Pettigrew's sadly shrewd policy observation, made more than three decades ago, that "in a real sense, integration has not failed in America, for it still remains to be tried as a national policy."[58] Where some of the poorest of the ghetto poor are concerned, HUD has had no evidence with which to respond to either Congress or local communities about

56. Sen (1999, p. 75). Sen also notes that "the sense of inequality may also erode social cohesion, and some types of inequality can make it difficult to achieve even efficiency" (p. 93).

57. Jackson (2000); Ellen (2000); Charles, chapter 3, this volume.

58. Pettigrew (1971, p. 297). Research evidence on the implementation and consequences of housing integration has been notably missing since the 1950s. But see Hughes and Watts (1964).

Box 6-1. *MTO Interim Evaluation: Summary of Significant Impacts*

—MTO had substantial, positive effects on the mobility of families in the experimental and Section 8 groups and on the characteristics of the neighborhoods in which they lived.

—There were a number of significant improvements in the neighborhood environment in which experimental group families lived and lesser improvements for Section 8 group families.

— Relative to the control group, the families that moved with program vouchers markedly improved their neighborhood conditions, reporting much less litter, trash, graffiti, abandoned buildings, and public drinking and fewer people "hanging around."

—The adults reported a substantial increase in their perception of safety in and around their home and a large reduction in the likelihood of observing a crime or of being a victim of crime.

—For adults, MTO participation was related to a large reduction in the incidence of obesity in both the experimental group and the Section 8 group and reduction in psychological distress and depression and increased feelings of calm and peacefulness in the experimental group.

—For girls under age fifteen, MTO participation brought about a moderately large reduction in psychological distress among those in the experimental group, a substantial decrease in the incidence of depression among those in the Section 8 group, and a very large reduction in the incidence of generalized anxiety disorder in both treatment groups.

—For girls aged fifteen through nineteen, participation in MTO resulted in a large reduction in the percentage in the Section 8 group who had ever been arrested for violent crimes, contributing to a significant reduction in the frequency of arrests for violent crimes.

—For girls aged fifteen to nineteen in the experimental group, there were reductions in marijuana use and smoking.

—For boys aged fifteen through nineteen in both treatment groups, there were increases in smoking but not in other types of risky behavior.

—MTO had significant but small effects on the characteristics of the schools that sample children attended but virtually no significant effects for either the experimental group or the Section 8 group on any of the measures of educational performance analyzed.

—Participation in MTO resulted in a large reduction in the proportion of female youth working and not in school, with a concomitant (though not statistically significant) increase in the proportion attending school.

—The only statistically significant treatment-control difference in any of the measures of adult employment or earnings analyzed was a slight reduction in the employment rate in the first two years after random assignment among adults in the experimental group.

what the effects of moving poor families into low-poverty communities would be like. There has been little systematic study to identify what types of city would be more or less amenable to various policy interventions aimed at deconstructing poverty and race isolation.[59] Knowing in which communities and neighborhoods, and for which families, a program like MTO might work best would greatly aid in developing alternatives to high-poverty ghettoized communities.

If Anthony Downs is correct in his assessment that efforts to revitalize high-poverty communities through community development have almost universally failed, then regional housing mobility efforts, such as MTO, are a necessary accompaniment to other policy options.[60] It is quite possible that receiving communities have different thresholds of tolerance and acceptance for children and adults of various racial and ethnic groups depending on their own racial and ethnic composition, their perceived vulnerability or susceptibility to other changes, and their access to social resources and programs that might help them to adapt to new families.[61]

Additional research is needed. To date, the evidence on racial integration portrays a cup that is worrisomely empty.[62] The persistence of negative stereotypes appears to be a potential political constraint on options for substantial movement of racially and economically diverse populations into a more diverse set of neighborhoods. There is little in public discourse today to suggest that people in general would be substantially more open than they were before to the prospect of thousands of public housing families relocating to low-poverty areas. There also is now the sense that middle-class African Americans are less willing to accept the costs of integration when those costs appear to outweigh the benefits likely to accrue to their children.[63]

Some predominantly white and middle-income neighborhoods also appear certain to oppose almost any housing relocation program, acting to protect their areas from perceived or actual threats. While such opposition can be better managed to reduce its occurrence or impacts, it is clear that efforts to offer minorities the choice to move out of their traditional communities will continue for some time to appear, for some number of minorities and whites, politically and socially suspect.[64]

MTO is not a silver bullet for eliminating ghetto poverty. However, at this middle stage in its life as a demonstration project, it appears to be essential to understanding both the operational challenges and the benefits to families of the

59. Abu-Lughod (1999); Glaeser, Kahn, and Rappaport (2000).

60. Downs (1999). See also Tegler, Hanley, and Liben (1995); Turner, Popkin and Cunningham (2000); Katz and Turner (2001); Briggs, chapter 14, this volume.

61. Guhathakurta and Mushkatel (2002).

62. Bobo and Zubrinsky (1996); Calmore (1999); Charles, chapter 3, this volume.

63. Hochschild (1995); Bobo (2001, pp. 285–90).

64. Husock (2000a, 2000b); Leigh and McGhee (1986); Meares (2003); Massey and Kanaiaupuni (1993).

choice to move out. A well-designed extension of MTO could offer opportunities to thousands of additional low-income and public housing families in communities whose social and institutional fabric is not so badly disjointed as in Baltimore County. As Owen Fiss argues for the black poor, "The only alternative to a program that seeks to expand choice is to condemn a sector of the black community to suffer in perpetuity for the devastating effects of our racial history."[65] And ghetto poverty does not of course affect blacks alone.

The policy issue—how to gradually deconcentrate, or "unpack," the poorest, most vulnerable families and children—has hardly been addressed. Recent cuts in funding for the Section 8 program by the Bush administration could preclude any new rentals, cause some families to lose their subsidies, and have the net effect of reversing previous gains in economic and racial integration. MTO's research legacy is, nonetheless, important and potentially powerful for U.S. public policymakers, as it stands as the solitary, rigorous research basis for understanding the contrasting effects of ghettoization and improved opportunity upon the lives of poor children and their parents remaining in and moving from public housing projects. We have only begun the process of understanding the balanced transitions—the mixture of positive and possibly negative impacts—of ending systematic social and economic isolation in our largest cities.

References

Abrams, Charles. 1955. *Forbidden Neighbors: A Study of Prejudice in Housing.* New York: Harper and Row.

Abu-Lughod, Janet. 1999. *New York, Chicago, Los Angeles: America's Global Cities.* University of Minnesota Press.

Andersson, Roger. 2003. "Settlement Dispersal of Immigrants and Refugees in Europe: Policy and Outcomes." Working Paper 03-08. Paper prepared for the Sixth National Metropolis Conference, Edmonton, March 20–24.

Aspen Institute. 2002. "Grow Faster Together or Grow Slowly Apart: How Will America Work in the Twenty-First Century?" Washington: Domestic Strategy Group.

Bickford, Adam, and D. Massey. 1991. "Segregation in the Second Ghetto: Racial and Ethnic Segregation in American Public Housing, 1977." *Social Forces* 69 (June): 1011–36.

Bipartisan Millennial Housing Commission Appointed by the Congress of the United States. 2002. *Meeting Our Nation's Housing Challenges.* U.S. Government Printing Office.

Blumstein, Alfred. 2000. "Disaggregating the Violence Trends." In *The Crime Drop in America,* edited by Alfred Blumstein and Joel Wallman, pp. 13–44. Cambridge University Press.

Bobo, Larry. 2001. "Racial Attitudes and Relations at the Close of the Twentieth Century." In *America Becoming: Racial Trends and Their Consequences,* edited by Neil Smelser, William Julius Wilson, and Faith Mitchell, pp. 264–301. Washington: National Academy Press.

65. Fiss (2000, p. 4). It is also clear that the United States is not alone in its interest in dispersing needy populations, suggesting that there may be opportunities for learning strategies from other countries. See Simon (2002); Andersson (2003).

Bobo, Larry, and Camille Zubrinsky. 1996. "Attitudes on Racial Integration: Perceived Status Differences, Mere In-Group Preference, or Racial Prejudice?" *Social Forces* 74 (March): 883–909.

Bonastia, Chris. 2000. "Why Did Affirmative Action in Housing Fail during the Nixon Era? Exploring 'Institutional Homes' of Social Policies." *Social Problems* 47 (November): 523–42.

Briggs, Xavier de Souza. 2003. "Housing Opportunity, Desegregation Strategy, and Policy Research." *Journal of Policy Analysis and Management* 22, no. 2: 201–06.

Briggs, Xavier de Souza, Joe Darden, and Angela Aidala. 1999. "In the Wake of Desegregation: Early Impacts of Public Housing on Neighborhoods in Yonkers, New York." *APA Journal* 65 (Winter): 27–49.

Calmore, John. 1979. "Fair Housing versus Fair Housing: The Conflict between Providing Low-Income Housing in Impacted Areas and Providing Increased Housing Opportunities through Spatial Deconcentration." *Housing Law Bulletin* 9 (November-December): 1–12.

———. 1999. "Viable Integration Must Reject the Ideology of 'Assimilationism.'" *Poverty and Race* 8, no. 6: 7–8.

Davis, Mary. 1993. "The Gautreaux Assisted Housing Program." In *Housing Markets and Residential Mobility*, edited by G. Thomas Kingsley and Margery Austin Turner. Washington: Urban Institute.

De Bernardo, Henry. 1979. "Analysis of HUD's Regional Housing Mobility Program." HUD library.

Devine, Deborah, and others. 2003. *Housing Choice Voucher Location Patterns: Implications for Participants and Neighborhood Welfare.* Office of Policy Development and Research, U.S. Department of Housing and Urban Development.

Dimond, Paul. 2000. "Empowering Families to Vote with Their Feet." In *Reflections on Regionalism,* edited by Bruce Katz, pp. 249–71. Brookings.

Downs, Anthony. 1973. *Opening up the Suburbs.* Yale University Press.

———. 1999. "Some Realities about Sprawl and Urban Decline." *Housing Policy Debate* 10, no. 4: 955–74.

Dreier, Peter, John Mollenkopf, and Todd Swanstrom. 2001. *Place Matters: Metropolitics for the Twenty-First Century.* University Press of Kansas.

Edsall, Thomas, and Mary Edsall. 1992. *Chain Reaction: The Impact of Race, Rights, and Taxes on American Politics.* New York: Norton.

Ellen, Ingrid Gould. 2000. *Sharing America's Neighborhoods: The Prospects for Stable Racial Integration.* Harvard University Press.

Farley, Reynolds, Sheldon Danziger, and Harry Holzer. 2000. *Detroit Divided.* New York: Russell Sage.

Finkel, Meryl, and Larry Buron. 2001. *Study on Section 8 Voucher Success Rates: Quantitative Study of Success Rates in Metropolitan Areas.* Final Report. Office of Policy Development and Research, U.S. Department of Housing and Urban Development.

Fiss, Owen. 2000. "What Should Be Done for Those Left Behind?" *Boston Review* 25 (Summer): 4–9.

Galster, George, ed. 1996. *Reality and Research: Social Science and U.S. Urban Policy since 1960.* Washington: Urban Institute.

Galster, George, Roberto Quercia, and Alvaro Cortes. 2000. "Identifying Neighborhood Thresholds: An Empirical Exploration." *Housing Policy Debate* 11, no. 3: 701–32.

Galster, George, Peter Tatian, and Robin Smith. 1999. "The Impact of Neighbors Who Use Section 8 Certificates on Property Values." *Housing Policy Debate* 10, no. 4: 879–917.

Galster, George, and others. 2003. *Why NOT in My Back Yard?* New Brunswick, N.J.: Center for Urban Policy Research.

Glaeser, Edward, Mathew Kahn, and Jordan Rappaport. 2000. "Why Do the Poor Live in Cities?" Working Paper 1891. Institute of Economic Research, Harvard University.

Goering, John, ed. 1986. *Housing Desegregation and Federal Policy.* Chapel Hill: University of North Carolina Press.

Goering, John, and Judith Feins, eds. 2003. *Choosing a Better Life? Evaluating the Moving to Opportunity Demonstration.* Washington: Urban Institute.

Goering, John, Ali Kamely, and Todd Richardson. 1997. "Recent Research on Racial Segregation and Poverty Concentration in Public Housing in the United States." *Urban Affairs Review* 32 (May): 723–45.

Goetz, Edward. 2000. "The Politics of Poverty Deconcentration and Housing Demolition." *Journal of Urban Affairs* 22, no. 2: 157–73.

Gramlich, Edward, Deborah Laren, and Naomi Sealand. 1992. "Moving into and out of Poor Urban Areas." *Journal of Policy Analysis and Management* 11, no. 2: 273–87.

Guhathakurta, Subhrajit, and Alvin Mushkatel. 2002. "Race, Ethnicity, and Household Characteristics of Section 8 Clients and Their Impact on Adjacent Housing Quality." *Urban Affairs Review* 37 (March): 521–42.

Hartman, Chester. 1963. "The Limitations of Public Housing: Relocation Choices in a Working Class Community." *AIP Journal* (November): 283–96.

Hays, R. Allen. 1995. *The Federal Government and Urban Housing.* State University of New York Press.

Heclo, Hugh. 1994. "Poverty Politics." In *Confronting Poverty: Prescriptions for Change,* edited by Sheldon Danziger, Gary Sandefur, and Daniel Weinberg, pp. 396–437. New York: Russell Sage.

Hirsch, Arnold. 1983. *Making the Second Ghetto: Race and Housing in Chicago, 1940–1960.* Cambridge University Press.

———. 2000. "Searching for a 'Sound Negro Policy': A Racial Agenda for the Housing Acts of 1949 and 1954." *Housing Policy Debate* 11, no. 2: 393–441.

Hochschild, Jennifer. 1995. *Facing up to the American Dream: Race, Class, and the Soul of the Nation.* Princeton University Press.

———. 2003. "Creating Options." In *A Way Out: America's Ghettos and the Legacy of Racism,* edited by Joshua Cohen, Jefferson Decker, and Joel Rogers, pp. 68–73. Princeton University Press.

Hughes, Helen, and Lewis Watts. 1964. "Portrait of a Self-Integrator." *Journal of Social Issues* 20: 103–15.

Husock, Howard. 2000a. "How Charlotte Is Revolutionizing Public Housing." *City Journal* (Spring): 52–59.

———. 2000b. "Let's End Housing Vouchers." *City Journal* (Autumn): 84–91.

Iceland, John, Daniel Weinberg, and Erika Steinmetz. 2002. *Racial and Ethnic Residential Segregation in the United Sates: 1980–2000.* CENSR-3, Census Bureau Series. U.S. Government Printing Office.

Jackson, Kenneth. 1985. *Crabgrass Frontier: The Suburbanization of the United States.* Oxford University Press.

———. 2000. "Gentleman's Agreement: Discrimination in Metropolitan America." In *Reflections on Regionalism,* edited by Bruce Katz, pp. 185–217. Brookings.

Jargowsky, Paul. 2003. "Stunning Progress, Hidden Problems: The Dramatic Decline of Concentrated Poverty in the 1990s." Metropolitan Policy Program, Brookings, May.

Jencks, Christopher, and Susan Mayer. 1990. "The Social Consequences of Growing up in a Poor Neighborhood." In *Inner-City Poverty in the United States,* edited by Laurence Lynn and Michael McGeary, pp. 111–86. Washington: National Academy Press.

Katz, Bruce, and Margery Turner. 2001. "Who Should Run the Housing Voucher Program? A Reform Proposal." *Housing Policy Debate* 12, no. 2: 239–62.

Leigh, Wilhelmina, and James McGhee. 1986. "A Minority Perspective on Residential Racial Integration." In *Housing Desegregation and Federal Policy,* edited by John Goering, pp. 31–42. University of North Carolina Press.

Lemann, Nicholas. 1991. *The Promised Land: The Great Black Migration and How It Changed America.* New York: Knopf.

Lief, Beth, and Susan Goering. 1987. "The Implementation of the Federal Mandate for Fair Housing." In *Divided Neighborhoods: Changing Patterns of Racial Segregation,* edited by Gary Tobin, pp. 227–67. Newbury Park, Calif.: Sage.

Lucas, Wendy. 1997. "Perry Hall, Baltimore, Maryland, Housing and Neighborhood Study: Putting FHA Housing on the Map." U.S. Department of Housing and Urban Development, April 23.

Massey, Douglas S., and Nancy A. Denton. 1993. *American Apartheid: Segregation and the Making of the Underclass.* Harvard University Press.

Massey, Douglas S., Andrew B. Gross, and Kumiko Shibuya. 1994. "Migration, Segregation, and the Geographic Concentration of Poverty." *American Sociological Review* 59 (June): 425–45.

Massey, Douglas, and Shaun Kanaiaupuni. 1993. "Public Housing, the Concentration of Poverty, and the Life Chances of Individuals." *Social Science Research* 20: 397–420.

Mayer, Susan, and Christopher Jencks. 1989. "Growing up in Poor Neighborhoods: How Much Does It Matter?" *Science* 243 (March 17): 1441-45.

McDougall, Harold. 1993. *Black Baltimore: A New Theory of Community.* Temple University Press.

Meares, Tracy. 2003. "Communities, Capital, and Conflicts." In *A Way Out: America's Ghettos and the Legacy of Racism,* edited by Joshua Cohen, Jefferson Decker, and Joel Rogers, pp. 51–56. Princeton University Press.

Moynihan, Daniel Patrick. 1971. "Toward a National Urban Policy." In *Urban Studies: An Introductory Reader,* edited by Louis K. Lowenstein, pp. 127–45. New York: Free Press.

Newman, Sandra. 1995. "Poverty Concentration as a Policy Strategy." Occasional Paper 17. Institute for Policy Studies, Johns Hopkins University.

Newman, Sandra, and Ann Schnare. 1997. ". . . and a Suitable Living Environment: The Failure of Housing Programs to Deliver on Neighborhood Quality." *Housing Policy Debate* 8, no. 4: 703–41.

Nyden, Philip, and others. 1998. "Neighborhood Racial and Ethnic Diversity in U.S. Cities." *Cityscape* 4, no. 2: 1–17.

O'Regan, Katherine, and John Quigley. 1999. "Accessibility and Economic Opportunity." In *Essays in Transportation Economics and Policy,* edited by Jose Gomez-Ibanez, William Tye, and Clifford Winston, pp. 437–66. Brookings.

Pattillo-McCoy, Mary. 1999. *Black Picket Fences: Privilege and Peril among the Black Middle Class.* University of Chicago Press.

Pettigrew, Thomas. 1971. *Racially Separate or Together.* New York: McGraw-Hill.

Polikoff, Alexander. No date. "Cabrini-Green to Willow Creek." Available from author.

———, ed. 1995. *Housing Mobility: Promise or Illusion?* Washington: Urban Institute.

Popkin, Susan, and others. 2000a. "The Gautreaux Legacy: What Might Mixed-Income and Dispersal Strategies Mean for the Poorest Public Housing Tenants?" *Housing Policy Debate* 11 (December): 911–42.

———. 2000b. *The Hidden War: Crime and the Tragedy of Public Housing in Chicago.* Rutgers University Press.

———. 2003. "Obstacles to Desegregating Public Housing: Lessons from Implementing Eight Consent Decrees." *Journal of Policy Analysis and Management* 22, no. 2: 179–99.

Rieder, Jonathan. 1985. *Canarsie: The Jews and Italians of Brooklyn against Liberalism.* Harvard University Press.

Roisman, Florence. 2001. "Opening the Suburbs to Racial Integration: Lessons for the Twenty-First Century." *Western New England Law Review* (Symposium): 173–221.

Rosenbaum, James E. 1992. "Black Pioneers: Do Their Moves to the Suburbs Increase Economic Opportunity for Mothers and Children?" *Housing Policy Debate* 2: 1179–213.

Rubinowitz, Leonard, and James Rosenbaum. 2000. *Crossing the Class and Color Lines: From Public Housing to White Suburbia.* University of Chicago Press.

Schill, Michael. 1992. "Deconcentrating the Inner City Poor." *Chicago-Kent Law Review* 67, no. 3: 795–853.

Sen, Amartya. 1999. *Development as Freedom.* New York: Anchor.

Shroder, Mark. 2000. "Social Experiments in Housing." *Cityscape* 5, no. 1: 237–59.

Simon, Patrick. 2002. "When Desegregation Produces Stigmatization: Ethnic Minorities and Urban Policies in France." In *Diversity in the City,* edited by Marco Martiniello and Brigitte Piquard. Bilbao: University of Deusto.

Sleeper, Jim. 2003. "Against Social Engineering." In *A Way Out: America's Ghettos and the Legacy of Racism,* edited by Joshua Cohen, Jefferson Decker, and Joel Rogers, pp. 92–101. Princeton University Press.

Tegler, Philip, Michael Hanley, and Judith Liben. 1995. "Transforming Section 8: Using Federal Housing Subsidies to Promote Individual Choice and Desegregation." *Harvard Civil Rights–Civil Liberties Law Review* 30 (Summer): 451–86.

Thompson, Phillip. 1999. "Public Housing in New York City." In *Housing and Community Development in New York City,* edited by Michael H. Schill, pp. 119–42. State University of New York Press.

Turner, Margery, Susan Popkin, and Mary Cunningham. 2000. *Section 8 Mobility and Neighborhood Health: Emerging Issues and Policy Challenges.* Washington: Urban Institute.

U.S. National Advisory Commission on Civil Disorders. 1968. *Report.* New York: Dutton.

Vale, Lawrence. 2000. *From the Puritans to the Projects: Public Housing and Public Neighbors.* Harvard University Press.

Venkatesh, Sudhir. 2002. "The Robert Taylor Homes Relocation Study." Center for Urban Research and Policy, Columbia University.

Vernarelli, Michael. 1986. "Where Should HUD Locate Existing Housing: The Evolution of Fair Housing Policy." In *Housing Desegregation and Federal Policy,* edited by John Goering, pp. 214–34. University of North Carolina Press.

Williams, E. Douglas, and Richard Sander. 1993. "The Prospects for 'Putting America to Work' in the Inner City." *Georgetown Law Journal* 81 (June): 2003–72.

Williams, Robin. 1964. *Strangers Next Door: Ethnic Relations in American Communities.* Englewood Cliffs, N.J.: Prentice Hall.

Winnick, Louis. 1995. "The Triumph of Housing Allowance Programs: How a Fundamental Policy Conflict Was Resolved." *Cityscape* 1, no. 3: 95–121.

7

New Capabilities in New Places: Low-Income Black Families in Suburbia

JAMES ROSENBAUM, STEFANIE DELUCA, AND TAMMY TUCK

Housing assistance traditionally aims only to provide shelter. However, recent research suggests that if housing is combined with residential mobility strategies, it also can provide families with access to social and economic opportunities and improve their lives. Through the Gautreaux program, low-income families were able to move to white middle-class suburbs throughout the six-county metropolitan area of Chicago. In the Moving to Opportunity (MTO) program, low-income families moved to low-poverty neighborhoods in five metropolitan areas (Baltimore, Boston, Chicago, Los Angeles, and New York City). Research on these residential mobility programs has discovered remarkable changes in participants' attitudes, behavior, and performance, but it also suggests important caveats about the limits of place as an arbiter of opportunity.[1]

However, as Xavier de Souza Briggs has stressed, that research focuses on outcomes, not process.[2] Most of the studies do not examine what features of the social environment are major influences or the underlying mechanisms that might explain observed outcomes. This is an important shortcoming, for it means that policymakers do not understand what it is about the residential moves that results in particular outcomes and that therefore they cannot be sure

1. Goering, chapter 6, this volume; Katz, Kling, and Liebman (1997); Ludwig, Hirschfield, and Duncan (2001); Rubinowitz and Rosenbaum (2000).
2. Briggs (1997).

when they replicate some features of the program that they capture the necessary elements.

Studies find that the presence of middle-class, affluent neighbors is positively related to adult employment and children's educational attainment and eventual earnings, some finding positive effects for whites, others for black male teenagers. Studies also show that youths achieve greater academic success if they live in areas with lower proportions of blacks; unemployed males; lower-income, female- headed households; or welfare-dependent families and higher proportions of managerial or professional workers. Further, the higher the percentage of unemployed males and welfare recipients in a given neighborhood, the fewer hours a person will work.[3] Many assume that resources by themselves—better schools, more activities, greater affluence—explain these results. If so, it is conceivable that low-income families could benefit from the superior resources in their new affluent communities without having any meaningful interaction with their neighbors. This tends to happen in some school busing programs: Children gain educationally even though their after-school interaction with their schoolmates is limited.[4]

The affluence hypothesis is the implicit model of the MTO program, which, in effect, randomly assigned low-income families to low-poverty or high-poverty census tracts so that research could focus on the effects.[5] If families benefited, it was assumed that they benefited simply by being surrounded by affluent neighbors. However, since families chose their own units within a tract, many aspects of their local circumstance were not controlled, and those effects have not been examined. Researchers are only beginning to examine the process by which residential mobility affects individuals or to consider whether outcomes might depend on certain conditions (enclaves, race or class of next-door neighbors, friendships, activities, and so forth).

However, having affluent neighbors may not be sufficient. Neighborhood affluence may not necessarily benefit all residents—low-income newcomers may not be included. Resource disparities could lead to competition, resentment, perceived deprivation, and negative outcomes, especially for young people.[6]

3. Sampson, Raudenbush, and Earls (1997); Sampson, Morenoff, and Earls (1999); Sampson, Morenoff, and Gannon-Rowley (2002); Brooks-Gunn and others (1993); Crane (1991); Datcher (1982); Corcoran and others (1990).

4. Wells and Crain (1997).

5. MTO assigned families resident in public housing projects to one of three treatment groups. The experimental group received counseling assistance and vouchers and was required, as a condition of voucher receipt, to choose a low-poverty neighborhood (based on 1990 census data), while a second group received vouchers without restriction, and a third group (the controls) did not receive any change in their housing assistance (though they were not restricted from leaving the projects on their own). See overview and research at www.mtoresearch.org (accessed September 24, 2004).

6. Jencks and Mayer (1990).

Families may have to have private transportation or to pay fees to benefit from the resources available in affluent suburbs, such as theaters, summer camps, a YMCA, or a superior public library. If a camp or program has a limited number of spaces, only people whose social networks provide early notification or people who have other useful connections may have access to them. Although a strong labor market means that jobs are available, employment is possible only for workers with the right skills and for those who have access to good child care and transportation.[7] Resources alone are not necessarily sufficient to guarantee access and improved outcomes.

The Social Capital Hypothesis

Social capital provides another explanation of the greater capabilities people show after they move to the suburbs. Social capital has been defined in a number of ways. Robert Lang and Steven Hornburg state that "social capital commonly refers to the stock of social trust, norms, and networks that people can draw upon in order to solve common problems. Social scientists emphasize two main dimensions of social capital: social glue and social bridges."[8]

While that definition covers a broad variety of socially supportive phenomena, James Coleman's original proposal refers to a more narrowly defined set of mechanisms, and he contends that they have powerful impacts on an individual's capabilities. He suggests that some aspects of social environments provide social capital, which enables people to take actions that they could not otherwise take. Social capital takes three forms: social norms that guide behavior; reciprocity—"people . . . doing things for each other"—which provides "credit" on which individuals can draw; and information channels—social networks that provide information about jobs and other resources. Social capital is more than merely social acceptance or social support. Coleman contends that "social capital is productive, making possible the achievement of certain ends that in its absence would not be possible."[9] In other words, social capital confers ability: It gives people capabilities that they would not have otherwise.

While Coleman provides convincing examples about the enhancing effects of communities, many questions remain. First, Coleman's examples are taken from close, tightly knit ethnic communities. Do more typical communities in modern America create useful social capital? Second, do middle-class white suburbs, which often are characterized as lacking in community cohesiveness, offer social capital to anyone? According to some stereotypes, suburbs are not real communities. They are "bedroom communities," where people come to sleep before

7. Rubinowitz and Rosenbaum (2000).
8. Lang and Hornburg (1998, p. 4).
9. Coleman (1988, p. S98).

returning to school or their job or visiting friends in some other location. Herbert Gans has presented evidence indicating that homeowner suburbs are communities; however, that has not been shown to be true in the kinds of suburban apartment complexes where the Gautreaux families lived, especially in recent years when so many women are working and rarely at home.[10]

Third, Coleman's examples mostly involve social insiders. The individuals who benefit are part of the social fabric of these closed communities—they were born there and have lived there all their life. It is not clear from his account whether newcomers would receive the same benefits. Fourth, inclusion is even more problematic if the newcomers are of a different income level and race, visibly distinct from the vast majority of residents. Do the more homogeneous suburbs offer acceptance to newcomers of different race and income? Do these outsiders become insiders in any meaningful sense and acquire any of the benefits of insiders?

Fifth, do low-income blacks choose to comply with middle-class white norms, even norms that conflict with their own experience? The adults in the Gautreaux program have typically lived their entire lives in housing projects, and they are accustomed to different social norms. Suburbs may impose norms and expect behaviors that are uncomfortable, undesirable, or impossible for low-income black families. Sixth, it is not certain that low-income black in-movers' compliance with norms will give them the same social capital benefits that other neighbors would get. Indeed, the opposite—the imposition of new costs—might occur. Despite the wild enthusiasm about social capital, the social norms and cohesion required for social capital could actually be harmful to some individuals.[11] In the enthusiasm about social capital, the aspects of social norms that sometimes coerce, ostracize, and constrain are often ignored. In the 1950s sociologists noted the ways that social norms suppress individualism, dissent, and disagreement; these critiques centered principally on the emerging affluence and conformity of postwar suburbs.[12] Such social processes may be particularly constraining for minorities.

Last, is social capital, if one can access it, beneficial for family outcomes? Previous analyses of surveys show that low-income black mothers and children did interact with their white suburban neighbors and that their level of interaction was similar to the amount of interaction of their counterparts who moved to mostly black city neighborhoods. We found that Gautreaux mothers talked with their neighbors and Gautreaux children played with their neighbors and did homework with their classmates. Contrary to our worst fears, these families were not ostracized; they had many kinds of interaction with their neighbors.[13]

10. Gans (1967).
11. Portes (1998).
12. Riesman (1950); Whyte (1956).
13. Rubinowitz and Rosenbaum (2000).

But interaction alone is not sufficient to demonstrate social capital. Social capital implies that social relationships confer capabilities, and that is hard to demonstrate with the survey data. Do these suburbs relieve mothers of anxieties and demanding obligations regarding social connections? Do the suburbs free up mothers' time or energy for other activities? Do the suburbs actually provide support, services, or social or material resources that enhance mothers' capabilities?

As Briggs notes, "geographic proximity does not a neighbor make—at least not in the social sense."[14] Social cohesion in the suburbs may be a mechanism for excluding outsiders, particularly those of another race and lower income. Social norms in white middle-class suburbs may constrain low-income blacks or prevent their access to activities. The social capital hypothesis seems highly problematic in this case. Rather than finding their new communities to be sources of social capital, new residents may feel that they are highly constraining and intolerant of the kinds of behaviors and attitudes with which they are comfortable. Consequently, in considering the applicability of Coleman's social capital explanation, the Gautreaux program studied here provides an opportunity to test the most extreme—and the most problematic—form of this question: Do middle-class white suburbs provide useful social capital to new low-income black residents?

The Analytic Approach

This chapter uses open-ended interviews that we conducted with sixty-nine mothers in 1989 and with eighty mothers in 1996, all black and all of whom had moved to mostly white, middle-income suburbs from high-poverty public housing in inner-city Chicago. The 1996 sample had been living in the suburbs for an average of thirteen years. We examined participants' reports about their interactions with their suburban neighbors, how it differed from their own experiences in the city, and how they believed those differences affected their behavior and their capabilities.

This study is one step in the larger process of understanding what the experience of moving entails and, in particular, what it means to become part of a very different community. We do not provide definitive evidence. We are trying to discover underlying processes about which social scientists and policymakers currently know very little. Unlike prior studies of the Gautreaux program, which used surveys on fairly large samples or administrative data on more than 1,500 families,[15] this study examines the statements volunteered by individuals. We take individuals' descriptions of changes and their interpretation of causality at face value. While we must be wary of methodological concerns that individuals

14. Briggs (1997, p. 197).
15. DeLuca and Rosenbaum (2000, 2001, 2003).

may misperceive or misinterpret their experiences, these respondents know more about their experiences than we do, so it is important that we learn from their reports and understand their subjective experiences of navigating a new environment. Nearly a decade ago, Briggs bemoaned the scarcity of qualitative data on these issues, and the intervening years have done little to change that.[16]

Although retrospective reports have shortcomings, they do provide information on long-term outcomes. Other research has shown movers' early difficulties (see John Goering, chapter 6, this volume), but some of these difficulties may be temporary problems of adjustment for movers or their new neighbors. Previous research finds that mothers and children gradually make friends over time and that any early harassment by neighbors gradually subsides or disappears over the first few years.[17] The long-term perspective presented here is especially pertinent for evaluating social outcomes from the moves. Unlike the vast majority of quantitative research on neighborhood effects, which focuses on individuals' academic or economic outcomes in the short term, this chapter focuses on social outcomes and interactions over the long term.

Recent findings have led some observers to conclude that residential mobility has no significant effect on receipt of public aid or employment. That hasty conclusion is probably not warranted, but even if it were there are several reasons for policymakers, public advocates, and researchers to focus intently on residential mobility programs. First, human development theory suggests that social programs are likely to have much larger effects on children than on adults,[18] and studies of both Gautreaux and MTO generally find larger changes in children than in adults. Second, temporary adjustment difficulties are likely to prevent individuals from benefiting from residential mobility in the first few years, especially when the move entails radical changes. We may discover the benefits of residential mobility only over the long term, after individuals have adjusted to their new environment. Third, program effects on social behaviors may be at least as important as the effects on economic behaviors. The United States has struggled over most of its history with the question of how to reduce race and class barriers in a society that espouses equality. The residential mobility program described in this study was designed to explore one approach, and this study emphasizes social outcomes and social interactions, quite apart from individuals' economic status. Moreover, this study finds that individuals can acquire new social competencies when they move to very different social environments, and it is quite possible that these competencies have a powerful impact on the next generation.

We focus on descriptions of concrete behaviors more than on impressions or attitudes, so the risks of distortion are reduced. We examine families' reports of

16. Briggs (1997).
17. Rubinowitz and Rosenbaum (2000).
18. Carneiro and Heckman (2003).

their experiences and whether families report any examples that illustrate important social processes—in particular, the development and use of useful social capital. If individuals act differently and have different capabilities in a new location—and if they attribute those changes to certain aspects of their location—then we have some indication that the new locations generated access to social capital.

The Gautreaux and MTO Programs

The Gautreaux program, a result of a 1976 Supreme Court decision, was created to allow Chicago public housing residents (and those on the waiting list) to receive Section 8 housing certificates and move to private apartments either in Chicago or in its mostly white suburbs. Between 1976 and 1998, more than 7,000 families participated. This program presents an unusual opportunity to see what happens when low-income black families accept an offer to move to middle-income white suburbs.

Participants avoided the typical barriers to suburbs not by virtue of their jobs, personal finances, or values but through a program that assigned them to suburbs through a quasi-random process, according to housing availability at the time and their position on the waiting list. In principle, participants could refuse an offer, but few did since they were unlikely to get another equivalent. Analyses in several studies suggest that placements also were largely unrelated to family attributes: Suburban and city movers were initially similar in many ways (age, number of children, education, marital status, welfare status).[19]

By necessity, the program excluded people who seemed unlikely to handle program demands. It eliminated about one-third of applicants because their families were too large for apartments or because they had poor rent payment records, which would likely lead to eviction. However, all participants were very poor, and they qualified for public housing. The best-documented pattern of black suburbanization involves working-class blacks moving to working-class suburbs, but Gautreaux moved low-income blacks into middle- and upper-income white suburbs. Only a few families moved to any one neighborhood, and participants moved to more than 115 suburbs in six counties around Chicago. Only a few high-rent suburbs were excluded.

The Moving to Opportunity program grew out of the Gautreaux program.[20] It assigned low-income families to one of three groups: a group moving to a low-poverty area, an open-choice Section 8 group, or a control group that remained in public housing in high-poverty areas. Gautreaux and MTO represent different models of leveraging potential neighborhood effects, and we can

19. Mendenhall, Duncan, and DeLuca (2004).
20. Turner (1998, p. 376).

learn from each. First, while Gautreaux moved families to distant suburbs, limiting interaction with former neighbors, many MTO moves were to city neighborhoods, sometimes clustered together or near poor neighborhoods. Second, while Gautreaux assigned families to specific addresses, MTO assigned them to specific census tracts, and families chose apartments in those tracts. Maps of MTO placements suggest that many moved near tract boundaries (perhaps to get affordable rents or to be closer to low-income neighbors) and some to high-poverty enclaves within the low-poverty tracts. Third, while Gautreaux created both racial and income integration (suburban movers went to areas averaging 90 percent white populations), MTO is a program for income, not race, integration: 32 percent of MTO movers to low-poverty areas went to areas with a black majority. If families are affected by attributes of place besides poverty rate or income mix (for example, racial composition, job opportunities), MTO does not systematically test those effects. These three factors—shorter moves, self-selection of address, and mixing of income but not race—make MTO more practically feasible than Gautreaux, but they may create smaller neighborhood effects. When MTO studies find neighborhood effects, therefore, these studies may underestimate the effects of a Gautreaux-type intervention. Other models are also possible. In Yonkers, New York, just north of the Bronx, an explicit enclave model was implemented, wherein residents live together in separate housing developments but potentially benefit from their middle-class community.[21] Each model has advantages and disadvantages (for example, political feasibility and applicability), and researchers need to examine various models in order to understand the dynamics of neighborhood effects.

Gautreaux and MTO also have distinctive features in research design. First, MTO was designed as an experiment, with random assignment, a no-change control group, and pre- and post-move data collection. Most evidence suggests that Gautreaux approximates random selection, but because it is not perfectly random, it leaves uncertainty about the initial comparability of suburb- and city-mover groups. MTO has a superior research design. Second, while MTO is a much newer program that (thus far) allows the study of short-term outcomes, Gautreaux studies report long-term effects almost two decades (seventeen years) after placement. Third, while MTO studies focus on quantitative outcomes, they are only now beginning to examine causal mechanisms (using survey data at the five- to seven-year mark and more recent qualitative interviews and ethnographic fieldwork).

Gautreaux research has long included qualitative observations about the ways social context affects individuals' behavior. A study of a random sample of 342 heads of household finds that five years after moving, suburban movers had

21. Briggs (1997).

higher employment rates than city movers.[22] A study of children finds that suburban movers were more likely than city movers to graduate from high school, to attend college, and to attend better colleges (four-year rather than two-year colleges); those who did not attend college were more likely to have a job, and their jobs offered higher pay and benefits. Examining social interaction, this survey found no significant differences between city- and suburban-mover adults on six interaction measures, the combined interaction scale, individual isolation, or number of friends. Suburban movers reported significantly more incidents of harassment when they first moved, but it declined over time, and there was no difference between city and suburban movers in their current reports of harassment. Regarding children's interaction, another study finds no difference between city and suburban movers in the time they spent with black friends and the amount of interaction they had with black friends, but suburban movers were significantly more likely than city movers to interact with white students in doing schoolwork, in engaging in activities outside school, and in visiting in their homes. These results provide quantitative evidence that the suburban moves led to a considerable amount of "bridging" social interaction that crossed racial lines.

The use of administrative data avoids two common problems in surveys: nonresponse and distorted responses. For instance, while previous surveys located about two-thirds of the initial respondents, this study located current addresses for 1,504 of 1,506 families.[23] Similarly, while families might be reluctant to report being on public aid, Illinois state records provided complete and valid data on public aid for all participants.

Encouragingly, the first study using administrative data finds that of families placed in suburbs, only about 30 percent had returned to the city an average of seventeen years later. Moreover, while virtually all suburbs in the program were less than 30 percent black, when those suburbs are divided into quintiles of black composition, the highest rates of return to the city come from the highest and lowest black quintiles and the middle quintile has the lowest return rate (25 percent). However, in no quintile do more than 33 percent return to the city.

The second study finds that families that moved to better neighborhoods, as defined by the education level of the placement census tract, were much less likely to be on public aid. Merging data from the Illinois state government with program records, we find that public aid rates went from 26 percent to 39 percent when families placed in the highest- and lowest-quintile neighborhoods are compared. The difference remains very strong and significant after controlling for years in the program, age, and premove public aid (see table 7-1). This

22. See Rubinowitz and Rosenbaum (2000) and the review there.

23. For the previous surveys, see DeLuca and Rosenbaum (2001, 2003); Rosenbaum and DeLuca (2000).

Table 7-1. *Logistic Regression, Aid to Families with Dependent Children Program, by Initial Placement, 1989*[a]

Variable	*Coefficient*	*Standard error*	*Significance*	*Exp(B)*
Neighborhood socioeconomic status	1.1563	0.4442	0.0092	3.1782
Years in program, 1989	–0.1793	0.0233	0.0000	0.8359
Age in 1989	–0.0521	0.0094	0.0000	0.9493
AFDC at entry[b]	1.4873	0.1903	0.0000	4.4251
Constant	0.3832	0.3806	0.3140	

Source:

a. N = 1,330; chi square = 282.04, $p < .000$.

b. Yes = 1, no = 0.

analysis is important because it suggests that initial placement has a long-term effect on family outcome (public aid receipt). The analyses also suggest that the suburb/city distinction was not an influence on this outcome, but the underlying social composition of suburb and city neighborhoods was a major influence. But even these analyses cannot examine *how* these composition factors influenced participants' behaviors. For that we must do qualitative analyses of social processes.

Qualitative Analyses

How might these effects have occurred? Families were placed far from their friends and family members in mostly white settings that initially were very uncomfortable. While jobs were plentiful, transportation and child care were not. While the large survey finds that many mothers or children had a great deal of interaction with suburban neighbors, survey data cannot tell us how this interaction arose or what consequences it had. We must turn to qualitative analysis to address those issues.

Normative Constraints

Contrary to the widespread enthusiasm about the effects of social cohesion and of compliance with shared social norms—both of which are important in social capital theory—Gautreaux participants in the suburbs were not always so happy about those effects. James Coleman emphasizes that social capital benefits come at the expense of being subject to informal social control. Suburban movers describe their new neighborhoods as more demanding than their previous neighborhoods. They speak of an uptight, highly constraining environment in which loud partying, public drinking, and other disturbances common in their previous neighborhoods are not tolerated. Some mothers describe struggling with the more restrictive environment, as the following indicate:

> I partied more freely in the old neighborhood, without fear of offending the neighbors. It was more relaxed. I felt more comfortable. I felt that I didn't have to explain anything about myself or about my background. It was accepted because we were all the same race.
>
> Suppression of self is necessary; I go to the city for release. I liked the freedom of movement and parties in my old neighborhood.
>
> I think more suburban now. I do. . . . I used to like to go out and stuff like that. But I don't do that anymore. I'm mostly just interested in church and stuff like that. It's a change within me.

These highly constraining norms were also difficult for some children. Some mothers reported that their children struggled with the strict expectations about their behavior:

> So he [her son] usually has more activity when he goes to the city with his friends. Because he can just let himself go—let his hair down, so to speak. Feel freer, I think.
>
> When we first moved out here, they would call the police when his [her son's] music was turned up.
>
> It makes me so upset. It's like these little kids out here, they're perfect. They don't do anything but go to school and come home. . . . I just can't understand it . . . [my son's misbehaviors are] just something that a ten-year-old boy is going to get into.

Similarly, mothers report feeling obligated to take care of their houses, buildings, yards, and neighborhoods. They perceived that they were regarded with suspicion and had to prove themselves, prove that they could meet the standards expected in the suburbs:

> When I first moved here, I had little problems with the people. But now they know what to expect from me. They know I'm clean. I think they were worried more about my coming in and messing up. Somehow, white people get the idea that black people are nasty . . . don't take care of anything. I think now they know I'm clean and they accept me more now. . . . I think the first few days we were living here they just wanted to see how nasty we were going to be. See if we going keep the house clean or have paper all over the yard. And when they saw we were going to keep our grass done, I think that they began to accept us.

Even as mothers struggled to meet expectations, they perceived that the normative constraints had many benefits. For example, the social norms in the Chicago suburbs prevented certain negative actions. Some mothers perceived less tolerance for drugs in the suburbs than in their city neighborhoods, a normative constraint that helped them to feel safer:

> I mean that it's zero tolerance out here. Especially over here on the side of town where I live.

> Because it was so easy to get drugs [in the city], a lot of kids are strung out on drugs because of their environment. . . . A single parent, you can't be with your child twenty-four hours a day. Some of the adults and older kids influenced them to do certain things that they might not do, and so by me moving away, it cut down the influence of them being in drugs.

Some mothers in the first study perceived the constraints as affecting them and their teenagers disproportionately and note instances in which police and neighbors treated their children with suspicion and bias and instances of police harassment, unwarranted detention, and arrests. Although it may be that these families were subjected to closer scrutiny than other neighbors and that their mistakes received a harsher response, their own reports suggest that norms were not selectively enforced.

Later, mothers reported that the constraints helped them to feel safer. High standards for safety were kept and enforced. They describe a strict, active, concerned police force and system of rules concerning curfews and loitering:

> Out here, they have a curfew. I think it's 10 o'clock. You don't see anybody on the streets. If the police are in the area, they will want to know what's happening.

> Here in the suburbs, the police are much stricter. I guess they have a smaller territory to cover. In the city they have so many things to do, but here they are very strict. And if you need any assistance from the police, or if any problems come up with these teenagers or anything, they're right on the spot and working with you as a concerned parent to alleviate the problem.

> In the city, [teens] hang on the corners. Here they can't hang on no corner, and he [my son] would be with his friends, and they'd be on the corner. Police would stop them. . . . They think they was being harassed by the police, and they just telling you to get off the corner.

> Here the policemen are much nicer. There's a difference in the city and 'burbs' policemen. My kids like policemen. In Chicago, kids do not like policemen. Out here they are really Officers Friendly. When you see them on the street, they wave. The kids are comfortable with them.

The police were not the only enforcers. Neighbors were constantly watchful, and they had a low tolerance for crime. Neighbors looked out for each other's safety and apparently succeeded in promoting informal social control, a phenomenon often attributed to a form of social capital known as *collective efficacy.*[24] Suburban Gautreaux participants reported that neighbors kept watch for them at night, watched over their homes and cars, and were willing to call the police or come to help in times of emergency. Specifically, suburban participants described how interaction with their neighbors led to looking out for one another's safety and how that type of community protection was different from what they experienced in the city, as these quotes from six mothers indicate.

> In the summer, most of the families in the complex look out for each other. In my old neighborhood in the city, I would run from the front door to back door, fearful about my kids' safety . . . but not here.
>
> I usually come in at 10:00 p.m., and the man down on the first floor, he knows what time I come in. He usually stands at the door when I come in.
>
> I mean, it's quiet, and they—I guess to a certain extent they will let me know if they see something or hear something. I do have a neighbor on the side of me that, you know, every now and then, you got someone coming around trying to break in, and we watch out for one another.
>
> Everybody spoke, and they really cared about what was going on with the other people—if somebody's car got broken into or something. People were concerned about what was going on with their neighbors.
>
> 'Cause she has grown up here, she had been here almost ten years now so she knows everybody, and basically everybody knows her, so when you know the people in your community you can come and go and feel safe and people look out for you.
>
> You can leave and rest assured that someone will watch your house. You can swap keys and neighbors will take care of your house.

Similarly, Gautreaux participants felt that, unlike their city neighbors, their suburban neighbors would call the police in an emergency or that they would come to help themselves:

> They seem to be concerned and look out for one another. In the suburbs, the whole neighborhood would call the police.
>
> They all came out [in response to a domestic disturbance]. It was like a big street thing. Everybody came out and was talking to the husband. The men took the husband to one side and the women took the wife. No one was hurt. He was just mad she had did something and she told him not to do it and she wasn't home when he got home or something like that. Some stupid thing.
>
> I was robbed [when she lived in the city]. My purse was snatched, and when I screamed, no neighbors called the police.

24. Sampson, Morenoff, and Gannon-Rowley (2002).

> They broke into my house [when she lived in the city], and the people next door said they didn't even hear it. They broke into our house, and a lot of more people's houses where I lived and nobody ever called for help. I've seen people . . . I've heard people saying that they've seen people getting beat up on the street and people won't even call for help. It's like they're afraid to even go to the phone and call.
>
> In my Chicago neighborhood, no one would call if I needed help because that was a common thing. Somebody was always down there fighting their girlfriend or somebody hollering, Help, help, help. That was a common thing. . . . You weren't sure whether you should, could get involved or not.

Even though the discriminatory actions by neighbors who already lived in the neighborhood were unfair and at times illegal, they also were predictable and flowed from processes similar to those Coleman describes so positively. However, those actions did not persist, and many participants now feel that their neighbors and the police are watching out for them. When norms are enforced in a discriminatory manner, and special scrutiny is given to a certain group of people, those norms are a constraint, not a protection, for that group. However, when norms are perceived to be enforced universally, then they constrain everyone's behavior and become a protection for all. These norms gave Gautreaux mothers peace of mind and reduced their concerns about their own safety and that of their children. Shared social norms, which were initially a barrier, became a form of social capital on which Gautreaux participants could draw.

Collective Child Care

Coleman contends that the collective caring for children that occurs in some cultures is an important example of social capital:

> A mother of six children, who recently moved with husband and children from suburban Detroit to Jerusalem, describes one reason for doing so as the greater freedom her young children had in Jerusalem. She felt safe in letting her eight-year-old take the six-year-old across town to school on the city bus and felt her children to be safe in playing without supervision in a city park, neither of which she felt able to do where she lived before. . . . In Jerusalem, the normative structure ensures that unattended children will be "looked after" by adults in the vicinity, while no such normative structure exists in most metropolitan areas of the United States. One can say that families have available to them in Jerusalem social capital that does not exist in metropolitan areas of the United States.[25]

Just as this type of social capital may be greater in Jerusalem than in suburban Detroit, as Coleman observes, it appears to be greater in the suburbs of

25. Coleman (1988, pp. S99—S100).

Chicago than in its inner city. Coming out of the inner city, Gautreaux mothers perceived that children were kept under better control in the suburbs than they were in their city neighborhoods and that those normative constraints reduced the risks that their children would get hurt or get in trouble. Gautreaux participants in the suburbs reported feeling significantly stronger that a neighbor would help their children if they were in trouble than did Gautreaux participants in the city.[26] The qualitative data support and extend this finding, suggesting how Gautreaux mothers became reassured that their children were safe:

> You know, from moving from [the city], you've got peace and you've got quiet. You got neighbors that would look or [say], "I see your daughter running in so and so . . . ." But [in the city] it was nothing like that.

> If they see your children participating in an activity and they figure you're the type of person that doesn't allow that, they'll come and tell you, or they will try to talk to your child about it.

> We speak and we talk. We all show concern about, you know, the neighborhood and keeping it safe for the children and for ourselves. We all kind of watch, too, for the kids because we don't want anything happening around here.

In the city, in contrast, Gautreaux suburban movers reported that requests for aid in an emergency were regarded with suspicion, out of fear of retaliation or creating dependence relationships.[27] One possibility is that individuals' expectations about what kind of support is possible may change with a new experience. Suburban movers came to see their previous experiences somewhat differently after being exposed to unimagined suburban experiences. Adults' perception of neighborly support and safety in the city changed once the adults experienced the suburbs. Herbert Gans argues that suburbs are different not because of any ecological feature but because of selection: Suburbs attract middle-class households raising children. Because of their life stage and resources, the focus of these households is their children. In moving from the city to the suburbs, low-income Gautreaux mothers seem to be picking up on this theme, which they report was not as salient in the city. James Coleman notes that "intergenerational closure" (parents knowing each other and acting collectively for children's benefit) is an important resource for childrearing: "When the parents' friends are the parents of their children's friends, a closed community is formed in which behavior can be monitored and guided. Parents decide on norms and sanctions, monitor each other's children, and aid in child raising."[28]

In the context of the Yonkers housing mobility program for low-income families, moving to safer neighborhoods changes how parents manage risk for

26. Rubinowitz and Rosenbaum (2000, table 7).
27. Rainwater (1970).
28. Coleman (1988, pp. S106–S107).

their children. Parents in more dangerous areas closely regulate their children's neighborhood peer relationships, but those living in safer neighborhoods feel less need to do so.[29] Gautreaux mothers also describe the suburbs as much freer of violent crime and gang activity than their city neighborhoods were. They could let their children go out and play without hovering over them:

> In the suburbs there are no gangs. I don't have to stand in the window and watch out for my kids. They know not to leave the complex. Any time I call, they can hear me.

> The violence in the area was shocking and scary. . . . I was always uneased. . . . Here in the suburbs I don't have to worry about people shooting at people, seeing people chase people and shooting, fighting. . . . I didn't care too much for letting my daughter go out for fear of her life. I was always afraid that a fight would break out when she was down the street. . . . My fear was that a stray bullet would come from one of the higher floors, and you would never know who shot you.

> In the city . . . we were often broken into, robbed. . . . I used to always carry knife. Not anymore, since I moved out to suburbs. I feel safe night and day.

Ironically, the city environment, where everything was permitted, was like living in a prison. As two Gautreaux mothers describe it:

> I think it was the richness in the atmosphere that the children realized . . . they no longer had to be in the projects. They no longer had to dodge bricks and things coming in the building where they lived. Here, they could just sit out and enjoy themselves, and they did. And they just fit right in. They was more happy than I was, I believe, you know, just to get out of there. Because it was like living in a prison, you know. And when you can't go out whenever you like and play or whatever—I had to go out with my kids—it's hard. But up here, it's a lot different; it's quieter, much quieter. I'm able to sleep at night.

> I give them more leeway, more freedom. I don't try to enforce some of the rules I tried to enforce on my other kids. The neighborhood was a violent place, so I had to keep them inside most of the time because I feared for their lives. It's just an entirely different breed of people around here. These people are hardworking; they make money. Therefore, you don't have that much fear.

Social and Material Benefits

Where competing ideas about the power of place are concerned, the affluence hypothesis is problematic, because it lacks a mechanism. Living in the midst of

29. Briggs (1998, p. 203).

affluent neighbors does not automatically confer benefits on low-income people. Indeed, there were unforeseen new costs. Gautreaux mothers were surprised to find that suburban public libraries charged a fee for library cards, which were free in the city, and suburban summer camps and YMCAs charged a fee for their programs, which also were free in the city. In addition, summer activities sometimes filled up quickly, even before they were formally announced in the local paper. Affluent suburbs offered many opportunities, but barriers to access existed.

However, mothers report that they received many benefits through their relations with neighbors. Gautreaux mothers say that they feel able to ask for help from their neighbors, and they describe a living environment in which people help one another:

> I think if I needed something and went to them, it would be okay. For example, if my car broke down or if I had a flat, if they had the time, they would help me with it.

> We have a list of everyone's name, address, phones. You feel free to call them if you want to. They are all very nice neighbors. If they have prejudice, they don't let you know it. We get along. I think that's the way it should be . . . very friendly.

> When something went wrong [in the city, neighbors] wouldn't help each other. Stuff like that. There's a big difference out here.

Suburban Gautreaux mothers describe incidents when neighbors picked up each other's mail, shoveled snow off each other's sidewalks or driveways, borrowed cooking ingredients from each other, and offered to pick things up for each other at the store, as these mothers report:

> I guess I'm the closest to the lady across the hall. . . . She will get my mail for me. and I do the same for her. She looks out for my house.

> They [neighbors in suburbs] shovel my walkway. It's hard for me to do it in my condition. They have those snowblowers, and they come over and blow the walkway. Sometimes I come home from work and my yard is all shoveled, my garage. He doesn't have to do it. I got locked out, and he climbed up on the roof and let me in.

> The suburbs help you out more, and they have more to offer. . . . Out here when Christmastime comes they help you. They help the needy . . . whereas in the city, you're on your own.

> If I need anything, I have neighbors I can go to and say, "Well, I need an egg." It's nice to know that there's someplace you can go other than the neighborhood grocery store fifteen minutes away.

Especially during times of need, Gautreaux mothers were often pleasantly surprised by the neighborly behavior of suburban residents, who would bring gifts at times of celebration or provide extra help. Some mothers received acts of kindness like gifts for their newborn babies and meals for housewarming occasions.

> We let each other know if we need anything. When I had my baby, I was surprised because everyone came and brought gifts for her. They were nice. Once when I went to the hospital, a neighbor cooked dinner. . . . When I lived in Chicago, nothing like that ever happened.

> My neighbor right next door, she made me a casserole the very first day I moved in. And her kids came over to talk to me and to try to help me get my house together.

> My neighbor across the street came over when we first moved in to offer to help.

Similarly, other mothers report receiving passed-down items that their neighbors did not want.

> I just accumulated stuff. People would throw away stuff and would always remember to ask me if I wanted it. Or they are going to have a moving sale or a garage sale, and they always give me a deal on things. I've been very blessed. And this house—all the stuff—look at it. I'm proud of it. When I moved out here I had nothing. I've been carrying in all the stuff since I've been here. Most of it's hand-me-downs, but I like it. I'm very proud of what I got.

> He didn't have a bike, so the people in the community provided one. There's always a bike being handed down.

In emergencies, other suburban Gautreaux mothers report that neighbors came to their rescue:

> At Christmas when I had to bury the [stillborn] baby that I had, they didn't know, but when they found out, the phone was ringing and they were offering all sorts of help. . . . They were extremely for real about help. They offered to keep the kids.

> When my water pipe busted, we had to get water from the neighbors next door, who had just moved in, and they were always bringing things over.

> Once my lights were turned off, and out of the clear blue sky, she [a neighbor] gave me $50 to put on my lights. Now, you hardly find friends like that. So I could put her in the category of a friend.

In some cases, there were bartering relationships. Some Gautreaux mothers saw the situation as a system of give and take:

> You do something for me and I'll do something for you. It helps considerably when people don't have money. When people didn't have money before, they did something for you, and you turned around and did something for them. This is the way it was at the time when money was not so important. You could very easily get someone to vacuum the halls and take some off of their rent for doing that. . . . If my car broke down and I couldn't make it to work, they'd see to it that I got to work. If I got stranded at any time . . . if I needed anything, they were always there, and vice versa, because with five babies you were always needing.

Given the meager public transportation in the suburbs, transportation was often a problem. Some mothers had cars, but they were old vehicles that sometimes broke down. Gautreaux mothers report participating in car pools and receiving rides from their neighbors:

> It was a white girl across the hall. Now, she went out of her way to be nice . . . and she was taking me to work. And she was always on hand trying to help me.

> Any time my car would break, they [my neighbors] would take us somewhere.

> One teacher, like if I didn't have transportation for her [her daughter] to get to school, he'd see to her getting there.

> My neighbor down the way there, she's real nice. Because like on some days, like I work late, and [my daughter] didn't have her car, she would go and pick her up for me. Like when I had problems with my car, she would help out.

School activities required money and transportation. That could have been an obstacle, but sometimes school staff took steps to remove such obstacles:

> A teacher paid the way for my child to go to a ranch for three days with his class because I couldn't afford it.

> The school counselor took my daughter and other kids on ski trip and brought her home afterwards. . . . I don't think we would have got that in Chicago.

Gautreaux mothers report that neighbors frequently watched over their children and that they themselves looked after their neighbors' children:

> They [neighbors] used to babysit my son, and I'd take care of their daughter for a couple of hours.

> My daughter babysits two little boys of the very nice neighbors next door.

> If I need a favor from a neighbor, I can get it babysitting. I had no contact with neighbors in Chicago.

By sharing obligations and returning favors, Gautreaux's suburban mothers were able to enjoy the benefits of their new neighborhoods. Through their neighbors' attitudes about property upkeep, tranquility and order, safety, childcare, and neighborly assistance, Gautreaux participants were able to check their own behavior against those of their middle-class role models. In addition, Gautreaux mothers and children took advantage of the clean, quiet neighborhoods and safe, caring environments in which they found themselves. There they could live freely, as they could not before because of bad conditions in the inner city.

Social Capital

Social norms and reciprocity obligations provide a form of capital that enhances people's capabilities. Indeed, social norms and reciprocity obligations permitted Gautreaux mothers and children to develop capabilities that they would not have otherwise. Some mothers and children perceive their city neighbors' behaviors of damaging and vandalizing buildings and their failure to maintain them as signs of a more general attitude of "not caring" and a fatalistic acceptance of deplorable conditions. They seem to sense that their city neighbors did not care about anything, based on the physical decay and disorder that they saw everywhere:

> Over there [in the city], the kids didn't care about anything, you know. They'd break windows out, tear up gardens and . . . the flowers, shrubs, and everything. . . . These are the types of things they were looking at every day. So I feel that they [my children] might have grew up and started doing some of the same stuff those kids was doing. And I was just glad to get them out of there. . . . Here [in the suburbs] people like to keep up the, you know, the house, the apartment, the building, the grounds around the building.

Some participants even describe learning how to keep things nice from the example of their suburban neighbors and their well-kept environment:

> I don't like it [in the city] because some of the people would throw their trash all over the place. . . . They have parties in the middle of the night and wake people up. . . . [In the suburbs] you learned how to be, you learned how to take care of things better.

It is possible that the clear physical evidence that neighbors cared and would take action may have taught participants how to take similar actions and, generally, how to make a difference in their own lives. Of course, it is speculation that people's attitudes about their physical surroundings generalize to their behaviors in other domains. Less speculatively, Gautreaux mothers' ability to go out to work was clearly affected by the various kinds of social capital accessible in suburban neighborhoods. For example, one mother reports that relationships with her neighbors made it possible for her to make a commitment to a job. It made no sense for her otherwise, if she had to rely on her old, undependable car. But her neighbors provided a dependable backup option: "They'd see to it that I'd get to work if my car broke down."

Similarly, while many Gautreaux mothers report that they did not take jobs in the city because of the risk of being attacked on their way home from work in the dark, one suburban mover reports that a watchful neighbor allowed her to take a job that required her to come home late. "I usually come in at 10:00 p.m., and the man down on the first floor, he knows what time I come in. He usually stands at the door when I come in. The parking lot is too dark." Neighbors also permitted other mothers not to worry about their children while they were at work:

> A couple of times I asked her [a neighbor] if my son could stay here until I get home from work because he's afraid to stay here by himself. . . . If I call her and ask her if my son could stay over there, she always says yes. She never turned me down for any favors or anything like that.

> In the city, if you leave your nine- or eight-year-old child to watch his baby brother, you always have to keep calling home more often than you do here. Because the neighbors out here, they kind of help watch, too. . . . When I was working, I had the neighbor next door to make sure my son was going to school and make sure my door was locked. But in the city you just can't do that because everything would be gone.

> Or if my children need something and I'm not here, I make sure I've got a backup to get somebody here within a matter of minutes to take care of it. And I've got that. I don't have to worry about a thing. If I'm at work and I have to work a sixteen-hour shift or if something jumps up, I can call the young lady that used to live next door to me and tell her, "Hey, my kids are in a rut. I need you to go over there." She will get her husband to come home from work to get her car and come get my kids. . . . So it gives me pretty good reassurance that they'll be taken care of. And there's someone there that cares.

> My daughter was the only child, and I worked. I had a neighbor that had an extra key to my house because my daughter was a latchkey child, so I had a good neighbor. I would watch her kids, and she had three, and I knew her whole family, so she could check on my kid in case anything had happened.

> In order for me to go back to school at that time . . . I had got a babysitter next door. The lady introduced herself to me. So I got a chance to go to school and get some skills.

Conclusion

It is important to point out that the housing mobility program presented here—one experiment in expanding the geography of opportunity available to low-income minority families—imposes no formal responsibility on receiving communities. The program selects and places families, but they must make their own way in their new neighborhoods. Nor are the communities informed about the program, which works through the private rental housing market. While this may not be ideal from a policy perspective, it provides a fascinating test of community reaction. Our research suggests that, even without encouragement, suburban neighbors are often receptive and more accepting over time. While some harassment occurred at the outset, it had largely subsided by the end of the first year in the suburbs.

The reader must remember that this is not a quantitative study, and it does not reliably indicate the frequency of various behaviors and experiences. In a previous large survey, we examine the frequency of social interaction in the suburbs, but that survey cannot tell us how those social outcomes arose or what their consequences were. In addition, despite the positive results demonstrated in multivariate studies associating placement neighborhood conditions with other child and family outcomes, we cannot know the causal mechanisms behind those findings.[30] This requires that we look more closely at detailed qualitative accounts by participants, and that is the purpose of the present study. By looking at the detailed reports of families, we discover processes that may have important implications for understanding the possibilities of class and race integration in American society and for understanding the consequences of such integration.

As an extensive review concluded, "we need a deeper focus on cultural, normative, and collective action perspectives that attach meaning to how residents frame the commitment to places."[31] We need to understand how residents react to social mores, to whom they apply, and how residents qualify for the benefits conferred by norms of reciprocity. Social norms can be constraining. Some mothers note difficulties in adjusting to suburban norms, which were unfamiliar and intolerant of some of their previous behaviors. However, many of those mothers, who had lived all their lives in housing projects where those norms did not exist, saw benefits to complying with them, and they decided to adopt them and to behave accordingly.

In addition, perhaps most surprisingly, many respondents report that they did in fact benefit from those norms. Although such results may not be inevitable or even prevalent, sometimes movers from the inner city do benefit from the social responsiveness and social capital of white middle-class suburbs.

30. Rosenbaum and DeLuca (2000); DeLuca and Rosenbaum (2003, 2004).

31. Sampson, Morenoff, Gannon-Rowley (2002, p. 474).

The constraining norms meant that mothers in the program did not have to spend all their time watching their children and allowed them to give their children more freedom. In other words, normative constraints can be a form of social capital, though this is not inevitable. Indeed, if the initial mistrust by neighbors and police had continued, Gautreaux mothers and children would not have benefited. However, the normative consensus, which initially regarded these families skeptically and excluded them, shifted to include them. What could have been an exclusionary process, reducing families' capabilities, instead became social capital that enhanced their capabilities.

Similarly, the mothers report a social responsiveness that provided resources to them. They received the benefits of reciprocal relations related to child care and of neighbors' general concern and watchfulness in promoting the safety of their children, their property, and themselves. They received favors in terms of transportation and acts of charity. The former examples resemble Coleman's discussions of reciprocity, whereby mothers received and gave in approximately equal measure. These social capital benefits depend more on generalized reciprocity than on what these particular mothers did for their neighbors.[32] However, it is remarkable that these new residents, who generally differed in race and class from their neighbors, were awarded that generalized reciprocity, although such inclusionary gestures appear to have depended on their showing their willingness to abide by community norms.

Transportation favors, it is true, were more one-sided. Some Gautreaux mothers could not supply transportation to others because they had either an unreliable car or none at all. Charity was also one-sided, though some bartering may have happened. But acts of charity may be influenced by social capital processes. At a time when national political discourse was disparaging low-income, black, single mothers and setting time limits on their receipt of federal benefits, charity toward welfare mothers cannot be taken for granted.

These outcomes are not inevitable, and the underlying social capital is not a given. Participants could have refused to comply with suburban norms; and even if they complied, suburban neighbors could have refused to accept and help participants. Indeed, some suburban neighbors did not accept participants, and a few even engaged in acts of harassment. Interestingly, these unwelcoming acts prompted other neighbors to repudiate those acts.

Coleman may be right about the productive power of norms. Participants' compliance with community norms probably enhanced the perception that they were members of the community. Harassers' breaking of norms of decency may also have forced other neighbors to back the neighborhood norms of acceptance. It is possible that the families that were generous in giving gifts or assistance would not have done so if they had felt that the Gautreaux families were

32. Putnam (1993).

not members of their community, and some might have ignored their neighbors if harassment had not forced them to take a stand. In turn, community membership may prompt acceptance and generosity.

Most important, the social context provides a form of capital that enhances people's capabilities. As Coleman points out, social norms and reciprocity obligations conferred capabilities on Gautreaux mothers and children that they would not have had otherwise. Just as eyeglasses are a form of physical capital that permits people to see, the social capital in suburban neighborhoods enabled mothers to engage in various activities because it freed them of the need to spend every moment watching their children. Some mothers report that they could count on neighbors if a child misbehaved or seemed at risk of getting into trouble, if a child was sick and could not attend school, or if there was some threat to their children, their apartments, or themselves. Social support that provides occasional assistance may be considered a form of social capital. It permits individuals to take individual actions when the opportunity presents itself, but it may not permit them to make an enduring commitment. A friendly neighbor's offer to watch a ten-year-old child permits a parent to make a quick trip to the store, but a neighborhood commitment to watching and protecting all children may permit a parent to make a commitment to a job. That is not just interpersonal support, it is systemic, and that is the form of social capital that enabled these mothers to take actions and make commitments that otherwise would be difficult or risky.

Many people assume that the effects of residential mobility experiments derive from an affluent context and greater material resources. We suggest another possible mechanism: Social capital provides benefits and even resources. Social normative support and the reciprocal benefits of safety, transportation, child care, and community watchfulness over children and property may be related to community affluence, but it is possible that they could occur in communities that are not highly affluent. Indeed, there may be trade-offs as families move away from the strong ties of low-income kin and old friends to the weaker ties of middle-class neighbors in a safe environment where they can count on their neighbors.[33] The relationship of social capital to affluence is not entirely clear at present. Now that these processes have been identified, research can quantitatively analyze their incidence and preconditions.

These findings also raise questions about the issue of individual preferences. Before moving to the suburbs, most participants were very reluctant to leave their city neighborhoods, and understandably so. They were moving to places far from their original neighborhoods and friends. They were moving to neighborhoods in which the social norms were radically different from theirs. The movers often expected racial harassment. Indeed, even after moving, many participants

33. Briggs (1998).

felt serious doubts about what they were doing, many had difficulty adjusting to the new set of expectations, many considered moving back to their old neighborhoods, and some actually did. However, we found that only 30 percent of suburb movers had returned to the city an average of seventeen years after placement. Why is that?

The present findings suggest that regardless of their initial preferences, participants came to accept the suburban norms. They decided to adopt these new norms, and they received substantial benefits from complying with them. These participants might not have chosen to live in the suburbs if they had been offered an alternative safe environment. But the vast majority did not return to the city. We believe that many Gautreaux participants became different people: They had different norms, different preferences, and different expectations. Just as Coleman suggests, they acquired capabilities from living in the suburbs and from becoming suburbanites, and if Coleman is correct, they would have lost those capabilities had they returned to their old city neighborhoods.

References

Briggs, Xavier de Souza. 1997. "Moving up versus Moving Out: Neighborhood Effects in Housing Mobility Programs." *Housing Policy Debate* 8, no. 1: 195–234.

———. 1998. "Brown Kids in White Suburbs: Housing Mobility and Social Capital." *Housing Policy Debate* 9, no. 1: 177–221.

Brooks-Gunn, Jeanne, and others. 1993. "Do Neighborhoods Influence Child and Adolescent Development?" *American Journal of Sociology* 99, no. 2: 353–95.

Carneiro, P., and James Heckman. 2003. "Human Capital Policy." Working Paper 9495. Cambridge, Mass.: National Bureau of Economic Research.

Coleman, James S. 1988. "Social Capital in the Creation of Human Capital." *American Journal of Sociology* 94 (supp.): S95–S120.

Corcoran, Mary, and others. 1990. "The Association between Men's Economic Status and Their Family and Community Origins." *Journal of Human Resources* 27, no. 4: 575–601.

Crane, Jonathan. 1991. "The Epidemic Theory of Ghettos and Neighborhood Effects on Dropping out and Teenage Childbearing." *American Journal of Sociology* 96, no. 5: 1226–59.

Datcher, Linda. 1982. "Effects of Community and Family Background on Achievement." *Review of Economics and Statistics* 64: 32–41.

DeLuca, Stefanie, and James E. Rosenbaum. 2000. "The Long-Term Effects of Residential Location." Paper prepared for the international meeting on socioeconomics, London School of Economics, London, July 7–10.

———. 2001. "Residential Mobility Effects on Women and Children." Paper prepared for the biennial meeting of the Society for Research on Child Development, Minneapolis, April.

———. 2003. "If Low-Income Blacks Are Given a Chance to Live in White Neighborhoods, Will They Stay? Examining Mobility Patterns in a Quasi-Experimental Program with Administrative Data." *Housing Policy Debate* 14: 305–46.

———. 2004. "Special Education and Neighborhoods: Does Social Context Affect Diagnosis?" Institute for Social Policy, Northwestern University.

Gans, Herbert. 1967. *The Levittowners.* New York: Vintage.

Jencks, Christopher, and Susan Mayer. 1990. "The Social Consequences of Growing up in a Poor Neighborhood." In *Inner-City Poverty in the United States,* edited by Laurence E. Lynn and Michael G. H. McGeary, pp. 111–86. Washington: National Academy Press.

Katz, Lawrence F., Jeffrey Kling, and Jeffrey Liebman. 1997. "Moving to Opportunity in Boston: Early Impacts of a Housing Mobility Program." Cambridge, Mass.: National Bureau of Economic Research.

Lang, Robert, and Steven Hornburg. 1998. "What Is Social Capital and Why Is It Important to Public Policy?" *Housing Policy Debate* 9, no. 1: 1–16.

Ludwig, Jens, Paul Hirschfield, and Greg Duncan. 2001. "Urban Poverty and Juvenile Crime." *Quarterly Journal of Economics* 116, no. 2: 665–79.

Mendenhall, Ruby, Greg Duncan, and Stefanie DeLuca. 2004. "Neighborhood Resources and Economic Mobility: Results from the Gautreaux Program." Institute for Social Policy, Northwestern University.

Portes, Alejandro. 1998. "Social Capital: Its Origins and Applications in Modern Sociology." *Annual Review of Sociology* 24: 1–24.

Putnam, Robert. 1993. *Making Democracy Work.* Princeton University Press.

Rainwater, Lee. 1970. *Behind the Ghetto Walls.* Chicago: Aldine.

Riesman, David. 1950. *The Lonely Crowd: A Study of the Changing American Character.* Yale University Press.

Rosenbaum, James E., and Stefanie DeLuca. 2000. "Is Housing Mobility the Key to Welfare Reform?" Survey Series. Metropolitan Policy Program, Brookings Institution, September.

Rubinowitz, Len, and James E. Rosenbaum. 2000. *Crossing the Class and Color Lines: From Public Housing to White Suburbia.* University of Chicago Press.

Sampson, Robert J., Jeffrey Morenoff, and Felton Earls. 1999. "Beyond Social Capital: Spatial Dynamics of Collective Efficacy for Children." *American Sociological Review* 64: 633–60.

Sampson, Robert J., Jeffrey D. Morenoff, and Thomas Gannon-Rowley. 2002. "Assessing Neighborhood Effects: Social Processes and New Directions in Research." *Annual Review of Sociology* 28: 443–78.

Sampson, Robert J., Stephen Raudenbush, and Felton Earls. 1997. "Neighborhoods and Violent Crime: A Multilevel Study of Collective Efficacy." *Science* 277: 918–24.

Turner, Marjorie Austin. 1998. "Moving out of Poverty: Expanding Mobility and Choice through Tenant Based Housing Assistance." *Housing Policy Debate* 9, no. 2: 373–94.

Wells, Amy Stuart, and Robert L. Crain. 1997. *Stepping over the Color Line.* Yale University Press.

Whyte, William H. 1956. *The Organization Man.* New York: Doubleday.

8

Beyond the Projects: Lessons from Public Housing Transformation in Chicago

SUSAN J. POPKIN AND MARY K. CUNNINGHAM

The 1990s brought a dramatic shift in federal policy affecting low-income households, most visible in the large-scale transformation of public housing nationwide. Nowhere has this happened on a grander scale than in Chicago. For decades, Chicago's high-rise "projects," clustered in inner-city ghettos, symbolized public housing's worst failures. Deliberately sited in racially segregated communities and cut off from the rest of the city by major expressways, these decaying developments were mired in what has been called the most destructive kind of poverty: thousands of extremely low-income, female-headed households struggling in communities dominated by gangs and drug traffickers.[1]

Under agreement with the federal government, the Chicago Housing Authority (CHA) is now demolishing these high-rise projects, relocating their residents, and planning to replace the projects with new, mixed-income housing. Thousands of extremely poor families still live in these developments, and what the transformation means for them is unclear. This process may offer residents new opportunities if policymakers make a serious effort to overcome the mistakes of the past and adopt regionwide strategies that prevent reconcentration and resegregation. However, successfully transforming these dysfunctional communities is extremely challenging, and there is the very real possibility that some proportion

This study was funded by the John D. and Catherine T. MacArthur Foundation.

1. Blank (1997).

of residents may end up worse off—living in other poor, minority communities, losing their housing assistance, or even becoming homeless.

By many measures, Chicago's situation was unusual. The CHA was one of the largest housing authorities in the country and faced some of the worst challenges. By the 1990s Chicago's high-rise public housing had become emblematic of the failures of federal housing policy. The agency's long history of management and maintenance problems left it with more distressed public housing than any other housing authority in the nation. As a result, the scope of the CHA's plan for transformation was far more ambitious than any other housing authority's plan. In addition to the sheer magnitude of the problems in Chicago, because of the agency's controversial history it faced a much higher level of public scrutiny than other housing authorities. In 1999, after more than five years of litigation and controversy, the CHA put in place a resident rights contract that called for continued independent monitoring throughout the transformation process.

In addition to these specific challenges, Chicago faced many of the same challenges as other housing authorities, such as impoverished residents with complex needs, the need for supportive services, tight rental markets, and the difficulties of negotiating the myriad federal and local regulations affecting the major federal initiative driving the transformation of distressed public housing developments, HOPE VI. Policymakers can draw a number of lessons from the Chicago experience. In particular, the transformation process in Chicago highlights the risks for residents and the struggles that housing authorities face in trying to balance concerns about residents' rights with local political pressures to remove blight, revitalize neighborhoods, and prevent the destabilization of other communities. Drawing on data from a longitudinal study of 190 households that entered the relocation process in 1999, we find that although some former residents have clearly benefited, many are still struggling. Despite the housing authority's stated intentions to promote mobility, thus far relocation has reinforced existing patterns of racial segregation. Further, many vulnerable families appear to be at risk of losing their housing assistance altogether.

The Federal HOPE VI Program

HOPE VI was created by Congress in 1992 to

—improve the living environment for residents of severely distressed public housing through the demolition, rehabilitation, reconfiguration, or replacement of obsolete projects (or portions thereof);

—revitalize sites on which such public housing projects are located and contribute to the improvement of the surrounding neighborhood;

—provide housing that will avoid or decrease the concentration of very-low-income families; and

—build sustainable communities.[2]

Since 1992 the U.S. Department of Housing and Urban Development (HUD) awarded 466 HOPE VI grants in 166 cities.[3] To date 63,100 severely distressed units have been demolished and another 20,300 units are slated for demolition.[4] In total, developments that were awarded HOPE VI grants through 2003 account for 94,600 public housing units; about two-thirds of these were occupied at the time of grant award. Current plans call for the construction of 95,100 replacement units, but only 48,800 of these will receive the deep, permanent public housing subsidies necessary to reach households with very low incomes. The remainder will receive shallower subsidies (and serve families not necessarily eligible for public housing) or no subsidies (and serve market-rate renters or even homebuyers). Although many of these subsidies will be replaced with rent vouchers, the potential loss of housing for the lowest income households remains one of the most controversial aspects of the HOPE VI program.[5]

The HOPE VI program came under fire during the fiscal year 2003 reauthorization process. The Bush administration proposed eliminating funding for the program in its fiscal year 2004 and fiscal year 2005 budget submissions, citing long delays between grant awards and the completion of revitalization projects at many sites; indeed, by 2003 only fifteen HOPE VI sites were complete.[6] Congress reauthorized the program through fiscal year 2006, but at a substantially lower level of funding. Despite this controversy, a comprehensive review by the Urban Institute and the Brookings Institution concludes that the evidence strongly supports continuation of the HOPE VI program. It also highlights critical areas where the program should be strengthened.[7] As of this writing the policy debate has expanded to encompass the rent voucher program, and the future of the HOPE VI program remains unclear.

Research on Public Housing Transformation

Because it targets developments with extremely low-income populations, the HOPE VI program affects some of the nation's most disadvantaged families, including large numbers of single female–headed households with young

2. Section 24 of the *United States Housing Act of 1937* as amended by section 535 of the *Quality Housing and Work Responsibility Act of 1998* (Public Law 105-276).

3. Popkin, Katz, and others (2004).

4. Holin and others (2003).

5. Popkin, Katz, and others (2004).

6. Holin and others (2003).

7. Popkin, Katz, and others (2004).

children. Many residents lack formal education, work experience, or marketable skills. In addition, there is evidence that a significant proportion of residents in the worst developments suffer from ills such as substance abuse, mental illness, domestic violence, and trauma from long-term exposure to violent crime.[8] As in Chicago, neighborhoods with HOPE VI developments are often isolated central-city communities with poor schools and inadequate city services. Because of their complex situations and lack of resources, many of these families may face special challenges in making a transition to a new housing development or to the private market.

Critics of HOPE VI argue that the program has actually made the situation worse for public housing residents.[9] They claim that the program has targeted developments that were not truly distressed, that it has substantially reduced the amount of affordable housing in many cities, and that former residents have been excluded from new, mixed-income developments. Further, these critics note that relatively little data are available to assess program performance, particularly data that would speak to how residents have fared during public housing transformation.

The research that does exist, including our site-based study, finds that relatively few original residents have returned to the revitalized sites.[10] However, many HOPE VI sites are only partially reoccupied, so the number of original residents who will ultimately return to the revitalized sites is unknown. An analysis of HUD administrative data for former residents at seventy-three HOPE VI sites in forty-eight cities shows that about one-third of former residents have received vouchers, half have relocated to other public housing developments, and the remainder have left subsidized housing.[11] This research suggests that residents may have ended up in at least somewhat better neighborhoods—the average census tract poverty rate for those who received vouchers dropped from 61 percent to 27 percent. About 40 percent were living in high-poverty tracts (greater than 30 percent poor); in contrast, 13 percent had moved to truly low-poverty neighborhoods, with poverty rates of less than 10 percent. The study finds less evidence of improvements in racial segregation, with the majority of households still living in tracts with predominantly minority populations.[12]

8. Popkin, Gwiasda, and others (2000).

9. Compare National Housing Law Project (2002).

10. Buron and others (2002); Keating (2000); Kingsley, Johnson, and Pettit (2000); Wexler (2000).

11. Kingsley, Johnson, and Pettit (2000). HUD is currently working on an analysis of the locations of all voucher holders nationwide.

12. Other studies, including the HOPE VI Retrospective Tracking Study (Buron and others 2002) and single-site studies in Chicago and Washington (Cunningham, Sylvester, and Turner 2000); Cunningham and Popkin (2002) find similar results.

The largest and most systematic study of outcomes for original residents is the HOPE VI Resident Tracking Study, a retrospective survey of former residents of eight HOPE VI sites where redevelopment began between 1993 and 1998.[13] The findings from this research suggest that many new housing environments for these relocated residents are an improvement over their former housing environments. A majority of the original residents in the study sample reported that they now lived in decent housing and in neighborhoods with lower poverty rates than their former neighborhoods. However, as in the national analysis, nearly all were still living in predominantly minority communities. Further, a substantial proportion of those who were living in public housing or had vouchers reported problems with drug trafficking and violent crime in their neighborhoods, and more than half of those in the private market—voucher users and unsubsidized households—reported having problems meeting housing expenses.[14]

The HOPE VI Panel Study is tracking residents from five housing developments over a four-year period as they go through the relocation process.[15] Baseline findings from this study indicate that residents have faced significant challenges. They were living in terrible conditions—worse than those reported by other poor renters nationwide. Further, the housing developments were extremely dangerous, with majorities of respondents reporting serious problems with drug trafficking and violent crime. These respondents—both adults and children—also faced numerous personal challenges, including physical and mental health problems, histories of domestic violence or substance abuse, criminal records, or poor credit histories.[16] Not surprisingly, fewer than half of these residents were employed before relocation. These findings suggest that for many current residents public housing transformation may be a difficult and risky process. Findings from the follow-up in 2003 indicate that residents who had been relocated—particularly those who had received vouchers—were living in substantially better housing in dramatically lower-poverty and safer neighborhoods and that their children were attending better schools.[17] However, the

13. Buron and others (2002).

14. However, the Resident Tracking Study has some significant limitations. Because it is retrospective, there is no information on residents' perceptions of their living conditions or economic struggles before HOPE VI. Further, because of the retrospective design, the sample underrepresents both unsubsidized tenants and others who were difficult to locate. In general, those who are difficult to find are those who move frequently, double up with another family, are homeless, or have moved out of the area—in other words, those who are likely to have experienced more problems than those the researchers were able to survey.

15. Popkin, Levy, and others (2002).

16. More than one-third of adult respondents reported having a chronic illness or health condition, such as high blood pressure, diabetes, or arthritis. Further, more than one-fifth of adults have asthma. Nearly one in three respondents (29 percent) reported poor mental health, almost 50 percent higher than the national average. Further, nearly one in six adults had experienced a major depressive episode within the past twelve months. See Popkin, Levy, and others (2002).

17. Comey (2004); Buron (2004); Popkin, Eiseman, and Cove (2004).

findings also highlight the severity of the health challenges facing these residents: Obesity was epidemic; three-quarters of the respondents suffered from a serious, chronic health problem; one in five suffered from depression; and many were still struggling to sustain employment.[18]

Public Housing Transformation, Chicago

Chicago, with its extraordinary number of distressed developments, has been by far the biggest beneficiary of the HOPE VI program. Since 1994 the CHA has received eight HOPE VI redevelopment grants and twenty-seven demolition grants, totaling over $327 million. Under its plan for transformation, the CHA will redevelop or rehabilitate 25,000 units of public housing; however, the plan calls for a substantial reduction in family public housing units (a net loss of 14,000 units). The original plan called for the relocation of as many as 6,000 families with housing choice vouchers (Section 8).[19] This plan, including relocation and revitalization, is estimated to cost at least $1.5 billion over ten years.

Numerous factors contributed to the CHA's exceptional problems with its housing. At the most basic level, the housing authority was simply very large, overseeing more than 40,000 family units, most poorly constructed, poorly maintained, and in desperate need of repair. Exacerbating its problems, the CHA had a long history of bad—and often corrupt—management. Finally, the size of the agency's developments and their location in isolated, high-poverty communities made them ideal environments for drug dealing and violent crime.

By the late 1980s, the CHA was in crisis, with its management in chaos and its developments rapidly deteriorating. Crime was so extreme that the agency was forced to devote the bulk of its capital and operating funds to security.[20] Despite these measures, the situation continued to deteriorate, precipitating a HUD takeover of the CHA in 1995. As part of the takeover, the new HUD-appointed administration contracted out the agency's housing choice voucher program.[21]

Since the CHA plan for transformation was approved in 1999 the agency has demolished nearly 7,000 units, including 2,199 in fiscal year 2002. It has rehabilitated over 2,000 units, primarily in buildings for senior citizens, and begun construction on several small, mixed-income developments.[22] Nearly 2,400 families have been relocated, about half in public housing and half with vouchers.[23]

18. Harris and Kaye (2004); Levy and Kaye (2004).

19. Based on its experience with the first three years of its plan, the CHA now believes that this figure will ultimately be lower than originally estimated. The *Quality Housing and Work Responsibility Act of 1998* merged the section 8 certificate and voucher program into one, to create the housing choice voucher program.

20. Popkin, Gwiasda, and others (2000).

21. For a detailed history of the CHA, see Popkin, Gwiasda, and others (2000). For more on the recent history of the section 8 program in Chicago, see Popkin and Cunningham (2000).

22. Chicago Housing Authority (various years: 2002).

23. Metropolitan Planning Council (2003).

The Relocation of Residents, Chicago

Unlike other cities, Chicago has a long history of attempts to offer public housing residents mobility opportunities. In principle, the CHA sought to take a regional approach to relocation and attempted to avoid creating new clusters of poverty. The Gautreaux mobility program, devised as a result of a settlement with HUD in the landmark housing desegregation case of that name, provided vouchers and counseling that helped more than 7,000 CHA families to move to nonminority areas between 1976 and 1999.[24] A similar program was started to serve suburban Cook County residents in the late 1980s. Chicago was also a site for the Moving to Opportunity demonstration in the mid-1990s. Building on that experience, CHAC Inc., the organization that administers the housing choice voucher program, initiated an in-house mobility program in 2000.[25] Given this history, it is not surprising that advocates, including the *Gautreaux* attorneys, began pressuring the CHA to emphasize mobility in its relocation planning.

The overarching goals of the CHA's relocation services reflect this emphasis on mobility and deconcentration; these goals are to help participants make good housing choices for themselves and their families, to help participants make a successful transition to the private market, and to prevent the creation of clusters of relocatees in other high-poverty neighborhoods. At this time the CHA and HUD contracted with the University of Illinois's Great Cities Institute to examine if there were enough units in the private market to absorb public housing families. The study revealed that, at least on paper, there were enough units. However, it was unclear if public housing relocatees had the capacity to find and obtain those units and if landlords would accept Section 8 vouchers in such a tight rental market. Designing an effective system to overcome these barriers and carry out the CHA's goals proved to be extremely difficult.

During the period of our study (1999–2002), the CHA continuously revamped its relocation services in response to problems and political challenges that arose during implementation. The agency's first attempt at relocation illustrates the enormous challenges involved. In September 1999 the CHA closed eleven buildings, moving many of their tenants to temporary units in "cluster buildings," which were located within the development but not yet scheduled for demolition. Over 800 of these households indicated on their housing choice surveys that they had selected housing choice vouchers as their first choice for relocation. (The families in our study sample are from this pool of residents.)

24. The primary cases involved were *Gautreaux* v. *Chicago Housing Authority,* 304 F. Supp. 736 (N.D. Ill. 1969), enforcing 296 F. Supp. 907 (N.D. Ill. 1969); *Gautreaux* v. *Landrieu,* 523 F. Supp. 665, 674 (N.D. Ill. 1981). Also see Rubinowitz and Rosenbaum (2000).

25. Cunningham and Popkin (2002).

The CHA contracted with three agencies to provide relocation counseling for these residents: Changing Patterns for Families, Family Dynamics, and the Leadership Council for Metropolitan Open Communities. The Leadership Council had administered the Gautreaux program; the selection of this agency indicated the CHA's intention to stress mobility in its relocation efforts.

This new relocation process did not go smoothly. First, by closing the eleven buildings all at once, the housing authority overwhelmed the counseling agencies and the housing choice voucher program. The agencies did not have enough time for start-up and staff training and simply could not cope with the sudden influx of clients. Inevitably, some relocatees slipped through the cracks and never received the services promised by the housing authority. Second, the agencies were not prepared for the difficulty of the task—most staff were unfamiliar with housing counseling, and the agencies were not equipped to deal with CHA residents' level of need for supportive services. Finally, there was a serious lack of coordination and communication—between the housing authority and its contractors, between the counseling agencies and the voucher program, and among the three relocation agencies themselves—which undermined the entire process.[26]

Because of the problems encountered during the first phase of relocation, the CHA's main resident organization, the Central Advisory Council, negotiated a formal contract to spell out the CHA's obligations to residents during the transformation process. The Relocation Rights Contract, signed in November 2000, states that all lease-compliant tenants living in CHA housing as of October 1999 were guaranteed a right to return to public housing.[27] In addition, the contract spells out the process for residents to select replacement housing and defines the services that would be offered to residents during the transformation, including supportive services, relocation assistance, and mobility counseling. Finally, the contract requires the appointment of a special monitor to audit the relocation process; however, this monitor did not begin work until the spring of 2002.

Following the signing of the Relocation Rights Contract, the CHA substantially reorganized its counseling services. In September 2000 the housing authority issued a new counseling request for proposals for a modified set of

26. For a thorough discussion of the problems encountered during the first phase of relocation, see Popkin, Cunningham, and Godfrey (2001).

27. The contract defines lease-compliant tenants as those who were up to date on their rent and utility payments or repayment agreement; were compliant with terms of the August 15, 2000, lease and federal requirements (including one-strike provisions that disqualify any tenant with household members who have evidence of involvement in drug or felony activity); had no unauthorized tenants in their units; and had a good housekeeping record, with no documented evidence of destruction, damage, or removal of CHA property in CHA files. See CHA Leaseholder Housing Choice and Relocation Rights Contract, November 2000. This document is available at the CHA website (www.thecha.org/partners/relocation/relocation_rights.html).

services, to include preparing relocatees for the private market, assisting them with the search for housing, and providing relocation counseling. In April 2001 the CHA contracted with two agencies (Changing Patterns and E. F. Ghoughan Inc.) to provide these services. Relocation counseling was supposed to include providing information on neighborhoods, identifying housing units, escorting clients to housing units, and assisting clients in completing the paperwork for the voucher process. In addition, the agencies were to provide budgeting and credit counseling, to assess clients' needs, and to follow up with visits after clients moved into their new housing. Finally, the CHA created two new supportive services that were to serve all residents and help them prepare for relocation: Good Neighbor workshops, to provide all residents with training in good tenant behavior, and the Service Connector, to do case management and referral to community services for residents who needed assistance in becoming lease compliant.

In addition to standard relocation counseling for residents who were moved out of the buildings slated for demolition and who chose vouchers, the CHA contracted with the Leadership Council to provide help to any CHA resident interested in moving to an opportunity area.[28] The Leadership Council began implementing this program in late 2001. The request for proposals for the third round of mobility counseling in 2002 placed even more emphasis on mobility, requiring all counseling providers to show clients at least one unit in an opportunity area.

Assessing the CHA Mobility Program

Despite the fact that the CHA plan for transformation, particularly its potential impact on residents, has been extremely controversial since its inception, there has been only limited information available about how residents have fared under the plan. The CHA Relocation and Mobility Counseling Assessment was intended to help address the need for information by systematically documenting the experiences of a sample of residents as they went through the relocation process.[29] The study involved multiple methods:

—A three-wave panel survey of a sample of approximately 190 CHA residents awaiting relocation through Section 8. The CHA relocatees in our sample were all leaseholders slated to move during the first phase of relocation. They had selected Section 8 rent vouchers as their first option for relocation in September 1999, when their buildings were closed, but they still had not relocated by the winter of 2000. A baseline survey was administered in spring 2000, with

28. These areas are defined as Chicago census tracts in which the poverty rate is less than 24 percent and the African American population is less than 30 percent; or as suburban census tracts that are less than 10 percent poor and less than 10 percent African American.

29. Popkin, Cunningham, and Godfrey (2001); also see Cunningham and Popkin (2002).

follow-up surveys occurring at approximately six-month intervals in fall 2000 and spring 2001.

—In-depth interviews with CHA relocatees, focusing on their experiences with the counseling programs in May 2000, March 2001, and March 2002.

—Administrative interviews with staff from CHA's contract counseling agencies.[30] Project staff conducted group interviews with CHA staff and counseling program administrators in January 2000 and held interviews and program observations from April to August 2000. Finally, project staff conducted follow-up interviews with program administrators and other key actors involved in the relocation process in the winter of 2001 and the spring of 2002.[31]

Because they were part of the first group of tenants referred for relocation, the respondents in our study sample were affected by all of the changes during the first phase of implementation of the transformation plan. They experienced the first attempt to provide relocation counseling services in 1999; some of them relocated during that period, but most ended up in "consolidation buildings" in their developments. Presumably, these residents—who had not left CHA housing—then went through Good Neighbor counseling, housing choice clinics, and the new housing choice survey, and some were assigned to new counseling agencies. For this reason, although they do not represent the full spectrum of CHA tenants and are probably among those facing the greatest challenges, their experiences illustrate the challenges facing residents affected by public housing transformation.[32]

Findings from the Relocation and Counseling Assessment

Research on national populations of low-income households suggests that those who live in public housing are generally more disadvantaged—having lower income, less work history, and lower levels of education—than other welfare

30. Between February 2000 and December 2001, these agencies were the Leadership Council for Metropolitan Open Communities, Family Dynamics, Changing Patterns for Families, and E. F. Ghoughan.

31. These key actors include CHA administrative staff; staff from the MacArthur Foundation working with the CHA; attorneys representing CHA tenants from Business and Professional People for the Public Interest (BPI), the Legal Assistance Foundation, and the National Center for Poverty Law; resident leaders from the Local Advisory Council and from the Coalition to Protect Public Housing; staff from the *Resident's Journal;* staff from the Metropolitan Planning Council; administrators from CHA's counseling agencies and CHAC; journalists writing about CHA-related issues; and researchers studying issues related to the CHA transformation plan.

32. Overall, we were able to complete follow-up surveys with about 73 percent of the original sample of 190, or 139 households. At the twelve-month follow-up, we were unable to locate 30 respondents; another 6 respondents had died, and 2 refused to participate. The whereabouts of the remaining respondents are unknown; some may have moved using a voucher, others may have moved to a different public housing unit, and some may have moved independently. See Cunningham and Popkin (2002) for a full discussion of survey methodology and response rates.

recipients.[33] The group of residents we tracked through the relocation process were significantly more disadvantaged than a similar group of residents participating in the housing choice voucher program during the same period.[34] All were African American, most were female, and over half (59 percent) had three or more children in their household. Most were long-term public housing residents, having lived in CHA housing for more than ten years. Nearly all (84 percent) had incomes below $10,000 a year, two-thirds had not finished high school, and only about a third were employed at the time of the survey.

These residents also faced significant personal challenges. Many were in poor health—34 percent reported that their health was only "fair" or "poor," and 50 percent reported that they or a family member had asthma. Further, these respondents had relatively low levels of personal efficacy, an indicator of how much control people have over their lives. Low levels of efficacy are associated with depression, long-term welfare recipiency, and very low expectations of improvement—in this instance, improving their housing situations.[35] Approximately 40 percent of the respondents scored themselves as "depressed," and 10 percent of these scored as "moderately" or "very" depressed.[36]

The findings from our study indicate how much more difficult the CHA's transformation process was to implement than originally anticipated. Most striking, although the CHA's annual plans call for the relocation of hundreds of families each calendar year, the number of households that moved was quite small.[37] At the six-month follow-up only thirty-six families (23 percent of the sample) had moved out of public housing into a private market unit. Six months later, only another seventeen households had moved successfully. Thus during the twelve months we monitored these families, just fifty-five (38 percent) managed to move to a private market unit with a voucher, while the rest remained in public housing—either in the same unit or in a consolidation building.

There are relatively few statistically significant differences between those who succeeded in moving and those who did not.[38] However, nonmovers did seem to

33. Zedlewski (2002).

34. See Popkin, Cunningham, and Godfrey (2001).

35. See Popkin (1990); Popkin, Cunningham, and Godfrey (2001).

36. The Center for Epidemiological Studies Depression Scale (CES-D) was used at the six-month and twelve-month follow-ups to assess respondents' degree of depression. The scale employs twenty questions about the frequency with which each of twenty events was experienced during the previous week. The weighted answers are added to create the depression score, which ranges from zero to sixty. Respondents with a depression score of sixteen or more are considered depressed.

37. CHA (various years).

38. At the twelve-month follow-up, the number of movers was large enough for us to be able to explore some of the factors associated with making a successful move. Those who moved tended to have fewer children and to report being employed at the time of the survey. However, they did not differ from nonmovers on a range of other characteristics, such as age, education, income, welfare receipt, health status, or access to a working car. See Popkin and Cunningham (2000) for more detail.

face personal barriers that likely made it more difficult for them to make a successful transition out of public housing. Nonmovers were consistently more than twice as likely as those who had moved successfully to report having paid their rent late in the past six months (40 percent versus 15 percent). Another indicator of possible credit problems was that twice as many nonmovers (42 percent) as movers (21 percent) said that they had not been able to afford a telephone in the past six months. Further, nonmovers were also significantly more likely to report worrying about not having enough food and cutting meals because they could not afford food. Because nonmovers had more lease-compliance problems than movers, they might well have had more problems with lack of resources or with budget management.

Our findings indicate that those residents who did succeed in moving ended up in better housing in safer and less poor neighborhoods than their original public housing community. Virtually all of the CHA's developments had poverty rates that exceeded 60 percent—indeed, nine of the poorest census tracts in the United States were in CHA housing.[39] Therefore, moving out of CHA housing almost necessarily meant at least minimal improvement. For our sample, the average reduction in neighborhood poverty for these households was 42 percentage points, meaning that there was a striking improvement in conditions for most of these families.

However, even with this substantial reduction, many of the neighborhoods these households are living in are still very poor. More than half (55 percent) are living in communities with poverty rates greater than 40 percent; only 11 percent (six households) are living in neighborhoods less than 20 percent poor, and only three of those households moved to extremely low-poverty neighborhoods (less than 10 percent). All of the moves were made within the city. Further, while many of these households have experienced a substantial reduction in poverty, there has been less change in racial segregation—the majority of movers are living in neighborhoods that are more than 90 percent African American.

One analysis of the neighborhood characteristics for *all* former CHA residents who have been relocated with vouchers since 1995 provides further indication that public housing transformation may simply be reconcentrating CHA residents in other poor, African American communities.[40] While racial segregation in Chicago has decreased slightly overall, it persists, particularly on the south and west sides of the city.[41]

Although they were still living in poor, racially segregated neighborhoods, the movers in our sample clearly perceived a substantial impact on their overall

39. Popkin, Gwiasda, and others (2000).
40. Fischer (2003).
41. Stuart (2000).

well-being as a result of these incremental improvements.[42] They consistently reported much better conditions than at baseline and than their counterparts who remained in public housing. In particular, these movers reported significant improvements in their housing conditions. At each wave, we asked respondents about a range of problems with their housing, including peeling paint, broken plumbing, rats or mice, roaches, broken locks, and heat that does not work. Findings from these follow-up surveys indicate that movers were significantly less likely to report any of these problems than those still living in CHA developments. Further, just 12 percent of movers reported having at least one "big problem" with their housing, compared with 53 percent of nonmovers.[43]

While most of the women we interviewed said that their new apartments were "much better," a few complained of problems such as lack of space or poor maintenance. Further, several spoke about the new challenges of living in the private market: less stable housing, difficulties in paying utility bills, and loss of the supportive services they had relied on.

> In [CHA] housing you can call in a work order. . . . They might not get to it right now, [but they will] in a week or so later. You don't worry about a gas bill, but you do worry about housing maintaining heat. You never worry about a threat that your water was about to get cut off. When you had a problem with your light bill, it was easier for you being in public housing to go to a program and get help, but it's not so [easy] once you're not there. You have the threat of [Section 8] inspectors coming around . . . harassing you about things . . . and you're not the landlord. You got threats of the water company coming and giving you cutoff notes. When the gas company cuts off your gas . . . it's off. It ain't like somebody's going to come in the middle of the night and see what's going on. Your lights, when they turn them off, then comes the panic.

In spite of such problems, movers were satisfied about other changes: neighborhoods substantially less dangerous than public housing, less graffiti and trash. Further, movers were about half as likely as those still in public housing to report "big problems" with drug trafficking and gang activity in their neighborhoods (about 50 percent versus over 90 percent). Even more important for their overall sense of well-being, movers were much less likely to report problems with violent crime: 41 percent of movers reported big problems with shootings and violence, compared with 90 percent of nonmovers.

42. Although our movers are still located in midrange poverty neighborhoods, it is possible that they will make incremental moves toward low-poverty neighborhoods. The Urban Institute is currently investigating the predictors of moves to low-poverty neighborhoods and will be releasing findings in early 2005.

43. This difference is statistically significant at the $p < .001$ level.

Confirming these findings, movers rated their neighborhoods as higher in "collective efficacy" than nonmovers.[44] Movers in our sample consistently rated their communities higher than nonmovers on social control (whether neighbors would take action if they saw someone causing problems) and on measures of social cohesion and trust (whether neighbors trusted each other and shared values). For example, 79 percent of movers said that people in their neighborhood were "willing to help their neighbors," compared with 51 percent of residents still in public housing.

Many of the respondents we interviewed spoke about the dramatic improvement in neighborhood safety and how this had affected their own—and their children's—lives:

> [My kids] love it. Because now they can have their friends come over and you don't want to be afraid that somebody's gonna jump on 'em or beat 'em up or do something like that. It's free. And there's no standing out in front of buildings. No hollering "Here comes the police" and stuff like that. It's very quiet where I'm at. Very quiet.
>
> I'm sleeping and resting and comfortable and everything. I ain't got to worry about my daughter leaving out, going to school, and something might happen. Worrying about her walking into gunfire, you know, all that. I'm glad. I used to get up every day, looking off my porch to see if my baby was safe. So I feel real good.

Finally, our results provide some indication that the improvement in conditions—and the successful transition out of public housing—may have had some short-term improvement on movers' mental outlook. Although we did not find differences at baseline, at the twelve-month follow-up, movers scored higher on self-efficacy. At the twelve-month follow-up, about half of movers—compared with about two-thirds of nonmovers—agreed with the statement, "Every time I try to get ahead, something stops me." Our longitudinal data indicate that there has been a substantial increase in self-efficacy for movers over time, while the scores for nonmovers had not changed.

Only about 40 percent of the respondents made a successful move from public housing during the twelve months that we tracked them. The rest remained in consolidation buildings. Conditions in these buildings were reportedly very poor throughout the study period. The majority of nonmovers reported at least one serious problem with their housing at the twelve-month follow-up. These reports remained essentially constant over time; for example, at each wave, about half of the respondents reported problems with peeling paint and broken

44. Sampson, Raudenbush, and Earls (1997). Collective efficacy is a factor associated with lower crime rates and neighborhood social organization; respondents' ratings measure the social cohesion and level of social control in a neighborhood.

plumbing, about one-third reported problems with rats or mice, and about one-fifth reported problems with heat or broken locks. One woman described more serious problems, saying she twice had sewage back up into her unit:

> Oh I had two floods. The worst flood I had, I lost all of my belongings. My TV, my microwave . . . about $800 or $900 worth of merchandise. . . . [But] I didn't have but $499 worth of receipts for some of the things I had purchased. And they [CHA] gave me, it's took about seven weeks, they gave me $400. . . . Then they gave me a voucher to go to the Salvation Army to get me a bed to sleep in. Because . . . my bed was closer to the floor, I don't put my bed way up because of the shooting.

Nonmovers' perceptions of problems with physical disorder and crime also remained constant over time. At each wave, nearly all—about 90 percent—reported problems with graffiti, trash, drug trafficking, drug sales, and violent crime. Several respondents described the dangers they or their children had experienced in their buildings. One woman said she was shot in the head by a stray bullet.

Finally, a number of respondents, particularly those from Robert Taylor public housing development, spoke of the dangers of having members from several gangs living in the same consolidation buildings. Several women mentioned that it was unsafe for their sons to visit them.

> Inside the building is where they sell their drugs. . . . Having to walk through there . . . sometimes it messes with me mentally, but I gather myself and go on upstairs. My son can't come see me, and my grandbabies, I can't see them like I want.

Residents face multiple barriers when moving, including finding an apartment with a Section 8 voucher, receiving adequate relocation assistance, and navigating the private market. We asked survey respondents in the two follow-up surveys why they had not moved since the baseline interview.[45] Their responses reflected the range and complexity of the barriers that made public housing transformation in Chicago so challenging. At the six-month follow-up, the most common reason cited for not moving was not finding an apartment they liked, in a neighborhood where they felt comfortable, and that had enough bedrooms. At the twelve-month follow-up, about a quarter of the nonmovers cited not being able to find an apartment; another quarter said that they had had "problems with Section 8"; and 13 percent said that they had not moved for "financial reasons." Although more than a third of nonmovers said that they had

45. At wave 2, this question was open-ended and the responses were grouped into categories for analysis. At wave 3, we used a closed-ended question based on the wave 2 responses.

paid their rent late in past six months, only a very small number (5 percent) said that they had officially been told that they were not lease-compliant. (We find little evidence that the nonmovers changed their minds about moving: At the twelve-month follow-up, only about 10 percent of nonmovers said they either had decided not to move or simply liked where they were, 75 percent said that they still planned on moving with a Section 8 voucher in the next six months, and 56 percent said they were actively searching for housing.)

Our qualitative data suggest several other barriers that may have made it difficult for these residents to relocate during the study period. One factor that may have inhibited moves, particularly early on, is that many of these residents reported that they did not receive the counseling services that the CHA intended during the first phase of relocation. At the baseline and six-month follow-up, 40 percent of the respondents could not identify their counseling agency: 7 percent named CHAC, the agency that runs the housing choice voucher program; 6 percent said "other"; and 31 percent said that they did not have a counseling agency. At the twelve-month follow-up, just 23 percent of nonmovers said they were still receiving mobility counseling, and almost half (45 percent) said that they had not been assigned to a counseling agency.

Some nonmovers who had received counseling services complained that these services were inadequate. For example, one woman said that she felt she needed more information and support than the two group meetings at her counseling agency and that many of the listings she received from her counselor were for units that had already been rented. Other respondents complained that the group briefings and housing listings were unhelpful, and several respondents complained that their counselors only offered them apartments in dangerous neighborhoods—neighborhoods they perceived as being as bad as the public housing developments they were trying to leave:

> They came and picked me up at the building. And then they took me around. They find apartments for you, you don't find it yourself. . . . And the neighborhoods were just like the neighborhood I'm in now.

The private rental market also presented major challenges for many of these residents. Many of the nonmovers in our sample had searched for housing, some of them intensively. In-depth interview respondents described calling counseling agencies regularly for listings, scanning the newspapers, and going out regularly to look at units. Those who had searched reported that the experience was difficult. They perceived discrimination against Section 8 voucher holders generally; against CHA relocatees, who are often perceived as troublemakers or criminals; and against families with children. They also encountered a tight rental market, which meant they had to compete for units in better neighborhoods.[46]

46. See Popkin and Cunningham (2000).

> Every place I find now and I call and asking where are you from and you tell them, and it's like, well, they don't come out and say, well you from CHA we are not going to have nothing to do with you . . . they'll say someone was looking at the apartment earlier and we're going to go with them. Then they said well how many children do you have. And I'll say well I have three small children. And they say well that's a problem. Do you have any teenagers? No I do not. If you got teenagers then they say that's a problem. They don't want teenagers in the building. They don't want small children in the building if they are not in school. . . . But I hope to get out.

In addition to problems with counseling agencies and rental market barriers, most of the residents we interviewed had profound fears about leaving their public housing communities. Bad as the conditions were, these developments were residents' long-term homes. Most of the residents in our sample—movers and nonmovers alike—had lived in public housing for more than a decade, and many had extensive networks of family and friends. As a result, for many, the prospect of leaving was very frightening.

Overall, the findings from our study highlight the risks to residents inherent in the CHA's transformation process. Although a few residents have been lucky enough to make successful moves and now feel they live in better housing in safer neighborhoods, most have not been as fortunate. Those residents are now living in public housing that is as bad or worse than their original units and are facing the prospect of multiple temporary moves while they wait for permanent relocation—or try to address their lease compliance issues so they can stay in public housing at all. And even those who have moved successfully are struggling with the challenges of the private market—higher utility costs, less stable housing, and lack of access to formal support systems.

The CHA has maintained that it is open to criticism and continuously seeks to improve its services, but its efforts—and the risks to residents—continue to be the subject of much public debate. The atmosphere has been made contentious by the long history of litigation and community activism involving the CHA. At the time the transformation plan went into effect, the CHA was already under several consent decrees that directly affected its revitalization plans, including the *Gautreaux* decree.

The situation became even more contentious with the release of the *Independent Monitor's Report* on relocation in January 2003.[47] Thomas Sullivan, a former U.S. attorney, was appointed independent monitor in 2002 under the provisions of the Relocation Rights Contract. He issued a series of highly critical reports on the CHA's relocation efforts during phase 2 of the plan for transformation,

47. Sullivan (2003).

culminating in the January 2003 summary report, which included fifty-four recommendations to improve the process. Some of the most serious criticisms are that the compressed timing of relocation in 2002 resulted in many residents having to move with very little notice into poor-quality units, that the Service Connector program failed to provide effective counseling, that relocation agencies failed to provide effective mobility counseling, and that the CHA lacked candor in addressing its shortcomings.

Shortly after the release of the January 2003 report, three legal advocacy groups jointly filed a suit against the CHA on behalf of current and former CHA tenants who have been or will be relocated as a result of the CHA's 1999 closing of buildings slated for demolition.[48] The suit (*Wallace* v. *The Chicago Housing Authority*) alleges that the CHA failed to provide adequate relocation assistance and effective social services to residents and that the result of this failure has been the perpetuation of segregation. The suit alleges that these families now live in neighborhoods that are just as racially segregated and nearly as poor as the public housing communities from which they were displaced.[49] The suit seeks the implementation of a new relocation program that would provide sufficient support to allow families to move to areas that could offer them greater opportunities. As of this writing, this suit has not yet been settled, and its long-term impact on CHA's relocation services and the implementation of the plan for transformation is still unclear.

Lessons from Chicago

The Chicago experience with public housing transformation illustrates the consequences of societal reluctance to deal with difficult problems such as racial segregation, the damage inflicted on families from the unintended consequences of federal policies and programs, housing the homeless, and the exclusionary housing policies in suburban areas. In Chicago, many of the poorest and least "desirable" tenants have been warehoused in CHA's developments for decades; as these developments are demolished, these tenants are being forced to move, and they face an uncertain future. Without serious attention to the issues raised in this chapter, the transformation of public housing is unlikely to realize its potential as a force for improving the lives of low-income families.

In some ways, Chicago should have been the best case for using public housing transformation to offer better opportunities for residents. The city has a long history of mobility efforts for public housing residents and at least three

48. The three groups are Business and Professional People for the Public Interest, which represents the *Gautreaux* plaintiffs; the National Center for Poverty Law (which also represents CHA tenants in a separate lawsuit, *Henry Horner Mothers Guild* v. *The Chicago Housing Authority*); and the Chicago Lawyers Committee for Civil Rights under the Law.

49. The suit cites Fischer (2003).

organizations with extensive experience in providing counseling and search assistance. There were multiple advocacy organizations interested in promoting mobility and desegregation, and the HUD takeover had put in place a process for addressing the existing segregation of housing voucher participants. But even with all of this experience and advocacy—and even with formal legal agreements to provide mobility services to residents—the CHA's efforts have met with little success. Residents are living in less poor neighborhoods, a very real benefit, but one that was almost inevitable given the high levels of poverty in the CHA's developments. Relatively few of those who moved are living in *low*-poverty neighborhoods; even fewer are living in neighborhoods that are not almost entirely African American.

Many factors have contributed to this outcome, including the CHA's ineffective management of the process, counseling agencies that were accustomed to working with volunteers and were unprepared to cope with the level of problems among CHA's general population, local politics that undermined implementation efforts, a tight rental market, and a lack of a regional commitment to offering alternative housing (for example, the resistance of suburban and working-class communities in the Chicago area to accepting relocatees). But the reality is that none of these problems is unique to Chicago—they are equally likely to occur in other large metropolitan areas attempting to transform their public housing. And indeed, the data available to date suggest that resegregation is the norm rather than the exception.[50] Unfortunately, the lesson of Chicago appears to be that, like so many efforts at "urban renewal," public housing transformation is unlikely to fundamentally address the problems of racial segregation and concentrated poverty, which have been caused by decades of exclusionary zoning policies, discrimination in the housing market, and lack of affordable housing regionwide.

In fact, rather than offering new opportunities for residents who have suffered the consequences of failed federal programs, public housing transformation may make things worse for at least one subgroup of residents. Residents who face multiple, complex problems may not be able to make a transition to either private market or new, mixed-income housing. Public housing—particularly distressed public housing like the CHA's developments—served as the housing of last resort for America's poorest for decades. A substantial proportion of those still living in these distressed developments are literally one step away from becoming homeless—and may become so if they are relocated to the private market. Without a fundamental refocusing of federal policy and a commitment to addressing the needs of our most vulnerable families, public housing transformation offers little hope for a better life for these residents.

50. Kingsley, Johnson, and Pettit (2000).

References

Blank, Rebecca. 1987. *It Takes a Nation: A New Agenda for Fighting Poverty.* New York: Russell Sage.

Buron, Larry F. 2004. *An Improved Living Environment? Neighborhood Outcomes for HOPE VI Relocatees.* A Roof over Their Heads Policy Brief 3. Washington: Urban Institute.

Buron, Larry, and others. 2002. *The HOPE VI Resident Tracking Study: A Snapshot of the Current Living Situation of Original Residents from Eight Sites.* Washington: Urban Institute.

Chicago Housing Authority. Various years (2000–2004). *MTW Annual Report* (March).

Comey, Jennifer. 2004. *An Improved Living Environment? Housing Quality Outcomes for HOPE VI Relocatees.* A Roof over Their Heads Policy Brief 2. Washington: Urban Institute.

Cunningham, Mary K., and Susan J. Popkin. 2002. *CHAC Mobility Program Assessment Final Report.* Report prepared for the John D. and Catherine T. MacArthur Foundation. Washington: Urban Institute.

Cunningham, Mary K., David J. Sylvester, and Margery A. Turner. 2000. *Section 8 Families in the Washington Region: Neighborhood Choices and Constraints.* Washington: Urban Institute.

Fischer, Paul. 2003. *Where Are the Public Housing Families Going? An Update.* Chicago: National Center for Poverty Law.

Harris, Laura E., and Deborah R. Kaye. 2004. *How Are HOPE VI Families Faring? Health.* Roof over Their Heads Policy Brief 5. Washington: Urban Institute.

Holin, Mary Joel, and others. 2003. *Interim Assessment of the HOPE VI Program: Cross-Site Report.* U.S. Department of Housing and Urban Development.

Keating, Larry. 2000. "Redeveloping Public Housing." *Journal of the American Planning Association* 66, no. 4: 384–96.

Kingsley, G. Thomas, Jennifer Johnson, and Kathryn Pettit. 2000. *HOPE VI and Section 8: Spatial Patterns in Relocation.* Washington: Urban Institute.

Levy, Diane K., and Deborah R. Kaye. 2004. *How Are HOPE VI Families Faring? Employment and Income.* Roof over Their Heads Policy Brief 4. Washington: Urban Institute.

Metropolitan Planning Council. 2003. "CHA Plan for Transformation: July 2003 Progress Report." Chicago.

National Housing Law Project. 2002. *False HOPE: A Critical Assessment of the HOPE VI Public Housing Redevelopment Program.* Oakland, Calif.

Popkin, Susan J. 1990. "Welfare: Views from the Bottom." *Social Problems* 37: 64–78.

Popkin, Susan J., and Mary K. Cunningham. 2000. *Searching for Rental Housing with Section 8 in Chicago.* Washington: Urban Institute.

Popkin, Susan J., Mary Cunningham, and Erin Godfrey. 2001. *CHA Relocation and Mobility Counseling Assessment Interim Report.* Washington: Urban Institute.

Popkin, Susan J., Michael Eiseman, and Elizabeth Cove. 2004. *How Are HOPE VI Families Faring? Children.* Roof over Their Heads Policy Brief 6. Washington: Urban Institute.

Popkin, Susan J., Victoria E. Gwiasda, and others. 2000. *The Hidden War: Crime and the Tragedy of Public Housing in Chicago.* Rutgers University Press.

Popkin, Susan J., Bruce Katz, and others. 2004. *A Decade of HOPE VI: Research Findings and Policy Challenges.* Washington: Urban Institute.

Popkin, Susan J., Diane K. Levy, and others. 2002. "HOPE VI Panel Study Baseline Report—Draft." Washington: Urban Institute.

Rubinowitz, Leonard S., and James E. Rosenbaum. 2000. *Crossing the Class and Color Lines: From Public Housing to White Suburbia.* University of Chicago Press.

Sampson, R. J., S. Raudenbush, and F. Earls. 1997. "Neighborhoods and Violent Crime: A Multilevel Study of Collective Efficacy." *Science* 277 (August): 918–24.

Stuart, Guy. 2002. "Integration or Resegregation: Metropolitan Chicago at the Turn of the New Century." Kennedy School of Government, Harvard University.

Sullivan, Thomas P. 2003. *Independent Monitor's Report No. 5 to the Chicago Housing Authority and the Central Advisory Council.* Chicago Housing Authority.

Wexler, Harry J. 2000. "HOPE VI: Market Means/Public Ends: The Goals, Strategies, and Midterm Lessons of HUD's Urban Revitalization Program." *Journal of Affordable Housing* 10, no. 3: 195–233.

Zedlewski, Sheila. 2002. *The Importance of Housing Benefits to Welfare Success.* Washington: Brookings Institution and Urban Institute.

9

The Persistence of Segregation in Government Housing Programs

PHILIP D. TEGELER

Some thirty years ago, after the passage of the federal Fair Housing Act and near the end of a twenty-five-year public housing development boom that created our most racially and economically isolated communities, civil rights advocates finally won the point that the U.S. Department of Housing and Urban Development (HUD) should no longer be permitted to routinely build new low-income housing in segregated, high-poverty neighborhoods.

HUD's site and neighborhood standards, developed in response to the 1970 case of *Shannon* v. *HUD,* were an important part of the implementation of the 1968 Fair Housing Act.[1] The *Shannon* case successfully challenged HUD's failure to assess and ameliorate the segregative effects of new housing projects, finding that the agency had failed in its duty, under the Fair Housing Act, "affirmatively to further" fair housing. These site and neighborhood standards recognized that restricting further development of low-income housing in the segregated, high-poverty areas was as important as creating new housing opportunities for minority families in less segregated neighborhoods.

The HUD site and neighborhood standards are still formally on the books, but they no longer apply to programs that create significant amounts of housing. Our most important low-income housing development programs are

1. 436 F.2d 809 (3d Cir. 1970). For a short history of the HUD site and neighborhood standards, see Vernarelli (1986).

largely unregulated from a civil rights perspective. Rules designed to prevent segregation in public housing and HUD-assisted private construction programs have been overlooked in the more recent federal Low-Income Housing Tax Credit (LIHTC) program and severely modified in the HOPE VI public housing redevelopment program. Other current programs that provide funds for assisted housing are similarly lacking in antisegregation controls. For example, the Community Reinvestment Act (CRA) has no siting controls and actually gives credit to banks for financing segregated low-income rental housing in high-poverty neighborhoods. The federal Housing Opportunities Made Equal (HOME) program disburses funds to cities and states, primarily for housing rehabilitation, but imposes few meaningful restrictions on where rehabilitated, low-income housing units should be placed. Even the Section 8 housing choice voucher program—a program that is designed, in part, to promote housing choice and mobility—has recently seen key program elements compromised and is at risk, paradoxically, of reducing choice and reconcentrating poor families in higher-poverty neighborhoods.[2]

How do we account for these oversights? They may be due in part to the compartmentalization of fair housing responsibility at HUD or to concerns about the legal vulnerability of race-based regulations.[3] But more important, they reflect a growing emphasis on community revitalization strategies (upgrading the places where disadvantaged people are already living), as efforts to promote residential integration (changing where people can and do choose to live) have faced repeated and seemingly intractable obstacles. But community revitalization is not inherently at odds with desegregation. Indeed, the two strategies are complementary, although desegregation is politically much harder to implement.

This chapter considers whether it is desirable to reinstitute some of the rules about where low-income housing may be placed and what the contours of those rules should be. Competing or conflicting policy objectives are an important

2. The ongoing restrictions on the tenant-based Section 8 voucher program are beyond the scope of this chapter, which deals with programs to fund physical development of housing. However, the current administration's actions to curtail mobility in the voucher program are indicative of HUD's priorities. HUD began restricting housing choice in the voucher program in the fall of 2003 by cutting back on the use of Section 8 "exception payment standards," which permit families to move to lower-poverty areas that have higher rents and requiring that all requests go through the HUD headquarters, which has led to a virtual freeze on exception rents. Then, HUD's decision in June 2004 to retroactively cut voucher funding increased incentives for public housing agencies to adopt policies that discourage or prohibit families from moving to higher-rent areas—including across-the-board reductions in payment standards that restrict the choice of available neighborhoods. HUD further restricted mobility in an official guidance issued in July 2004 that would permit public housing agencies to restrict voucher holders' portability rights where the agencies make a showing of financial hardship. This guidance was extended in 2005, despite protests from housing and civil rights organizations. For more detail, see www.prrac.org/mobility.

3. See Bonastia (2000); David Freund, "Democracy's Unfinished Business: Federal Policy and the Search for Fair Housing, 1961–1968" (www.prrac.org.policy.php [2004]); Pindell (2003).

part of the challenge, though a lack of attention by policymakers is the much greater hurdle. We have learned a great deal in the thirty-five years since *Shannon:* We have learned about the long-term benefits possible for families who move to substantially lower-poverty neighborhoods; we have learned about the potential harms to families who live in high-poverty neighborhoods; and we have learned something about which strategies work best to revitalize poor neighborhoods. How to apply these findings in a way that balances the competing demands of neighborhood revitalization and integration is the key challenge for a new generation of housing policy.

HUD Site and Neighborhood Standards

The current HUD site and neighborhood standards govern both conventional public housing and project-based Section 8 housing (housing developments that use HUD vouchers to support rehabilitation).[4] These standards also apply to some other HUD programs, to the extent that these programs incorporate the standards by reference. The siting regulations for the public housing and Section 8 programs are almost identical.[5] They generally prohibit building new low-income housing in racially concentrated neighborhoods, but at the same time they include broad exceptions that permit such housing to be developed if "sufficient, comparable opportunities" exist outside areas of minority concentration or if a showing is made of "overriding need" for housing that cannot otherwise be met in the region.[6]

The site and neighborhood standards reflect a range of policy tensions and assumptions about the effects of racial segregation and poverty concentration. They also reflect different perspectives on the problem of segregation. For example, the basic restriction set out in the HUD regulations—that low-income housing is not to be placed in predominantly minority communities—is focused largely on the neighborhood impact of segregation and poverty concentration.

On the other hand, the first major exception to the rule, which permits housing to be placed in a segregated neighborhood if "comparable opportunities" exist outside segregated areas, is primarily focused on the perspective of the individual

4. See 24 CFR §§ 941.202 (c) (public housing); § 983.6 (Section 8). In contrast to the portable, tenant-based Section 8 voucher program, project-based Section 8 programs assign vouchers to physical units that have been rehabilitated or newly constructed. Project-based vouchers are commonly used in conjunction with other sources of government housing financing, such as the LIHTC and HOME programs. In the 1970s and 1980s, when the site and neighborhood standards were developed, project-based Section 8 housing included new construction, substantial rehabilitation, and moderate rehabilitation programs. See also 24 CFR §§ 92.02 (HOME program).

5. Site and neighborhood standards for the project-based Section 8 program provide more criteria for assessing when exceptions can be made to the standards. See 24 CFR §§ 983.6(b)(3)(iii) and 983.6(b)(3)(iv).

6. 24 CFR §§ 941.202(c)(i)(A); 983.6(b)(3)(ii)(A); 941.202(c)(i)(B); 983.6(b)(3)(ii)(B).

family seeking housing: Do they have adequate housing choices available outside the segregated neighborhood? If this test is satisfied, it appears that HUD is less concerned if the minority neighborhood becomes more racially or economically isolated.[7] The second exception, for "overriding need," acknowledges the possibility that low-income housing development may in some cases have positive effects for a low-income community and also shows concern for the absolute shortage of housing, and the need of poor families to have somewhere to live, in the short term.[8]

In both sets of regulations, the standards for rehabilitated housing are significantly laxer than for new construction, reflecting an assumption that preserving existing housing is more important in some cases than creating desegregated housing. Both sets of regulations seek to avoid new construction of assisted housing in minority areas, reflecting an assumption that such housing will be primarily occupied by minority families and will thus increase racial segregation and concentration. However, the regulations are also designed to avoid increases in poverty concentration without regard to race: Both new and rehabilitated developments must "avoid undue concentration of assisted persons in areas containing a high proportion of low-income persons."[9] During the Clinton administration an effort was made to clarify this standard to bar assisted housing developments in neighborhoods of over 40 percent poverty; however, the proposed regulation was withdrawn.[10]

As Michael Vernarelli suggests in his brief history of the site and neighborhood standards, ambiguity was built into the siting regulations from the outset, both in the definition of "area of minority concentration" and the scope of the rule's exceptions.[11] This ambiguity resulted in substantial litigation and weakening of the standards over time to the point where they were no longer effective in controlling segregated housing development.

The Weakening of Civil Rights Restrictions in Key Programs

Although the legal basis for the consideration of race in the siting of low-income housing has not diminished since the early 1970s, the enforcement of the anti-

7. This emphasis is especially clear in the project-based Section 8 regulations, which place an emphasis not just on the availability of assisted housing but also on the success rates of families seeking housing outside segregated neighborhoods. 24 CFR § 983.6(b)(iii)(c)(6).

8. The project-based Section 8 regulations spell out some of HUD's specific policy concerns, requiring that any low-income housing investment in a poor neighborhood only be undertaken as part of an "overall local strategy" for the "preservation or restoration of the immediate neighborhood" or where the development is needed to protect residents from gentrification. 24 CFR § 983.6(b)(iv).

9. 24 CFR §§ 983.6(a)(3); 941.202(d).

10. 58 Fed. Reg. 8187 (February 11, 1993) (notice of proposed rulemaking); 60 Fed. Reg. 23381, 23383 (May 8, 1995) (noting withdrawal of the proposed rule on December 9, 1994).

11. Vernarelli (1986).

segregation rules has been relaxed in current HUD programs, and siting rules have not been formally applied to housing development programs overseen by other federal agencies.

The Low-Income Housing Tax Credit Program

The LIHTC Program, currently the nation's largest low-income housing production program, has operated with little civil rights oversight since its inception in 1986.[12] The mandate of the Fair Housing Act, that all federal agencies take steps affirmatively to further fair housing, is not expressly incorporated in the LIHTC statute, and the Department of the Treasury has provided no guidance on fair housing to the state housing finance agencies that administer the program.[13] The program's responsibilities to provide fair housing are alluded to only once in Internal Revenue Service (IRS) regulations, in a broad incorporation by reference to HUD regulations.[14] There are no specific site selection requirements in the LIHTC regulations, and decisions about which projects to fund are entirely delegated to state housing finance agencies.

The failure to explicitly require compliance with fair housing policy is accompanied by specific competing incentives in the LIHTC statute that promote low-income housing development in "qualified census tracts," which are often the poorest census tracts in a jurisdiction.[15] The statute also directs states to give priority to projects that serve "the lowest income tenants . . . for the longest periods" and further encourages developers to fill these projects with the poorest of the poor.[16] The LIHTC statute fails to give direction as to how much priority to assign these two goals or how to reconcile them with the compelling goals of poverty deconcentration and racial integration.

12. 26 USC § 42. The LIHTC program was created by the Tax Reform Act of 1986. HUD reports that the program generates "the equivalent of nearly $5 billion in annual budget authority to issue tax credits for the acquisition, rehabilitation, or new construction of rental housing targeted to lower-income households," with "an average of about 1,300 projects and 90,000 units . . . placed in service in each year of the 1995 to 2001 period" (www.huduser.org). The failure of the LIHTC program to promote fair housing is extensively reviewed in Roisman (1998).

13. Roisman (1998). See also Orfield (2005).

14. 26 CFR § 1.42-9.

15. Qualified census tracts are HUD-designated areas "in which 50 percent or more of the households have an income which is less than 60 percent of the area median gross income for such year or which has a poverty rate of at least 25 percent." 26 USC § 42 (d)(5)(C)(ii). The LIHTC statute recognizes qualified census tracts in two ways. First, developments within these tracts are entitled to substantial (130 percent) increase in "eligible basis." 26 USC § 42(d)(5)(C)(i). Second, the LIHTC statute requires that state allocation plans give "preference in allocating housing credit dollar amounts among selected projects to . . . projects which are located in qualified census tracts . . . and the development of which contributes to a concerted community revitalization plan." 26 USC § 42(m)(1)(B)(ii).

16. 26 USC § 42(m)(B)(ii). See Roisman (1998, p. 1015): "The tax credit statute mandates that preference be given to 'projects serving the lowest income tenants . . . for the longest periods of time.'"

Predictably, the lack of civil rights controls in the LIHTC program has led to a geographic distribution of LIHTC housing in many states that mirrors existing conditions of racial and economic segregation. As Florence Roisman concluded in 1998, based on the first national study of the program by Abt Associates, by 1995 most LIHTC units were located in central cities, and of these units, 74 percent were located in predominantly low-income neighborhoods.[17] These findings are reinforced by a more recent national assessment of the LIHTC program, which documents a continuation of this trend between 1995 and 2000, with substantial numbers of tax credit units still placed in predominantly low-income and minority communities, especially in the Northeast.[18] The report concludes, with some understatement, that "neighborhoods containing tax credit projects tend to have more low-income households, higher poverty rates, minority populations, and proportions of female-headed families with children, and more renter-occupied units than neighborhoods generally."[19] Although this pattern of concentration is not present in all states, it appears to predominate in states of the Northeast, Mid-Atlantic, West Coast, and parts of the Midwest. Local analyses of locations of tax credit properties in Massachusetts, New Jersey, and Connecticut have confirmed these trends.[20]

In response to the concerns raised by Florence Roisman and others, some efforts to bring the LIHTC program into conformity with the Fair Housing Act were undertaken during the Clinton administration by HUD secretary Andrew Cuomo. The result, a Memorandum of Understanding between the Treasury Department, the Justice Department, and HUD, signed August 11, 2000, was designed as a first step in this process, committing these agencies to better coordinate and share civil rights enforcement information. After the 2000 election, little additional progress was made on the national level.

Since the administration of the LIHTC program is delegated to state housing

17. Roisman (1998); also see Heintz, Anderson, and Doyle (1996); Orfield (2005).

18. Nolden and others (2002, pp. 44, 50). For example, in the northeastern states, between 1995 and 2000, 62 percent of all LIHTC units (including units for the elderly, which are disproportionately white and suburban) were located in central cities, 46 percent were in predominantly minority neighborhoods, and 43 percent were in predominantly poor neighborhoods.

19. Nolden and others (2002, p. iii). The LIHTC location data understates the degree of concentration in the program, because locations of family and elderly housing are counted together, rather than disaggregated, and many LIHTC developments for the elderly are located in suburban areas.

20. In Massachusetts, Barbara Rabin's 2002 testimony to the Department of Housing and Community Development on behalf of the Fair Housing Center of Greater Boston indicates that "almost two-thirds of LIHTC projects within Boston are very heavily concentrated in census tracts whose residents are predominantly black and Hispanic," and "almost half (49 percent) of TC projects within the city of Boston are in census tracts in which the median income is below 50 percent of area median income." Testimony of Greater Boston Legal Services before Massachusetts Department of Housing and Community Development, December 18. See also Testimony of Massachusetts Law Reform Institute, January 26, 2001. For New Jersey, see *In re Adoption of the 2002 Low Income Housing Tax Credit Qualified Allocation Plan,* A-10-02T2 (N.J. App. Div. 2003), plaintiffs' appendix. For Connecticut, see Nolden and others (2002, appendix A).

finance agencies, which are required to develop procedures for allocation of tax credits in a so-called qualified allocation plan, much of the attention to civil rights compliance has come on the state level. In response to the failure of state housing finance agencies to develop siting procedures to avoid further racial and economic segregation, civil rights advocates have brought legal challenges to state administration of the LIHTC program in New Jersey and Connecticut.[21] The basic theory of these cases is simple: The Fair Housing Act (specifically, 42 USC § 3608(d)) creates affirmative obligations on the Department of the Treasury. The duty to "affirmatively further fair housing" includes promotion of nondiscrimination and integration as well as consideration of racial concentration effects and less segregative alternatives.[22] Under the Fair Housing Act this duty is delegated to state and local housing agencies, including state housing finance agencies.[23] The duty to affirmatively further fair housing is also delegated to state housing finance agencies by IRS regulations, which incorporate HUD fair housing regulations (although the tax credit agencies have ignored the HUD site selection rules).[24] Both cases also included important state fair housing claims.[25]

While these and other state cases may establish important legal precedents, it is clear that real national reform will need to come from the Treasury Department itself and a recognition that the community revitalization language in the LIHTC Act does not preclude siting controls consistent with the Fair Housing Act.[26]

The Community Reinvestment Act

The CRA was passed in 1977 to address the problems of redlining and community disinvestment in low-income minority neighborhoods.[27] The CRA is

21. In New Jersey, a panel of the state Appellate Division recently ruled against the plaintiffs in a decision that acknowledges that the state is subject to the duty to affirmatively further fair housing but then goes on to give great deference to the many competing goals of the state Housing and Mortgage Finance Agency, without considering how those goals could be molded to a more proactive regional fair housing agenda. See *In Re Adoption of 2003 Low Income Housing Tax Credit Qualified Allocation Plan,* 848 A.2d 1 (N.J. Super. App. Div. 2004). For an excellent summary of the case and its background, see Kenneth H. Zimmerman, "The Low Income Housing Tax Credit Program and Civil Rights Law. Updating the Fight for Residential Integration" (NIMBY Report, fall 2004, National Low Income Housing Coalition, www.nlihc.org). In Connecticut, a similar case brought by a local community organization has been stalled on procedural grounds and is now on appeal to the Connecticut Supreme Court. See *Asylum Hill Problem Solving Association* v. *King,* 36 Conn. L. Rptr. 422 (Superior Court, 2004). The author is a former attorney for the plaintiffs in the Connecticut case.

22. See *Shannon* v. *HUD.*

23. See *Otero* v. *NYCHA.* 484 F.2d 1122 (2d Cir. 1973).

24. 26 CFR § 1.42-9.

25. The Connecticut litigation is based in part on a 1991 state law that requires state housing agencies to "affirmatively promote fair housing choice and racial and economic integration in all programs." Public Act 91-362, codified in part at Conn. Gen. Stat. § 8-37cc(b). The New Jersey litigation was based in part on the "Mount Laurel" doctrine, a claim also rejected by the Appellate Division.

26. Roisman (1998); Orfield (2005).

27. 12 USC § 2901-2907. See generally Overby (1995). See also Marsico (2000).

generally viewed as a positive incentive to encourage home mortgages, small businesses, and banking services in low-income minority communities, and this purpose is reflected in the statute's language and legislative history.[28]

At the present time, CRA-regulated institutions are involved in a decreasing share of home mortgage loans for minority homebuyers, and "predatory lending" has emerged as a more pressing civil rights concern than access to single-family mortgages (see William Apgar and Allegra Calder, chapter 5, this volume). However, the CRA also includes incentives promoting assisted rental housing that need to be examined for their consistency with fair housing goals. Specifically, the CRA's current implementing regulations, adopted in 1995, place a strong emphasis on (and reward banks for) investment in community development lending, which may include financing for low-income rental housing developments in high-poverty neighborhoods.[29] The CRA regulations do nothing to discourage banks from such investments and actually seem to encourage it.[30] The regulations do not appear to encourage banks to invest in rental projects for poor families outside high-poverty neighborhoods or outside areas of minority concentration.[31] In this sense, the CRA regulations are, on their face, at odds with the Fair Housing Act's emphasis on promoting housing choice and integrated housing patterns. The CRA's emphasis on directing housing loan funds to specific geographic places (rather than to enhance the housing choices of persons living in those places) is also responsible for the loan concentration in single-family home mortgages that has been observed by some observers of the program.[32]

To the extent that CRA regulations encourage segregation, they are in conflict with the duty to affirmatively further fair housing, as set out in the Fair Housing Act, specifically in 42 USC § 3608(d), which imposes this duty on all "executive departments and agencies [in] their programs and activities relating to housing and urban development." This provision expressly applies to the federal banking

28. See Overby (1995).

29. The CRA regulations are set out separately for each of the federal agencies that regulate different types of banking institution. See 12 CFR part 25 (Comptroller of the Currency), part 563 (Office of Thrift Supervision), part 345 (Federal Deposit Insurance Corporation, or FDIC), and part 228 (Board of Governors of the Federal Reserve System). The regulations for the different agencies are essentially similar, but fewer requirements are imposed on small state-chartered banks by the FDIC. Community development loans (which include loans for low-income rental housing) are an important component of the heavily weighted lending test and the investment test, which are both reviewed when banks apply for mergers.

30. For example, the grading factors for low-income rental housing investment include "activities that revitalize or stabilize low- or moderate-income geographies." The regulating agencies also place weight on the bank's responsiveness to community development corporations, the vast majority of which promote low-income housing development in poor neighborhoods.

31. Indeed, the enforcement dynamic is in the opposite direction: Commitment agreements with community-based organizations challenging CRA certifications commonly include promises to invest in assisted multifamily housing in poor neighborhoods. See Marsico (2000).

32. See Schill and Wachter (1995).

agencies that oversee CRA compliance.[33] Under this analysis, the Fair Housing Act would require modification of the CRA regulations to more carefully circumscribe low-income rental housing investment in poor neighborhoods and also to reward lenders for investments in suburban low-income housing developments that directly benefit residents of the poor inner-city neighborhoods the CRA is intended to help.[34]

There is nothing in the text or the legislative history of the CRA that suggests a mandate for banks to encourage the intensification of concentrated poverty, and new fair housing requirements would be fully compatible with, and supportive of, the community development emphasis of the act.

HUD Retrenchment on Desegregation

While the Department of the Treasury and federal banking agencies have been casually disregarding the Fair Housing Act in their promotion of assisted housing development, HUD has taken a more active role in dismantling the protections of the site and neighborhood standards. In several key programs (HOPE VI, HOME, and its deconcentration rule), and in cooperation with Congress, HUD has diluted or carved away significant exceptions to these requirements and at the same time has cut the few programs that helped poor families locate housing outside of high-poverty neighborhoods. Like its sister agencies, HUD has taken these steps, at least in part, in the name of community development.

HOPE VI. The HOPE VI program was intended to eliminate and replace the most severely distressed and segregated high-rise public housing developments with mixed-income housing and to assist poor public housing families in finding housing outside high-poverty areas (42 USC § 1437; see Susan Popkin and Mary Cunningham, chapter 8, this volume). In no other HUD program have the competing goals of community revitalization and deconcentration been so explicitly conjoined. However, while the program has succeeded in revitalizing dozens of public housing communities, it has largely failed to deliver on the promise of access to low-poverty communities and desegregation.[35] As Ngai

33. Other federal laws reach outright discrimination by lending institutions, but it is unclear whether these fair lending laws can be applied to bank investments that result in obvious perpetuation of segregation in a community.

34. Another interesting trend in CRA compliance is the use of the act to assist moderate-income families in leaving poor neighborhoods. This incentive was triggered by the change in CRA regulations in 1995 to "count" (for CRA compliance purposes) loans to minority individuals purchasing housing outside of predominantly minority communities. While this trend may promote greater integration in predominantly white areas, it also encourages middle-class flight from the inner city. See Friedman and Squires (forthcoming).

35. The most recent research on HOPE VI is summarized in Popkin and others (2004) and in Buron and others (2002). Most original residents are living in areas with substantially lower poverty rates than the neighborhood of their original public housing development. However, this change is largely a function of how extraordinarily high the original poverty rates were; in fact, the average census tract poverty rate for all participants was as high as 27 percent after relocation or

Pindell, a former observer-participant in the Baltimore HOPE VI process, points out, "HOPE VI focuses on bringing higher-income residents in but does a correspondingly poor job of facilitating moves by affected public housing residents to better neighborhoods."[36]

The relaxation of fair housing rules was built into the HOPE VI program from the outset and was viewed as central to the program's twin goals of deconcentration and neighborhood revitalization. Most important, HOPE VI developments are exempt from traditional HUD site and neighborhood standards as long as the total number of new public housing units on site is "significantly" less than those in the original public housing development.[37] This exception was incorporated in HOPE VI program notices and was also added generally to public housing site and neighborhood standards, creating a rebuilding-on-site exception to the rules for all public housing demolition and replacement.

Legislation adopted at the outset of the HOPE VI program repealed the one-for-one public housing replacement requirement for most public housing demolitions.[38] It was argued that the one-for-one replacement requirement was a significant obstacle to demolition of highly distressed, segregated public housing and that the repeal of this provision was necessary to permit the HOPE VI program and other needed public housing demolitions to go forward.[39] However, the repeal of the one-for-one replacement requirement has also eliminated the possibility of substantial scattered-site housing developments outside of areas of minority concentration.[40]

These loopholes in the HOPE VI statute were ultimately tolerated by some civil rights advocates because of the promise that the most segregated and disinvested public housing developments might be permanently eliminated and their residents finally given a chance to live in decent housing in neighborhoods with access to opportunity. But as the program has matured, the pragmatic need to complete development has often outweighed the program's original goals of deconcentration and desegregation. For example, the waiver of racial siting standards for rebuilding public housing was ultimately extended to a large area around the former public housing site (in some cases, up to three miles from the site), so that the program can now include a virtually citywide waiver of the site and neighborhood standards for replacement public housing. Also, while the HOPE VI program has been heavily reliant on Section 8 vouchers to rehouse

return to the former site, which can hardly be characterized as low poverty. Among former residents who did not return to the former site, about 40 percent were living in neighborhoods with greater than 30 percent poverty. The report also observes that HOPE VI has achieved far less success in increasing racial integration than in deconcentrating poverty. See Popkin and others (2004, p. 29).

36. Pindell (2003, p. 385).

37. 42 USC § 1437p(d).

38. 42 USC § 1437p; HUD notice PIH 99-19.

39. See for example Schill and Wachter (1995).

40. See Roisman (1995a)

former public housing tenants, these vouchers have often not included enhanced rents or special mobility features that would permit wider geographic choices to participating families.[41] Recent changes in the housing voucher program have further exacerbated this situation, with HUD restricting the use of "exception payment standards" and cutting permissible rents in a number of metropolitan areas.

Combined, these rules have led to the rebuilding of substantial concentrations of low-income housing in segregated neighborhoods, with inadequate replacement housing created to accommodate the tenants voluntarily displaced by the redevelopment and the placement of most tenants relocated with vouchers into predominantly minority neighborhoods.[42] While the long-term impacts of HOPE VI are not yet clear, as Ngai Pindell warns, "The danger for HOPE VI is that twenty years from now it will be one more policy intervention that contributed to higher degrees of racial separation. . . . The signs and foundation of this future are already visible."[43] For a program partly rooted in the desegregation goals of *Brown* and *Gautreaux,* these initial results are disappointing.

HOME. The HOME program was established in 1990 as part of the Cranston-Gonzalez Affordable Housing Act. HOME is an annual block grant program that distributes housing-related funds to eligible jurisdictions, including the fifty state governments. Housing-related funds may, and often do, include assistance for low-income family rental housing.

The HOME regulations, at 24 CFR part 92, recite the requirement that recipients must affirmatively further fair housing as a condition of receiving funds, but the regulations expressly limit the application of HUD site and neighborhood standards to "new construction of rental housing." Other housing development (including, apparently, substantial gutting and rehabilitation of a long-vacant structure) is subject only to the admonition that it be consistent with the Fair Housing Act and that it "promote greater choice of housing opportunities."[44] Since little HOME-funded housing is new construction, this standard means that most HOME housing will not be scrutinized or rejected for its contribution to segregation and higher concentrations of poverty.

The HOME program, like the Community Development Block Grant program, also suffers from a geographic bias inherent in a voluntary government

41. The lack of adequate housing relocation for families relocated from HOPE VI and other developments slated for demolition has been challenged in civil rights litigation in Chicago brought by the National Center for Poverty Law, the Chicago Lawyers Committee, and Business and Professional People for the Public Interest. *Wallace* v. *Chicago Housing Authority* (N.D.Ill., filed Jan. 23, 2003; served 2005).

42. As an Urban Institute report notes, "nearly all original residents who moved with vouchers ended up in neighborhoods that were at least 90 percent African American." Popkin and others (2004, p. 29).

43. Pindell (2003). See also Buron and others (2002).

44. 24 CFR § 92.205(a)(3).

program targeted to "entitlement" communities above a certain size.[45] The targeting of these funds primarily to central cities, without any requirement of collaboration with surrounding municipalities (or indeed without any requirement that some funds be used to create housing for city residents outside the city) naturally tends to perpetuate regional housing segregation.

HUD's Deconcentration Rule. HUD's Rule to Deconcentrate Poverty and Promote Integration in Public Housing is another example of HUD's failure to meaningfully address racial and economic segregation.[46] This rule, adopted in 2000 in response to the Quality Housing and Work Responsibility Act of 1998, mandates that local public housing agencies adopt income deconcentration goals, requiring that these agencies adopt admissions procedures to prevent wide differences in median incomes among housing complexes. Unfortunately, in spite of pointed advance comments about the futility of such a strategy without a regional component, the regulation limits its scope to projects that are within each public housing agency's geographic area.[47] Although there is nothing in the Quality Housing and Work Responsibility Act that requires such a limitation, no efforts are made in the regulations to bridge the demographic divide between urban and suburban public housing agencies. The American Civil Liberties Union's commented as follows on the proposed rule:

> Most of the deconcentration and fair housing provisions of the proposed rule are designed for housing authorities that are internally segregated by income and race. To the extent that this is a problem, the proposed rule offers a partial solution. In many parts of the country, however, the real problem is segregation among housing authorities within a housing market, with lower-income, minority-occupied projects located in the city, while surrounding suburbs are home to smaller-scale, higher-income, predominantly white developments. There is no effort in the proposed regulation to encourage cross-jurisdictional or cross-program opportunities within a housing market.[48]

The Council of Large Public Housing Authorities was more blunt, asserting that "virtually all families in public housing are very poor. There are no rich or high-income buildings as fantasized in the proposed rule."[49] The proposed regulation also refuses to link racial desegregation with the income deconcentration goal of the Quality Housing and Work Responsibility Act of 1998. The reason,

45. See Tegeler (1994).

46. 24 CFR § 903. See generally Hendrickson (2002).

47. These comments are catalogued by Hendrickson (2002, nn. 297, 355, 357) and include formal comments submitted by the ACLU, the NAACP Legal Defense Fund, and the National Low-Income Housing Coalition. (The comments of the ACLU were drafted in part by the author.)

48. Letter on file with the author.

49. Hendrickson (2002, p. 72).

according to HUD, is that the two obligations (poverty deconcentration and nondiscrimination) come from different statutes and thus must also be kept separate in the regulations.[50] Thus rather than meld these two standards together in a meaningful way, the regulation's reference to racial discrimination is limited to reciting the truism that the Fair Housing Act applies to the admissions policies of public housing authorities.

Site Selection and Concentrated Poverty

The original site and neighborhood standards operated on the assumption that housing segregation is harmful—or at least contrary to national civil rights policy. Since the early 1970s, substantial additional research has been done, and while there may no longer be a national consensus that segregation is "wrong," there is a growing social science consensus that segregation is harmful, particularly the severe poverty-concentrated segregation associated with subsidized housing in the central city.

> Research during the past decade has demonstrated that poverty in the United States has become increasingly concentrated into high-poverty neighborhoods and that such concentrations appear to have a range of detrimental effects on the well-being and future opportunities of residents of those areas. . . . The harmful effects of high-poverty areas are especially severe for children, whose behavior, choices, and prospects are particularly susceptible to neighborhood-based events and characteristics such as peer group influences, school quality, and the level of violent crime.[51]

In light of this research, before adopting new siting rules several compelling questions must be asked. First, how will choosing to remain in a high-poverty neighborhood likely affect the average family in the long run, particularly the children? Second, does the family have a real choice in terms of location; that is, can they realistically select housing outside of the poor neighborhood where the apartment is being offered? Third, is this a neighborhood where the family would choose to live if they were actually offered the option of an apartment in a lower-poverty community? Finally, if additional units for low-income families are added to a neighborhood already burdened with poverty, what impact will this additional housing have on existing neighborhood residents?

The answers to the first of these questions—the likely effects of a desegregative move—are increasingly clear: Moving from high-poverty to low-poverty environments can enhance life outcomes for families and children (see James

50. 65 Fed. Reg. 81214 (Dec. 22, 2000). See also Hendrickson (2002, n. 358).

51. Goering, Feins, and Richardson (2002, p. 1). See also Goering and Feins (2003); Massey and Denton (1993); Wilson (1987); Jargowsky (1997).

Rosenbaum, Stefanie DeLuca, and Tammy Tuck, chapter 7, this volume; John Goering, chapter 6, this volume).[52] The answers to the second and third questions have rarely been sought, but the evidence strongly suggests that the demand for housing among poor families outside of poverty-concentrated areas far exceeds the supply. The final question, assessing the impacts of new low-income housing development on existing residents in a neighborhood, is a more difficult problem and is discussed in depth below in an effort to posit appropriate guidelines for site selection in current and future assisted housing programs.

Measuring Demand

In a society obsessed with public opinion polling and market research, it is remarkable that poor people have rarely been asked where they want to live. It is sometimes assumed that because low-income families stay behind when higher-income families leave urban neighborhoods, the former must be exercising a "choice" to remain. Similarly, when housing mobility programs fail to attract large numbers of families, it is posited that "many voucher recipients want to remain in the central city, close to their friends and relatives, near community and religious services, and in close proximity to public transit."[53] While this pattern may need to be taken into account in the design of housing mobility programs, it should not necessarily guide public policy about the siting of assisted housing developments. Although some families may wish to stay in high-poverty segregated neighborhoods where low-cost housing is relatively plentiful, evidence shows that a substantial number of families are interested in leaving these neighborhoods—and at least some are desperate to leave. But for these families there are relatively few places to move, and each assisted development placed in a poor neighborhood both intensifies neighborhood poverty and uses up scarce housing resources, diminishing the prospects of finding housing elsewhere.

What is the demand among poor families for desegregated housing? This is a difficult question to answer and may vary by geographic region. One approach has been to look at the number of families who take advantage of suburban housing opportunities where they are offered.[54] The best evidence we have of this type of demand is from the current Moving to Opportunity research, which shows that 25 percent of public housing residents offered an opportunity to live in a low-poverty neighborhood voluntarily gave up their public housing apartment to volunteer.[55]

Local estimates of demand vary widely. In Chicago's Gautreaux program, "after some initial uncertainty about whether eligible families would be interested . . . the demand for the program increased dramatically and remained high

52. See also Turner and Acevedo-Garcia (2005)
53. Varady and Walker (2003, p. 26).
54. See Hendrickson (2002, p. 59). See also Roisman and Botein (1993).
55. Goering and Feins (2003).

throughout more than two decades of its existence," and by the early 1990s the program was receiving ten thousand calls or more from prospective applicants on its annual registration day.[56] In Minneapolis, initial demand for suburban placements was low, with only 6 percent of eligible residents responding.[57] It is likely that these variations relate to the reputation of the local program, the types of counseling assistance offered to relocated tenants, and the difficulty of the local rental market (see Margery Turner and Stephen Ross, chapter 4, this volume). Until a more comprehensive survey is completed, in planning for future demand policymakers should rely on the Moving to Opportunity program's somewhat conservative estimate of a 25 percent participation rate for housing mobility programs among residents in high-poverty communities.

Even with the limited research that has been done, several important hypotheses can be advanced. First, the concept of housing choice as a basic kind of liberty—the right of every family to move into a community and school system of their choice—has deep support in many low-income communities, far beyond the number of persons who are ultimately willing to take advantage of such a choice. Second, however demand is measured, the demand for desegregated housing options far exceeds the limited supply. Third, moving is difficult for any family but especially so for a poor family with little information, few choices, little or no experience outside of government-run housing, and health and other obstacles in their path.[58] Until an adequate supply of lower-cost housing is created outside of poor neighborhoods, and offered to inner-city residents with the support services necessary to facilitate their moving, we will never know the true extent of demand for desegregated housing.

Recent Evidence—and Unanswered Questions

In spite of the apparent consensus on the general harms of concentrated poverty, it is more difficult to assess the particular harms to existing residents of adding additional low-income housing to a poor neighborhood. As Lance Freeman and Hilary Botein remind us in their overview of the literature of neighborhood effects, "as with much nonexperimental social science research, the most vexing problem is designing methods that can satisfactorily answer the question at hand."[59] As they point out, the question of impact is highly contextual, depending on the types of impact being measured and the type of neighborhood being impacted.

56. Rubinowitz and Rosenbaum (2000, pp. 6, 54). Similarly, a 1992 telephone poll of a sample of Hartford Section 8 voucher holders shows that 68 percent had an interest in moving to suburban towns, though the results of that poll were not necessarily reflected in participation rates in the local housing mobility program. See Donovan (1994).

57. Goetz (2003, pp. 180–81).

58. See, for example, Popkin and Cunningham (1999).

59. Freeman and Botein (2002, p. 360).

The incremental effects of adding additional low-income housing to a poor neighborhood are less well understood than the overall harmful effects of poverty concentration, and the specific ways that concentrated neighborhood poverty adversely affects families is still being studied. As John Goering and colleagues note in their summary of Moving to Opportunity research:

> The harmful effects of living in poverty-concentrated neighborhoods have been evident for a long time, but evidence and discussion about how neighborhood environments may exert positive influences on behavior and life chances has developed only recently. . . . Despite considerable research progress during the past decade, there is only limited understanding of which neighborhood effects most likely will appear first, what types of households or family members are affected and under what circumstances they are affected, and the durability or persistence of neighborhood effects.[60]

Developing a better understanding of these mechanisms is crucial in assessing site selection policies. One of the most important questions is what type of neighborhood qualifies as "low poverty" so as to obtain the documented benefits of living in such a neighborhood. Is it a neighborhood with less than 10 percent poverty, as in the Moving to Opportunity (MTO) experimental group? Or will some benefits accrue to low-income families in neighborhoods with somewhat higher poverty levels, as suggested by some of the initial results for the MTO comparison group? A related question is the threshold neighborhood poverty level at which harmful effects begin to be felt. George Galster and colleagues have begun to explore this question, suggesting a methodology for analyzing threshold effects associated with a variety of neighborhood composition measures, including percentage of single-parent households, recent unemployment, and percentage of (current) high school dropouts.[61] The answers to these questions could help develop a more graduated site selection policy, which might prohibit new low-income housing in the most isolated poor communities but permit limited, targeted development that supports community renewal in viable mixed-income communities (15–25 percent poverty levels).

The potential benefits of certain types of low-income housing development need to be taken into account. In light of the stark evidence on the harms of poverty concentration, it would seem counterintuitive that adding housing units for poor families in high-poverty areas would contribute to neighborhood revitalization. Yet this proposition has been advanced by a number of researchers and is a basic assumption of the community development movement.[62] At the

60. Goering, Feins, and Richardson (2002, p. 2).
61. Galster, Querica, and Cortes (2000). See also Galster and others (2003).
62. See for example Van Ryzin and Genn (1999).

same time, there is evidence that investment in low-income rental housing development appears to be less effective as a strategy for neighborhood revitalization in inner-city neighborhoods than other strategies, such as homeownership and economic development approaches.[63] In a recent study for HUD, researchers from Abt Associates caution that "states should be skeptical about claims that a [low-income housing tax credit] project will revitalize a neighborhood" and that "construction of affordable housing is a relatively weak tool to influence that change," especially where the proposed housing development is the only intervention: "The choice of LIHTC developments in such areas should be made only when part of a well-designed revitalization strategy for that neighborhood. Where such strategies are not present, the LIHTC resource may be better used to expand housing opportunities for low-income families in relatively higher-income parts of the metropolitan area."[64]

In light of this research, the community development value of a low-income rental development may be dependent on what type of development is being proposed, how it relates to an overall neighborhood revitalization plan, and to what extent it is designed to address existing poverty-related neighborhood deficits.

Toward a Future Site Selection Policy

The social science consensus on the harms of poverty-concentrated living environments, especially for children, strongly suggests that site selection guidelines be reinstituted in all current housing and community development programs, whether they originate at HUD, the Treasury Department, or the federal banking agencies. Based on what we know about demand for desegregated housing, these site selection requirements can be imposed without interfering with individual housing choice. At the same time, the policy emphasis on community revitalization that is built into programs such as CRA, HOPE VI, and LIHTC can be furthered without undermining fair housing goals, if community development funds are spent more wisely and a substantial portion of development funds are set aside for housing outside the central city, to satisfy the substantial unmet demand among inner-city residents for desegregated housing.

In creating these new siting guidelines, it will be important to avoid the rule-versus-the-exception dynamic that undermined the original site and neighborhood standards.[65] New siting guidelines, to the extent that they authorize

63. Ding and Knaap (2002); Newman and Schnare (1997); Rusk (1999).

64. Kadduri and Rodda (2004, p. 19)

65. I am indebted to Alan Mallach, an urban planner (and former director of Housing and Community Development in Trenton), for some of the ideas in this section, versions of which appear in his draft proposal for the Low-Income Housing Tax Credit program in New Jersey. See "Toward a Policy Framework for the Allocation of Low-Income Housing Tax Credits," New Jersey Institute for Social Justice (www.njisj.org [March 2004]).

low-income housing development in higher-poverty areas, should focus on measurable community development rather than on a questionable "finding" that the housing will assist in community development. To the extent possible, similar guidelines should be adopted across program lines, to provide predictability to developers and permit the use of multiple programs in a single project.

The first lesson of recent research on race and poverty is that site and neighborhood standards must be refocused on neighborhood poverty levels in addition to race.[66] A single national standard should be adopted to identify neighborhoods that are both racially segregated and severely impacted by poverty (for example, areas of minority concentration, under the current HUD definition, that also exceed 20 percent poverty).[67] In these neighborhoods, low-income housing development should be permitted only where community development and housing mobility programs are built into the program design. To achieve this, the lenient "overriding need" and "comparable opportunity" exceptions to the HUD site selection requirements, which have effectively swallowed the rule, should be replaced with specific requirements to ensure that the goals embodied by these exceptions are realized.

For example, instead of the "overriding need" exception, which recognizes that in some circumstances low-income housing may actually promote community revitalization, new site selection goals should require housing in higher-poverty neighborhoods to include community enhancements—such as a homeownership component or a retail and office component—that will improve the neighborhood over time. Likewise, the siting of new low-income housing should be prohibited or extremely limited in those neighborhoods where it is likely to have little positive effect.[68] In addition, government-assisted rental developments in the poorest communities should be required to market to slightly higher-income working families, not only to the poorest of the poor.

Similarly, instead of the "comparable opportunity" standard, which seeks to promote the values of housing choice by creating an exception to site selection

66. Similarly, Florence Roisman (forthcoming) suggests that low-income housing development should be restricted in neighborhoods served by schools identified as "failing" under the federal No Child Left Behind legislation. See also John Goering, chapter 6, this volume, where he suggests that any future expansion of the Moving to Opportunity program should include labor market and school performance characteristics.

67. The cutoff of 20 percent poverty was used by HUD to implement the mandate of Congress to deconcentrate poverty and expand housing opportunities, in the 2001 amendments to the Section 8 voucher program's rules for project-based vouchers. See "Revisions to PHA Project-Based Assistance Program; Initial Guidance," 66 Fed. Reg. 3605, 3608 (January 16, 2001).

68. Kadduri and Rodda (2004, pp. 19, 20). This perspective is reflected in HUD's project-based Section 8 site standards, which stress that low-income housing development in a poor neighborhood must be part of an "overall local strategy," and also in the LIHTC statute that directs states to adopt a preference for qualified census tracts only where the housing "contributes to a concerted community revitalization plan." As noted earlier, these types of standards have not been particularly effective, and it may be appropriate to consider moving from a rule-based approach to performance standards that include the desired elements in the housing that is approved.

guidelines, each housing development should require a specific percentage (at least 50 percent) of annual housing development funds in each metropolitan area to be set aside for housing in low-poverty areas, including suburban communities. This was the original intent of the "comparable opportunity" standard designed by HUD some thirty years ago, and it should be reinstated and enforced. If this approach is coupled with strong, affirmative marketing and housing counseling targeted to poor neighborhoods and city-based housing waiting lists, it could help to guarantee that low-income families that choose to move to less segregated housing have affordable housing choices at least as extensive as their neighbors who choose to remain.

References

Bonastia, Chris. 2000. "Why Did Affirmative Action in Housing Fail during the Nixon Era? Exploring 'Institutional Homes' of Social Policies." *Social Problems* 47: 523–24.

Buron, Larry, and others. 2002. *The HOPE VI Resident Tracking Study: A Snapshot of the Current Living Situation of Original Residents from Eight Sites.* Washington: Urban Institute.

Ding, Chengri, and Gerrit-Jan Knaap. 2002. "Property Values in Inner-City Neighborhoods: The Effects of Homeownership, Housing Investment, and Economic Development." *Housing Policy Debate* 13, no. 4: 701–27.

Donovan, Shaun. 1994. "Moving to the Suburbs: Section 8 Mobility and Portability in Hartford." Working Chapter W94-3. Joint Center for Housing Studies, Harvard University.

Freeman, Lance, and Hilary Botein. 2002. "Subsidized Housing and Neighborhood Impacts: A Theoretical Discussion and Review of the Evidence." *Journal of Planning Literature* 26 (February): 359.

Friedman, Sandra, and Gregory Squires. Forthcoming. "Does the Community Reinvestment Act Help Minorities Access Traditionally Inaccessible Neighborhoods?" *Social Problems.*

Galster, George C., Roberto G. Querica, and Alvaro Cortes. 2000. "Identifying Neighborhood Thresholds: An Empirical Exploration." *Housing Policy Debate V* 11, no. 3: 701–32.

Galster, George C., and others. 2003. *Why Not in My Backyard? Neighborhood Impacts of Deconcentrating Assisted Housing.* Center for Urban Policy Research, Edward J. Bloustein School of Planning and Public Policy, Rutgers University.

Goering, John, Judith D. Feins, and Todd M. Richardson. 2002. "A Cross-Site Analysis of Initial Moving to Opportunity Demonstration Results." *Journal of Housing Research* 13: 1.

Goering, John, and Judith Feins, eds. 2003. *Choosing a Better Life? Evaluating the Moving to Opportunity Demonstration.* Washington: Urban Institute.

Goetz, Edward. 2003. *Clearing the Way: Deconcentrating the Poor in Urban America.* Washington: Urban Institute.

Heintz, Kathleen, Andrea A. Anderson, and Heather Doyle. 1996. *Development and Analysis of the National Low-Income Housing Tax Credit Database: Final Report.* Cambridge, Mass.: Abt Associates.

Hendrickson, Cara. 2002. "Racial Desegregation and Income Deconcentration in Public Housing." *Georgetown Journal on Poverty Law and Policy* 35 (Winter): 35–88.

Jargowsky, P. A. 1997. *Poverty and Place: Ghettos, Barrios, and the American City.* New York: Russell Sage.

Kadduri, Jill, and David Rodda. 2004. *Making the Best Use of Your LIHTC Dollars: A Planning Paper for State Policy Makers.* Cambridge, Mass.: Abt Associates.

Marsico, Richard D. 2000. "Enforcing the Community Reinvestment Act: An Advocate's

Guide to Making the CRA Work for Communities." *New York Law School Journal of Human Rights* 129: 129–98.
Massey, Douglas S., and Nancy A. Denton. 1993. *American Apartheid: Segregation and the Making of the Underclass.* Harvard University Press.
Newman, Sandra, and Ann Schnare. 1997. ". . . and a Suitable Living Environment: The Failure of Housing Programs to Deliver on Neighborhood Quality." *Housing Policy Debate* 8, no. 4: 703–41.
Nolden, Sandra, and others. 2002. *Updating the Low-Income Housing Tax Credit Database: Projects Placed in Service through 2000.* Cambridge, Mass.: Abt Associates.
Orfield, Myron. 2005. "Racial Integration and Community Revitalization: Applying the Fair Housing Act to the Low Income Tax Credit." *Vanderbilt Law Review* 58 (November, forthcoming).
Overby, A. Brooke. 1995. "The Community Reinvestment Act Reconsidered." *University of Pennsylvania Law Review* 143: 1431–531.
Pindell, Ngai. 2003. "Is There Hope for HOPE VI? Community Economic Development and Localism." *Connecticut Law Review* 35: 385.
Popkin, Susan J., and Mary K. Cunningham. 1999. *CHAC Section 8 Program: Barriers to Successfully Leasing Up*. Washington: Urban Institute.
Popkin, Susan J., and others. 2004. *A Decade of HOPE VI: Research Findings and Policy Challenges.* Washington: Urban Institute.
Roisman, Florence. 1995a. "Intentional Racial Discrimination and Segregation by the Federal Government as a Principal Cause of Concentrated Poverty: A Response to Schill and Wachter." *University of Pennsylvania Law Review* 143: 1351.
———. 1995b. "The Lessons of American Apartheid: The Necessity and Means of Promoting Residential Racial Integration." *Iowa Law Review* 81 (December): 479.
———. 1998. "Mandates Unsatisfied: The Low-Income Housing Tax Credit Program and the Civil Rights Laws." *Miami Law Review* 52: 1011.
———. Forthcoming. "Keeping the Promise: Ending Racial Discrimination and Segregation in Federally Financed Housing." *Howard Law Journal* 48.
Roisman, Florence, and Hilary Botein. 1993. "Housing Mobility and Life Opportunities." *Clearinghouse Review* 27: 335.
Rubinowitz, Leonard, and James Rosenbaum. 2000. *Crossing the Class and Color Lines: From Public Housing to White Suburbia.* University of Chicago Press.
Rusk, David. 1999. *Inside Game/Outside Game: Winning Strategies for Saving Urban America.* Brookings.
Schill, Michael, and Susan Wachter. 1995. "The Spatial Bias of Federal Housing Law and Policy: Concentrated Poverty in Urban America." *University of Pennsylvania Law Review* 143: 1285.
Tegeler, Philip. 1994. "Housing Segregation and Local Discretion." *Journal of Law and Policy* 3: 209.
Turner, Margery, and Dolores Acevedo-Garcia. 2005. "Why Housing Mobility? A Summary of the Current Evidence." *Poverty and Race* (January-February): 1.
Van Ryzin, Gregg, and Andrew Genn. 1999. "Neighborhood Change and the City of New York's Ten-Year Housing Plan." *Housing Policy Debate* 10, no. 4: 799–838.
Varady, David P., and Carole Walker. 2003. "Housing Vouchers and Residential Mobility." *Journal of Planning Literature* 18, no. 1: 17–30.
Vernarelli, Michael J. 1986. "Where Should HUD Locate Assisted Housing?" In *Housing Desegregation and Federal Policy,* edited by John Goering, pp. 214–34. University of North Carolina Press.
Wilson, William Julius. 1987. *The Truly Disadvantaged: The Inner City, the Underclass, and Public Policy.* University of Chicago Press.

PART III

Metropolitan Development and Policy Coalitions

10

Connecting Smart Growth, Housing Affordability, and Racial Equity

ROLF PENDALL, ARTHUR C. NELSON,
CASEY J. DAWKINS, AND GERRIT J. KNAAP

During the economic boom of the 1990s, developers and builders urbanized unprecedented amounts of rural land throughout the United States. They also redeveloped downtowns in cities that had been all but written off as dead only a decade earlier. Land use planners, concerned about the first trend and excited about the second one, began to broaden their agendas, no longer concentrating solely on managing growth at the fringe, in activities commonly known as growth management, but also on providing incentives and encouragement for growth and redevelopment within existing cities and inner suburbs. As they broadened their scope, physical planners embraced a new label for their activities: *smart growth.*[1] Smart growth provides new techniques and perhaps a new orientation for land use planning. But in most of the United States it has been grafted onto a regulatory framework that has evolved only slowly since the early 1900s.

Land use regulations sort out the urban landscape, allowing some uses, encouraging combinations of some uses, and excluding other uses based on their relationship to the public health, safety, and welfare. This sorting provides useful economic coordination, protects public health, safeguards the environment, and arguably maintains the long-term viability of the building industry itself.

1. Burchell, Listokin, and Galley (2000); Downs (2001); Nelson (2002).

Because of these useful functions, few observers argue that land use regulations ought to be eliminated altogether.[2]

But land use regulation also has a long association with racial and class-based discrimination, segregation, and exclusion. In the early years of regulation, many cities used zoning as a tool for de jure segregation, designating exclusive black and white zones. Then, and now, jurisdictions have zoned African American and Latino neighborhoods in permissive ways, allowing noxious uses that other residents will flee. In more recent years a wide array of land use regulations have been associated with higher housing prices and, by extension, with exclusion of African American and Hispanic residents, who tend to have lower incomes and thus can less easily afford housing in such neighborhoods or jurisdictions. Furthermore, any inflationary effects of land use regulations will be a disproportionately heavy burden on African Americans and Hispanics. The majority of African Americans and Hispanics rent their housing; land use regulations that raise housing prices indirectly reduce home ownership opportunities for racial minorities and burden them with unaffordably high rents.

As the most recent manifestation of the underlying desire to sort out land uses, smart growth must contend with the legacies of exclusionary and inflationary land use regulations. This chapter addresses that legacy by reviewing the research evidence on connections between land use regulation and racial exclusion and segregation, concentrating primarily on the effect of land use regulations on African Americans and to a lesser extent Latinos. Regulations also exclude other racial and ethnic minorities, but most of the literature to date focuses on black-white segregation. It centers much of its attention on whether (and how) land use regulations raise housing prices, thereby indirectly influencing housing markets within which all residents search for a place to live.

Prelude: Racial Zoning

Long before land use zoning became widespread, jurisdictions throughout the United States used racial zoning to segregate neighborhoods. California was a pioneer in this respect; various municipalities adopted explicitly anti-Chinese laws in the 1870s and 1880s, during the height of violence and discrimination against Asian immigrants. San Francisco's 1884 ordinance regulating the operation of laundries—which were both a source of employment and a community gathering place for Chinese immigrants—withstood several legal challenges but was eventually struck down by the U.S. Supreme Court in *Yick Wo* v. *Hopkins* because of its obvious anti-Chinese motivation.[3]

2. See, however, Ellickson (1973).

3. *Yick Wo* v. *Hopkins,* 118 U.S. 356 (1886); Kosman (1993).

A generation later, after the Supreme Court endorsed "separate but equal" facilities for blacks and whites in *Plessy* v. *Ferguson*, municipalities throughout the United States but especially in the South began to adopt explicit racial zoning ordinances, designating districts for exclusive black, white, and sometimes mixed occupancy. Properties in these zones could not be legally sold to a member of any race except those specified in the ordinance. Baltimore, Atlanta, Louisville, Richmond, and other large and midsized cities throughout the South and mid-South adopted racial zoning between 1910 and 1915.[4] Law reviews and many state supreme court rulings endorsed the practice of racial zoning, generally contending that racial zoning was an appropriate exercise of the local police power.[5] In 1917, however, the U.S. Supreme Court ruled racial zoning unconstitutional (*Buchanan* v. *Warley*, 245 U.S. 60) because it interfered with the ability of property owners to dispose of their property as they saw fit.

Even though racial zoning was ruled unconstitutional in 1917, municipalities continued to adopt and enforce racial zoning ordinances for years afterward.[6] Indeed, Birmingham, Alabama, adopted a racial zoning ordinance in 1944, which was struck down by federal courts in 1949.[7] Even had this not been true, in the 1910s, when racial zoning was first adopted, the black population had grown in urban areas throughout the United States; poor agricultural conditions in the mid-1910s and the growth of urban manufacturing during World War I encouraged the rapid migration of blacks from farms to cities.[8] And many municipalities that abandoned racial zoning simply replaced the racial designations with use designations that would help maintain racial segregation. Atlanta, for example, adopted an ordinance in 1922 that designated formerly white zones R1, black zones R2, and mixed zones R3, but this scheme was too transparent to pass muster with the state supreme court.[9] Other cities were probably more successful at hiding the racial intentions behind their ostensibly race-neutral zones.

Post-*Buchanan* examples of racial zoning notwithstanding, the effort to exclude people from neighborhoods on the basis of their ethnicity shifted after

4. Higginbotham, Higginbotham, and Ngcobo (1990).

5. *Plessy* v. *Ferguson,* 163 U.S. 537 (1896); Bernstein (1998); Kosman (1993). Many southern states were subject to Dillon's rule, the principle that municipalities had no authority not expressly granted by state government. Hence some states had to pass enabling legislation to allow racial zoning. Virginia did so in 1912, but North Carolina never did so, and the North Carolina Supreme Court invalidated Winston's racial zoning ordinance as a consequence of this lack of authorization. See Higginbotham, Higginbotham, and Ngcobo (1990).

6. Silver (1997).

7. *Monk et al.* v. *City of Birmingham et. al,* 87 F. supp. 538 (1949), upheld on appeal in *City of Birmingham et al.* v. *Monk et al.,* 185 F.2d 859 (1950).

8. Massey and Denton (1993).

9. Bernstein (1998).

1917 toward private deed restrictions and covenants between land developers, homeowners associations, and property buyers. These racially restrictive covenants were rendered unenforceable by a 1948 U.S. Supreme Court decision (*Shelley* v. *Kraemer*, 334 U.S. 1), but like racial zoning they persisted afterward. New developments in Kansas City, for instance, carried racially restrictive covenants well into the 1960s.[10]

The idea that minorities, especially African Americans but also Latinos and Asians, threaten property values was not just conventional wisdom but also adopted federal and state policy until the 1960s. From the armed forces to public housing to transportation to urban renewal, most major institutions at the federal level were, before then, explicitly designed to separate non-Hispanic whites from minorities. The Federal Housing Administration (FHA), created in 1934 to provide low-cost mortgage insurance, favored the most "stable" neighborhoods.[11] The FHA's system downgraded mixed-race and minority neighborhoods. It also promoted "modern" subdivision controls and zoning ordinances, both of which were thought to maintain neighborhood stability and thereby guarantee property values.[12]

Land use regulations were therefore initially designed in part to separate people by ethnicity; in other words, they were meant to construct an American version of apartheid.[13] It is therefore only natural to suspect that land use regulations might still be complicit in the construction and maintenance of racial and ethnic segregation, even though they have many other overt objectives. But the pathway from land use controls to racial exclusion is now generally more indirect—and thus more difficult to trace—than the mapped-out apartheid of racial zoning.

The Path from Land Use Regulation to Racial Inequity

After *Buchanan,* land use regulations would not have direct racial impacts. Rather, their effects on race—whether intentional or not—would have to occur indirectly, via their intermediate effects on land use and the built environment. The indirect links from land use regulation to racial impact require further explication.

On average, African Americans and Latinos have several disadvantages compared to whites in housing markets. First, their incomes are substantially lower than those of whites; at the median, non-Hispanic white households earned about $46,300 in 2001, compared to $29,740 for black households and $33,560 for Hispanic households, which tend to be larger than those of the

10. Gotham (2000).
11. Jackson (1985).
12. Weiss (1987).
13. Massey and Denton (1993).

other two groups.[14] As a consequence, a smaller share of African Americans and Latinos than of whites can afford housing in neighborhoods or jurisdictions whose housing prices require relatively high incomes. Second, African Americans and Latinos have considerably lower homeownership rates than do non-Hispanic whites; only about 45 percent of each group owned their own homes in 2000, compared to 73 percent of whites.[15] For all these reasons, any regulation that either raises the price or limits the availability of rental housing can indirectly exclude African Americans or Latinos, solely because they tend to have lower incomes and tend to rent their housing rather than own it. Furthermore, African Americans and Latinos are likely to suffer disproportionately in jurisdictions with strict land use controls because of the likely limited supply of affordable housing.

The primary analytic task for those seeking to make the connection between land use regulations and racial equity, then, begins with determining whether a particular regulation or a combination of regulations raises housing costs or limits the availability of rental housing. It continues with the determination of how higher housing costs or limited rental housing availability, on either the local level or the regional level, affect African Americans and Latinos. At the local level, regulations can indirectly exclude African Americans and Latinos from some jurisdictions when they raise housing prices or limit rental housing. And at the regional level, regulations can increase housing costs for all residents, but the costs of higher housing costs may fall disproportionately upon low-income people, who are disproportionately African American and Hispanic.

A History of Land Use Regulation

Land use regulation emerged in the United States in the late 1800s and early 1900s. The earliest forms of public regulation were zoning and subdivision control.

Zoning specifies permitted and prohibited uses for private land, limits the intensity (density) of development, and sets a maximum building envelope. Starting with the earliest zoning ordinances, there has always been a distinction between hierarchical (or Euclidean) zoning and exclusive-use zoning. Hierarchical zoning permits all, or almost all, uses in its least restrictive category, protecting single-family residential homes in a category of their own. Industrial zones, that is, can also usually accommodate all other uses in a Euclidean zoning scheme. Exclusive-use zoning, by contrast, prohibits residential uses in industrial zones, commercial uses in residential zones, and so on. By the 1990s over

14. U.S. Census Bureau (2002).

15. African Americans and Latinos also face substantial discrimination and higher fees when they attempt to obtain housing, mortgages, and homeowner's insurance. These contributors to segregation and exclusion are less directly connected to local land use practices, however, than high housing costs and a lack of rental housing.

90 percent of the municipalities in large U.S. metropolitan areas had adopted zoning ordinances, with notable exceptions in and around Houston, Texas.[16] Zoning is required in some states, including California and Oregon.

Subdivision control governs the division of land for resale and primarily ensures the availability of adequate infrastructure (streets, water supply, sewage disposal, and so on).[17] Subdivision regulation also provides a process through which local governments review development applications. Subdivision regulation became popular in the wake of rampant land speculation in the 1920s. When this boom collapsed, thousands of people owned "paper lots" they could not reach because they were not served by roads.[18] When the Great Depression of the 1930s caused widespread delinquencies in payment of the special assessments that funded infrastructure construction in platted subdivisions, many more local governments adopted subdivision ordinances requiring physical improvements.[19]

Land use zoning and subdivision regulation have clear and straightforward objectives. Zoning, in particular, helps to minimize negative externalities such as noise and odors. Subdivision regulations were designed to protect housing consumers, who frequently bought lots sight unseen, and to ensure that local governments would not bear the long-term costs of providing infrastructure to areas with legal lots but without infrastructure. By requiring that public services be provided as a precondition of development, subdivision regulation helps to reduce public fiscal costs. Major real estate interests and early planners embraced both zoning and subdivision regulation because they promised to protect the stability and property value of residential neighborhoods and avoid nuisance lawsuits against industrial users.[20] While both zoning and subdivision regulation would ostensibly be carried out in accordance with a comprehensive (physical) plan for municipal development, such plans tended to be rudimentary and advisory rather than specific and binding, at least until the 1960s.

The suburbanization that swept the United States between World War II and 1965 occurred within the framework set out by local zoning and subdivision control ordinances. These ordinances fostered extensive development of single-use neighborhoods, separation between workplaces and housing, increases in driving, and other hallmarks of urban sprawl. They also proved costly to provide with public services and converted large amounts of open space to urban development. To reduce sprawl, some local governments adopted urban containment programs. These programs ranged from permanent and inflexible greenbelts to

16. Siegan (1978).

17. Site plan review is analogous to subdivision regulation and ensures infrastructure adequacy for land development when there is no subdivision.

18. Smith (1987).

19. Smith (1987).

20. Weiss (1987).

urban growth boundaries, which can be expanded to ensure an adequate land supply to allow markets to function.[21] Other local governments adopted measures to ensure infrastructure capacity. These measures include adequate public facilities ordinances, which provide that growth may not occur unless and until certain public facilities related to the development meet local standards for quality and capacity.[22] They also include impact fees, which require developers to pay a pro rata share of the cost of new capital facilities. A smaller number of local governments placed annual limits on residential building permits to smooth the pace of development.

Coincident with the new interest in growth management, states began reforming their planning laws to require more local planning. California required its local governments to adopt general plans starting in 1971 and soon thereafter required them to bring their zoning ordinances into conformity with their plans. In 1973 Oregon adopted statewide growth management legislation requiring local governments to adopt comprehensive plans that were consistent with a series of state goals.[23] Florida, following a model proposed by the American Law Institute, adopted a comprehensive program of "critical area" protection and "development of regional impact" review and for the first time required local governments to join in the planning.[24] Starting in the late 1980s, another wave of states—Washington, New Jersey, Vermont, Maine, Rhode Island, and Maryland—passed growth management legislation, again requiring or giving stronger incentives for local planning, consistent with state goals.[25]

Smart growth expands upon growth management in several ways without abandoning the tools of growth management.[26] First, it directs attention beyond land use regulation and direction of growth at the suburban fringe to all the practices that guide growth, including not only regulation but also investment in infrastructure, open-space protection, and crucially, investment in inner cities. Second, smart growth devotes much more attention to urban design at the site, neighborhood, and regional scale. Third, smart growth concentrates on reinvesting and improving established neighborhoods and on preserving historic resources. Fourth, smart growth relies more than growth management on incentives and guidance and less on regulation and mandates. This retreat from command and control applies equally to the relationship between the public and private sector and the relationship between state and local government. For example, smart growth open-space programs tend to respect private property rights by purchasing land and development rights or allowing density transfers

21. Pendall, Martin, and Fulton (2002).
22. Godschalk and others (1979).
23. Leonard (1983).
24. American Law Institute (1976); Read (1987).
25. Bollens (1992); Gale (1992); Innes (1992).
26. Burchell, Listokin, and Galley (2000); Downs (2001); Nelson (2002).

rather than reducing development capacity. And state-level smart growth programs (such as that in Maryland) attempt to shape local development decisions by targeting investments and coordinating state programs rather than by requiring that local plans meet state goals and penalizing them if they do not.

Land use regulations are adopted not in isolation but as components of local regulatory regimes, that is, the sum of formal and informal institutions that regulate the delivery of housing and community services in a locality. These institutions include not only land use regulations but also affordable housing programs, infrastructure investment, and initiatives to protect open space. Together, these components of the regional regulatory regime probably affect affordability more than any particular local land use regulation.

There is substantial variation among regulatory regimes in the United States.[27] The Northeast and Midwest are dominated by metropolitan areas in which a large number of small municipalities use large-lot zoning to control growth; these municipalities seldom adopt affordable housing programs to mitigate the price effects of their land use regulations. Metropolitan areas in the South (outside Florida) and the Great Plains tend to be more laissez-faire; they seldom impose growth controls of any kind, nor do they adopt affordable housing programs. County governments are important, especially in the South, but their regulatory role is often very slight and usually designed to facilitate development rather than to control it.[28] Local governments in the West—and in Florida and Maryland—all have stronger growth management programs, often coordinated at the county level, with combinations of such techniques as urban growth boundaries, building permit caps, and adequate public facilities ordinances. Exclusionary zoning is very rare in these regions; municipalities and especially counties tend to use large-lot zoning primarily to protect productive farming and forestry lands and open space rather than to create low-density residential environments. Many municipalities in the West also adopt a large number of creative, local, affordable housing programs.

Housing Costs

At the broadest level, land use regulations can affect housing costs from two directions, supply and demand. Strict regulations, that is, are likely to limit the supply and increase the quality of housing, but they are also likely to provide benefits—such as a lower tax rate, more protected open space, and adequate infrastructure—for which prospective residents are willing to pay.[29]

27. Pendall (1995).

28. Lowry and Ferguson (1992).

29. A lower tax rate would result from a regulatory system that raises land or property values; when a jurisdiction's tax base rises, it can provide the same quantity of constant-quality public services at a lower tax rate.

Most of the literature on land use regulations and housing affordability concentrates on the supply side. These regulations can affect the quantity of housing supplied; zoning and urban growth boundaries, for example, can limit the amount of land available for housing and thereby limit the amount of housing supplied by the market, and building permit caps can limit the number of housing units provided. Ordinances requiring adequate public facilities can limit housing supply if infrastructure capacity cannot accommodate development. The impact of a supply constraint will be more pronounced in locations with few acceptable substitutes; in open metropolitan regions, on the other hand, housing consumers will simply search for housing in their price range, bypassing controlled locations whose prices are too high.[30]

Beyond their impacts on supply, regulations can also raise the quality of housing supplied, including its size, structure type, construction, and infrastructure. Building codes, zoning, subdivision regulations, and development impact fees do this by imposing direct requirements on residential builders. Building codes can require expensive materials that add to construction costs. Zoning ordinances usually designate specific zones in which only single-family detached residences are allowed; sometimes entire municipalities, or even blocs of municipalities, are zoned exclusively for single-family detached homes. Zoning ordinances can also ban the construction of secondary dwellings in single-family zones and often place severe limits on manufactured housing and mobile homes or even prohibit these housing types entirely.[31] And zoning ordinances in many states can set a minimum house or apartment size. Subdivision regulations can raise housing costs by imposing demanding and sometimes overengineered infrastructure requirements on housing developers.[32] And impact fees tend to be passed on to buyers or renters of new housing, with established homeowners and landlords receiving windfall gains because their housing already has the infrastructure for which new buyers or renters must pay.[33]

30. Courant (1976); Katz and Rosen (1987).

31. Since housing markets are often segmented by location, type, style, and density, it is often difficult to predict how supply restrictions imposed on certain housing types will affect the entire regional housing market. Because customers and housing producers can substitute among various housing submarkets in response to submarket supply restrictions, the ultimate price impact of land use regulations will depend on the type of regulation imposed (for example, density restriction, allowable-use restriction, lot size restriction) and the elasticity of demand for housing in each submarket (Grieson and White 1981). If the submarkets operate independently of one another, and the demand for the restricted land use is more elastic than the demand for the unrestricted land use, then the regulation may actually serve to reduce the aggregate price of new housing. This results from the fact that the supply of land available for the unrestricted land use increases, which causes prices in that market to fall by an amount that is greater than the higher price in the restricted market (Ohls, Weisburg, and White 1974).

32. Seidel (1978).

33. In some markets, landowners indirectly pay impact fees or share their costs with home buyers or renters, but at least in theory, landowners can simply withdraw their property from the market and wait for prices to rise if they prefer not to accept lower prices from builders.

Regulations can also have a series of indirect impacts on housing and infrastructure quality. Land-supply constraints can encourage builders to shift toward higher-density housing types if they are permitted to do so. The housing stocks in Seoul and London, both of which are encircled by inflexible greenbelts, have shifted decisively toward multifamily structures.[34] Building permit caps or quotas, by contrast, sometimes indirectly encourage builders to build large houses rather than attached housing units; since they are not guaranteed permission to build the volume of attached housing necessary to attain a desired profit level, they may shift to up-market housing, for which they can obtain a higher total profit per unit. Permit caps are also sometimes implemented through "beauty contest" systems, which favor large houses and encourage builders to load expensive amenities into their houses and subdivisions.

Land use regulations also raise housing prices by reducing the responsiveness of local builders to increases in price. A highly regulated system, in which subdivision approval requires seven or eight months, for example, is likely to approve fewer subdivisions before periodic housing price spikes abate than an unregulated system, in which approval requires only a few weeks. The long-term effects of these response lags on the total amount of new housing supplied—and thus on prices—can be significant.[35]

Land use regulations and growth management can also affect the demand side of the housing equation by increasing local amenities and thereby increasing the price that residents are willing to pay to live there. Some growth management programs can elevate the value of an entire region by making more efficient use of infrastructure, creating or enhancing agglomeration economies, and improving the quality of life; values will rise because demand rises. This expectation can increase housing prices even though changes in demand or supply may never actually occur.[36] Furthermore, a regulatory regime that encourages high-density, mixed-use development focused on mass transit may increase demand because of the convenience that such development patterns offer and because people may be able to avoid purchasing vehicles (thereby allowing them to devote more income to housing).

Housing Tenure and Expulsive Zoning

Land use regulations have an indirect but important connection with housing tenure that derives in part from their effects on agricultural, structural, infrastructure, and supply values. Single-family houses tend to be owned by their occupants; multifamily dwellings tend to be rented. Any regulation that promotes the construction of single-family houses and discourages the development

34. Bae (1998); Evans (1991).
35. Mayer and Somerville (2000).
36. Titman (1985).

of attached dwellings will also tend to attract more owner-occupants and limit opportunities for renters. Zoning ordinances can also exert a direct influence on the occupancy of housing units by reserving certain zones for narrowly defined families, further limiting options for unrelated low-income individuals who wish to share a house.

Zoning can be used not only to exclude minorities from neighborhoods and jurisdictions where they do not yet live; it can also be used to encourage them to leave areas where they do live. Yale Rabin documents at least twelve cases in which local governments used industrial zoning designations to reduce property values of, and introduce toxic or hazardous land uses into, predominantly African American neighborhoods, even some predominantly composed of single-family houses.[37] For example, Hamtramck, a Michigan city surrounded by Detroit, designated black neighborhoods for the expansion of automobile manufacturing plants, resulting in displacement of thousands of African American families. Baltimore County, Maryland, designated several historically black neighborhoods for exclusive industrial and commercial use, limiting or eliminating replacements or additions to the housing stock. These zoning designations do not always eliminate African Americans entirely, but those who remain experience not only lower property values but also hazardous conditions.

Uncovering examples of expulsive zoning is difficult; it is even more difficult to identify cases in which local governments neglect to use zoning in a way that protects residents from health and safety threats irrespective of their race. Such nondecisions, however, may be the rule rather than the exception, since protective zoning is often conferred upon those with more wealth and power.[38] Hundreds of environmental justice cases throughout the United States arguably would not have arisen had land use controls been operating in ways that ensured people of color the same protections that white non-Hispanics often enjoy in the same jurisdictions.

Exclusion

Thus far, our main focus has been on the ways in which land use regulations can increase housing prices, limit the entry of renters into local jurisdictions, and introduce insalubrious land uses into minority neighborhoods. These exclusionary and expulsive impacts may be motivated by the desire to exclude or eliminate low-income residents and racial minorities, but local governments also adopt land use controls to maximize or at least balance the local budget (so-called fiscal zoning), to create and sustain amenities for local and even regional constituencies, to ensure that adequate infrastructure is available, to safeguard against natural hazards, to smooth the rate of change, to support agricultural

37. Rabin (1989).
38. Dubin (1993); Kaswan (2003).

and forest land productivity, and to create positive externalities (for instance, by encouraging complementary land uses to locate close to one another). Many of these purposes reinforce one another, hindering efforts to distinguish unethical or even illegal exclusionary land use regulation from regulation to promote the public welfare.

Yet a growing body of evidence permits some generalizations about the extent to which land use regulations of various sorts are primarily motivated by the intent to exclude. Broadly speaking, this literature suggests that when large-lot zoning is the primary land use control, it is likely to have been adopted to exclude low-income households. There is strong support from case law, popular accounts, and the academic literature that local governments adopt large-lot zoning, minimum house size requirements, and bans on secondary units precisely to make their housing more expensive and thereby exclude lower-income racial and ethnic minorities.[39] Two studies delve into the history of conflicts in Mount Laurel, New Jersey, that led to the best-known legal decisions overruling exclusionary zoning ever to be handed down by a court in the United States.[40] Federal courts, by contrast, have been more deferential to local zoning and have tended to uphold the right of communities to exclude low-income residents, at least on constitutional grounds, as long as there is no direct evidence that they intended to exclude racial or ethnic minorities.[41] The adjudication of these cases and their tendency to be decided in favor of exclusionary jurisdictions show that local governments not only know that their large-lot zoning ordinances will exclude but also embrace them for precisely that reason.

Barbara Rolleston, studying the intensity of local residential zoning ordinances in metropolitan Chicago, finds that communities with smaller minority populations than surrounding communities tend to practice restrictive zoning, supporting the idea that exclusionary motivations contribute to local zoning decisions.[42] But other motivations, especially the desire to maximize or at least balance the local budget, are simultaneously at work in many cases; Rolleston also finds that communities with growing tax bases practiced less restrictive residential zoning.

39. Babcock (1966); Danielson (1976).

40. See Kirp, Dwyer, and Rosenthal (1995); and Haar (1996). These cases, known as Mount Laurel I (*Southern Burlington County NAACP* v. *Mount Laurel,* 336 A.2d 713, N.J. 1975) and Mount Laurel II (*Southern Burlington County NAACP* v. *Township of Mount Laurel,* 456 A.2d 390, N.J 1983), set forth the statewide fair-share housing system that was modified and incorporated into state law in 1985 as the New Jersey Fair Housing Act (N.J. Stat. Ann. 52:27D-301 to 329).

41. In *Village of Arlington Heights* v. *Metropolitan Housing Development Corp.,* 429 U.S. 252 (1977), the U.S. Supreme Court established a nearly impossible standard for exclusionary zoning cases brought under the equal protection clause of the Constitution. Proof of disproportionate impact on minorities is not enough to invalidate a zoning ordinance for constitutional violations; plaintiffs are required to demonstrate intent to exclude.

42. Rolleston (1987).

For other residential controls, by contrast, it is difficult to distinguish such narrow motivations; indeed, other controls are often adopted in concert with affordable housing programs that blunt the exclusionary impact of land use regulations. Studies of jurisdictions that adopt growth measures of certain kinds find that growth-controlled jurisdictions tend to be growing faster and to have more professional and white-collar residents, wealthier households, and fewer minorities, but these results are neither universal nor are they direct evidence of exclusionary intent.[43] Some places adopt growth measures after a spurt of rapid growth in response to the desire of newcomers to maintain the quality of the environment and public services that were present when they arrived.[44] Comparing voters for and against a growth-control ballot measure in Riverside, California, M. Gottdiener and Max Neiman find no relationship between support for the measure and socioeconomic status; rather, support tends to correlate with "liberal" sentiments "generally favoring more government activity in providing public services."[45] Jeffrey Dubin, D. Roderick Kiewiet, and Charles Noussair, analyzing precinct-level returns from competing 1989 growth measures in San Diego City and County, support the Gottdiener and Neiman results.[46] They also find that minority voters—even holding constant their tenure—tend to oppose the measures much more often, and that homeowners—holding race constant—tend to support them. This finding tends to support exclusionary models based on both race and class (to the extent that class corresponds to tenure).

Attitude surveys, which ask people about their positions on growth control, also support the idea that slow-growth sentiments respond to perceptions that growth has been too fast and that infrastructure is deteriorating.[47] Perceptions sometimes matter more than the real rate of growth.[48] Liberalism also tends to associate with support for controls in many attitude surveys; the surveys lend less support, however, to the idea that people who favor controls are wealthier than those who oppose them. A retrospective on these surveys suggests that the sources of support for growth control and management may change through time, producing contradictory results even within jurisdictions, not to mention among different jurisdictions.[49]

The intentions of local regulation—both explicit and implicit—may matter little to economists who study the price effects of land use regulations, but intentions are crucial. Jurisdictions whose residents and elected officials wish to exclude low-income people and racial minorities can use a huge array of devices

43. Donovan and Neiman (1992); Dowall (1984); Protash and Baldassare (1983).
44. Dubbink (1984); Rosenbaum (1978).
45. Gottdiener and Neiman (1981, p. 62).
46. Dubin, Kiewiet, and Noussair (1992).
47. Anglin (1990); Baldassare and Wilson (1996).
48. Baldassare (1985).
49. Baldassare and Wilson (1996).

to do so, ranging from such legal approaches as large-lot zoning to illegal violence and intimidation. Exhorting such jurisdictions to allow smaller lots and to adopt affordable housing programs is a wasted effort. Local governments that want simply to manage their growth but also wish to build diverse communities, by contrast, can take actions and adopt policies to do so, embracing a regime that both manages growth and actively pursues a diversity of housing in ways that the market alone would not provide.

Inclusion

Land use regulations can indeed be used to include and protect racial minorities. First, they can ensure wider housing opportunity and more mixed neighborhoods and communities. Some regulatory regimes include affordable housing and inclusionary elements that are designed to lower the costs of construction and broaden choices to more housing segments. Some programs include measures to ensure an adequate supply of land for dwellings of many types. By permitting, or encouraging, the construction of smaller and denser forms of housing, housing units are made available at lower prices and rents, even though the cost per unit of housing services may be higher. Local governments sometimes complement strategies to ensure adequate land supply and a range of housing types with housing subsidy programs and programs that encourage or require provision of affordable housing by private sector builders.

Second, land use regulations and growth management can reduce the cost of infrastructure per unit, thereby lowering housing costs. Infrastructure controls can indirectly increase housing densities, creating housing in structure types (attached units and small-lot single-family homes, for example) that are less expensive and open to rental occupancy and thus more often occupied by lower-income racial and ethnic minorities. They can also ensure that existing capacities are fully employed before new facilities are built and help capture economies of scale through regionalization.[50] Ordinances requiring adequate public facilities and fees based on the impact of the growth can favor the construction of attached or higher-density housing to make more efficient use of the infrastructure, whose costs are borne by landowners and new residents instead of the general public.

Third, land use regulations and other growth programs can be designed in ways that protect and enhance the health, safety, and quality of life for African Americans and Hispanics. In particular, they can enact zoning that avoids the siting of noxious facilities in minority neighborhoods and near schools, hospitals, and other necessary facilities. Regulations and growth programs can also help ensure convenient access to shopping, transportation, schools, parks, and other necessities of urban life.

50. Knaap and Nelson (1992).

Testing Theories about Regulation, Price, and Exclusion

Studies of how land use regulations affect housing can be divided into local studies and regional studies. Most studies, whether local or regional, suggest that strict control of growth is associated with a tighter housing supply and higher housing prices, but the relationship is not as straightforward or as consistent as economic theory would predict. In particular, land use regulations tend to have less severe effects on affordability if they are adopted within a context that also accommodates higher-density development and places few explicit restrictions on the pace of growth.

Local Effects

Local zoning clearly affects land prices: Land zoned for high-density development tends to be more costly than land zoned for agriculture. Zoning also affects the rate and intensity of housing development. Communities with very low-density zoning tend to have slower growth rates, accommodate fewer new multifamily dwellings, and shift toward rental occupancy, compared to jurisdictions with higher-density zoning.[51] Based on case studies of local regulations in North Carolina and New Jersey, which tend to regulate with standard zoning and subdivision regulations rather than with smart growth techniques, Michael Luger and Kenneth Temkin contend that many regulatory requirements impose "excessive" costs that range from $10,000 to $20,000 for each new housing unit.[52] Studies of local regulations in the coastal areas of California and Maryland find that reductions in zoned density have displaced housing to areas fairly distant from the coast; in the California case, displacement to cities and counties is as far as fifty miles from the controlled communities.[53]

A series of studies also shows that jurisdictions with strong growth controls have higher single-family housing prices than weakly controlled or uncontrolled jurisdictions.[54] For example, Petaluma, California, a national leader in capping residential building permits, has higher housing prices and lower production of low- and moderate-income housing than two nearby jurisdictions without growth controls.[55] But the building permit caps that most of these studies analyze are fairly uncommon even in California.[56]

Studies gauging the direct impact of local growth management programs and growth controls on housing construction levels, however, produce more mixed and ambiguous results than studies on the correlation between land use controls

51. Pendall (2000).
52. Luger and Temkin (2000).
53. Feitelson (1993); Levine (1999).
54. Dowall and Landis (1982); Elliott (1981); Katz and Rosen (1987); Rosen and Katz (1981).
55. Schwartz, Hansen, and Green (1981, 1984).
56. Glickfeld and Levine (1992).

and housing prices. John Landis, for example, finds that three out of seven "growth-controlled" jurisdictions grew more rapidly than a non-growth-controlled matched jurisdiction.[57] In a regression analysis of most California jurisdictions, Madelyn Glickfeld and Ned Levine find that the annual number of growth-control measures enacted did not affect the value of construction (an indicator of construction activity) three years later.[58] A Southern California study also finds that growth control does not always make much difference in the level of construction among jurisdictions.[59] A California-wide study using spatial statistics finds that urban growth boundaries, building permit caps, and adequate public facility ordinances have no significant effect on the location or supply of housing.[60] But a study of the spatial impacts of growth controls in the San Francisco Bay area alone finds that they displace growth to both outlying and infill locations.[61] A study of over a thousand jurisdictions nationwide also finds no consistent supply-side effect from urban growth boundaries, adequate public facilities ordinances, building permit caps, or even building permit moratoriums.[62]

Evidence from Boulder, Colorado, by contrast, shows fairly clearly that the most extreme forms of growth control raise housing prices and displace development to other areas. Boulder has one of the least flexible greenbelts in the United States, has imposed a citywide thirty-five-foot building height limit, and limits the pace of growth. Within Boulder, housing prices have risen dramatically. An early study suggests that some of the price increase was an impact of amenities conferred by open space.[63] But more recent price increases are a consequence of both reduced housing supply and increased housing demand,[64] even though the city has adopted other programs to promote and require the production of moderately priced dwelling units.[65] About 55 percent of the city's workforce lives outside the city limits.[66]

The effects of new growth management and growth control are more inconsistent than those of exclusionary zoning in part because used (existing) housing dominates many regional markets.[67] Land use regulations apply mainly to new housing. Furthermore, local land markets are complicated and fragmented. A

57. Landis (1992).
58. Glickfield and Levine (1992).
59. Warner and Molotch (1992).
60. Levine (1999).
61. Shen (1996).
62. Pendall (2000).
63. Correll, Lillydahl, and Singell (1978).
64. Lorentz and Shaw (2000).
65. Miller (1986).
66. Berny Morson, "Boulder Looks at Harm Tied to Costly Housing: Council Adopts Report that Urges More Affordable Homes," *Rocky Mountain News,* February 21, 1999, p. 35A.
67. DiPasquale and Wheaton (1994).

study of three large but expanding California cities suggests that complex and strict land use regulations may raise housing prices because they restructure the residential construction and development industry in ways that allow builders to command monopoly rents.[68] Another California comparison finds that housing prices rose more moderately in Napa in the late 1970s, despite its inflexible urban growth boundary, than in nearby Santa Rosa, which allocated sufficient land; Napa had slack demand, while large developers in Santa Rosa hoarded land.[69] New town developments in California (Irvine) and elsewhere (Columbia, Maryland; Woodlands, Texas) have also commanded premium prices in part because their large developers could release land slowly.[70] In metropolitan areas, where control over land is more fragmented (either in ownership or among jurisdictions), one would expect housing consumers to be able to limit the effects of local supply restrictions by shopping next door.

The effect of land use regulations also depends on how local governments carry them out. Building permit caps, for example, are often enacted in response to unusually high growth rates in previous years—rates that would not have been attained even without the controls in later years. Furthermore, growth controls often have loopholes that preclude stringent implementation, including exemptions for affordable housing and small projects.

These ambiguities about the relationship between land use regulations and housing prices cast doubt upon the clear-cut conclusions derived from the studies of the effects of growth control on the price of housing, since land use controls can raise prices only indirectly—by restricting land and housing supply.

Regional Effects

Housing demand rises, and prices go up accordingly, in uncontrolled jurisdictions near controlled jurisdictions[71] and in less-regulated parts of regulated jurisdictions.[72] Frequently, residents in the locations to which growth is displaced respond by imposing restrictions of their own. And when many jurisdictions within a county adopt exclusionary zoning or put caps on building permits, the county's built density drops over time.[73]

Entire metropolitan areas can thus become highly restricted as a consequence of these unconnected growth-control decisions on the local level; when this happens, housing prices are likely to rise throughout the region. Studies generally find higher housing prices in regions with more tightly controlled housing markets. The challenge in these empirical studies has been to measure the various

68. Landis (1986).
69. Dowall (1984).
70. Forsyth (2002).
71. Katz and Rosen (1987).
72. Pollakowski and Wachter (1990).
73. Pendall (1999).

aspects of constraint. Physical constraints, such as steep slopes and water bodies, undoubtedly play some role. Regulations are also important. The availability and pricing of infrastructure play their part, as does the metropolitan pattern of landownership.

Using measures of restrictiveness based on interviews with builders and developers, four studies find higher lot prices in regions with more restricted developable land.[74] Two of the studies estimate that constraints of all kinds explain about 40 percent of the variation in house prices among metropolitan areas, with about three-quarters of the effect attributable to natural constraints and one-quarter attributable to regulatory constraints.[75] Using more systematic survey data, Stephen Malpezzi and colleagues developed a measure of restrictiveness based on the time required to secure development approval, the availability of residential land compared to demand, and the adequacy of infrastructure.[76] This measure, like the others, correlates with higher prices at the median and low end.

All of the studies suggest that restriction corresponds with higher housing prices or rent, but none of them tests the regulation-to-price relationship through time. Hence none of the studies offers a complete enough model to gauge how much a region's housing prices or rents would rise or fall after it adopts or eliminates land use regulations, because most of them are cross-sectional rather than longitudinal. Furthermore, the models do not use specifications that account for endogeneity between prices and regulations; regulations are likely to be adopted more frequently in high-value regions because such property owners have more investment to protect. And finally, few of the studies account for demand-side influences on housing prices beyond income- and job-related measures. Land use controls promise benefits ranging from fiscal stability to environmental quality to infrastructure capacity, so regions that are more controlled may also have more of these benefits. Since land use regulations can both restrict supply and increase demand, it is important to account more fully for the demand side before making definitive statements about the supply-related impact on lot or housing prices or supply.

Most of these studies, furthermore, do not distinguish the price effects of different regulatory regimes. Most of Malpezzi and colleagues' restrictiveness variables, for example, would appear to apply mainly to exclusionary zoning regimes, which put limits on the amount of land zoned for multifamily housing, reduce opportunities for rezoning, and lengthen approval times. But San Francisco, San Jose, and Honolulu, well-known for growth control but not for exclusionary zoning, score highest on the Malpezzi index; Boston, Newark, and New

74. Black and Hoben (1985); Segal and Srinivasan (1985); Rose (1989a, 1989b).

75. Rose (1989a, 1989b).

76. Malpezzi (1996, 2002); Malpezzi, Chun, and Green (1998); Malpezzi and Green (1996).

York, all of which are characterized by exclusionary zoning, also score high. Richard Green, an exception, examines the impact of various zoning constraints on the price of housing and other aspects of housing affordability (such as tenure and rent) and share of new housing constructed within an "affordable" price range.[77] He finds that zoning sets a minimum price floor for housing construction, making small, inexpensive houses unprofitable relative to large, expensive houses, thereby limiting their production.

Surprisingly few studies measure the direct connection between regulation at the regional level and regional housing supply. One exception, the study by Christopher Mayer and C. Tsuriel Somerville, concentrates on how land use regulations affect regional housing supply.[78] Using the same regulatory database on which Malpezzi and Green rely, Mayer and Somerville find that housing markets in highly regulated metropolitan areas—in particular, those in which subdivision approval takes a long time—both produce less housing generally and are less responsive to price increases than those in less-regulated areas. Although the difference is small in any particular year, the cumulative difference can be fairly extreme.

Case study research provides a deeper, if less generalizable, picture of how regulatory regimes affect housing affordability and opportunity. Ira Lowry and Bruce Ferguson, for example, examine the aggregate impacts of land use regulation in Sacramento, California; Nashville, Tennessee; and Orlando, Florida.[79] Here again, land supply made the difference between eroding affordability in Sacramento, where land was scarce compared to demand, and in Orlando, where the land supply kept pace with demand and housing inflation did not erode despite the city's complex web of state, regional, and local regulations. Interestingly, housing prices rose more rapidly in Nashville's unregulated market than in Orlando's regulated market. Despite abundant land, Nashville developers engaged in rampant land speculation during the 1980s and constructed far more homes than buyers would buy at the high prices the developers had to ask to recover their speculative investments. Lowry and Ferguson conclude that Nashville residents and builders alike would have benefited if land use regulations had limited land speculation.

A case study still in progress is that of the effect of metropolitan and state-level land use regulation in Portland, Oregon. Oregon statutes require its local governments to adopt urban growth boundaries to curb sprawl; in Portland, the boundary is regional, taking in three counties, and is mirrored by a similar boundary across the Columbia River in Vancouver, Washington. Urban containment in Oregon (and to an extent in Washington) is designed not to limit

77. Green (1999).
78. Mayer and Somerville (2000).
79. Lowry and Ferguson (1992).

the total amount of housing—in fact, local governments are required to demonstrate that their growth boundaries contain enough land to satisfy market demands for new development well into the future—but rather to increase density, enhance development mix, and provide more transportation options in urban areas so as to reduce pressure on historic productive lands and undeveloped areas.

The main purpose of Portland's regional growth management system (of which its urban growth boundary is a part) is to produce a more compact, mixed, and efficient metropolitan area. To satisfy market demands, Oregon has substantially reduced regulatory constraints and increased housing densities inside of the boundaries. Oregon municipalities are not permitted to enact moratoriums or to cap building permits. Furthermore, jurisdictions in metropolitan Portland are subject to the Metropolitan Housing Rule, which requires them to zone in such a way that half of their potential dwellings are multifamily housing units. Furthermore, the state places a strong emphasis on a fast and predictable permitting process.[80] All of these features, combined with continuous monitoring of buildable land, raise hopes among supporters of the Oregon system that its brand of growth management will lend predictability to development, create an urban form that has fewer harmful and more beneficial effects on people and the environment, and still provide a range of housing types at affordable prices for the region's residents.

Portland's boundary was drawn expansively when it was created in the early 1980s; furthermore, Portland's economy was depressed throughout much of the 1980s and 1990s. Housing prices were therefore among the lowest on the West Coast until the early 1990s. But Portland's single-family housing prices rose markedly in the 1990s, just as its urban growth boundary began to constrain regional housing supplies. Following this increase, Samuel Staley, Jefferson Edgens, and Gerard Mildner speculated that the region would be in a housing deficit situation by 2017 if the boundary was not expanded. For this reason, homebuilders and development interests strongly supported relaxing the boundary.[81]

Other analysts suggest that Portland had previously been undervalued, perhaps because of the prolonged economic recession. Justin Phillips and Eban Goodstein contend that Portland's price escalation has merely allowed it to catch up with average levels among thirty-seven western cities, and they suggest that speculative bidding may have been more important than the urban growth boundary in raising housing prices.[82] In any event, they found no statistically significant association between the boundary and housing prices.

Anthony Downs, using different data, concludes: "The mere existence of [an urban growth boundary], even a stringently drawn one, does not necessarily cause

80. Knaap and Nelson (1992); Nelson and Duncan (1995).
81. Staley, Edgens, and Mildner (1999).
82. Phillips and Goodstein (2000).

housing prices in a region to rise faster than those in other comparable regions without any kind of [boundary]."[83] Downs notes that the much-advertised spike in housing prices seen in the early 1990s was attributable principally to substantial increases in employment and incomes, not to the supply-restricting effects of its regional urban growth boundary and other growth management efforts. Furthermore, some of Portland's growth undoubtedly consisted of equity-rich Californians, whose wealth helped inflate the Portland housing market. And finally, Portland has a high quality of life, which has arguably been boosted by growth management, underscoring the likelihood that if regulations have indeed raised housing prices, they have done so at least as much by enhancing demand as by restricting supply.

Empirical research on Portland also confirms that land uses have shifted and densities have increased since the urban growth boundary took effect. A 1991 study found that the volume of multiple-family and attached single-family development had increased dramatically in the previous decade, and the average lot size of single-family houses had dropped by nearly half.[84] This shift apparently resulted from both market factors (a prolonged economic downturn that increased demand for affordable dwelling types) and the combined effects of the growth boundary and the Metropolitan Housing Rule. More recent data for Portland show that the trend toward higher density continued during the economic boom of the 1990s, with average lot sizes falling 14 percent in Clackamas and 20 percent in Multnomah County.[85]

In summary, there is little argument that a region dominated by local governments whose regulations choke off the supply of housing and limit the construction of high-density dwellings will experience housing price increases. This inflationary effect will be stronger yet in regions where development is made more unpredictable by infrastructure deficits and ad hoc local development approval processes. Portland may appear to be such a region to some of its detractors, but compared with any other metropolitan area in the United States with even a modicum of regulation, Portland's system is designed to do everything possible to make compact development happen and not simply to reduce development capacity.

Conclusion

At the local level, the evidence is fairly clear that exclusionary and expulsive zoning "work": That is, they exclude and expel racial and ethnic minorities by changing the built environment and rearranging land values. The indirect effects of other land use regulations, by contrast, are much less clear.

83. Downs (2002).
84. ECO Northwest, David J. Newton Associates, and MLP Associates (1991).
85. Phillips and Goodstein (2000).

Although local regulations associate with higher housing prices, the research evidence does not consistently support the contention that urban growth boundaries, permit caps, adequate public facilities ordinances, or moratoriums influence the housing stock. Sometimes, in fact, they create more opportunity for low-income people and renters, thereby expanding choice for racial minorities, who predominantly earn low incomes and rent their housing. Urban growth boundaries and adequate public facilities ordinances, in particular, can promote a higher-density land use pattern, which makes multifamily rental housing more economically viable for builders; they are sometimes (as in Portland) adopted in concert with powerful deregulatory mechanisms, which allow builders to respond quickly to surges in demand. Both adequate public facilities ordinances and impact fees can also prevent the infrastructure backlogs that fuel local dissatisfaction with growth and precipitate development moratoriums, actions that can be at least as damaging to housing supply and thus to inclusion as the price effects of infrastructure charges.

Often, however, so-called growth controls do not influence the housing stock at all. When this is the case, an association between regulations and higher housing prices may be a sign that high-priced localities enact more land use regulations than low-priced localities. Alternatively, land use regulations may associate with higher housing prices either because they serve as proxies for unobserved, perhaps nonregulatory, phenomenons or because they improve local amenities enough to raise demand.

Whatever the reason for the association, however, local governments can probably mitigate many price effects of land use regulations by carrying them out in an environment that encourages the construction of more affordable and higher-density housing. Rolf Pendall reports that municipalities with adequate public facilities ordinances, urban growth boundaries, and building permit caps tend to allow higher-density housing—at least in their zoning ordinances if not in designated on-the-ground sites—and also to adopt a wide range of affordable housing programs.[86] This finding is consistent with other findings that more "liberal" constituencies support growth controls; rather than being motivated by a desire to exclude, such constituencies are likely to seek intervention in land markets that are producing negative externalities.

At the metropolitan level, the final link in the indirect relationship between land use regulation and racial and ethnic equity is much more obscure than it is at the local level. Black and Hispanic residents have lower homeownership rates in metropolitan areas with high housing prices.[87] Black home ownership is higher in metropolitan areas where more jobs have decentralized from the central business district.[88] Deregulated and sprawling metropolitan areas may thus

86. Pendall (1995).
87. Flippen (2001).
88. Kahn (2001).

have lower prices and higher minority homeownership than controlled and contained ones. Yet minority residents in these areas may also face higher exposure to environmental hazards and noxious land uses, lack of access to amenities, lack of transportation choices, and lower housing-value appreciation. More research is needed to help clarify the costs and benefits of sprawl—and of the land use regimes that either promote it or curtail it—for racial and ethnic minorities. Furthermore, more research is needed to understand the historic connections between regulation and racial and ethnic exclusion of almost all minority groups and to identify new patterns of regulatory exclusion that emerge as the nation's ethnic and racial diversification intensifies.

What of smart growth? The movement is still in its early phases, making it difficult to forecast whether it will be exclusionary, inclusive, or neutral in its class-based and ethnic impacts. Some organizations that advocate smart growth contend that it will reduce income and racial segregation because of its focus on density, mixed-use neighborhoods, and urban revitalization. If mixed uses, mixed housing types, higher density, transit, and other components of the smart growth agenda are enacted at the local and regional level, low-income people, African Americans, and Hispanics may indeed realize important benefits from smart growth.

But while neighborhoods with mixed uses and housing types may be more integrated, smart growth may also result in gentrification. Where this happens, as evidence suggests is the case in many American metropolitan areas, smart growth may help displace minority residents unless local governments take measures to protect the neighborhood against gentrification.[89] The degree to which density-driven neighborhood and even jurisdictional sorting outweighs the density-derived benefits of a more diverse housing stock is an empirical question and will likely vary within and among metropolitan areas and through time.[90]

Smart growth tends to avoid state mandates and limits on local home rule. This makes it categorically different from earlier growth management systems, which change the calculus of local decisionmaking and thereby help overcome parochialism.[91] Indeed, William Fischel observes that a regional growth management hearing board in Washington State overturned a local government's downzoning of land as inconsistent with the state's Growth Management Act.[92] Under smart growth, local governments are free to choose from a menu of tools. Those with exclusionary motivations may simply use the tools that protect open space, requiring development to pay its own way, while rejecting the tools that promote higher-density, mixed-income, pedestrian-oriented development. Other local governments, however, may take advantage of state and federal

89. Glaeser and Shapiro (2003); PolicyLink, "Equitable Development Toolkit: Beyond Gentrification" (www.policylink.org/EDTK/default.html [February 3, 2005]).

90. Pendall and Carruthers (2003).

91. Knaap (1998).

92. Fischel (1999).

incentives to promote a different and more balanced development pattern; that is, they may adopt smart growth as a new planning regime rather than merely using its tools to reinforce its existing, exclusionary, regulatory regime.

References

American Law Institute. 1976. *A Model Land Development Code*. Philadelphia.

Anglin, Roland. 1990. "Diminishing Utility: The Effect on Citizen Preferences for Local Growth." *Urban Affairs Review* 25: 684–96.

Babcock, Richard F. 1966. *The Zoning Game: Municipal Practices and Policies*. University of Wisconsin Press.

Bae, Chang-Hee Christine. 1998. "Korea's Greenbelts: Impacts and Options for Change." *Pacific Rim Law and Policy Journal* 7: 479–502.

Baldassare, Mark. 1985. "The Suburban Movement to Limit Growth." *Policy Studies Journal* 4: 613–27.

Baldassare, Mark, and Georjeanna Wilson. 1996. "Changing Sources of Suburban Support for Local Growth Controls." *Urban Studies* 33: 459–71.

Bernstein, David E. 1998. "Philip Sober Controlling Philip Drunk: Buchanan v. Warley in Historical Perspective." *Vanderbilt Law Review* 51: 797–879.

Black, Thomas J., and James Hoben. 1985. "Land Price Inflation and Affordable Housing: Causes and Impacts." *Urban Geography* 6: 27–47.

Bollens, Scott A. 1992. "State Growth Management: Intergovernmental Frameworks and Policy Objectives." *Journal of the American Planning Association* 58: 454–66.

Burchell, Robert W., David Listokin, and Catherine C. Galley. 2000. "Smart Growth: More than a Ghost of Urban Policy Past, Less than a Bold New Horizon." *Housing Policy Debate* 11: 821–79.

Correll, Mark R., Jane H. Lillydahl, and Larry D. Singell. 1978. "The Effects of Greenbelts on Residential Property Values: Some Findings on the Political Economy of Open Space." *Land Economics* 54: 207–17.

Courant, Paul N. 1976. "On the Effects of Fiscal Zoning on Land and Housing Values." *Journal of Urban Economics* 3: 88–94.

Danielson, Michael N. 1976. *The Politics of Exclusion*. Columbia University Press.

DiPasquale, Denise, and William C. Wheaton. 1994. "Housing Market Dynamics and the Future of Housing Prices." *Journal of Urban Economics* 35: 1–27.

Donovan, Todd, and Max Neiman. 1992. "Citizen Mobilization and the Adoption of Local Growth Control." *Western Political Quarterly* 45: 651–75.

Dowall, David E. 1984. *The Suburban Squeeze: Land Conversion and Regulation in the San Francisco Bay Area*. University of California Press.

Dowall, David E., and John D. Landis. 1982. "Land Use Controls and Housing Costs: An Examination of San Francisco Bay Area Communities." *AREUEA Journal* 10: 67–93.

Downs, Anthony. 2001. "What Does "Smart Growth" Really Mean?" *Planning* 67: 20.

———. 2002. "Have Housing Prices Risen Faster in Portland than Elsewhere?" *Housing Policy Debate* 13: 7–31.

Dubbink, David. 1984. "I'll Have My Town Medium-Rural, Please." *Journal of the American Planning Association* 50: 406–18.

Dubin, Jeffrey A., D. Roderick Kiewiet, and Charles Noussair. 1992. "Voting on Growth Control Measures: Preferences and Strategies." *Economics and Politics* 4: 191–213.

Dubin, Jon C. 1993. "From Junkyards to Gentrification: Explicating a Right to Protective Zoning in Low-Income Communities of Color." *Minnesota Law Review* 77: 739–801.

ECO Northwest, David J. Newton Associates, and MLP Associates. 1991. "Urban Growth Management Study: Case Studies Report." Salem: Oregon Department of Land Conservation and Development.

Ellickson, Robert C. 1973. "Alternatives to Zoning: Covenants, Nuisance Rules, and Fines as Land Use Controls." *University of Chicago Law Review* 40: 681–733.

Elliott, Michael. 1981. "The Impact of Growth Control Regulations on Housing Prices in California." *AREUEA Journal* 9: 115–33.

Evans, A. W. 1991. "Rabbit Hutches on Postage Stamps: Planning, Development and Political Economy." *Urban Studies* 28: 853–70.

Feitelson, Eran. 1993. "The Spatial Effects of Land Use Regulations: A Missing Link in Growth-Control Evaluations." *Journal of the American Planning Association* 59: 461–72.

Fischel, William A. 1999. "Does the American Way of Zoning Cause the Suburbs of Metropolitan Areas to Be Too Spread Out?" In *Governance and Opportunity in Metropolitan America,* edited by A. Altshuler and others, pp. 151–91. Washington: National Academy Press.

Flippen, Chenoa. 2001. "Residential Segregation and Minority Home Ownership." *Social Science Research* 30: 337–62.

Forsyth, Ann. 2002. "Planning Lessons from Three US New Towns of the 1960s and 1970s: Irvine, Columbia, and the Woodlands." *Journal of the American Planning Association* 68: 387–415.

Gale, Dennis E. 1992. "Eight State-Sponsored Growth Management Programs: A Comparative Analysis." *Journal of the American Planning Association* 58: 425–39.

Glaeser, Edward L., and Jesse M. Shapiro. 2003. "Urban Growth in the 1990s: Is City Living Back?" *Journal of Regional Science* 43: 139–65.

Glickfeld, Madelyn, and Ned Levine. 1992. *Regional Growth, Local Reaction: The Enactment and Effects of Local Growth Control and Management Measures in California.* Cambridge, Mass: Lincoln Institute of Land Policy.

Godschalk, David R., and others. 1979. *Constitutional Issues of Growth Management.* Washington: Planners Press.

Gotham, Kevin Fox. 2000. "Urban Space, Restrictive Covenants, and the Origins of Racial Residential Segregation in a US city, 1900–50." *International Journal of Urban and Regional Research* 24: 616–33.

Gottdiener, M., and Max Neiman. 1981. "Characteristics of Support for Local Growth Control." *Urban Affairs Quarterly* 17: 55–73.

Green, Richard K. 1999. "Land Use Regulation and the Price of Housing in a Suburban Wisconsin County." *Journal of Housing Economics* 8: 144–59.

Grieson, Ronald E., and James R. White. 1981. "The Effects of Zoning on Structure and Land Markets." *Journal of Urban Economics* 10: 271–85.

Haar, Charles M. 1996. *Suburbs under Siege: Race, Space, and Audacious Judges.* Princeton University Press.

Higginbotham, A. Leon, Jr., F. Michael Higginbotham, and S. Sandile Ngcobo. 1990. "De Jure Housing Segregation in the United States and South Africa: The Difficult Pursuit for Racial Justice." *University of Illinois Law Review* 1990: 763–877.

Innes, Judith E. 1992. "Group Processes and the Social Construction of Growth Management." *Journal of the American Planning Association* 58: 440–53.

Jackson, Kenneth. 1985. *Crabgrass Frontier: The Suburbanization of the United States.* Oxford University Press.

Kahn, Matthew E. 2001. "Does Sprawl Reduce the Black/White Housing Consumption Gap?" *Housing Policy Debate* 12: 77–86.

Kaswan, Alice. 2003. "Distributive Justice and the Environment." *North Carolina Law Review* 81: 1031–148.

Katz, Lawrence F., and Kenneth T. Rosen. 1987. "The Interjurisdictional Effects of Growth Controls on Housing Prices." *Journal of Law and Economics* 30: 149–60.

Kirp, David L., John P. Dwyer, and Larry A. Rosenthal. 1995. *Our Town: Race, Housing, and the Soul of Suburbia.* Rutgers University Press.

Knaap, Gerrit J. 1998. "The Determinants of Residential Property Values: Implications for Metropolitan Planning." *Journal of Planning Literature* 12: 267–82.

Knaap, Gerrit J., and Arthur C. Nelson. 1992. *The Regulated Landscape: Lessons on State Land-Use Planning from Oregon.* Cambridge, Mass.: Lincoln Institute of Land Policy.

Kosman, Joel. 1993. "Toward an Inclusionary Jurisprudence: A Reconceptualization of Zoning." *Catholic University Law Review* 43: 59–108.

Landis, John. 1986. "Land Regulation and the Price of New Housing." *Journal of the American Planning Association* 52: 489–508.

———. 1992. "Do Growth Controls Work? A New Assessment." *Journal of the American Planning Association,* 58: 489.

Leonard, H. Jeffrey. 1983. *Managing Oregon's Growth: The Politics of Development Planning.* Washington: Conservation Foundation.

Levine, Ned. 1999. "The Effects of Local Growth Controls on Regional Housing Production and Population Redistribution in California." *Urban Studies* 36: 2047–68.

Lorentz, Amalia, and Kirsten Shaw. 2000. "Are You Ready to Bet on Smart Growth?" *Planning* 66: 4–9.

Lowry, Ira S., and Bruce W. Ferguson. 1992. *Development Regulation and Housing Affordability.* Washington: Urban Land Institute.

Luger, Michael I., and Kenneth Temkin. 2000. *Red Tape and Housing Costs: How Regulation Affects New Residential Development.* New Brunswick, N.J.: Center for Urban Policy Research.

Malpezzi, Stephen. 1996. "Housing Prices, Externalities, and Regulation in U.S. Metropolitan Areas." *Journal of Housing Research* 7: 209–41.

———. 2002. "Urban Regulation, the 'New Economy,' and Housing Prices." *Housing Policy Debate* 13: 323–49.

Malpezzi, Stephen, Gregory H. Chun, and Richard K. Green. 1998. "New Place-to-Place Housing Price Indexes for U.S. Metropolitan Areas, and Their Determinants." *Real Estate Economics* 26: 235–74.

Malpezzi, Stephen, and Richard K. Green. 1996. "What Has Happened to the Bottom of the U.S. Housing Market?" *Urban Studies* 33: 1807–20.

Massey, Douglas S., and Nancy A. Denton. 1993. *American Apartheid: Segregation and the Making of the Underclass.* Harvard University Press.

Mayer, Christopher J., and C. Tsuriel Somerville. 2000. "Land Use Regulation and New Construction." *Regional Science and Urban Economics* 30: 639–62.

Miller, Thomas I. 1986. "Must Growth Restrictions Eliminate Moderate-Priced Housing?" *Journal of the American Planning Association* 52: 319–25.

Nelson, Arthur C. 2002. "How Do We Know Smart Growth When We See It?" In *Smart Growth: Form and Consequences,* edited by T. S. Szold and A. Carbonell, pp. 82–101. Cambridge, Mass.: Lincoln Institute of Land Policy.

Nelson, Arthur C., and James B. Duncan. 1995. *Growth Management Principles and Practices.* Chicago: Planners Press.

Ohls, James C., Richard C. Weisburg, and Michelle White. 1974. "The Effect of Zoning on Land Values." *Journal of Urban Economics* 1: 428–44.

Pendall, Rolf. 1995. "Residential Growth Controls and Racial and Ethnic Diversity: Making and Breaking the Chain of Exclusion." Ph.D. dissertation, University of California at Berkeley.

———. 1999. "Do Land Use Controls Cause Sprawl?" *Environment and Planning B: Planning and Design* 26: 555–71.

———. 2000. "Local Land Use Regulation and the Chain of Exclusion." *Journal of the American Planning Association* 66: 125–42.

Pendall, Rolf, and John I. Carruthers. 2003. "Does Density Exacerbate Income Segregation? Evidence from United States Metropolitan Areas, 1980–2000." *Housing Policy Debate* 14, no. 4: 541–90.

Pendall, Rolf, Jonathan Martin, and William Fulton. 2002. "Holding the Line: Urban Containment in the United States." Metropolitan Policy Program, Brookings Institution.

Phillips, Justin, and Eban Goodstein. 2000. "Growth Management and Housing Prices: The Case of Portland, Oregon." *Contemporary Economic Policy* 18: 334–44.

Pollakowski, Henry O., and Susan M. Wachter. 1990. "The Effects of Land Use Constraints on Housing Prices." *Land Economics* 66: 315-324.

Protash, William, and Mark Baldassare. 1983. "Growth Policies and Community Status: A Test and Modification of Logan's Theory." *Urban Affairs Review* 18: 397–412.

Rabin, Yale. 1989. "Expulsive Zoning: The Inequitable Legacy of *Euclid*." In *Zoning and the American Dream: Promises Still to Keep*, edited by C. M. Haar and J. S. Kayden, pp. 101–21. Chicago: Planners Press.

Read, Tod. 1987. "Environmental Permit Coordination in Florida." *Journal of Land Use and Environmental Law* 3: 54–74.

Rolleston, Barbara Sherman. 1987. "Determinants of Restrictive Suburban Zoning: An Empirical Analysis." *Journal of Urban Economics* 21: 1–21.

Rose, Louis A. 1989a. "Topographical Constraints and Urban Land Supply Indexes." *Journal of Urban Economics* 26: 335–47.

———. 1989b. "Urban Land Supply: Natural and Contrived Restrictions." *Journal of Urban Economics* 25: 325–45.

Rosen, Kenneth T., and Lawrence F. Katz. 1981. "Growth Management and Land Use Controls: The San Francisco Bay Area Experience." *Journal of the American Real Estate and Urban Economics Association* 9: 321–43.

Rosenbaum, Nelson. 1978. "Growth and Its Discontents: Origins of Local Population Controls." In *The Policy Cycle*, edited by J. V. May and A. B. Wildavsky. Beverly Hills, Calif.: Sage.

Schwartz, Seymour I., David E. Hansen, and Richard Green. 1981. "Suburban Growth Controls and the Price of New Housing." *Journal of Environmental Economics and Management* 8: 303–20.

———. 1984. "The Effect of Growth Control on the Production of Moderate-Priced Housing." *Land Economics* 60: 110–14.

Segal, David, and Philip Srinivasan. 1985. "The Impact of Suburban Growth Restrictions on U.S. Housing Price Inflation, 1975–78." *Urban Geography* 6: 14–26.

Seidel, Stephen R. 1978. *Housing Costs and Government Regulations: Confronting the Regulatory Maze.* New Brunswick, N.J.: Center for Urban Policy Research.

Shen, Qing. 1996. "Spatial Impacts of Locally Enacted Growth Controls: The San Francisco Bay Region in the 1980s." *Environment and Planning B: Planning and Design* 23: 61–91.

Siegan, Bernard. 1978. *Land Use without Zoning.* Lexington, Mass.: Lexington Books.

Silver, Christopher. 1997. "The Racial Origins of Zoning in American Cities." In *Urban Planning and the African American Community: In the Shadows*, edited by J. M. Thomas and M. Ritzdorf, pp. 23–42. Thousand Oaks, Calif.: Sage.

Smith, R. Marlin. 1987. "From Subdivision Improvement Requirements to Community Benefit Assessments and Linkage Payments: A Brief History of Land Development Exactions." *Land and Contemporary Problems* 50: 5–30.

Staley, Samuel R., Jefferson G. Edgens, and Gerard C. S. Mildner. 1999. "A Line in the Land: Urban Growth Boundaries, Smart Growth, and Housing Affordability." Policy Study 263. Los Angeles: Reason Public Policy Institute

Titman, Sheridan. 1985. "Urban Land Prices under Uncertainty." *American Economic Review* 75: 505–14.

U.S. Census Bureau. 2002. *Median Income of Households by Selected Characteristics, Race, and Hispanic Origin of Householder, 2003.*

Warner, Kee, and Harvey Molotch. 1992. "Growth Control: Inner Workings and External Effects." Berkeley, Calif.: California Policy Seminar.

Weiss, Marc A. 1987. *The Rise of the Community Builders*. Columbia University Press.

11

The Rise and Fall of Fair Share Housing: Lessons from the Twin Cities

EDWARD G. GOETZ, KAREN CHAPPLE,
AND BARBARA LUKERMANN

This is a story about the rise and fall of an exceptional effort to offer affordable housing throughout a racially changing metropolitan area. In the late 1970s, the Minneapolis–Saint Paul region created a national model for fair share housing that significantly increased the availability of subsidized, low- and moderate-income housing in suburban areas throughout the region.

Local governments in the area worked with the regional planning body, the Metropolitan Council, to promote the development of low-cost housing to meet their share of the regional need for such housing. The effort resulted in a dramatic dispersal of subsidized housing in less than a decade. The program's ability to achieve such rapid change in the geography of opportunity suggested a promising strategy for circumventing suburban exclusionism and for creating a more racially inclusive region. The fair share housing program, combined with the existence of the Metropolitan Council and the program of tax-base sharing the region had initiated a few years earlier, put the Minneapolis–Saint Paul area far ahead of others in acting regionally to address metropolitan-wide issues. Indeed, the area gained a national reputation as a leader in regional approaches that persists even today.

Yet despite the accomplishments of the fair share system, it was by the end of the 1980s all but dismantled, and what remained was largely ignored by local and regional officials. Ironically, fair share was undermined in part by the very dynamic it was meant to manage: the increasing racial diversity of the metropolitan area and the increasing concentration of poverty. Just as important, however, failures of leadership at federal, state, and regional levels reduced the fair share program to an empty paper requirement not seriously regarded by those to whom it applied or by those given responsibility for its implementation. Thus despite being regarded as a model of regionalism nationwide, the Twin Cities metropolitan area has fallen victim to the self-fulfilling prophecy constraining most regions in America: Low-cost housing supply expands where such housing is already concentrated, and racial inclusion gains are marginal at best.

In this chapter, we examine the twenty-five-year evolution of fair share housing efforts in the Twin Cities. We chose twenty-five high-growth suburban municipalities for in-depth study. In each municipality, we reviewed official plans and zoning practices. We interviewed housing, community development, and planning officials along with real estate developers and current and past officials of the Metropolitan Council. We also constructed a database of 7,463 suburban land parcels that had been designated for high-density housing in 1980 and tracked their redesignation to other uses or to lower densities over a twenty-year period. For a sample of the parcels, we examined the actual development outcome after twenty years. Our approach provides a rich, multidimensional perspective both on the factors that led to the development of the region's model fair share program of the late 1970s and on the reasons for the system's precipitous decline in the 1980s and 1990s.[1]

1. The study focuses on suburban communities that experienced the greatest rates of growth over the past three decades and, among those, also includes the communities poised for the greatest rate of growth in the next twenty years. We selected 25 of the 144 municipalities in the seven-county Twin Cities region for detailed study. Of those, we selected the 15 that had added the most population between 1970 and 1990. The final 10 were chosen based on both past growth and projected growth; that is, municipalities that were in the top thirty in both historic and projected growth. Each municipality was the subject of a case study examining the correlation between comprehensive plans, zoning practices, development approval practices, and other processes and standards with implications for affordable housing development. All of the approved comprehensive plans between 1976 (the year the state's planning law was enacted) and 2001 were reviewed for each municipality in the sample. The oldest comprehensive plan we examined was approved by the Metropolitan Council in 1979.

Plans were evaluated on the basis of four issues. First, did communities calculate the existing and projected need for low- and moderate-income housing and their share of the regional need for such housing? Second, how does the plan define income levels and land allocated to different housing densities, and does the plan explicitly or implicitly link high-density housing to the objectives related to low- and moderate-income housing? Third, does the plan lay out a series of steps to be taken by the community to achieve the low- and moderate-income housing goals established? Finally, does the plan explicitly state how many acres of high-density, developable land have been set aside, and can this amount accommodate enough low- and moderate-income housing to meet the stated goals?

Interviews were conducted with housing and community development or planning officials in the twenty-five communities. The interviews were used to determine what types of effort the communities made to promote low- and moderate-income housing and to provide a means of

We find that a combination of important demographic changes in the region, federal reductions in housing subsidies, and changes in the leadership of the Metropolitan Council undermined the legitimacy that a regional approach to affordable housing enjoyed during the late 1970s. Many of the governments in our sample no longer acknowledge a responsibility to meet their share of regional affordable housing needs, and the Metropolitan Council has been quite reluctant to leverage local affordable housing activity. Much of the land originally designated for high-density, low-cost housing has been redesignated or developed at lower densities, reducing the supply of land available to would-be developers of affordable housing. By 2001, of the acreage set aside in 1980 for high-density housing, only 6 percent actually saw new, affordable housing built. Given the enormous growth that has taken place in the twenty-five communities we studied, this retreat from fair share housing constitutes a missed opportunity of tremendous proportions—but not an irreversible one.

Policy Background

In the late 1960s, in the wake of urban disturbances in several larger American cities, no fewer than four national and presidential commissions called for a greater dispersion of federally subsidized housing and, more specifically, for greater development of such housing in suburban areas.[2] Congress provided federal funding and support for the creation of metropolitan councils of government to develop regional planning approaches and authorized the councils to review local applications for federal aid to ensure that proposed projects were consistent with regional development plans. These efforts led to the creation of "fair share" housing programs in several localities, including Dayton, Chicago, San Francisco, Washington, and the Twin Cities.

This first generation of regional housing programs (to be distinguished from the second generation of mobility programs developed during the 1990s) was created in the context of the fair housing movement of the late 1960s and early 1970s and of various local and national efforts to "open up" the suburbs to people of color.[3] Though fair share programs typically identified the dispersal of "affordable" or subsidized units as their goal, the concentration of these units in central cities was seen as a significant impediment to the residential desegregation of racial minorities. Thus fair share serves both desegregation and dispersal objectives.

checking on the implementation of standards, plans, and programs identified in earlier comprehensive plans. In addition, we conducted interviews with several housing developers to get their perspectives on developing affordable housing in the sample communities.

2. See Danielson (1976); John Goering, chapter 6, this volume.

3. Goetz (2003).

The framework for implementing the fair share housing program is the Minnesota Land Use Planning Act (LUPA) of 1976 (Minn. Statute § 473.859). LUPA provides for mandatory land use planning in the Minneapolis–Saint Paul region and requires that the comprehensive plans adopted by communities include a housing program "which will provide sufficient existing and new housing to meet the local unit's share of the metro area need for low- and moderate-income housing."

The Metropolitan Council and Implementation of Fair Share

The Metropolitan Council, created by the Minnesota legislature in 1967, is one of few multipurpose regional agencies in the United States. The council's responsibility for shaping growth in the region and its authority over the Twin Cities' unique regional tax-base sharing program made it one of the leading examples of regional leadership on issues of metropolitan disparities in the 1970s. The distribution of low-cost housing in the region was a central element in the council's early perception of its mandate. Even before passage of LUPA, the Metropolitan Council had adopted a policy of dispersing "modest-cost" housing throughout the region over five years. To implement this policy, the council weighed each community's record in producing modest-cost housing when it reviewed applications for federal infrastructure grants.[4] After LUPA was adopted in 1976, the council created a housing allocation plan that provided numerical goals for all communities within the region's growth boundaries. The allocation plan was based on a count for each community of present and projected households and jobs and nonsubsidized low- and moderate-income housing units. This system of individual community allocations was in place through the early 1980s.

The council provided the allocation figures to each community, and these were in turn incorporated into local planning documents. The Metropolitan Council judged the adequacy of local housing plans based on the amount of land set aside for high-density residential development. The assumption used by the council was that high-density development was the most likely to produce affordable units. (Subsequent experience in the development of affordable housing in the region has borne this out.)[5] The council, however, lacked (and to this day still lacks) authority to require communities to plan for a specific amount of low- and moderate-income housing. As one staff member told us, "We can't say . . . you have to provide affordable housing. All we can say is that you have to provide the opportunity to not discriminate against affordable housing."

4. This review process is dubbed A-95, for the federal Office of Management and Budget circular of that number that provides regional councils of government the power to review grant applications of communities.

5. Goetz, Chapple, and Lukermann (2002).

By the end of the 1970s, the council had several tools available to promote a fair share approach to affordable housing. First, LUPA required that communities make plans for meeting their share of regional housing needs. Second, the allocation plan was a means of establishing regional needs and local shares. Third, the council had adopted a set of zoning and land use guidelines aimed at promoting more affordable housing opportunities. The guidelines included suggestions related to lot size, garages, square footage of living area, and other items that have a direct impact on housing prices. Fourth, the council's power of review gave it input into the grant-making decisions of the federal government. Finally, the council's willingness to take into account the affordable housing performance of communities when they reviewed grant applications gave it leverage over local housing efforts.

When this system was in place and functioning, the region's affordable housing profile changed significantly. From 1975 to 1983, the central cities' share of the region's total of subsidized units fell from 82 to 59 percent. This impact made the Twin Cities' fair share program one of the highest-performing regional programs in the entire nation.

Yet at just the time when the region was establishing its promising fair share effort, changes in national policy, local political leadership, and regional demographics combined to undermine it. The first shock to the system was a change in federal housing policy. Dramatic budget cuts endured by the U.S. Department of Housing and Urban Development in the early 1980s, totaling an 80 percent reduction in budgetary authority over a six-year period, significantly reduced the availability of housing subsidies that local governments could use to build low- and moderate-income housing. Before these budget cuts, most of such housing in the region (and in the nation) was dependent upon direct and sizable federal subsidies. As federal subsidies declined, so did the ability of local governments to directly produce such housing. Because the Metropolitan Council equated low- and moderate-income housing with federally subsidized housing, federal budget cuts caused the council to discontinue its practice of allocating fair share housing obligations to suburban communities.

This decision by the council followed not only a reduction in federal subsidies but also a change in leadership at the council. Democrat Rudy Perpich was elected governor in 1976 and took office early the next year. Perpich, who had little interest in metropolitan planning and tended to ignore the Metropolitan Council on important decisions in which it might have been involved, appointed council members who shared his disinterest in regional planning.[6] Though much of the fair share structure was in place before Perpich's election, the council that he appointed was less enthusiastic than the old council about regional control of housing policy and not inclined to insert itself directly into

6. Johnson (1998).

local development issues. This trend accelerated with the election of Perpich's successor to office, Republican Arne Carlson. Carlson's base of electoral support was in the more affluent developing suburbs of the Twin Cities region, the same areas that were becoming increasingly reluctant to provide affordable housing.

The decline of fair share coincided with a shift in the perspective of metropolitan officials. Myron Orfield argues that the era that produced fair share housing and regional tax sharing was dominated by what he calls progressive regionalists. These officials included both Republican and Democratic lawmakers who "were interested in . . . shaping a more cohesive, cost-effective, efficient, and equitable region." Their support for these positions, however, was based on a "hard-headed calculation of the costs of inequity and the destructive competition for development among municipalities in a region." In contrast, the 1980s and 1990s were dominated by "consensus-based regionalists" for whom "the greatest evil was not defeat, but controversy."[7] The consensus-based approach characterized the work of the Metropolitan Council in the area of affordable housing throughout these decades. More directive council actions, such as the provision of fair share housing goals, were dropped as the council shied away from prescribing a particular path of action for suburban municipalities. Repeated proposals at the state legislature aimed at limiting or abolishing the Metropolitan Council during this period only reinforced the institutional timidity that had set in. In this environment, the council steadily backed away from intervening in local decisionmaking in affordable housing.

Fundamental, however, in the retreat from fair share were the changing demographics of the central cities during the 1980s. More people of color moved to the area, and greater concentrations of poverty and the attendant social problems emerged in core neighborhoods. The number of people of color in the region nearly doubled during the 1970s and again during the 1980s. Most of these families settled in the core areas of the metropolitan area. The social and economic homogeneity that had been the foundation of almost two decades of regional problem solving began to disappear. By the end of the 1980s, the region had the sixth highest level of wealth disparity between central city and suburb among the twenty-five largest metropolitan areas in the country. The poverty rate, which stayed virtually the same for the region, nevertheless increased dramatically in Minneapolis and Saint Paul.

The decline in the central cities, furthermore, spread into older suburban areas during these years. In the 1990s, 41 percent of the region's population lived in what Orfield calls at-risk suburban communities.[8] Together with the central cities, these areas had 65 percent of the region's population but 83 percent of the poor. These trends in suburban decline were readily evident as some

7. Orfield (2002b, pp. 239, 245).
8. Orfield (2002a).

communities undertook strategies to improve their images and upgrade their housing stock in efforts to limit low-income household growth.[9]

The racial dimension of the region's economic polarization was widely evident. Blacks living in areas of high poverty increased from 27 percent to 47 percent during the 1980s. As the 1990s began, minorities in Minneapolis and Saint Paul were more likely to live in poor neighborhoods than were minorities in any other major metropolitan area in the country.[10] The neighborhoods of high minority concentration came to be identified with a range of social problems from poverty and high social service needs to violent crime and drug use. African American gangs fought over the city's illicit drug trade. A high-profile execution-style murder of a white policeman by African American gang members in 1992 brought racial tensions in the region to a peak. Fear of crime, most of which was associated with drug-related violence in the central cities, was the region's most important issue for several years over the late 1980s and early 1990s. Local news media covered the central city's crime trends in detail, whites pulled their children out of the public schools (in Minneapolis, close to 70 percent of the students in the public schools in the 1990s were of color—in a city that was 77 percent white), and local police initiatives began to target communities of color in the central neighborhoods.[11]

The Retreat from Fair Share

In less than a decade, the system of fair share housing created by the Minnesota legislature and the Metropolitan Council lay partially dismantled, and the part not dismantled was ignored. The reduction in housing subsidies led the council to stop calculating fair share obligations for local governments. At the same time, the volume of federal infrastructure grants declined, reducing the number of opportunities the council had to exercise leverage over local housing performance through the review process. In the face of these changes, the council decided to no longer hold local governments accountable for low-cost housing. Eventually, the council withdrew its zoning and development guidelines, which, though never binding on any community, had provided a standard against which local actions could be judged.

All that remains, in fact, of the fair share infrastructure that was in place in the region at the start of the 1980s are the LUPA planning requirements. Municipalities are still required to have a plan that establishes the local share of regional needs for low- and moderate-income housing and an implementation strategy to meet that share. This requirement, however, has become largely an empty one.

9. See Goetz (2000a).

10. Norman Draper, "Twin Cities' Core Has Worst Poverty Rate for Minorities," *Minneapolis Star Tribune,* December 13, 1993, p. 1A.

11. Goetz (2003).

LUPA did not grant the Metropolitan Council any authority to force compliance with the low- and moderate-income housing elements of the statute. Lacking the authority to force compliance, the council never established a system for monitoring whether local zoning conforms to comprehensive plans. As a result, according to one council staffer, the council had "no systematic way of knowing that a plan was being followed or how it was being followed." In fact, in the years following the enactment of LUPA, the council has not monitored cities on several dimensions: whether zoning conformed to the approved plan, whether land designated for high-density housing was in actuality set aside, whether the housing built on such land was actually affordable to low- and moderate-income families, whether communities otherwise impeded low- and moderate-income housing goals, and whether the amount of low- and moderate-income housing that was built met the goals set out in the fair share allocation (for those years when the council was providing allocation numbers). There is, in essence, no centralized information on whether or how communities have followed up on the fair share plans created as a result of LUPA. In the face of this inattention, local governments no longer take the LUPA housing planning requirements seriously.

In fact, the low- and moderate-income housing elements of LUPA have been so thoroughly ignored over the past twenty years that the Minnesota legislature created a new law in 1995, the Livable Communities Act (LCA), to generate regional activity in the area of affordable housing. LCA was the result of State Representative Myron Orfield's three-year effort to resurrect a regional affordable housing program.[12] Orfield, a Democrat from a Minneapolis district with significant poverty and physical decline, pushed through a package of bills aimed at reducing regional inequities. Though his bills narrowly passed the legislature (thanks to a coalition of inner-city and first-ring suburban legislators), they were vetoed by the governor each year. Finally, LCA (not authored by Orfield) was passed as a compromise bill and signed by the governor. LCA establishes housing goals based not on need, however, but rather on how much affordable housing already exists in each community and its immediate neighbors. Paradoxically, the program (the details of which were designed by the Metropolitan Council of the mid-1990s, a council not inclined toward meaningful redistribution of affordable housing opportunities in the region) creates lower benchmarks for areas that have the least affordable housing. This counterintuitive benchmark system was established to reflect and reinforce prevailing market trends in the various subregions of the metropolitan area, not to challenge them. Even these benchmarks, however, have been routinely ignored by communities and by the Metropolitan Council in the minority of cases where they call for an increase in affordable housing.[13]

12. See Orfield (1997).
13. See Goetz (2000b).

Planning for Low- and Moderate-Income Housing

The history of planning for fair share in the Twin Cities is characterized by three distinct waves. The first wave began when LUPA was created and lasted until 1982 and includes, for most of the high-growth communities we studied, the first plan submitted pursuant to LUPA. The second wave covers the years from 1982 to 1995. There are very few plans from this wave; most communities simply continued to operate under the plans approved during the first wave. The third and final wave began in 1995, the year LCA was passed and provided a different framework for establishing local housing plans.

LUPA language suggests that in order to identify a community's share of the metropolitan need for low- and moderate-income housing the comprehensive plan must make reference to regional needs—or if not explicitly to regional needs, then to the local share of regional needs. The first round of plans meets this requirement by referencing the fair share allocation established by the Metropolitan Council. Almost without exception, the plans we reviewed from this era identify the municipalities' share of regional low- and moderate-income housing needs. Furthermore, the plans indicate an acceptance of the fair share methodology. Some plans even indicate that the regional allocation system was the best way to determine local needs. The plans submitted in the third wave have a decidedly different orientation toward regional allocation systems.

The south suburban community of Apple Valley provides an example of the shift in planning priorities. In 1979 Apple Valley's plan specifically cites the superiority of a regional approach to defining housing needs: "The need for low- and moderate-income housing within Apple Valley must be identified on a regional basis because Apple Valley is a suburb within the Minneapolis/Saint Paul Metropolitan area and there is nothing of particular significance within the community that would cause it to stand apart from regional considerations" (Apple Valley Comprehensive Plan, 1979). The Apple Valley plan of twenty years later reads, "the City is in the best position to determine the most responsible option for meeting the future needs of Apple Valley rather than the Metropolitan Council, especially as it relates to residential densities" (Apple Valley Comprehensive Plan, 1999). In fact, not a single plan submitted later than 1990 that we reviewed identifies local share of regional low- and moderate-income housing needs. Instead, these plans rely upon LCA-related goals negotiated with the Metropolitan Council that are neither "low-mod" in nature nor based on need.

Interviews with planners from our sample communities indicate that about half (incorrectly) regard LCA goals as the working statement of low- and moderate-income housing needs in their cities. With the exception of only two communities, none of the later plans we reviewed identifies existing or projected low- and moderate-income housing needs at all. Interviews indicate that most planners in our twenty-five communities shifted their vocabulary about low-cost housing from low-mod, which is typically used in reference to subsidized housing, to affordable, which is the term of use in LCA. (The definition of affordable is a housing cost not greater than 30 percent of income for those at 80 percent of the area median income for a family of four for homeownership and at 50 percent of the median for rental housing. It is not adjusted for actual household size, however, resulting in a more inflated definition of affordable.) When asked what their working definition of "low- and moderate-income housing" was, more than two-thirds of the suburban planners we interviewed referred to the LCA guidelines. One respondent indicated that his community used the LCA affordability guidelines, though they are "a joke" because they are so high. In general, it is clear that the current wave of comprehensive plans violate LUPA in that there is typically no calculation of local and regional needs for low- and moderate-income housing and there is no attempt to identify each locality's share of regional needs.

Plans from the first wave typically identify subsidized housing programs from all three levels of government—local, state, and federal—as important implementation tools. While this represents the easiest statement to make in the implementation section (it merely obligates the locality to investigate the use of existing subsidy programs), during the last wave of plans most communities fail to mention programs from even two of the three levels of government. One city official attributes this to a changed political environment, saying, "More programs were available in 1981 when people wanted to change the world. . . . Today there is the idea that government shouldn't be involved in private developments with public monies, so there is less public support."

There is even a greater disparity between first-wave and third-wave plans when one looks at the various local regulatory initiatives listed. Local regulatory barriers to affordable housing are an important contributor to the nation's inability to meet housing needs.[14] The degree to which municipalities revise their local land use regulations in ways that promote the development of lower-cost housing is an important indicator of their commitment to meeting low- and moderate-income housing needs. To cite just two examples: Increasing allowable densities reduces the per-unit cost of housing; and reducing minimum square-footage requirements allows the building of smaller, and therefore less costly, housing. Among the comprehensive plans we examined, these and other regulatory reforms were much more evident in the first wave than in the third wave. For example, 58 percent of first-wave plans mention increasing densities and reducing square footage requirements, compared to just 19 percent and 12 percent of third-wave plans.

14. See Downs (1993); Advisory Commission on Regulatory Barriers to Affordable Housing (1991).

From Planning to Implementation

The Twin Cities' fair share housing program failed not only as a planning exercise but in its implementation as well. No effective means of monitoring the implementation of local housing plans was ever put in place, nor is there widespread monitoring of local affordable housing. The implementation of specific steps called for by suburban housing plans was sporadic at best. Finally, few of the suburban communities we studied have taken active steps to produce low- and moderate-income housing.

Monitoring Housing Production

LUPA envisions a system in which local governments plan for low- and moderate-income housing within a regional context. In such a regional system, tracking the building of such housing is an important, if minimal, step toward achieving program goals. A given community, its municipal peers, and the regional authority all should know what housing each community has produced, whether it is on track to meet its obligations, and if not, what kinds of changes are needed. The Metropolitan Council established no such monitoring system for the region as a whole.

As for the local communities, two-thirds of the communities in our sample do not have an inventory or database indicating the amount of low- and moderate-income housing they have. Ten of these communities indicated that the county housing authority would have information on the number of such units within their jurisdictions. Of the municipalities that did keep track, three have been doing so only since LCA was created in 1995, and only one indicated that its list went back as far as the mid-1970s, when LUPA was initiated. Another community planner reported that her city had only eight subsidized units and that keeping track of them did not require anything as formal as an inventory or database.

Promoting Housing Production through Regulation

We asked our interviewees whether any of a series of specific regulatory techniques was in place in their communities for enhancing the production of low- and moderate-income housing. Seventeen (71 percent) of the communities we studied had in place some version of a planned unit development (PUD) ordinance allowing for lot sizes and densities negotiated between developers and city officials. In most places, however, these ordinances had no impact on low- and moderate-income housing. One of the considerations that limited the effectiveness of PUD ordinances—and of increases in allowable densities—is the starting point from which communities worked. One southwest suburb was able to increase from an average of 1.80 units an acre to 2.86 in one project and 2.47 in another. These densities, though technically an increase over the previous average, were insufficient to produce more affordable housing.

Local regulatory reforms that were less often achieved were specific changes to zoning and development guidelines. Changes in zoning or development guidelines, while rarer than other steps, have the potential for long-term benefits in that they change the rules under which residential development takes place. Some specific promises—to reduce lot widths, to increase the maximum units per acre in townhome districts, and to eliminate the minimum floor-area requirements for single-family housing and the garage requirements for multifamily housing—were met by communities in our sample. One community changed its zoning to provide for a greater range of density (up to thirty units an acre is now allowed in high-density areas), and another community fast-tracked developers' proposals for modest-cost housing and also increased mobile home densities. Half of the city officials we interviewed indicated that they allow accessory apartments as a means of promoting affordability.

More frequently, however, communities simply failed to carry out specific zoning and regulatory changes intended to facilitate lower-cost housing. Promises to reduce minimum lot-size requirements, to increase density requirements for single-family housing, to adjust the garage and minimum floor-area requirements, and to ensure that a substantial portion of residential land be made available for multifamily housing were frequently left unmet over twenty years.

For example, one 1980 plan states that the community would establish an ongoing subcommittee to make periodic (at least every three years) reviews of the city's housing program and to make recommendations for change as necessary to the City Council and the Planning Commission. The subcommittee was never established. Our interview contact commented, "I couldn't have told you that was in the plan. Sounds like one of those great consultant ideas." Just under half of the communities allow smaller lot sizes in certain circumstances. Only seven communities (29 percent) report that they use set-asides, in which developers are required to build a certain percentage of units suitable for low- and moderate-income families. None of the communities allow expedited approval for low- and moderate-income housing projects, only five (21 percent) reduce development fees for affordable housing, and only three (12 percent) allow density bonuses to promote affordability. Finally, just five of the communities allow for variances to their zoning ordinance in order to allow low-cost housing.

Implementing Housing Plans

In summary, there is a wide range in the degree to which communities implement their housing plans. It is clear that a housing plan adopted in one year is not necessarily embraced by city councils in subsequent years. One of our informants said it was typical for her city council to participate in workshops to help develop the comprehensive plan. "The problem is that the council members that may have worked on these things are not necessarily the same ones as we have today." As a result, proposals made by staff pursuant to the plan can be killed by council members elected subsequent to adoption of the plan. Though this is perhaps an endemic weakness of planning tools in an environment controlled by political figures and market actors, it is made worse in the Twin Cities case by the lack of enforcement authority in LUPA and the utter lack of initiative on the part of the Metropolitan Council to monitor local actions.

Follow-through on comprehensive plans is not always a simple yes or no proposition. Compliance on some items means more than a single action over a fifteen-year period. In addition, the experiences of these twenty-five communities indicate the important difference between passive reduction of barriers and the active encouragement of low- and moderate-income housing development. Several communities passed PUD ordinances as their plans suggested they would, but our informants clearly indicated that these had no impact on low-cost housing development. Similarly, respondents indicated that some costs had been reduced by the measures taken by the city, but the total amount of cost reduction was insufficient to generate low-cost housing development.

Our interviews also revealed that in some cases communities were operating under plans that had language with which officials were not familiar. In one community, our respondent, the city's top housing and community development official, was surprised to hear that the 1999 plan states that his city will "notify developers of single-family homes that about 8 percent of homes in their developments should be affordable to lower-income homebuyers; provide any zoning or regulatory concessions needed to facilitate this." In this case, the "policy" is just another "great consultant idea" that was never seriously entertained by the community, despite being in the comprehensive plan.

Many communities have made some good-faith efforts to follow up on specific items in their housing plans. It is clear that some communities have used the plans as frameworks for action. In other cases, however, the plan is seemingly not "owned" by the staff or the city council in any meaningful way. We present these data not as a definitive scorecard of promises kept, because our ability to determine the degree of community follow-up is inexact, especially thirty years removed from the time that most of these plans were adopted. There is, however, little doubt that an ongoing system of monitoring community compliance would have provided greater and more consistent information on this issue. Such a monitoring system is also likely to have encouraged local actions that are more uniformly in line with the plans that were approved.

More active steps to create low- and moderate-income housing are relatively rare in the cities we studied. Only one-third of them regularly solicit proposals for such housing. A slightly lower percentage has ever acted as a developer of this housing. In only two of the cities do officials both solicit proposals and actively develop this type of housing.

Persistent Barriers

Despite twenty-five years of planning for low- and moderate-income housing, both local officials and private sector housing developers readily identify local land regulations as significant barriers to more affordable housing development. Planners and developers agree that in the twenty-five high-growth suburbs we studied restrictions on the amount of land zoned for high-density housing, minimum lot-size requirements, and other zoning restrictions leading to high land costs limit the development of affordable housing. One developer stated that "the most difficult [obstacle] is the environmental regulations, especially requirements to preserve wetlands, trees and provide buffer zones. These regulations decrease the effective use of the property."

Developers frequently mentioned neighborhood opposition to their proposals for lower-cost housing in suburban areas. Developers reported record turnouts at public meetings, neighborhood distributions of flyers and leaflets urging residents to attend meetings and to oppose a proposed development, and one instance of the developer getting threatening phone calls at home. "Nitpicking the project design," as one developer put it, has been one of the neighborhood strategies, together with opposition to rental units. Active opposition of neighbors is so prevalent that developers expressed surprise when a project of theirs did not attract vocal opposition. One developer reported that when he arrived at the city council meeting for the vote on his development, the absence of a crowd led him to believe he had shown up on the wrong night.

On the other hand, almost all of the developers found city staff members supportive and helpful in pursuing projects. In some instances assistance in project design was provided to make the development fit better into the neighborhood; in two instances the staff supported use of tax increment financing funds; and in one community the staff actually helped the developer find an appropriate site. According to one developer, city staff "pushed on the Met Council and lobbied the Minnesota Housing Finance Agency for tax credit designation. . . . MHFA tax credits were critical. . . .[I] couldn't have done it without them." Another developer credited city staff with trying to "help with elected officials and countering neighborhood opposition."

Typically, however, elected officials were not as uniformly supportive of the projects proposed by these developers. Comments on support from elected officials were more tentative, ranging from "quieter support," "passive support," and "generally supportive" to instances of opposition when a project was proposed in a council member's district.

Developers are well aware of the reluctance of communities to accept affordable housing. None relishes the opportunity to be reviled by neighbors at a public meeting. Furthermore, most developers can ill afford to devote time and resources on projects that are blocked by local governments. Therefore, developers select their cities carefully in an attempt to minimize costs associated with projects that die. As one said, "We don't bother to go out and work in communities where we are not wanted." What results is a cycle in which the difficulties of low- and moderate-income housing development become self-perpetuating. Developers avoid certain communities and concentrate new low-cost housing development in communities that have a better track record of approving such projects, thereby increasing the concentration of this housing in those places. Eventually, the more receptive communities become concerned that they have "too much affordable housing" and, with the region in mind, perhaps more than their fair share. These communities then become less receptive, and the pool of eligible and willing communities shrinks further.

The Impact of Fair Share Housing

Over a period of twenty years the Metropolitan Council dramatically retreated from implementing fair share housing in the Twin Cities region. In the absence of prodding from the council—indeed, in the absence of any significant attention to the issue at all on the part of the regional entity—local suburban governments quickly retrenched their efforts to promote low- and moderate-income housing. They did so by ignoring the implementation strategies they had adopted as part of early planning efforts, and by removing from their planning documents any true commitment to low- and moderate-income housing production. The cumulative effect of this retreat from fair share housing has been dramatic.

As a way of quantifying the impact, we tracked what actually happened to land designated for high-density housing from 1980 to 2000. Using maps from the planning and zoning documents of the twenty-five cities in our study, we identified 7,463 parcels (8,590 acres) of land set aside for high-density residential use in the first-wave plans. The identification of these parcels was taken by the Metropolitan Council as evidence of the communities' commitment to promoting low- and moderate-income housing. The record of what happened to these parcels over the period 1980–2000 shows, however, almost a complete lack of new, affordable housing having been developed.

The most common outcome for the parcels that were set aside for high-density residential development in the first wave was redesignation to another land use. Approximately 38 percent of the acreage designated for high-density housing was redesignated for low- or medium-density residential development. An additional 16 percent was redesignated for PUDs at indeterminate densities. Seventeen percent of the land is now zoned for nonresidential use. Only 22 percent of the acreage has remained high density or has been redesignated for higher-density development. By assuming the maximum possible units under the zoning guidelines for these communities, a potential 58,681 units were lost on these parcels.

There was wide variation in the degree to which communities redesignated their high-density residential land. Just eleven cities account for 95 percent of down-designated acreage, and these eleven are significantly more likely to be in the lower-income group of communities ($p < .10$). Likewise, just six communities account for most of the redesignation to PUD or nonresidential use. In terms of the lost capacity for high-density housing, just thirteen communities account for over 99 percent of these lost units.

Of course, municipalities can also move land from other zoning categories into high-density residential uses. Though this occurred in our sample, it did not match the rate at which land was being removed from high-density use. The amount of current acres set aside for high-density housing indicates a net loss of 17 percent of the original total (assuming that the original comprehensive plan designations corresponded to zoning designations).[15]

To determine what has been built on the land designated for high-density housing, we studied a sample of 243 parcels. Only 55 percent of the land set aside for high-density housing actually had housing in 2001. Thirty percent of these parcels, however, already had housing on them in 1980; that is, they could not have been intended for new, low- and moderate-income housing and therefore should not have been counted as part of the communities' commitment to meeting future fair share housing needs.

Of the new housing that was built between 1980 and 2000 on the land initially set aside by the twenty-five municipalities in our study, only 33 percent were affordable to low- and moderate-income households.[16] Given our examination of the sample parcels, we are able to estimate the rate at which high-density land set aside in year one yielded new affordable housing units twenty years later. This estimate is given by the equation

$$X = a * .83 * .24 * .7 * .33,$$

where a is the number of acres set aside for high-density housing in year one and X is the estimated number of acres on which new, low- and moderate-income, high-density units will have been built over a twenty-year period. The equation adjusts for

—the net rate at which high-density land is redesignated for low-density or other uses (a 17 percent reduction of the original amount of land set aside),

—the percentage of land zoned for high density that actually has housing on it (24 percent, according to our sample),

15. This rate of reduction is based on the twenty-three communities for which we were able to gather data on current high-density residential acreage.

16. We use rents charged by other providers of subsidized low- and middle-income housing in the Twin Cities region as a guideline for what constitutes affordable.

—the percentage of the acres with housing on which the housing had been built after 1980 (70 percent),

—the percentage of those acres with new housing that was affordable to low- and moderate-income households (33 percent).

We estimate, then, that given the experience of these twenty-five high-growth municipalities over the period 1980–2001, for every hundred acres of land set aside for high-density residential development in 1980 roughly five acres contained new, low- and moderate-income, high-density housing in 2001. The importance of this figure is twofold. First, it is an estimate of the degree to which communities have not followed through on their initial commitments to meeting their fair share of affordable housing needs. Second, to the extent that the Metropolitan Council used high-density housing as a surrogate for affordable housing, the experience in the Twin Cities between 1980 and 2000 suggests that to develop a given number of acres as high-density, low- and moderate-income housing, the municipalities in our sample would have had to designate twenty times that number for high density in their initial land use plans.

Conclusion

Given the dynamics of racial relations in the United States, efforts to build more inclusive communities through housing policy require a strong combination of policy design, political will, leadership, and institutional commitment. For a brief period of time in the late 1970s, such a combination existed in Minneapolis–Saint Paul. The newly formed Metropolitan Council actively implemented a fair share housing program that achieved promising results in the dispersal of low-cost housing throughout the region. Uninterrupted, such a program could have had a significant impact on the racial and economic inclusiveness of suburban areas during a period of rapid growth for the metropolitan area.

From these very promising beginnings, however, fair share housing promotion in the Twin Cities has seemingly disappeared with little trace. The region has lost ground quite literally, in the sense that ninety-five of every hundred acres set aside for promoting new, low- and moderate-income housing has been used for something else. The region has lost ground politically, as well, in effect squandering the legislative and administrative consensus that produced the region's fair share program of the late 1970s. The language of regional commitment to low-cost housing needs has disappeared—and with it a vital tool for expanding the geography of opportunity across racial and ethnic lines. This is particularly tragic in light of the region's growing racial diversity.

Evidence of regional cooperation in defining and meeting housing needs is nonexistent in the official plans of suburban communities after the mid-1980s. What shortly followed were high-profile cases of developing suburbs resisting subsidized housing and ugly scenes of suburbanites packing hearing rooms to denounce efforts to bring "those people" into their communities.[17] The falling fortunes of fair share housing in Minneapolis–Saint Paul have been dramatic indeed. The failure (to this point) of fair share in Minnesota highlights several important lessons for efforts to create racially inclusive communities.

First, the case illustrates the need to expand efforts beyond government-subsidized housing. Because the Twin Cities' program equated fair share housing with the distribution of subsidized housing, the dramatic reduction in federal housing subsidies in the 1980s meant, in effect, the end of the fair share effort. The role of regulatory barrier reduction was never afforded a prominent place, leaving the fate of fair share housing dependent on the highly unstable funding base of subsidized housing.

Second, a failure of leadership at multiple levels of government undermined the program. At the federal level this was manifest in budget cutbacks; at the state level, in reduced gubernatorial support for regional initiatives. These two failures of leadership led to the third and most devastating failure, the abandonment of any effort to implement the program by the area's regional body. The Twin Cities' case shows that merely having the institutional infrastructure (in this case a regional governance body) in place is no guarantee that effective policy implementation will take place.

Third, weaknesses in the statute itself, most prominently the lack of enforcement or monitoring powers, produced a situation in which local governments could ignore the provisions of the program without penalty. Had state land use policy contained specific requirements for enforcement of fair share requirements, the precipitous decline of the program might have been avoided.

Fourth, significant demographic changes that polarized the region in race and class terms produced an environment in which local governments had the motivation to ignore the provisions of the program. As race and class became more salient and more highly charged issues regionally, the political will to achieve racial inclusion declined.

Conversely, these lessons also remind us that, under certain circumstances, fair share can work. Even with the weaknesses of policy design identified above, the Minneapolis–Saint Paul effort did accomplish a significant change in the geographic distribution of subsidized housing in the early years of the program. The Metropolitan Council did at one point use its powers to leverage more inclusive housing efforts. Suburban communities did adopt the language of regionalism in their housing plans. They did identify regulatory reforms and subsidy programs that would expand housing opportunities. The lesson is not that fair share cannot work to create more inclusive communities but that such efforts require a supportive political and institutional environment, a multiplicity of strategies (spanning subsidized and market housing as well as regulatory and subsidy approaches), and strong policy design.

17. Goetz (2003).

References

Advisory Commission on Regulatory Barriers to Affordable Housing. 1991. *"Not in My Backyard": Removing Barriers to Affordable Housing.* U.S. Department of Housing and Urban Development.

Danielson, Michael N. 1976. *The Politics of Exclusion.* Columbia University Press.

Downs, Anthony. 1993. "Reducing Regulatory Barriers to Affordable Housing." In *Housing Markets and Residential Mobility,* edited by G. Thomas Kingsley and Margery Austin Turner, pp. 255–81. Washington: Urban Institute.

Goetz, Edward G. 2000a. "The Politics of Poverty Deconcentration." *Journal of Urban Affairs* 22, no. 2: 157–74.

———. 2000b. "Fair Share or Status Quo? The Twin Cities Livable Communities Act." *Journal of Planning Education and Research* 20, no. 1: 37–51.

———. 2003. *Clearing the Way: Deconcentrating the Poor in Urban America.* Washington: Urban Institute.

Goetz, Edward G., Karen Chapple, and Barbara Lukermann. 2002. *The Affordable Housing Legacy of the 1976 Land Use Planning Act.* Center for Urban and Regional Affairs, University of Minnesota.

Johnson, William C. 1998. *Growth Management in the Twin Cities Region: The Politics and Performance of the Metropolitan Council.* Center for Urban and Regional Affairs, University of Minnesota.

Orfield, Myron. 1997. *Metropolitics: A Regional Agenda for Community and Stability.* Brookings.

———. 2002a. *American Metropolitics: The New Suburban Reality.* Brookings.

———. 2002b. "Politics and Regionalism." In *Urban Sprawl: Causes, Consequences and Policy Responses,* edited by Gregory D. Squires, pp. 237–54. Washington: Urban Institute Press.

12

Fair Housing and Affordable Housing Advocacy: Reconciling the Dual Agenda

MARA S. SIDNEY

How is it that some civil rights advocates get trapped in a cycle of dependence, keeping them and their cause invisible, while others are able to push issues of race and racial inequality onto regional housing and community development agendas? This chapter addresses that efficacy question in the context of two very different cities with distinct advocacy movements.

Proponents of a regional housing agenda often frame their discussion of metropolitan inequalities, and their advocacy, in terms of class. They describe the social problems that emerge from economically segregated metropolitan areas, where the poor are concentrated in central cities and the affluent in outlying suburbs. Housing advocates point out that affordable housing, concentrated in central cities, is scarce in the parts of metropolitan areas experiencing the most population and job growth. They argue that the dearth of affordable housing harms both the rich and the poor. Low-income people, and particularly low-income people of color, face limited educational and employment opportunities in central cities, perpetuating the social inequities that accompany the spatial pattern of urban sprawl. Housing advocates also argue that labor shortages threaten the economic viability of growing centers of commerce in outlying areas; the economy needs low- and moderate-wage workers, but the scarcity of affordable housing in these areas means that these workers cannot live near their jobs.

To date, many discussions of uneven development describe the racial and ethnic segregation that coexists with the economic divide, but when researchers and advocates move from describing the problem to prescribing solutions, few recommendations explicitly and directly address these racial dimensions.[1] Some authors deemphasize their importance relative to socioeconomic disparities,[2] while others remain silent about racial inequality. Advocates sometimes choose silence as a political strategy, thinking that raising racial issues will provoke opposition to regional initiatives.

Why does race drop off the regional agenda when it comes to policy prescriptions? One reason is that fair housing groups do not typically partner with the affordable housing movement in local movements for regional justice, although fair housing groups are the advocates most likely to focus on the racial dimensions of the problem. This chapter argues that the value of a fair housing–affordable housing coalition seems clear from a policy-analytic perspective but faces political obstacles. That is, building a coalition that places racial and socioeconomic justice equally at its core faces barriers rooted in the characteristics of the fair housing movement on the one hand and the affordable housing movement on the other. I explore some of these obstacles below, comparing two very different metropolitan contexts. I suggest that national fair housing policy has produced a population of local fair housing groups that have trouble developing allies and do little to mobilize the public behind their cause. In effect, they are not well positioned to build a coalition with affordable housing advocates. At the same time, for a variety of reasons, affordable housing advocates may not perceive fair housing or civil rights advocates as natural allies.

In the discussion that follows, I draw on research about the fair housing movement to illustrate some of the challenges and prospects for creating a coalition of fair housing and affordable housing advocates. Two case studies illustrate contrasting outcomes in local fair housing movements. In Denver, fair housing groups have trouble building political alliances beyond a small but long-standing circle of public and private sector supporters. Building a coalition for regional housing initiatives that would address both race and class disparities is unlikely to happen there. In the Twin Cities, initiatives by fair housing and affordable housing advocates do add up to a regional housing movement. Emergence of fair housing advocates in the 1990s combined with interest from affordable housing groups in fair housing problems to produce this outcome. Yet even here racial inequalities take a backseat to class inequalities in much of the policy discourse. These two case studies serve an analytic purpose rather

1. See for example Orfield (1997); Rusk (1999).
2. For example Dreier, Mollenkopf, and Swanstrom (2001).

than an inferential one. All cities will not be like these two, but groups in every city will confront the barriers to coalition building posed by national fair housing policy and will attempt to reconcile national policy and local context. These two cases, with their contrasting movements, show advocacy groups responding to local obstacles and opportunities.

The Role of Race in Regional Housing Inequality

Social scientists know that race operates independently of class to restrict individuals' housing choices. Evidence of the prevalence and persistence of racial discrimination in housing markets is overwhelming. The U.S. Department of Housing and Urban Development (HUD) has sponsored audit studies in more than twenty large metropolitan areas every ten years since the late 1970s. The 1989 study led to the estimate that 54 percent of racial minorities faced discrimination of one kind or another when seeking housing. The 1999 audits show that black and Hispanic homeseekers experienced adverse treatment in more than half of their visits to sales and leasing agents. Although consistent adverse treatment was estimated to occur about 22 percent of the time, the study finds that Hispanic renters faced the highest prospect of discrimination and that geographic steering of prospective buyers based on their race occurred more often than in previous studies.[3]

Racial segregation in housing and schools remains at high levels in metropolitan areas across the country, especially between African Americans and whites, although the white-to-Asian and white-to-Hispanic segregation rates increased during the 1990s.[4] White and Asian people can translate higher incomes into better neighborhoods, whereas black and Hispanic people cannot.[5] Studies that analyze neighborhood differences for black and white HUD Section 8 voucher holders point to the independent effect of race on housing options; for example, black households with housing assistance are more likely to live in distressed neighborhoods than other assisted households.[6] Evaluations of the few mobility programs that exist (programs that aim to enable poor people and often racial

3. See Margery Turner and Stephen Ross, chapter 4, this volume; Turner, Struyk, and Yinger (1991); Margery Turner and others, "Discrimination in Metropolitan Housing Markets: National Results from Phase I HDS 2000 (www.huduser.org/publications/hsgfin/phase1.html [November 2002]).

4. See for example Massey and Denton (1993); Yinger (1995); Lewis Mumford Center, "Ethnic Diversity Grows, Neighborhood Integration Lags Behind" (www.albany.edu/mumford/census [December 2001]); John Logan, "Separate and Unequal: The Neighborhood Gap for Blacks and Hispanics in Metropolitan America" (www.albany.edu/mumford [October 2002]). Note that by white I refer to non-Hispanic white.

5. John R. Logan, Jacob Stowell, and Dierdre Oakley, "Choosing Segregation: Racial Imbalance in American Public Schools, 1990—2000," Lewis Mumford Center (www.albany.edu/mumford [2002]).

6. Pendall (2000).

minorities to relocate to wealthier suburbs or neighborhoods with predominantly white populations) often emphasize the importance of housing counseling to a program's success. The need for counseling in part relates to the impact of race on the operation of housing markets; minority families need assistance if they are to find housing in white neighborhoods.[7]

This body of evidence means that programs to address the supply of affordable housing constitute only part of the solution to metropolitan housing inequality. We also need to reduce the incidence of the discriminatory practices that limit housing options for minority households and address a range of other factors that give rise to racial segregation. These include attitudes and information about neighborhoods, perceptions of schools, and differences in school quality and quality of life across neighborhoods and towns within metropolitan areas.[8]

There are several reasons why, despite the evidence of racial discrimination, proponents of regional housing equality talk more about class than about race. Some may not know of the research or despite their awareness remain convinced that income outweighs race in limiting housing options. They understand metropolitan housing inequality as a function of uneven distribution of affordable housing and think that increasing supply would, by extension, increase housing choices for racial minorities and decrease segregation. Sometimes advocates avoid explicit discussion of racial segregation as a political strategy; by not discussing the racial composition of the low-income population in need of housing, they attempt to limit opposition to such housing from white suburbanites. Still others contest the relevance of racial segregation and discrimination in increasingly multiethnic urban areas, or they point out the complex attitudes that black people hold toward housing desegregation measures.[9]

Characteristics of the fair housing movement itself also explain why advocates for regional affordable housing overlook or downplay the importance of racial inequalities. The work of fair housing does not often bring advocates of that cause into contact with affordable housing advocates and does not require them to persuade local or state government decisionmakers, affordable housing advocates, or the general public of the importance of decreasing racial inequality in housing. Rather, the nuts and bolts of fair housing work consists of investigating claims of discrimination and presenting these claims in specialized arenas such as the courts or administrative hearings, often out of view of the general public. This mode of action stems from features of national fair housing policy itself. That is, policy aimed at addressing racial discrimination in housing has produced a population of fair housing groups with low visibility. Fair housing

7. John Goering, chapter 6, this volume; Rubinowitz and Rosenbaum (2000).

8. Camille Charles, chapter 3, this volume; Yinger (1995).

9. Jennifer Hochschild, "Creating Options" (bostonreview.net/br25.3/hochschild.html); Powell (2000).

policy encourages groups to acquire a set of technical skills but does not encourage groups to develop skills in building coalitions, advocating in the legislative arena, or mobilizing the public. Yet these sorts of political skills are what fair housing advocates need if they are to convince affordable housing advocates that regional housing agendas should include attention to, and remedies for, racial inequality.

Linking Fair Housing Policy and Advocacy

These claims emerge from research conducted over several years on the influence national policy has on local advocacy and, more specifically, on how policy resources interact with local contexts to weaken or strengthen nonprofit groups.[10] This work is rooted in a theoretical perspective that understands public policies as "designs," institutional frameworks of ideas and tools.[11] Scholars using this perspective show how public policies capture, or institutionalize, a set of ideas about a problem that prevailed in a political process. They then analyze how such a set of ideas and tools shapes subsequent politics and problem-solving efforts. Put another way, any public policy offers a distinctive set of resources to advocacy groups. The policy design approach asks how this resource "package" shapes patterns of political participation and advocacy. But local groups confronted with national policy designs are situated in distinctive contexts, which mediate how they employ policy resources and to what effect. Thus attention to political, social, and historical features of localities is also needed to fully understand patterns of local housing advocacy.

This chapter thus begins by analyzing the resources that national fair housing policy offers local groups. It then turns to a comparison of housing movements in Denver and Minneapolis–Saint Paul. Faced with the same national fair housing policy, groups in Denver and the Twin Cities behaved quite differently. Denver groups forged quiet partnerships with private industry, whereas the Twin Cities groups confronted and opposed government practices. Aspects of fair housing policy itself explain the challenges that fair housing groups such as those in Denver face in drawing attention to and support for fair housing issues. In the Twin Cities, however, advocates have used fair housing resources to craft a regional fair housing agenda, partially succeeding in bridging the gap between race and class. When affordable housing advocates took up fair housing issues, they raised the visibility of fair housing on the public agenda. Racial and class inequalities thus became part of a regional housing agenda, although class remained privileged in policy recommendations.

10. Sidney (2003).
11. Schneider and Ingram (1997).

Elements of local context—including the rate of racial change, the state political context, and the presence of historical fair housing networks—help explain why Denver's fair housing movement differs from that in Minneapolis–Saint Paul. Local context pushed Denver groups to rely primarily on national policy resources, keeping them barely visible to the general public. In Minneapolis–Saint Paul, local context enabled groups to build a broader, more inclusive approach to fair housing that addressed both racial and economic inequalities in housing. I argue that national fair housing policy pushes local advocacy groups in directions that make them less likely to become part of regional housing coalitions. Some local contexts exacerbate these tendencies. But in others, fair housing has the potential to become a component of regional housing advocacy. On the ground, local advocacy groups engage in a process of adapting national policy resources to their local context.

Fair Housing Resources: Civil Rights and Affordable Housing

Public policies contain sets of resources that nonprofit groups use to implement them. Using these resources transforms groups because resources push groups to engage in particular kinds of activity, to act in particular arenas, and to adopt particular understandings of a problem. A first step in understanding the actions and orientations of local fair housing groups must be to examine the set of resources that fair housing policy offers them. Funding is an obvious and important resource that policies may offer groups, but it is only one resource. We also can think of problem definitions, procedures, and information as resources that policies provide to local groups. Problem definitions specify the contours of a problem—its causes, consequences, and victims. Procedural resources offer opportunities or arenas for group action; they give groups a role in implementation and usually require particular skills and knowledge. Informational resources provide groups with the expertise and data they may use to exert influence. Analysis of the fair housing policy design shows two sets of resources, a dominant set related to civil rights and a subordinate set related to affordable housing. Table 12-1 summarizes the discussion.

Civil Rights Resources

The bulk of fair housing policy resources rest here. Funding, procedures, and information are available to groups adopting an understanding of fair housing rooted in identifying and punishing discriminatory practices in housing transactions and in compensating victims. HUD's Fair Housing Initiatives program (FHIP) funds nonprofit fair housing organizations on a competitive basis to undertake enforcement activities. Groups receive funding to take claims, investigate them through use of fair housing tests, and represent clients in the administrative process that HUD operates regionally or that state civil rights agencies

Table 12-1. *Fair Housing Resources*

Resources	*Civil rights*	*Affordable housing*
Ideas	Discriminatory practices in housing transactions identified Perpetrators punished Victims compensated (made whole)	Affordable housing provided on a nondiscriminatory basis
Funds	FHIP Legal damages	Legal damages
Procedures	Administrative enforcement Courts	Administrative enforcement Courts
Information	FHIP conferences Technical assistance	(None)

run with HUD subsidies. FHIP offers limited funding for education and outreach activities as well. HUD holds annual conferences for FHIP grantees to promote information sharing and to provide technical assistance. An alternative procedural resource for fair housing groups is the court system. Groups may choose to litigate on behalf of a client rather than use HUD's administrative enforcement process. Both administrative law judges and trial judges and juries may award attorney's fees and damages to local fair housing organizations.[12]

Local groups using these resources typically develop legal and investigative expertise and work on fair housing case by case in their cities. Their work takes them into courtrooms and classrooms, filing lawsuits and training real estate agents. As they prepare complaints and guide clients through the administrative enforcement process, advocates learn to interact with state and federal civil servants. In general, they are likely to establish partnerlike relationships with HUD, which funds them to enforce the law and helps them, through annual conferences, to develop their skills. Indeed, HUD has come to rely on nonprofits to undertake certain enforcement activities it finds difficult, given its political vulnerability—namely, fair housing testing. Yet testing is critical to enforcement because minority homeseekers often need to know how a housing professional treats clients of different races if they are to recognize discrimination in the post–Fair Housing Act era. Fair housing groups that do this civil-rights-oriented work, focused on the private housing sector, are less likely to develop skills in coalition building either with elected officials or with the public. Much of their operational support and technical assistance comes from the federal government, and they do their work in specialized arenas out of the public eye, such as courtrooms and administrative offices.

12. Bensinger (1996).

Affordable Housing Resources

A second set of fair housing resources is rooted in an understanding of fair housing as the provision of affordable housing on a nondiscriminatory basis. Only procedural resources are available to groups who adopt this definition of the problem, not direct funding or information. The Fair Housing Act requires HUD to integrate "fair housing" into its existing housing programs "in a manner to affirmatively further the purposes of this title" (Section 808). Thus it directs attention to the operating procedures and outcomes of federal programs such as public housing (Section 8 and Community Development Block Grants). Groups may file a fair housing lawsuit against HUD or against a recipient of federal housing subsidies, such as a public housing authority or a local government. Or groups may try to show that local governments have not "affirmatively furthered" fair housing in their use of federal housing and urban development funds, as the Fair Housing Act requires of them. FHIP funding is not available for use in claims against government.

Local groups using these resources will typically become adversaries of government rather than partners in enforcement. They are more likely than civil-rights-oriented groups to develop skills to build coalitions and to mobilize the public because they need allies to help fund litigation and may need to generate public support in their struggle against government adversaries. In other words, they need to generate the funds and the information on which to base a legal claim before they can use fair housing's procedural resources. In addition, these claims tend to be class-action lawsuits, so advocates need to convince a "class" to join the effort; thus they must be able to communicate in broad terms how racial discrimination has harmed a group of people.

Contrasting Cases of Local Fair Housing Advocacy

Examples of fair housing movements in Denver and the Twin Cities illustrate some of the ways groups respond to national fair housing resources and the political consequences these responses have for fair housing groups. These observations are grounded in two years of field research in Washington, Denver, and the Twin Cities that consisted of interviews, participant observation, and archival research.[13] In Denver, fair housing groups focused on civil rights enforcement,

13. Data were collected during field research in Minneapolis, Denver, and Washington from August 1998 through January 2000. Data consist of interviews, archival research, and participant observation. I conducted seventy-seven in-person, semistructured interviews with past and present civil rights, fair housing, and housing activists and with government officials at the local, state, and federal levels, both elected and civil servants. I attended related events and workshops, including national meetings of advocacy groups, and consulted archival materials, including government documents, local newspapers, and advocacy group archives.

relying on one set of fair housing resources. These groups faced challenges in generating local political support for their work. Their dilemmas show why fair housing groups may not be working to build coalitions with affordable housing advocates in supporting a regional housing agenda and why they may not be a strong voice for the inclusion of racial justice in a regional agenda.

Twin Cities fair housing advocacy differs dramatically from that in Denver. Fair housing efforts focus on affordable housing provision, using a strong base of local resources to leverage the procedural resources fair housing policy offers. Indeed, the Twin Cities movement redefined fair housing advocacy into the pursuit of regionally dispersed affordable housing, thus blending the race and class dimensions of metropolitan inequality into their reform agenda. Still, race holds a subordinate position in this agenda, highlighting the difficulties of moving race into a regional movement. Table 12-2 summarizes the differences across Denver and Twin Cities advocacy.

Denver: Civil Rights and a Cycle of Dependence and Invisibility

Fair housing advocacy enjoys deep roots in Denver. A cadre of committed advocates has worked for decades to advance racial equality in housing. But Denver's fair housing groups have few local allies, are relatively invisible to the general public, and have generally overburdened staff.

Denver advocates have engaged in fair housing activity since the late 1950s. Well before the 1968 national law was enacted, one of the country's largest nonprofit fair housing centers operated there. Although it closed in the early 1970s, a small cadre of advocates retained their interest in the issue, keeping it alive in government and industry arenas and in a neighborhood organization. When federal funding became available in the late 1980s for fair housing planning, these advocates secured a grant and undertook a process that led to the creation in 1987 of a new fair housing center. This center, Housing for All, has been joined by two additional fair housing groups—Housing Opportunities Made Equal (HOME) and the Community Housing Resource Board. Housing for All and HOME receive FHIP funds to engage in enforcement. They investigate individual claims using fair housing testing, and advocate on behalf of victims spanning the protected classes of racial minorities, families with children, and disabled people. They conduct workshops for homeseekers and teach real estate professionals about fair housing law.

Denver's fair housing movement thus uses federal policy's civil-rights-related resources, working to decrease discrimination in private housing transactions. Advocates have responded to nearly every opportunity for federal funding, securing money to examine discriminatory practices in home rentals, sales, lending, and insurance. They have conducted special demonstration projects, participated in nationwide housing audits, undertaken fair housing planning projects, and won FHIP grants year after year to support the two fair housing centers. In

Table 12-2. *Two Models of Fair Housing Advocacy*

	Denver	*Twin Cities*
Goal	Protecting civil rights	Providing affordable housing for all households
Primary target	Private sector practices	Public sector practices
Strategies	Investigating and filing claims of discrimination Partnering with private sector (such as the Insurance Council) Educating private sector actors (for example, fair housing training)	Investigating and filing claims of discrimination Litigating (regarding, for example, public housing siting, educational inequity) Mobilizing (as through the Metro Sabbath)
Arenas	Behind-the-scenes, specialized (such as administrative agencies, real estate trade associations)	Public (such as the state courts, the state legislature)
Visibility	Low	High

doing so, fair housing activists in Denver have adapted their strategies to incorporate changes in national law and HUD priorities.

Clearly these national policy resources enable Denver advocates to engage in a range of fair housing activities; but they also pose several challenges to local groups. These challenges are not unique to Denver; they also emerge within other FHIP-funded groups. Using FHIP resources traps Denver groups in a cycle of invisibility. Grantees are grateful for the funds they receive, but as in other government grant programs these funds deprive local groups of the autonomy to control their agenda, require time-consuming reporting and applications, and often come with pressures to produce a certain number of discrimination claims (which some staff members believe reduces the quality of their enforcement). This occurs with HUD's funding for state civil rights agencies as well; one state staffer said that investigators prefer to work on employment discrimination cases. "The requirements [HUD] has for final investigative reports are so meticulous . . . that to write up a housing case takes much longer than to write up an employment discrimination case. The investigators get really testy if they feel like they are being given more housing cases than their fair share."

Groups shift their priorities from funding cycle to funding cycle, in accordance with HUD's changing priorities for fair housing implementation. One year groups may receive extra "points" for reaching out to new immigrant communities, another year they get credit for focusing on building standards for accessibility to disabled tenants. "We're like puppets on a string for HUD," according to a state civil rights official. "I have no idea how they decide what they're going to emphasize this year and how they're going to divvy up the money. They rename the grants every year so you can't figure out what they say."

As is the case with nonprofit grantees in a range of policy sectors, federal funds are necessary but insufficient. Staff members are stretched thin, and maintaining morale is difficult. Yet paid staff members are extremely busy taking and processing claims, finding testers and coordinating tests, and representing clients. They would like to cultivate a diversity of funders to reduce dependence on government and to limit their vulnerability to federal budget cuts, but they have little time to do so. The terms of their FHIP grants prohibit them from lobbying, which some activists define quite broadly. Consequently, in Denver many government officials and local elites are unaware of the fair housing movement's work; among those I interviewed, many are not convinced that racial discrimination is a problem in Denver.

Indeed, lack of public awareness of racial discrimination represents a key challenge that fair housing groups face when trying to generate alliances. In addition to constraints that federal resources place on a group's time and ability to lobby, federal resources also channel advocates into specialized arenas rather than into more public arenas. And enforcement's reliance on fair housing testing creates disincentives for groups to publicize the prevalence of the problem in their communities.[14]

A fair housing test is a paired-comparison experiment in which individuals similar in all ways but race or ethnicity seek to buy or rent a home (see Margery Turner and Stephen Ross, chapter 4, this volume). These "testers" complete reports about their experiences—how they were treated and the information they were given. Comparing these reports can identify disparate and discriminatory treatment. The anonymity of fair housing testers clearly is critical to the success of this method of identifying discrimination; if a leasing agent or broker suspects someone to be a tester, he or she may behave differently during a housing transaction. Thus fair housing groups must keep their testing initiatives and personnel confidential. Confidentiality also is a condition of many fair housing cases settled out of court. The public may never learn the details of the discriminatory practices a defendant engaged in or the damages won by the plaintiff and nonprofit group. Nonprofits' work thus remains invisible to most city residents.

Another reason fair housing groups keep the details of their testing programs private is that local real estate agents tend to fear the practice and worry that they may be "entrapped" unfairly. When real estate brokers talk at industry training sessions, it is clear that their sense of the size of a fair housing group's testing program is exaggerated. Nonprofits actually struggle to maintain a qualified pool of volunteer testers and conduct a rather limited number of tests each

14. Testing is the method that nonprofits use to identify discriminatory practices. It is recognized by the courts and HUD as proof of discrimination, and HUD funds groups to engage in testing.

year relative to the number of housing transactions that occur. Yet advocates think that if housing professionals fear they may be "tested" at any time they may be more likely to comply with fair housing laws. Nonprofits are thus less likely to publicize the weaknesses of their testing programs as a way of attracting more support for them and are more likely to work behind the scenes to garner more resources.

The incentive to keep testing results confidential diminishes a fair housing group's ability to convert volunteer testers into political advocates. Because the results of any test may become evidence in litigation, and a tester may be called as a witness to describe his or her experience, fair housing groups do not inform testers about the outcome of a test because they fear contaminating the evidence. Volunteer testers rarely know whether they have helped to uncover and punish discrimination or if the tests found no illegal practices at all. These volunteers may gain little sense of the extent of discrimination in their own communities, yet unlike the nonprofit staffers, whose lobbying activities are restricted by federal funding, volunteers could freely lobby or attempt to mobilize support.

Finally, mechanisms of allocating fair housing funds create disincentives for cooperation among fair housing groups in a community. Federal funding is awarded on a competitive basis, pitting local groups against one another. Some Denver advocates were unhappy that, with the founding of HOME, the city had two FHIP-funded groups. They saw federal support in zero-sum terms, fearing that HUD would not maintain adequate funding levels for both groups over time.[15] Another barrier to cooperation is that legal damages and attorney's fees must be shared among groups if several work together on a successful lawsuit. Federal enforcement's reliance on testing and its funding mechanisms lead some groups to work alone and to keep a low profile. Doing so may help them develop strong fair housing cases and claims and may act to deter the private real estate industry from some discrimination, but it also keeps the problem off the public agenda, thus undermining the development of public support.

Twin Cities: Regional Housing on the Public Agenda

The political dilemmas that Denver groups face in gaining attention and support for efforts to reduce racial discrimination explain why local fair housing groups will have trouble bringing racial inequality into a regional housing reform agenda or, indeed, spearheading such an effort. This is especially true of fair housing groups that tap civil-rights-oriented policy resources. The example of fair housing advocacy in the Twin Cities shows another path through which racial and economic housing justice might be joined: the entrance of affordable

15. By contrast, a local HUD official welcomed the presence of an additional enforcement group, comparing it to having more state troopers on the highways to catch speeding drivers.

housing advocates into the fair housing arena. These "new" fair housing advocates bring a strong network of connections to elected officials and experience working in the legislative arena and educating and mobilizing the public. But their views of housing problems and the political landscape also pose challenges to injecting race into the regional housing agenda.

In the Twin Cities, a wide range of groups have taken up fair housing issues, using a variety of strategies to pursue their goals. In general, either these groups rely on the federal fair housing resources related to affordable housing, or they do not use federal resources at all. As such, they have evaded the cycle of invisibility that challenges Denver's activists and other civil-rights-oriented fair housing groups and have succeeded at publicly articulating the problem of economic disparities in the metropolitan area and, to a lesser extent, the problem of racial disparities.

The contemporary fair housing movement emerged only in the 1990s and consists of a wide range of groups, from legal advocates to faith-based organizations to affordable housing and poor people's advocacy groups. The Minnesota state legislator Myron Orfield brought the regional concept of fair housing to the legislative agenda in 1993, when he sponsored a series of bills to reduce concentrated poverty in the Twin Cities. In addition, lawyer-activists founded two fair housing groups and launched two lawsuits with fair housing dimensions.[16] *Hollman* v. *Cisneros* charged HUD, the Minneapolis Public Housing Authority, the city, and the state with intentionally segregating African Americans in public housing.[17] The second lawsuit, against the state, charged that racial and class segregation created inadequate education for Minneapolis–Saint Paul children. Plaintiffs sought a metropolitanwide housing integration policy as part of the relief, although they were not successful. To generate support for this lawsuit, the NAACP founded the Education and Housing Equity project, which organized and facilitated "community circles" to discuss and act on schools, housing, and race.

Affordable housing advocates began to undertake fair housing advocacy as well. Growth in the Twin Cities' minority population converged with a shortage of affordable housing; affordable housing advocates recognized that they could use fair housing tools to work toward their goal of preserving and increasing the supply of affordable housing. Because of the disparate impact on people of color, lack of affordable housing in a Twin Cities suburb constitutes "unfair" housing. As one organizer put it, "You can't organize on housing issues without looking at fair housing issues."

16. The Housing Discrimination law project receives FHIP funds to engage in enforcement on behalf of low-income protected classes. The Minnesota Fair Housing Center conducts research.

17. This lawsuit resulted in a negotiated consent decree under which spatially concentrated public housing units are being replaced with units scattered throughout the metropolitan area, and a community planning process is guiding redevelopment of the public housing site.

Since then, the Affordable Housing Stabilization project was formed (in 1998), with support from the local Family Housing Fund. Affordable housing activists and lawyers were developing fair housing and other litigation strategies to prevent Section 8 prepayment, which threatened affordable units. This approach to fair housing focuses on government compliance with fair housing regulation in its use of federal funding for affordable housing. According to one legal activist, "Fair housing tools can often be used to preserve affordable housing or to open up doors for affordable housing. Not easily, and never without huge struggles, but affordable housing advocates should look for every tool that they can use." Another advocate had begun to examine the fair housing requirements of the Community Development Block Grant program and described a low-rent apartment building in Saint Paul that the city was threatening to demolish. Using a fair housing argument helped to preserve the building. "Ninety-three families out of ninety-four were African American," she said. "The fair housing angle has been underused [in housing advocacy]."

Other innovative strategies included commissioning a play to use as a tool to mobilize congregations around fair and affordable housing. The Metropolitan Interfaith Coalition on Affordable Housing won FHIP funds for this work. Performances of the play were followed by group discussions, during which coalition members passed out postcards to the state legislature and sign-up sheets to identify volunteers for further affordable housing activities in the congregation's community. Yet another example is Metro Sabbath, the Catholic archdiocese Office of Social Justice's lobbying campaign to increase state funding for affordable housing: Materials on racial and income polarization are sent to congregations throughout the metropolitan area to educate congregations and to generate political action.

In this quest for reducing metropolitan inequalities, the problem of racial inequality takes a backseat to the problem of economic inequality in the work of many advocates. For example, although Orfield calls his proposals "fair housing" bills, and although he and others describe problems in the Twin Cities area in terms of racial and class disparity, the compromise legislation focuses on encouraging suburbs to develop affordable housing, without provisions for reducing racial discrimination or otherwise guaranteeing access to racial minorities.[18] Additionally, during interviews with affordable housing activists, they most often described metropolitan inequalities in terms of class rather than race. Those who acknowledge that racial discrimination is part of the problem perceive discussion of it as a political barrier to winning support for affordable housing and therefore refrain from doing so in public arenas. That is, because of racial prejudice and discrimination, affordable housing advocates consciously avoid discussing the racial composition of the low-income population when

18. Orfield (1997).

they promote affordable housing in public arenas; in one advocate's terms, the strategy is to "take the black face out of affordable housing."

For example, a community development corporation director explained that, when addressing the city council in a Twin Cities suburb to seek approval for a housing development, he would not say "we expect 70 percent of these folks will be black." Race, he said, "is still a very delicate subject in Minnesota." A housing organizer concurred with this approach. "Most of the time you take the most expedient route to get something done. Whatever argument I have to use to get housing built, I will use. But that still doesn't address the race issue." The racial dimensions of housing issues, she said, "are topics of conversations to have probably outside of a heated battle to get some affordable housing built." A foundation official noted that people of color are not well represented on the staffs of housing advocacy groups. "Most of the people served by affordable housing programs are people of color," he said, but the organizations providing those services are staffed mostly by white people.

Affordable housing advocates in the Twin Cities, adept at publicizing and securing resources for affordable housing and at providing technical assistance to housing providers, now see themselves as fair housing advocates. They could tap their resources more directly on behalf of racial justice as they work to preserve and increase the supply of affordable housing. That is, they could work explicitly to ensure that people of color will have access to housing, and more generally they could promote the ideal of racial and ethnic diversity in the suburbs. But their assessment of the political landscape bars them from doing so.

The Influence of Local Context

Federal policy does not act alone in shaping fair housing advocacy; advocates respond to their local contexts as well. In Minneapolis–Saint Paul and Denver, groups facing the same set of policy resources and incentives chose very different courses of action. Three local factors seemed to condition fair housing advocacy groups' responses to the national policy design: the rate of change in racial diversity and poverty, the state political context, and the presence and nature of historical organizational networks. To some degree, we can understand the features of Denver's fair housing movement as responses to a local context relatively hostile to their cause. Whereas advocates in Denver use federal resources to compensate for lack of local support for fair housing efforts, advocates in Minnesota use federal resources to complement a local array of actors and institutions supportive of affordable housing.

Changing Racial Diversity and Poverty

Differences in the rate of demographic change help explain why fair housing activism in Minneapolis–Saint Paul focused on low-income minorities and why activism was more visible to the public in the Twin Cities than in Denver. Although in both cities a majority of residents are white, Denver is a historically multiethnic city, with a sizable Latino population and somewhat smaller black population. The proportion of Denver residents who are black remained essentially the same from 1980 to 2000. The proportion of Denver residents who are Latino, however, grew from 19 percent in 1980 to 23 percent in 1990, a 23 percent increase. By 2000 Latinos made up 34 percent of the population, a 40 percent increase over 1990. Latinos have not been as active on fair housing issues as whites and blacks in Denver.

Minneapolis–Saint Paul, on the other hand, experienced during the 1980s and 1990s much more rapid and dramatic shifts in the racial composition of its population. The minority population grew by 32,000 people during the 1980s, a 69 percent increase, and continued to increase in numbers and diversity in the 1990s.[19] The city's 2000 census shows that minorities and immigrants account for all of the city's population growth.[20] The nonwhite population grew by 54,000 people, or 68 percent. In addition, the minority population became more impoverished during the 1980s, although there is evidence that the 1990s brought some improvement. One study concludes that whereas poverty declined slightly among blacks nationwide during the 1980s, in Minnesota it grew from about 24 percent in 1980 to about 36 percent in 1990.[21] Indeed, black poverty rates in the Twin Cities have been among the highest in the nation. In 1980 about one quarter of Twin Cities blacks lived in ghetto neighborhoods; by 1990 nearly half of them did, and the poverty rate grew from 30 percent in 1980 to 41 percent in 1990.[22] By 2000 the rate had dropped to 32 percent, still significantly higher than the rate of 10 percent for whites. In Denver, the black poverty rate changed from 21 percent in 1980 to 27 percent in 1990; for Latinos, the rate changed from 24 percent to 31 percent. By 2000 both of these rates had dropped; 19 percent of blacks were poor, and 23 percent of Latinos, lagging behind the white rate of 11 percent.

These differences in the rate of racial change and the relative impoverishment of minorities have two implications for fair housing action. First, they drive the convergence of fair housing and affordable housing issues in the Twin Cities. Affordable housing advocates in the 1990s became interested in the incentives to participation that fair housing policy design offers. Second, the novelty of diversity means that race is news, so the media focus on racial issues. To some extent, media images of minorities are associated with crime and welfare and thus fuel negative stereotypes, making advocacy more challenging. Most activists interviewed thought that media coverage of race hurt their advocacy

19. Goetz (1998).
20. Minneapolis Planning Department (2001).
21. Ahlburg (1998).
22. Korenman, Dwight, and Sjaastad (1997).

efforts, and they tend to frame housing issues in terms of class—for example, when trying to persuade suburban jurisdictions to build affordable housing (Edward Goetz, Karen Chapple, and Barbara Lukerman, chapter 11, this volume, describe suburban opposition). On the other hand, the publicity gives race and housing issues agenda status in a way not experienced by activists in Denver. Ironically, the increasing salience of race in Minneapolis–Saint Paul has prompted many housing advocates to keep race out of their public rhetoric.

State Political Context

The differing political contexts in the two states help account for the focus on private sector practices in Denver and public sector policies in Minneapolis–Saint Paul; this difference also influences the visibility of fair housing issues. Although both cities have histories of liberal, progressive leadership, Colorado is generally conservative and Republican compared to liberal Minnesota, where even Republicans have a tradition of progressivism. Republicans controlled both houses of the Colorado legislature from 1976 to 2000, when Democrats gained a one-seat lead in the Senate. In Minnesota, Democrats have controlled the state senate for twenty-nine years, and the state house for a decade until the 1998 elections. In Minneapolis–Saint Paul, affordable and fair housing activists turn to the state for policy changes and funds, but Colorado fair housing activists do not see the state as a viable source of support, either in terms of programs or funding.

In Denver, where fair housing activism is oriented toward protecting civil rights, activists and government agency staff report that they purposely try to keep a low profile. The higher visibility of fair housing activities could attract negative attention. A good example of Denver's orientation to partnerships rather than litigation is its Residents' Insurance Council. After conducting an FHIP-funded homeowners insurance audit, a fair housing group convened a working group that included industry and government representatives to examine the findings. The resulting Residents' Insurance Council won a grant from the Ford Foundation to undertake a loss mitigation program in the neighborhoods that the audit found to be suffering from redlining. In general, Denver's advocates have chosen to pursue claims through administrative channels rather than litigation; this reflects their interest in minimizing opposition by limiting their use of what one advocate called "the big stick" of litigation, their limited resources (which are not adequate to fund a large-scale legal effort), and their anticipation that the federal district court with jurisdiction would not be sympathetic to fair housing cases.

The state context constrains a regional affordable housing–fair housing agenda in Colorado. Denver activists do not see fair share legislation, for example (which succeeded in the Minnesota legislature, albeit in a weak form) as even in the realm of possibility in Colorado. In Minnesota, with a stronger tradition of using redistributive policy, activists view the state as the locus of government with the most resources to contribute to affordable housing. The state thus represents a viable resource and instrument for Minnesota advocates. The Minnesota Fair Housing Center, though denied HUD funds, secured research grants from the state Social Services Department to study the link between homelessness and fair housing and helped secure a special appropriation for the Human Rights Department for fair housing testing.

Organizational Networks

Fair housing advocacy in each of these cities is embedded in different historical networks, with implications for contemporary movement orientations in each place. Fair housing activism in Denver is rooted in a civil rights tradition, whereas in Minneapolis–Saint Paul the current fair housing efforts largely consist of activists from other spheres adapting to new circumstances by engaging fair housing policy tools. In Denver, current fair housing activity is part of a long and continuous history of fair housing activism, which emerged in the late 1950s in the city's Park Hill neighborhood. Residents of this neighborhood mobilized to fight blockbusting and racial turnover and to promote stable integration. Their efforts led to passage of the state fair housing law in 1959, preceding national law by nine years—and the first law in the nation to cover private housing. Activists who got their start in these early fair housing battles still lived in Park Hill, and many made careers of fair housing, civil rights, and related pursuits, in government and nonprofit settings. Former employees of Denver's original fair housing center, which had fifty employees before the national law ever existed, are now scattered in careers both public and private, forming a network of advocacy. They serve in the city and state governments, in Denver's Community Development Agency, in the Colorado Housing Finance Authority; they work as real estate agents in the city, are active on industry fair housing training, and serve as board members of Housing for All and the Community Housing Resource Board. With such a network, it is not surprising that Denver groups have taken advantage of most funding opportunities from HUD since 1968.

Minneapolis–Saint Paul has nothing like this continuity of activism and expertise on fair housing. Rather, the current movement drew on the network of affordable housing activists that developed and gained strength during the 1970s and 1980s. Although a local fair housing movement in the late 1950s and early 1960s secured passage of state and city fair housing laws, these activists moved on to other causes. Many became involved in the national civil rights movement. Some, including churches, became involved in housing development. Civil rights groups turned to employment issues, policy brutality, and neighborhood revitalization. Many of the federal fair housing resources that Denver activists took advantage of were untapped in the Twin Cities. But in the 1990s, as demographic changes converged with a shortage of affordable housing, affordable housing advocates and advocates for the poor became fair housing activists as well. These activists are comfortable with public engagement, are oriented toward mobilization strategies that have worked for them on affordable housing issues, and bring these orientations to the fair housing issue.

Conclusion

This chapter explores why local fair housing movements differ from one another and also why some movements may not be equipped to push racial inequality into a regional housing agenda. Fair housing groups relying heavily on national policy resources, like those in Denver, may become trapped in a cycle of invisibility, sacrificing their autonomy and access to the public. When affordable housing advocates with a regional perspective enter the fair housing arena, as they did in Minneapolis–Saint Paul, they tend to use fair housing tools to secure more affordable housing, often stopping short of advocating for guarantees that racial minorities will have access to such housing or promoting the value of diverse communities. Indeed, they may consciously avoid such advocacy, since their efforts to win affordable housing are difficult enough without facing implicit or explicit racial prejudice as part of the opposition (see Goetz, Chapple, and Lukerman, chapter 11, this volume). These patterns in advocacy emerge as groups select national policy resources in light of local contextual factors, such as demographic change, political constraints, and organizational histories.

Can solutions that explicitly focus on overcoming racial inequalities in housing access and patterns become part of the menu of regional policy recommendations? Such a menu might include initiatives such as significantly boosting fair housing enforcement (including much more frequent and widespread fair housing testing and preparation of class-action litigation in the public and private housing sectors); affirmative marketing and housing counseling strategies to ensure that people of color learn about housing opportunities outside of central cities; prointegration initiatives in the suburbs that would build commitment to creating diverse neighborhoods and send the message that all people are welcome. It is my conclusion that the political process to generate such a menu of policy proposals will rely on effective coalitions between affordable housing and fair housing advocates—and specifically between those who recognize and address the external barriers that keep these potential allies apart. A failure to forge such coalitions will leave fair housing groups and the racial dimensions of regional inequality marginalized in regional housing movements.

As these case studies show, the barriers to coalition building include national policy resources and adaptive behavior to local context. But groups, aware of the barriers, can think creatively about ways to bridge them. In particular, discovering mechanisms and means of talking about racial inequalities—rather than accepting that "political reality" precludes such discussion—seems an important though challenging step toward generating policy proposals to reduce racial inequality in metropolitan areas. The Twin Cities case offers examples of possible mechanisms. Class-action litigation used (race-based) fair housing law to generate regional affordable housing opportunities for people of color; study circles aimed to build popular support for regional racial and class integration, though without tangible results in this case. Perhaps leadership development efforts for people of color in the housing arena might mean that, unlike in the Twin Cities, the advocacy community reflects their voices and demands.

Continuing to avoid public discussion of race in order to win political support for housing measures does little to advance our political system's ability to address real racial injustices. It keeps the problem of racial discrimination in housing off the public agenda and offers no corrective to the scant awareness that the public has about the independent role of race in limiting housing choice. It also perpetuates the myth that limits on housing choice merely reflect what various racial groups can afford.

Scholarship on public policy demonstrates that "policy talk" influences the features of the policies and programs that emerge from the political process.[23] Thus, in practical terms, if race is not a major part of the public discourse about regional housing inequalities, then policies that emerge to fight them are not likely to offer mechanisms or resources explicitly targeted at racial discrimination. From the 1950s forward, fair housing has been called the stepchild of the civil rights movement; unless advocates, officials, and scholars find ways to bring race into the discussion of regional housing policy, we implicitly accept this status and offer little hope for changing it.

References

Ahlburg, Dennis A. 1998. "Characteristics of Poverty in Minnesota." *CURA Reporter* 28: 7–11.

Bensinger, Sarah R. 1996. "Maximizing Damages for Fair Housing Organizations under the Fair Housing Act." *Journal of Affordable Housing* 5: 227–35.

Dreier, Peter, John Mollenkopf, and Todd Swanstrom. 2001. *Place Matters: Metropolitics for the Twenty-First Century*. University Press of Kansas.

Goetz, Edward G. 1998. "Race, Class, and Metropolitan Housing Strategies: A Look at the Minneapolis–St. Paul Region." Paper prepared for Urban Affairs Association annual meeting, Fort Worth, Texas, April 22–25.

Korenman, Sanders, Leslie Dwight, and John E. Sjaastad. 1997. "The Rise of African American Poverty in the Twin Cities, 1980 to 1990." *CURA Reporter* 27: 1–12.

Massey, Douglas S., and Nancy A. Denton. 1993. *American Apartheid: Segregation and the Making of the Underclass*. Harvard University Press.

Minneapolis Planning Department. 2001. *2000 Census Report: Population, Race, and Ethnicity*.

Orfield, Myron. 1997. *Metropolitics: A Regional Agenda for Community and Stability*. Rev. ed. Brookings.

23. Rochefort and Cobb (1994); Schneider and Ingram (1997).

Pendall, Rolf. 2000. "Why Voucher and Certificate Users Live in Distressed Neighborhoods." *Housing Policy Debate* 11: 881–910.

Powell, John A. 2000. "Addressing Regional Dilemmas for Minority Communities." In *Reflections on Regionalism,* edited by B. Katz, pp. 218–48. Brookings.

Rochefort, David A., and Roger W. Cobb. 1994. *The Politics of Problem Definition: Shaping the Policy Agenda*. University Press of Kansas.

Rusk, David. 1999. *Inside Game/Outside Game: Winning Strategies for Saving Urban America.* Brookings.

Rubinowitz, Leonard S., and James E. Rosenbaum. 2000. *Crossing the Class and Color Lines: From Public Housing to White Suburbia.* University of Chicago Press.

Schneider, Anne L., and Helen Ingram. 1997. *Policy Design for Democracy*. University Press of Kansas.

Sidney, Mara S. 2003. *Unfair Housing: How National Policy Shapes Community Action.* University Press of Kansas.

Turner, Margery Austin, Raymond J. Struyk, and John Yinger. 1991. *Housing Discrimination.* U.S. Department of Housing and Urban Development.

Yinger, John. 1995. *Closed Doors, Opportunities Lost: The Continuing Costs of Housing Discrimination*. New York: Russell Sage.

PART IV
Conclusions

13

Equitable Development for a Stronger Nation: Lessons from the Field

ANGELA GLOVER BLACKWELL AND JUDITH BELL

The longer America takes to achieve full racial inclusion and participation, the more complex the task becomes. What was once the province of civil rights activists seeking removal of explicit racial barriers to housing, education, and jobs has become a twenty-first-century conundrum for metropolitan planning and development: how to create economically viable, livable, sustainable regions. Among other things, the strategy that accomplishes this will have to rebuild and reclaim the vibrancy of the urban core and address the geographic dimensions of racial exclusion.

Our organization, PolicyLink, has been in the forefront of an emerging movement called equitable development—anchored by the fair distribution of affordable and racially inclusionary housing. In this chapter, we provide an overview that movement, outline its core strategies, and connect efforts in the field—many of them still unfolding—to the timely studies found in this volume. We conclude with a focus on developing the leadership that this all-important work will require.

Why Equitable Development

Even as people of color gained rights, sprawling, poorly planned development patterns drew resources out of the urban core communities where African Americans and recent immigrants were increasingly being concentrated. Now, regions, fueled by the decentralization of urban growth, have emerged as the dominant economic and demographic units, rather than cities. Economic clusters extend beyond, or completely outside of, long-established city business centers. Transit systems cut across neighborhoods and towns with an emphasis on linking suburban workers to jobs. And new census analyses show that, over the last decade, many older suburbs experienced a growth in minority residents and in poverty and a loss of white and higher-income residents, suggesting new challenges for these communities and a continuation of the sprawling pattern.

As this volume reminds us, the emerging regional economies have ushered in new barriers to opportunity, particularly for low-income people of color. Inner-city public schools have deteriorated as suburban migration draws tax revenue and political clout away from the urban core. The lack of affordable housing in surrounding neighborhoods with higher-performing schools further isolates low-income city residents from quality public education. Finding housing near new job opportunities has been difficult for people of color, since job growth has frequently been focused in outlying communities with little, if any, rental housing and with restrictive land use policies requiring large lot sizes and other exclusionary zoning practices, along with a host of other not-in-my-backyard (NIMBY)-oriented policies and practices. The Millennial Housing Commission's report notes that "restrictive zoning practices" and the "adoption of local regulations that discourage housing development" are key elements to the spatial mismatch between job growth and job seekers' places of residence.[1]

In the regional economy, housing is the linchpin to quality of life: access to high-quality schools, jobs, services, and recreation. Increasing the supply of affordable housing is essential to improving housing opportunity, but achieving racial equity will require more. To reach equity goals, affordable units must be spread across the region. Planning for these units must accomplish the following:

—Anticipate the dislocation that accompanies gentrification as well as the white and middle-class flight that often follows the entry of low-income people of color, particularly African Americans;

—Coordinate with regional transportation services;

—Focus on workforce development and circumvent a jobs-housing mismatch; and

—Incorporate asset- and wealth-building strategies.

In short, planning must address all of the race-filled challenges of metropolitan development.

Advocates for racial economic and social equity have begun to understand this new regional paradigm and to grapple with the opportunities and challenges that it presents. New relationships and partnerships are being sought and built, and coalitions are emerging to develop strategies to achieve equity in the

1. Bipartisan Millennial Housing Commission (2002, p. 2).

local and regional context. In November 2002, PolicyLink collaborated with the Funders' Network for Smart Growth and Livable Communities to host a meeting on promoting regional equity. The original plans were to attract 250 participants; the overwhelming response, however, forced us to close registration at 650. As a result of generous contributions for scholarships, particularly by the Ford Foundation, and attention to racial and geographic diversity, over half the participants were people of color and thirty-five states were represented. An array of policy issues was explored during in-depth strategic discussions, which highlighted and dissected specific experiences and specific places. The need for affordable housing as a key part of local, regional, state, and federal agendas was clear, as was the need for comprehensive approaches.

The newly emerging equitable development paradigm aims to ensure that low-income people and communities of color benefit from local and regional economic activity by requiring that housing development and distribution are seen as the centerpiece of geographic and racial fairness. Further, it collectively targets transportation, asset and workforce development, and public and private investment policies and practices.

Equitable development is also relevant in a variety of community contexts, ranging from weak urban markets with neighborhoods suffering from years of severe disinvestment to economically vibrant regions surrounding vital urban centers with "hot" housing markets that fuel gentrification in once-neglected neighborhoods. This agenda has currency whether the goal is reducing concentrated poverty, avoiding displacement of existing residents in revitalizing communities, or promoting mixed-income, mixed-race neighborhoods across the region. This comprehensive approach is guided by the following goals:

—To integrate people-focused and place-focused strategies. Community and regional development and revitalization policies and practices must integrate people-focused strategies—efforts that support low-income community residents and families—with place-focused strategies—those that stabilize and improve housing, commercial establishments, and environments.

—To reduce local and regional disparities. One's home address should not be the determinant of one's life chances. The services, amenities, and opportunities that are essential for healthy, livable communities should be accessible to all neighborhoods. Though some trade-offs will exist in the near term, win-win solutions must be crafted that simultaneously improve conditions in low-income communities of color and build healthy metropolitan regions. Metropolitan areas that pay attention to *both* regional growth and central city poverty are more likely to thrive.

—To promote double bottom-line investments. Public and private investments in low-income communities are key to revitalization, but to reduce poverty and promote advancement these investments must produce a double bottom line: financial returns for investors and also economic and social benefits for residents (for example, jobs, needed services, entrepreneurial opportunities, and access to desirable, affordable housing, including ownership options).

—To ensure a meaningful community voice, participation, and leadership. Broad, well-supported participation of community residents and organizations in planning and development helps ensure that the results benefit the community, respond to the needs of low-income people and people of color, and reflect the principles articulated above. To accomplish this, community residents and organizations must have access to the tools, knowledge, and resources that can guarantee meaningful participation in development. This last principle goes beyond metropolitan policy analysis and planning ideas to the new civics of regional leadership.

Equitable Development in Practice

In the new regional paradigm, development, to be fair and racially inclusive, must place the highest priority on promoting sound, comprehensive housing policies and strategies that provide desirable, safe, affordable housing for all residents all over the region. The principles of equitable development raise the challenge to simultaneously address the needs of the people in the community while improving the quality of the housing stock and commercial and service environment. This means city and county officials, nonprofit and for-profit developers, and local leaders paying attention, from the beginning of a neighborhood improvement process, to finding ways to keep housing affordable over time. It also means that commercial and residential development outside of poor urban neighborhoods should seek ways to create affordable housing. Further, transportation and other regional public investments should enhance the value of housing throughout the region by making jobs and recreational activities broadly accessible.

There must also be a focus on making sure that revitalization efforts create jobs and opportunities for those in need and promote wealth building. Unfortunately, attention in this latter arena, if disconnected from housing affordability, may lead to displacement. Below, in the discussion of the Market Creek Plaza experience, we look at efforts to expand housing choices and regional opportunity across lines of race and income, addressing gentrification and displacement in revitalizing areas, equitable development in weaker markets, and links to transportation and other metropolitan growth issues.

Market Creek Plaza, located on a former abandoned factory site in the diverse yet underserved Diamond Neighborhoods of San Diego, embodies many of the principles of equitable development. Conceived through a partnership between the Jacobs Center for Neighborhood Innovation (JCNI) and local residents, Market Creek is a thriving twenty-acre, mixed-use commercial and cultural center anchored by a Food 4 Less supermarket. In 1997 JCNI—an operating foundation established by the Jacobs Family Foundation with the mission of strengthening neighborhoods—decided to locate and focus its work in the Diamond Neighborhoods, whose 88,000 residents are 43 percent Hispanic, 30 percent African American, 12 percent Asian, 11 percent white, 3 percent non-Hispanic mixed race, and 1 percent Hawaiian–Pacific Islander.[2] Nearly a quarter of the area's residents earn less than $15,000 annually, and an estimated 30 percent do not have access to a car, making travel to retail facilities or job opportunities in other neighborhoods difficult. Accordingly, the project initially focused not on affordable housing (which at that time was amply available in the historically disinvested community) but on attracting economic activity and retail and cultural amenities to the Diamond Neighborhoods. The resident planning and ownership philosophy guiding Market Creek Plaza's design and construction exemplifies equitable development in practice.

With the support and collaboration of JCNI, Diamond residents organized into teams and crafted development plans, which included a large, well-stocked supermarket, local grocery and construction jobs (as well as small business opportunities), and a plaza design reflecting the cultural diversity of the neighborhood. The construction team, a diverse coalition of trade and youth organizations, engaged in comprehensive recruiting, training, and business development efforts to achieve a hiring rate of 69 percent women-owned or people-of-color-owned contractors for the Market Creek Plaza construction (compared to a rate of 2 percent for the city of San Diego at large). Another team negotiated an agreement with Food 4 Less to hire and train Diamond residents at its other San Diego locations, thereby building the skills necessary for them to successfully transition to employment at the Market Creek site; when that store opened in January 2001, 91 percent of employees hired to fill the 110 union positions were local residents. This partnership produced benefits for both the community and the supermarket; according to Food 4 Less, the Market Creek Plaza store is one of the two best performers of any of its San Diego locations.[3]

These two aspects of the project—resident engagement and economic viability—demonstrate how equitable development can not only revitalize neighborhoods but also ensure that local residents of color benefit. With Market Creek Plaza as a catalyst for neighborhood reinvestment and visibility, the Diamond Neighborhoods are now vulnerable to rising housing values, which threaten the ability of community residents to stay and reap the very benefits of development they worked to create. Since only one-third of homes in the immediate neighborhood of Market Creek Plaza are owner occupied, rising housing costs may eventually force longtime renters out. Anticipating this threat, JCNI is

2. Jacobs Center for Neighborhood Innovation (undated).

3. To learn more about the process and accomplishments of Market Creek Plaza, including the innovative design and the local businesses that are finding space in the plaza, see McCulloch and Robinson (2002; 2005).

exploring housing stabilization strategies—such as limited equity co-ops and community land trusts—with a particular focus on resident ownership. As the Market Creek Plaza story continues to unfold, the fair distribution of affordable housing, including maintaining the stock of such housing as a neglected area improves, must remain the cornerstone of equitable development in the Diamond Neighborhoods and beyond.

Equitable Development and Housing

The realization that, to be equitable, access to affordable housing must always be paramount in the development process led PolicyLink to launch, in 2001, the Equitable Development Toolkit: Beyond Gentrification. The tool kit points advocates to strategies, policies, and practices being used around the country to enable low-income residents to remain in their neighborhoods and reap the benefits of revitalizing communities. It provides access to information about promising approaches organized under the headings of affordable housing, controlling development, financing strategies, and income and asset creation. However, the majority of the organizations, networks, and coalitions with which PolicyLink interacts—spanning community development, civil rights, transportation, housing, and environmental groups—have identified the expansion and fair distribution of affordable housing as the key target of their work.[4]

The fact that such a diverse array of groups has landed on the equity (fair) and geographic (distribution) challenges of affordable housing reveals a strategic opportunity to bring new constituencies into housing policy and into the quest for full racial inclusion. It also opens the door to the need for regional equity as an overarching goal. For reasons outlined above—and indeed, throughout this volume—we would argue that a focus on race and housing in the context of regional development and growth is the only way to achieve regional equity.

Regional development patterns play a significant role in housing gentrification and displacement. Yet as contributors to this volume show, without political will and a strategic agenda, little progress will be made toward achieving regional equity through housing advocacy. Many jurisdictions shun responsibility for producing affordable housing, and external enforcement mechanisms are the exception. To make matters worse, public commitment to housing affordability problems in the United States has significantly diminished—as Xavier de Souza Briggs argues (chapters 1 and 14, this volume), housing affordability is the most invisible social policy issue in America—placing greater dependence, but no pressure, on the private sector to address the challenge.

4. Responding to this need, sixteen of the twenty-four tools in the tool kit are focused on housing strategies and their catalyst role in equitable development.

Building a coherent housing strategy that responds to geographic concerns and promotes racial equity requires bundling a number of tactics, policies, and practices together. The tool kit identifies and explains some of these: expiring-use features of laws and regulations, just-cause evictions, code enforcement, infill incentives, developer exactions, rent controls, inclusionary zoning, limited equity housing co-ops, community land trusts, housing trusts funds, transit-oriented development, and real estate transfer taxes, to name a few.

Isolated from the local and regional development process and disconnected from a goal of racial equity, though, these strategies produce piecemeal results. But as part of a conscious equitable development agenda working in partnership with a multi-issue coalition and in concert with a broad spectrum of government agencies—housing, economic development, transportation, parks and recreation, zoning—these strategies begin to build a meaningful response to the years of uncontrolled, sprawling inequity. These substantive strategies get nowhere without political will and financial and other resource commitments.

In response to the toolkit and our work in equitable development, PolicyLink began to hear from advocates living and working in communities with weak markets who felt that the equitable development framing had application in their communities. Although gentrification was not a factor in their cities, these advocates were particularly attracted to principles that guide the development process in the areas of concentrated poverty where residents had little voice and little hope of seeing benefits from development beyond a space in public housing (which also seemed to be vanishing). These inquiries led us to scrutinize the tools to determine how they interact in these weak market environments. What we found, of course, is that different tools are appropriate at different times and that using some tools together can produce the best result. Most important, it is clear that if the development process is successful, sooner or later the issue of dislocation—whether full-blown gentrification or not—will surface. Setting up the development process with that reality in mind, taking advantage of land and property that may be quite affordable at the beginning of the process, and integrating benefits for existing residents will lead to equitable results.

The following sections focus on the possibilities for addressing affordable housing that are available to communities in different stages of development. The cities of Washington and Boston have attracted significant economic development and have experienced significant revitalization in many of their neighborhoods, yet there are steps that can be taken to ensure that low-income communities of color benefit from that development. Baltimore, by contrast, is a "weak market" city, still seeking revitalization, but it may well have greater opportunities to incorporate a range of affordable housing tools into its development plans. In California, a variety of organizations worked together to mount a multi-issue campaign to address infrastructure investment throughout the state. Affordable housing is the core issue in each of these places; an examination of efforts currently taking place in them demonstrate the possibilities of equitable development strategies.

Race, Space, and Equitable Development in Washington

In the past several years, Washington has experienced a dramatic economic turnaround, heating up a dampened housing market and igniting displacement in some newly desirable low-income neighborhoods. Further, the housing construction market has reignited. These changes have led organizers and advocates to look to inclusionary zoning as a strategy to address the city's critical affordable housing needs. In this city, embracing inclusionary zoning comes as a next step after the establishment of a housing trust fund.

A healthy regional economy and successful local policies, including strategic public investments, have transformed some Washington neighborhoods from economically depressed areas with concentrations of low- and moderate-income residents—many of whom are African American—to neighborhoods highly sought after by higher-income renters and buyers—many of whom are white. The resulting interplay of race and geography make Washington a laboratory for understanding how equitable development tools and strategies can lead to housing equity.

The neighborhoods in the District and their development course over the last decade mirror what has happened in many regions across the United States. Growth, prosperity, and opportunity are located on one side of the Anacostia River, while population loss, community distress, and poverty are concentrated on the other. The Anacostia River is both a geographical boundary and a metaphor for the great divide between the affluent and the economically depressed residents of Washington.

The new vitality in some low-income neighborhoods has sparked significant displacement dynamics, with low-income residents being pushed out by escalating rents and condominium conversions just as their neighborhoods have begun to have the very conveniences and amenities that they fought for. Much of this displacement occurs along racial lines, revealing inequity issues that can be effectively addressed by equitable development strategies. Indeed, the combination of housing that is affordable to a wide range of income categories as well as situated across the region in a manner that affords accessibility to jobs, schools, and shops is a critical measurement of equitable development.

The time is right for applying equitable development tools in Washington. The city is experiencing an unprecedented surge in private investment: its Office of Planning, which tracks major housing projects, estimates that since 2000 approximately 30,000 units have been planned or completed or are under construction. If all these units are finished, the potential impact of an inclusionary zoning policy is substantial. A mandatory strategy for affordable housing is in order. But developing an appropriate proposal and strategy for successful adoption—with agreed targets for the policy's impact—is challenging. Differing views on the political realities of the District and its elected officials shape how advocates define the parameters of a potential inclusionary zoning policy. Moreover, meeting the range of needs of low-income residents will take strong and innovative skills in organizing and maintaining coalitions as well as developing policy.

Typically, affordable housing construction occurs in neighborhoods that already have a high concentration of affordable units and does not facilitate a pathway to greater opportunity. Mandatory inclusionary zoning can provide a counterweight to this pattern by designating where affordable units must be located and who must benefit; organizers and advocates in Washington decided to focus on achieving such a policy. The campaign, however, is vulnerable to the pitfalls common to grassroots struggles that seek a broad coalition including low-income residents, organized labor, researchers, policy advocates, and business and civic leaders. Finding points of agreement among the differing perspectives of those involved in the development of campaign strategies is critical.

Organizing groups tend to represent low- and very low-income residents. Leaders of these groups have experienced similar campaigns and are wary of efforts that may dilute campaign goals. Housing policy groups lack a strong grassroots constituency, which is a challenge for national and regional organizations. Moreover, policy groups, while desiring meaningful change, frequently are concerned with broader constituencies (from the working poor to low- and very low-income renters) and multiple political and economic dynamics (for example, will this negatively impact developers' bottom line, thereby decreasing political viability?). Politically savvy leaders of these groups may deem it best to focus on bigger picture issues, seemingly at the expense of the needs of individuals represented by the organizers.

As the Washington campaign for inclusionary zoning got under way, the challenge was to reconcile these points of view, to develop a consistent strategy, and to seek agreement on targets and tactics for reaching campaign goals. One "hot spot" for these differing perspectives involves targets for affordable units mandated by the proposed inclusionary zoning policy. To meet the needs of organizers' primarily low-income African American constituencies, the target needed to be as low as possible. The Washington area's median income is $82,800. Targeting 80 percent of area median income—or $66,000—for inclusionary units would not have ensured that low-income residents were guaranteed benefits. But as Karen Brown shows in her study of the thirty-year experience with inclusionary zoning in the District's growing suburban communities, inclusionary public policy is largely a market strategy.[5] How much added flexibility an inclusionary zoning policy can actually grant a private developer while

5. Brown (2001).

still allowing him to view development as attractive (profitable) is an important question. Reducing the area medium-income percentage to make units more available to residents with lower incomes might drive away developers who fear that lower prices would cut too deep into their profits.

Organizers and their constituents in communities of color shared a lack of faith in whether implementation of the plan would ensure actual, tangible benefits: Would they actually end up renting or owning one of the newly built, affordable units? The success of inclusionary zoning policies and communities' enthusiasm about implementation seem tied both to the provisions of the ordinance and to the designated management of the units and use of the revenues created by the policy. Some jurisdictions with a strong, well-respected, well-connected (to communities of color and policymakers) nonprofit housing sector have given these organizations ongoing responsibility for the management of new affordable units, thus helping to ensure that implementation of inclusionary zoning helps to advance racial justice goals. In other jurisdictions, public agencies help ensure that low-income communities of color benefit by virtue of their connection to—and relative trust by—residents. In the District, where the housing authority has lacked a positive public will, the key was the engagement of the nonprofit sector, its connection and credibility with communities of color, and its capacity to ensure successful implementation.

While a long-standing distrust between organizing and policy advocacy groups could have made the discussions and strategic decisionmaking more difficult, the strong commitment of both groups to addressing housing needs has brought all voices to the table. The continued dynamic of the alliance among the organizations plays out against a backdrop of the need for housing and the determination to create it. Advocates recognize the possibilities that an inclusionary zoning policy can offer to a community desperately in need of the benefits that accompany affordable housing. In Boston, such a tool has been in place for over thirty years, but current political realities make it necessary to vigilantly struggle to maintain and strengthen it.

Boston: Safeguarding Tools for Housing Equity

Advocates from the greater Boston area came together in November 2002 to explore regional challenges and the possibilities of working together on the intersection of housing, transportation, and equitable development. This initial convening was far more representative of the city of Boston than of the overall region. In fact, many of the participants in the first convening were skeptical of the notion of engaging in a regional effort. These were seasoned organizations and leaders, and they were not sure that they were ready to embrace the whole region as the focus for any of their efforts.

Communities in the Boston region are highly segregated by race and income; the increasingly multicultural and multiracial nature of the region has not translated into integrated neighborhoods. The 2000 census shows that one-fifth of the census tracts in the region have at least 15 percent of their population living in poverty, and almost one-third of these tracts have a poverty rate of 30 percent or more. These high-poverty neighborhoods are concentrated in Boston, though aging suburbs also contain large pockets of vulnerable families, including newer immigrant groups. The concentration of low-income populations reflects significant racial disparities. The population in the tracts with more than 30 percent poverty was 52 percent people of color, including 17 percent black, 27 percent Hispanic, and 9 percent Asian.

The discussions of the challenges in affordable housing, transportation, environmental justice, and workforce development crystallized the regional realities for the Boston leaders. Community organizations tend to focus their work on achieving equity in specific areas, such as housing, transportation, land use, and economic development. But recognizing that the achievement of regional equity will require focusing on the intersection of many issues and developing an integrated strategy for addressing them, by April 2003 a core group of committed regional players had emerged, calling itself Action for Regional Equity (Action!). The group represents seventeen organizations with strong advocacy bases in the ethnic, social equity, and community development fields. These include organizations focused on organizing, policy analysis and advocacy, affordable housing, and economic development. Outreach efforts netted strong organizations representing suburban communities as partners with the Boston-based groups. A menu of policy opportunities emerged for Action! to consider. One of those policies—Chapter 40B—represents many of the promises and challenges to achieving regional equity and was the catalyst for determining future action.

As Spencer Cowan finds in a study of antisnob zoning in several states, Massachusetts' Chapter 40B was an early attempt to undermine exclusionary housing practices and is potentially one of the state's most effective policy tools for ensuring that affordable housing is spread fairly across all communities.[6] Enacted in 1969, 40B is meant to encourage the production of affordable housing in all communities throughout the commonwealth. The law addresses the shortage of affordable housing statewide by reducing unnecessary barriers created by local approval processes, local zoning, and other restrictions. Towns in Massachusetts have considerable freedom to make siting and other decisions, which mitigates against reversing intense segregation through regional action. The program is controversial, like antisnob zoning in other states, because it gives developers the right to override local zoning laws through a state appeals

6. Cowan (2001).

process if the jurisdiction does not provide 10 percent of its housing stock as affordable. A developer could go to the state, for example, and be approved to build a hundred-unit apartment complex if 20 percent of the proposed units were affordable to low-income residents. Controversy aside, 40B has a positive intended effect, expanding the geography of affordable housing.

Action! endorses a community-based policy agenda for achieving equitable development goals across the region. It embraces the need for comprehensive action, including environmental justice and social equity concerns, and recognizes the connections among public transit, affordable housing, workforce development, and open-space issues, seeing these aspects as closely linked and requiring integrated regional change. Finally, the group wants to ensure that the needs of low-income residents are addressed and that equitable development objectives are met through balanced land use decisions across jurisdictions. While research shows that the best outcomes for low-income families are realized in mixed-income communities, the region's development trends continue to concentrate poverty and racially segregate communities. Low-income people of color who are concentrated in high-poverty neighborhoods are prey to economic disinvestment and political neglect, exposed to crime, and isolated from good jobs, quality education, health services, and even essential amenities such as supermarkets. Strengthening 40B could lead to the creation of mixed-income communities that could help alleviate these problems.

At the same time, the political landscape shifted. A new Republican governor was elected in Massachusetts and took office in January 2003. He established a state Office of Commonwealth Development and appointed a longtime smart growth advocate from the New England region as chief of the new office. The state cabinet-level position was charged with coordinating the fragmented policies and programs of multiple agencies, including Environmental Affairs, Transportation, and the Department of Housing and Community Development, and the state's fiercely independent cities and towns. This new smart growth "czar" was potentially leading a dramatic shift in government receptivity to cross-issue and cross-jurisdictional action.

Meanwhile, opposition to 40B resulted in multiple attempts to weaken the legislation. In 2002 the legislature passed a compromise measure; it was supported by affordable housing advocates but was ultimately vetoed by the governor. In 2003 more than seventy bills were introduced to amend 40B, causing the governor to form a diverse task force, including some members of Action!, to develop a legislative compromise. Public discussion of 40B gave Action! a tangible organizing focus with the potential for real policy impact. As originally drafted, Chapter 40B contained no language specific to race, though in its thirty-four-year history, as Cowan shows, 40B has proven to be a vital tool for racial inclusion by creating a more varied and affordable mix of housing types—entry points for diverse families—in local communities. Like the not-in-my-backyard furor elsewhere in America, current debates about 40B are studded with codes for racial exclusion, such as "community character" and "declining [school] test scores," making clear that some opponents intend to dismantle or weaken the legislation.

Action! targeted hearings on 40B for some of their efforts. Leaders came to testify and brought their members to fill hearing rooms. Equity voices were heavily represented, framing the issues and setting the stage for the challenges that any effective measure ought to address. As part of these efforts, groups sought to raise the specter of racial exclusion, always present but seldom acknowledged in the Boston region and many other parts of our nation. These advocates want the issues examined through a racial lens, among others, to highlight the segregated and racially polarized nature of the region and to broaden support for their efforts among advocates of racial equity. This includes developing a media strategy that targets ethnic and mainstream media as part of the comprehensive agenda to build support for maintaining and strengthening 40B.

These efforts are ongoing and are indicative of the multifaceted approach and time commitment required to add or strengthen equity objectives in major housing and land use policies and practices that have developed over time. Action! exemplifies the challenges of coalition building and the opportunities inherent in framing issues with equitable development in mind to ensure that race is not left out of the equation. The new regional effort represents a stretch for most of the involved leaders and organizations. The groups that make up the coalition are very sophisticated and known for taking strong positions. The fifteen-month process to hammer out a regional strategy and to convince their constituents of its efficacy should not be overlooked. As Peter Dreier reminds us in a paper on successful housing advocacy in Los Angeles, communities that take on affordable housing campaigns should be prepared for the strenuous efforts that may be needed to successfully incorporate the points of view of all groups necessary to achieve campaign goals.[7] This means acknowledging the need for organizations to maintain commitments to their missions, which are typically focused at the neighborhood and city level, while pursuing a regional agenda for affordable housing. In most instances, such organizations will have a local and single-issue focus; working at the regional level often means entering brand new territory.

Working through the issues and conflicts that coalition building requires can develop the capacity of the coalition and its leaders, thus enabling them to successfully advance equitable development throughout the region. The seeds are there for Action! to develop into a deep and cohesive coalition. Moreover, the multi-issue nature of Action! suggests new opportunities, as well as different challenges, to develop more cross-issue coalitions with the strength, flexibility,

7. Dreier (2001).

and trust to carry out multiple campaigns. In Boston, the Barr Foundation has brought new resources to Action! and its members, providing hope that the group will be able to embrace its new equitable development approach with support for enhanced organizational efforts.

Equitable Development in Weak Market Cities

The discussions about Washington and Boston reveal how useful a framework equitable development is in forming housing strategies that stabilize and secure low-income and working families in communities seeing an influx of new investment. According to the 2000 census, approximately one-quarter of all large cities (those with populations of more than 100,000) continue to face significant population decline and the attendant disinvestment that follows.[8] These Rust Belt cities are primarily located in the Northeast and Midwest and just a few decades ago were thriving industrial and manufacturing centers that drove economic growth in their regions as well as the national economy. In recent years organizations such as the Community Development Partnership Network have worked to bring greater national attention to the challenges that these "weak market" cities face, such as declining home values and equity, diminishing tax bases that lead to fewer public amenities, large-scale vacant and abandoned property, brownfields, racial concentration of poverty, loss of social networks, and lower median incomes.[9]

Rebuilding neighborhoods in weak market cities so that they become or remain vibrant communities is a fundamental equitable development challenge.[10] All communities in a region should be "places of choice," with the services and supports that individuals and families need to be economically and socially stable. Many weak market cities lack the most basic amenities (for example, banks, grocery stores, neighborhood parks, cultural centers) that families need to lead healthy, productive lives. Transforming distressed communities requires understanding the competitive advantage of these places relative to the region, then tailoring strategies to attract reinvestment, while connecting existing low-income residents to the benefits of future revitalization.

Housing investments can be a key vehicle for promoting equitable development in weak market cities. However, the tools and strategies employed may be quite different than in their "hotter market" counterparts. An exploration of Baltimore, Maryland, reveals the differences. Baltimore is a weak market city in a region that is doing well. As of the 2000 census the median household income

8. Glaeser and Shapiro (2001).

9. Brophy and Burnett (2003).

10. PolicyLink and the Community Development Partnership Network are collaborating on a research report (to be released in mid 2005) that will articulate the policy and action agenda for promoting regional equity in weak market cities.

in the city of Baltimore is 60 percent of the region ($30,078 versus $49,938) and has declined approximately 9 percent since 1990. In 2000 the average home price in Baltimore was 53 percent of the regional average ($69,900 versus $132,400) and declined by 5 percent from 1990. The disparity across the region is quite great, with suburban communities such as Anne Arundel County ($156,500) and Howard County ($198,600) having median housing values well above the regional average.[11] The region is characterized by high levels of racial segregation and concentrated poverty, with low-income people and communities of color disproportionately living in the central city.

A key equitable development goal for Baltimore is to stimulate the real estate market in the central city in a manner that brings new investment but that also secures and stabilizes existing residents so they enjoy the benefits of revitalization, such as appreciating home values and improved neighborhood services. One important housing strategy that tries to strike this balance is the Healthy Neighborhoods Initiative in Baltimore, which recognizes the critical role that healthy, attractive neighborhoods play in making the city and region thrive. The initiative focuses on "in the middle" neighborhoods, which usually do not have compelling enough problems to attract headlines yet also fail to attract investment dollars because of troubled properties. The Healthy Neighborhoods Initiative draws on neighborhood strength, harnessing assets and utilizing market forces to reinvigorate neighborhoods in the middle. Housing investments that build home equity and appreciation are coupled with civic engagement activities that strengthen the social fabric of the neighborhood. In the Belair-Edison neighborhood, for instance, median sales prices for homes on target blocks increased over 9 percent from 2002 to 2003; it is long-term, existing residents who are benefiting from this revitalization. Foundations such as the Goldseker Foundation and the Baltimore Community Foundation have made strategic investments in the Healthy Neighborhoods Initiative, recognizing the importance of this approach to building thriving neighborhoods that are connected to the broader region.

At the same time, Baltimore needs housing strategies that will create more affordable housing options in more advantageous communities in the region so that lower-income residents are better connected to a web of vital services and supports. One promising effort that is under way is being led by the Citizens Planning and Housing Association and the Baltimore Regional Initiative Developing Genuine Equality, which are partnering on an inclusionary zoning campaign for the Baltimore region. In the near term they are focusing on getting mandatory inclusionary zoning in Anne Arundel and Howard Counties—and then trying for adoption of a statewide ordinance.

11. For the regional numbers we use statistics for the Baltimore primary metropolitan statistical area.

As the Baltimore experience shows, weak market cities must reinvigorate the real estate market in the central city, while promoting affordable housing opportunities across the region. It is, indeed, a hard balance to strike. Promoting affordable housing in suburban communities will require reforming exclusionary land use practices that preclude the development of more affordable housing types. And producing affordable housing in the central city needs to be done in a manner that does not further concentrate poverty in these communities. When affordable housing is constructed in the central city, it must be connected to broader efforts aimed at neighborhood revitalization.

Using Multi-Issue Coalitions to Expand Affordable Housing Resources

In California, support for a new multi-issue, equity-focused coalition sparked efforts at the state level to develop strategies and resources to engage an array of organizations and constituencies. The James Irvine Foundation provided multi-year support for the Sustainable Communities Working Group. This group included organizations that had never worked together and some that had only recently come to the issues of land use and equity. The working group included American Farmland Trust, Mexican American Legal Defense and Educational Fund, Surface Transportation Policy Project, California Works Foundation (a labor-based research organization), and more recently PolicyLink. Together, these organizations focused on developing an agenda to link the interests of environmental, housing, civil rights, and transportation advocates.

In 2003 the working group supported new incentives for multisector development. Typically, localities fund and support development for specific infrastructure investments, such as a new freeway or expanded sewer lines. While a multisector approach to such development seems prudent, the reality is that funding comes either in project- or sector-specific amounts. This approach has presented particular challenges in California, where the state's constitution requires a two-thirds supermajority for passage of bonds and local special taxes.

California's exponential growth, coupled with inefficient land use patterns, poses critical challenges to the state's quality of life. Its population has grown 200 percent over the past fifty years, totaling nearly 34 million residents, and is expected to grow by another 12 million by 2020. Housing prices and rents in many regions are exorbitantly high because of inadequate affordable housing production. Poorly planned residential and commercial developments have resulted in increased traffic, exposing 80 percent of the population to unhealthy levels of air pollution. The state suffers from a severe lack of infrastructure improvements due to the lack of much-needed public investments. Areas that have sought to raise revenues to make needed improvements have met with very mixed success. Between 1986 and 2002, 1,438 tax measures that would fund a broad range of community needs were proposed; of these, slightly less than half (46 percent) passed. Analysts note that if the voter approval threshold had been 55 percent—still a healthy majority—rather than two-thirds, the passage rate would have been 57 percent, with over 25 percent more measures approved and billions of additional dollars available for vital local community investments.

The working group sought a constitutional amendment to reduce the voter threshold—from two-thirds to 55 percent—for localities seeking bonds and special taxes linking affordable housing, transportation, parks and open space, and general infrastructure investments. The campaign allowed the group to make the linkage between the issues and local, regional, and statewide needs. It also allowed them to point to the need for multiple strategies and to argue that the proposed measure would push localities to take a more integrated, and effective, approach to infrastructure investment. The campaign also laid the foundation for arguing that isolated transportation investments would not solve regional congestion challenges, that solutions require multisector strategies.

Lowering the threshold holds the promise for greater success. In 2000 voters approved Proposition 39, a ballot initiative that decreased the threshold for education bonds, and the passage rate for proposed measures dramatically improved. Proposition 39 lowered the voter approval threshold from two-thirds to 55 percent for local school bonds for repair, construction, or replacement of aging and overcrowded school facilities. Communities that had been previously unable to pass bonds were able to do so because of Proposition 39. Since its passage, 147 school districts have successfully passed bond measures. Of these, 82—or over half—had never passed any school bond measure. The successful use of Proposition 39 offers strong evidence that a majority of California residents are frequently willing to support public investments when they have the power to do so.

While both houses of the California legislature are primarily Democratic, they do not have two-thirds majorities in either house. An impressive coalition emerged to support the proposed measures. The initial coalition of transportation, housing, environmental, and civil rights organizations expanded to include strong voices from the business community. Unfortunately, despite strong and increasing support across issues, geography, and constituency, Republican legislators threatened to run primary challengers against any member who showed support for measures connected to tax increases, even for measures such as these, which would place the ultimate decision with voters.

Republicans clamped down because they did not want to facilitate any measures that could be tied to increased state revenues, and they demanded unity behind their strategy. No cracks appeared in the Republican's strategy. Because this is California, one group seriously considered moving the measures in some form on to the ballot through a signature-gathering process. (There are multiple ways to qualify an initiative for the ballot—through the legislature or with a large number of voters' signatures to a petition.) But with the legislative and political stalemate, the effort stalled. Groups are reviewing their options and planning for the continuation of this multisector approach to regional issues.

Lessons from the Field

The Washington, Boston, and California coalitions described above include strong representation from affordable housing advocates and rely on them for their technical knowledge and political and legislative lobbying skills. The California coalition also includes groups with strong litigation skills, a strength typical of fair housing advocates. However, none of these coalitions has made reaching out to fair housing advocates a major objective. This is because fair housing and affordable housing suffer a common limitation: a lack of strong, organized constituencies. In the cities cited above, and in others where PolicyLink has worked, the challenge has been balancing the needs of constituency-based groups with those that have a policy or industry focus. The comprehensive nature of equitable development speaks to the need for diversity of constituency, skill, and race, but the ability to mobilize expanded efforts is most hampered by capacity issues at the organization, coalition, and leadership levels.

Beyond the coalition issues lie questions about racism and racial preferences, as discussed in the study by Camille Charles (chapter 3, this volume). Will efforts like those in Boston, for example, help to change how people think about race and neighborhoods? To the extent that these efforts spur new relationships, the data suggest that they should. And to the extent that these efforts visibly take on polarized views and political dynamics, they should help to spark important public debates. But as Charles herself notes in an overview of long-run trends in racial attitudes, whether indicators of racism decrease or simply shift is a question that can only be answered over time. None of the efforts described in this chapter, or anywhere else in this book, suggests that the rate of change can be dramatically accelerated.

Instead, this and other chapters offer new road maps—and key caveats on older ones—for reaching the goals of greater equity and full inclusion and participation in our society. Though the processes of coalition building and advocacy may be occasionally fraught with tension and discord, seeing them through to resolution is critical to change. Success requires that the voices of leaders of color, and neighbors of all colors, are heard and that they have the resources to be meaningful and regular participants in policy campaigns and debates. We turn our attention last to the leadership question.

Leadership for Policy Change

Successful campaigns that benefit low-income communities and people of color need organized constituencies, coalitions, and alliances to carry them out.

Organizing requires leadership to gather forces, facilitate discussion, guide strategy development, and be an active presence in policy formation. Before efforts like those described above in San Diego, Washington, and Boston took off, leaders saw the need and took steps to address it.

In campaigns across the country, leaders of color are making a critical difference in the evolution of policy development and implementation by forming alliances and bridging divides that often exist between organizing groups and policy organizations. Even with the backing of strong organizations and engaged constituencies, many, however, continue to find it difficult to access policy venues, those critical places where decisions are made that have direct impact on the daily lives of people of color in low-income communities. These barriers led PolicyLink to interview over a hundred leaders and to survey the literature on leadership and leadership development.[12] The study reveals a great deal about the special roles that leaders of color can and must play and about the best available options for overcoming the barriers they face.

Leaders of color can make the decisive difference in ensuring that affordable housing initiatives are built on principles of equitable development. More often than not, these are leaders who possess the following: a set of values focused on justice, equity, and inclusion; a passionate commitment to improving the quality of life of everyone in the community; a willingness to bridge boundaries of race, ethnicity, class, and gender; and a deep understanding of the importance of an organized constituency and how to build it. Leaders who come from and are rooted in communities of color understand the issues confronting their communities and can bring a new perspective to discussions about housing, health, employment, education, and the environment. The policies that result from such inclusion are likely to be beneficial to the communities they are designed to serve.

Yet there are only a few people of color in public, private, or nonprofit sector positions where policy is made or influenced. More than 80 percent of congressional leaders, 94 percent of state governors, and 96 percent of university presidents in the United States are white men. In the entire history of the United States Congress, there have been only eighteen senators of color—and only three African American senators since Reconstruction.[13] Only one African American and one Asian American—L. Douglas Wilder of Virginia and Gary Locke of Washington, respectively—have been elected to gubernatorial positions (although several African Americans have run unsuccessfully for governor in recent years, and Indian American Bobby Jindal narrowly lost the 2003 race for Louisiana governor before his landslide election to the U.S. House of Representatives in 2004). Throughout the 1990s, white men constituted 97 percent

12. McCulloch and Robinson (2003).

13. Numbers are from U.S. Senate web page "Minorities in the Senate" (www.senate.gov/artandhistory/history/common/briefing/minority_senators.htm).

of Fortune 500 chief executive officers (CEOs).[14] In philanthropy, 94 percent of all CEOs and 90 percent of all chief financial officers (CFOs) are white.[15] And while media play a critical role in influencing policy, newspaper newsrooms are 88 percent white.[16]

The exclusion of people of color from policy discussions and decisions has repercussions beyond communities of color. It deprives the nation of the wisdom and experience these communities could bring to bear in solving some of the country's most seemingly intractable problems.

Leadership development programs can be an effective way to ameliorate this situation. However, to be successful, such programs must go beyond training to provide access to policy arenas as well as to support networks that help remove the isolation faced by many leaders of color. The PolicyLink study finds that the best leadership programs include mentors for program participants and focus not only on the leader but also on building the capacity of the leader's organization and constituency, which are necessary to successfully engage policymaking. This triple focus—on leader, organization, and constituency—offers the best means of supporting the policymaking involvement of communities of color.

The inequities so apparent today have been long in the making and will not be quickly made right. Still, strategies for addressing those inequities are available and can speed the day when regions truly are the economically viable, livable communities they should be, providing the basics for quality of life: a place to live, a place to learn, and a place to earn. By addressing the need for and location of affordable housing, equitable development strategies provide the foundation for education and jobs. The more intentional organizers and advocates are in applying equitable development principles and in building the public will required to spread those principles from regions to the states and the nation, the more likely it is that policies on fair and affordable housing—as well as health, education, transportation, and other issues—will be inclusive of the racial and ethnic diversity that increasingly defines our nation and puts its ideals to the test.

References

Bipartisan Millennial Housing Commission Appointed by the Congress of the United States. 2002. *Meeting Our Nation's Housing Challenges.* U.S. Government Printing Office.

Brophy, Paul, and Kim Burnett. 2003. *Building a New Framework for Community Development for Weak Market Cities.* Denver: Community Development Partnership Network.

Brown, Karen D. 2001. "Expanding Affordable Housing through Inclusionary Zoning: Lessons from the Washington Metropolitan Area." Metropolitan Policy Program, Brookings.

14. CEO data from Fortune 500.

15. Burbridge and others (2002).

16. American Society of Newspaper Editors, 2003 Newsroom Employment Census (www.asne.org/index.cfm?id4446 [2003]).

Burbridge, L., and others. 2002. *The Meaning and Impact of Board and Staff Diversity in the Philanthropic Field.* Washington: Joint Affinity Groups.

Cowan, Spencer. 2001. "Anti-Snob Land Use Laws and Suburban Exclusion." Paper prepared for Conference on Housing Opportunity, Civil Rights, and the Regional Agenda. Urban Institute, November 16.

Dreier, Peter. 2001. "Expanding the Political Constituency for Affordable Housing: Tentative Lessons from Los Angeles." Paper prepared for Conference on Housing Opportunity, Civil Rights, and the Regional Agenda. Urban Institute, November 16.

Glaeser, Edward, and Jesse Shapiro. 2001. *City Growth and the 2000 Census: Which Places Grew, and Why.* Metropolitan Policy Program, Brookings.

Jacobs Center for Neighborhood Innovation. Undated. "Profile of the Diamond Neighborhoods." Fact sheet. San Diego.

McCulloch, Heather, and Lisa Robinson. 2002. "Market Creek Plaza Case Study." Paper prepared for National Community Economic Development Symposium. Southern New Hampshire University.

———. 2003. *Leadership for Policy Change: Strengthening Communities of Color through Leadership Development.* Oakland, Calif.: PolicyLink.

———. 2005. *Market Creek Plaza: Toward Resident Ownership of Neighborhood Change.* Oakland, Calif.: PolicyLink.

14

Politics and Policy: Changing the Geography of Opportunity

XAVIER DE SOUZA BRIGGS

Whatever the prevailing mood has been at the national level, America's local communities have a long history of ambivalence toward new arrivals and minority groups, whether immigrant or native born. As early as 1750, for example, Benjamin Franklin suggested that German immigrants arriving in numbers in Philadelphia "will never adopt our language or customs," and, perhaps surprisingly from our current vantage point, he added, "any more than they can acquire our complexion."

Much of this ambivalence has been expressed through housing exclusion, from government-sanctioned segregation in the era of Jim Crow and ongoing discrimination by realtors, banks, and other private parties to the everyday acts of racial avoidance—perfectly legal, but costly—that thwart the creation of a more integrated society. In this book, we outline why unequal housing choices and the uneven metropolitan development patterns associated with segregated growth continue—and also what those patterns imply as economic inequality persists and America rapidly becomes more racially and ethnically diverse than ever before. Rapid immigration makes some segregation by race or ethnic group inevitable in the years to come, because newcomers tend to arrive in particular places faster than they can diffuse through the housing market. But more worrisome is the growth of class segregation within racial groups over the past generation, as well as the fact that many immigrants and native-born minorities are "making it" to suburbs that no longer offer secure ladders to education or job opportunity.

The prospect of a dual society, officially welcoming but socially gated, looms. More than any other factor, high levels of segregation by race and class, by neighborhood and municipality, determine the quality of schools and other public services, rates of street crime and associated levels of fear and insecurity, geographic access to jobs, exposure to environmental hazards, and prospects for building assets through property investment. We are well beyond the folk wisdom about "bad neighborhoods" or the stereotypes about people who live in them. Beyond the carefully researched consequences for education and economic opportunity on which I focus in chapter 2, compelling new evidence from criminology and public health indicates specific ways that segregation by race and income contributes to many of the nation's most persistent health disparities and the propensity—of young males, in particular—to perpetrate violence.[1] These links between place and well-being are deeply disturbing in a society that declares equality of opportunity a core value, and so are the broad trends: In at least some of these dimensions, such as educational opportunity and geographic access to jobs, the social costs of segregation appear to have increased sharply since 1970. Low- and moderate-income families, particularly if they are racial minorities, are not only more likely to live in high-risk, low-resource places but also are more likely to bounce among such neighborhoods, moving frequently due to rent increases, divorce, the death of a wage earner, or other life shocks. Long-run exposure to poor neighborhoods is especially high for African Americans, and race is a much stronger predictor of this pattern than income, household type, or other factors.

Tied to the forces that produce and reproduce this segregation, the extent of sprawl—relatively low-density, car-reliant, unplanned growth on the undeveloped fringe of metropolitan areas—has begun to frustrate even middle- and upper-income families, who can afford to live at a safe distance from many of the problems of cities and older, at-risk suburbs. The nation's current strategy for handling race and class differences at the local level is, paradoxically, what we might call containment-plus-sprawl. It is a strategy that disperses and subsidizes new development while concentrating social and economic advantage. This system permits, and in fiscal and other terms actually encourages, some communities to function as exclusive and exclusionary clubs. Consistent with these patterns, white Americans, who have the widest housing choices, report increasing tolerance of racial and ethnic diversity in principle but little enthusiasm for policies aimed at reducing racial inequality.[2] Meanwhile, segregated jurisdictions obscure the possibilities of forging a common-interest politics, without which basic reforms to the dominant investment and development model are all but impossible.

1. Sampson, Morenoff, and Raudenbush (2005).
2. Bobo (2001).

What are the prospects for changing these patterns, given such lukewarm support for efforts to attack inequality, and what kinds of change should we emphasize? In this final chapter, I analyze the politics, principles, and policy choices needed to create a more equitable geography of opportunity in America, beginning with a look at the central dilemmas that change will confront.

Core Dilemmas

We should think about prospects for change in the context of four dilemmas. First, traditional civil rights strategies, including strategies for enforcing antidiscrimination "fair housing" laws, are necessary but woefully insufficient to expand housing choice. Civil rights strategies must evolve significantly to address that fact. Second is the thorny dilemma of competing public objectives, which are common in race-conscious policy debates and rarely resolvable by invoking rights alone. Third, our public life should anticipate the important—but often unspoken and uncomfortable—tension between the integrationist agenda and what we might call the agenda for group empowerment. Put differently, this is the tension between integrating all groups and empowering particular groups, often defined by race and by historical disadvantage. Group empowerment often hinges on hopes that concentration has powerful advantages, that "separate"—if it leads to better targeting—can lead to "equal." Fourth is the dilemma of local, exclusionary politics and the need to build broader-based support for inclusionary policy: The central political challenge is to create coalitions and other mechanisms of change powerful enough to overcome exclusion by local communities.

The Power and Limits of Civil Rights

Traditional civil rights strategies for protecting housing choice, while important, offer surprisingly little leverage on the problem of changing the geography of opportunity. Why? For one thing, the forces that produce class segregation in our communities are, for the most part, perfectly legal, since they encourage discrimination by income (ability to pay), which is what competitive markets do by design. As many urban observers emphasize, any meaningful solutions to class segregation must address where people can afford to live, a matter shaped in important ways by government policy, not just by compliance with antidiscrimination protections that regulate transactions in the private market. Where the racial dimension of segregation is concerned, even if most acts of racial discrimination in housing markets—the acts that *are* illegal—were detected, and even if the violators were effectively prosecuted, fair housing enforcement alone would have a limited impact on the racial makeup of America's communities, for reasons I detail below. Vigorously enforced fair housing laws are important in a society that declares a commitment to equal opportunity regardless of one's background *but not because those laws contribute significantly to desegregating the society.*

This fact reflects a wider challenge associated with how we act on complex social problems. All too often, we rely on policy fixes that seem to connect to the problems we care about or that some trusted advocate has earlier endorsed. But smart, legitimate strategies should come before the policies they help to justify. Good strategies embody particular ideas about cause and effect—what business strategists and designers of social programs call "logic models," which explain why the state of the world will change in a particular direction if some action is taken. Specific sets of causes and effects, outlined in sequences or chains of necessary conditions, expose assumptions and contingencies that decisionmakers, interest groups, and implementers alike should understand. These strategies help us avoid costly, unintended consequences as well as policies that come to be more symbolic than effective for meeting a specific aim.

Consider again the example of enforcing laws against housing discrimination. Here is a logic model (a chain of conditions) outlining what an impact on levels of segregation would in fact require:

—Condition 1. *A wide range of potential victims (housing consumers) are aware of their rights under law.* Survey data indicate that most Americans know that housing discrimination is illegal, and also think it is wrong, but feel that it is not much of a problem any more.[3] The threshold condition—knowing that we all have the right to receive equal treatment in the marketplace—clearly depends on ongoing public education, because foreign-born immigrants and low-income people are generally less familiar with civil rights protections and also because violators of housing rights rely on this ignorance.

—Condition 2. *In a given act violating fair housing laws, the victims are aware that they have been victimized (for example, by real estate professionals, financial institutions, others).* Using federal testing and enforcement data, George Galster estimates that only about 1 percent of the two million acts of housing discrimination each year even generated complaints during the 1980s, and the evidence is that housing discrimination has become more subtle since then.[4] For example, realtors commonly "editorialize" about neighborhoods to provide more information to white homebuyers and to encourage them to choose areas with fewer poor or nonwhite households. What is more, the language realtors use with testing agents suggests that they know that this form of steering is illegal but do not fear being caught.[5]

—Condition 3. *The victims are willing and able to report their perceived victimization to public authorities.* In fact, the data above indicate that many perceived acts go unreported—and for a wide array of reasons that are challenging

3. Abravanel and Cunningham (2002).
4. Galster (1990); see also Turner and Ross, chapter 4, this volume.
5. Galster and Godfrey (2003).

to address. Other obligations seem more pressing, one fears retribution, or one doubts that anything good will come from filing a complaint.

—Condition 4. *Adequate resources are in place for processing, investigating, and adjudicating legitimate claims (the operational element of enforcement).* Yet these resources have been inadequate from the start, that is, since 1968, when federal fair housing protections were hastily enacted after the assassination of Martin Luther King Jr.[6] All the key functions are chronically understaffed: sorting claims effectively, investigating appropriate claims vigorously, and then acting on the evidence.

—Condition 5. *For those claims that produce a finding of guilt, penalties are adequate to deter or limit future violations of the law.* We have no direct evidence on these effects in the fair housing arena, but evidence on regulatory effects in other fields suggest little reason for optimism that current enforcement efforts have a significant effect on the incidence of housing discrimination.[7] Two factors drive the effectiveness of any enforcement effort: success at *detecting* and reliably prosecuting bad behavior; and penalties sufficient to *change* the bad behavior. Fair housing enforcement scores low on both, and in general, equal opportunity enforcement—in labor and other domains, on race, disability, and other bases for discrimination—struggles with both.

—Condition 6. *Reductions of discriminatory behavior will have a significant effect on housing choices, thus enabling more inclusive and integrated communities to emerge.* Yet acts of discrimination in the marketplace, especially since they often go undetected, have a limited effect on the kinds of neighborhoods that people of various backgrounds prefer. Simply put, reducing bad behavior in the market will not clearly change what people desire, only their ability to realize those desires.

Conditions 1 through 3 show why fair access to housing will always be a difficult civil right to enforce, and conditions 4 and 5 indicate that the prospects for significantly limiting future bad behavior (reducing the target) are likely very modest, at least through law enforcement. Broader changes in societal attitudes and practices could certainly help there. But the final condition is the clincher: Segregated communities result not just from frustrated attempts by minority homeseekers to find more integrated settings but also from preferences of whites and minorities alike that undermine a more residentially integrated society. Even small differences in these preferences (by race of homeseeker) can lead to very segregated outcomes in a marketplace offering a limited supply of available housing units and given the preexisting condition of segregation.[8] What this means is that segregation stems not only from illegal acts of discrimination but also from perfectly legal, if segregative, choices—"self-steering" by whites and

6. Cashin (2004).
7. Cooter and Ulen (2004).
8. Ellen (2000); Schelling (1971).

minorities—as well as a limited, geographically concentrated supply of affordable housing choices.

This is not a blame-the-victim argument about fault, and the preferences of people of color that Camille Charles examines in detail (chapter 3, in this volume)—looking for a racial comfort zone, wariness about being the pioneer in possibly unwelcoming territory—appear to capture the legacy of past injustice, of social exclusion, and even of the physical risk faced by early pioneers of color in formerly all-white communities. Moreover, people of all backgrounds seem to value the benefits of living among a critical mass of "people like me"—however that may be defined. Wanting that is not illegal, nor is avoiding particular neighborhoods because of that desire. But as a practical matter, we should disabuse ourselves of the notion that mere enforcement of antidiscrimination law is a powerful tool for reducing segregation by race and class in America.

As Margery Austin Turner and Stephen Ross explain in chapter 4, fighting contemporary patterns of housing discrimination is nevertheless key to ensuring that people can make full and informed housing choices, and the fight will need to adapt to changing patterns of behavior—over-the-phone discrimination in which landlords and rental agents respond to accents and ethnically identifiable names, more education of immigrants about their housing rights, and education and testing to combat unequal assistance by realtors with mortgage finance. Regulation strategy expert Malcolm Sparrow offers a compelling argument for picking important problems on such a list and problem solving creatively around them, rather than continuing a broad and diffuse, procedure-focused compliance effort that seems destined to continue failing.[9] Finally, beyond the specific domain of consumer rights in the housing market, other rights-based strategies—addressing transportation equity and a host of issues relevant to metropolitan development patterns—may turn out to be significant in the years ahead.

Competing Objectives

Some barriers to opportunity in America—discrimination in the housing market on the basis of race, for example—are simply wrong. The law says so. We should ensure that rights are well understood and improve the mechanisms for detecting violations, and violators should be held accountable. But many of the choices that confront America's communities, including those that tap into sharply conflicting interests related to real estate or turf, are far more discretionary and distributional in character. These choices do not juxtapose minority and majority rights in a straightforward standoff. Rather, the most important choices that will define the future of our communities involve difficult trade-offs among a host of competing public objectives: for example, making housing

9. Sparrow (2000).

more affordable for a wide variety of households, especially for working families, while specifically promoting equitable access regardless of race (since neither objective ensures the other); preserving the quality of life of built-up communities while accommodating new population growth across a range of incomes (perhaps through smarter growth); and ensuring an appropriate degree of local decisionmaking—in a country that cherishes localism—while addressing urgent, higher-level goals that will shape the fortunes of entire metropolitan regions, states, and the nation (achieving what we might term home-rule-plus). These housing-related dilemmas, and the imperfect resolutions that most policies and programs represent, are analogous to the difficult education dilemmas that have stirred so much public debate of late—for example, public university admissions plans that seek to both reward merit and reduce inequality by race and income, promoting diversity in the educational experiences of all students.[10]

Mara Sidney, in her chapter analyzing the politics of fair housing and affordable housing in two very different metropolitan areas (chapter 12), shows why competing objectives require careful political strategies, not just clever policy measures. One reason that laundry lists of reform spur too little action is that too often advocates sidestep the thorny issue of trade-offs or demonize the opposition. In saying this, I am not arguing that all views on race, space, and opportunity are equally valid—rather that competing objectives call for creativity in reframing problems to be less zero-sum (win/lose) where possible, finding ways to mitigate costs and compensate those who disproportionately bear them, adding issues to the mix to make more valuable trades possible among the parties in conflict, and organizing new constituencies for important ideas, not just cutting deals with the parties and interests already in play.[11] In the final part of this chapter, I illustrate how such stakeholder and issue analyses can lead to innovative problem solving.

Integrating All Groups versus Empowering Some Groups

Since the uneven geography of opportunity is, as Camille Charles puts it, color coded, we face the puzzle of defining an agenda for public action that balances the important aims of integration—not forced but available for those who choose it—with those of group empowerment. Even if it enjoyed more public attention and wider support, the traditional integrationist agenda, whether focused on integration by race or class or both, is clearly no cure-all. No agenda for public policy and public action can address itself strictly to the integration of privileged communities—what economist Anthony Downs analyzed as "opening up the suburbs" some thirty years ago—at the expense of those who continue to

10. Guinier and Torres (2002); Clotfelter ((2004).

11. See Xavier de Souza Briggs, "We Are All Negotiators Now: An Introduction to Negotiation in Community Problem-Solving" (www.community-problem-solving.net [October 25, 2004]); Susskind and Cruikshank (1991).

live in, or who move into, disadvantaged areas.[12] Improving life and expanding opportunity for members of disadvantaged groups *who do not move* is also critical. Downs acknowledged that, and so have other careful observers, often to promote community development (place upgrading) but more recently to advance race-targeted programs, such as charter schools designed to focus on the learning needs of minority students.

Fierce arguments over these contrasting aims go back to the upheaval of the 1960s—to the politics of the War on Poverty, the civil rights movement, and the claims of ethnic nationalism. Not only have race-conscious public policies lost considerable support in recent decades, so too have efforts to promote racial integration specifically—and not just the controversial federal efforts focused on low-income housing that John Goering recounts in chapter 6. One oppositional school of thought, more popular with white Americans but enjoying minority support as well, argues that "affirmative," race-conscious policies, including some that promote residential integration by race, undermine the very equal opportunity standards that advocates of racial equity claim to promote—that affirmative amounts to discriminatory. In the 1990s the argument that affirmative policies discriminate against whites scored significant victories in the courts and legislatures, for example, as well as in the court of public opinion.

A second oppositional school, more often minority led, argues that integration has either been oversold (in its benefits) or comes at too great an opportunity cost for individuals, minority groups, and the society at large (in terms of other goods or objectives traded off). Should a minority renter or homebuyer family move into a neighborhood composed mainly of another racial or ethnic group, risking harassment and managing the costs of adjustment, for the sake of a complex bundle of benefits that living in a particular community *might* confer over time? The evidence is that people differ in their calculus of these costs and benefits and thus in their willingness to make such choices. Should precious public resources emphasize the creation of mixed-income housing and other investments to attract middle-income, racially diverse housing consumers to urban neighborhoods, when housing affordable to low-income households is at crisis scarcity levels in many communities? Should we address the increasing segregation of schools across lines of city and suburb (between-district segregation) if that focus somehow diverts attention from the strengthening of urban schools for the children they currently enroll?

As Camille Charles underlines in her chapter, there is some evidence that "integration fatigue" has grown among minorities, even as white attitudes show greater racial tolerance and, at the same time, less support for the notion that minorities deserve special help to overcome ongoing disadvantages. Racial integration efforts confront opposition from strange political bedfellows, then,

12. Downs (1973).

including some minorities and liberal whites, who think integration too costly and less urgent than other needs, and conservatives—of all racial and ethnic backgrounds—who think the available means of promoting greater integration are unfair.

Meanwhile, in the group empowerment domain, the cause of community development—and the impressively developed industry of mostly nonprofit organizations that work to advance it—has thus far been given a paper cup, as the saying goes, to bail out an ocean. Most of the conditions that make inner-city America such a consistent nexus of social problems, for example, are orchestrated by social and economic forces operating at a metropolitan or larger scale. These are forces that small community developers targeting particular neighborhoods, and likewise faith institutions and secular social welfare groups that do important work with disadvantaged individuals and families, are simply not equipped to change.[13] All too often, community development simply "holds up the bottom"—that is, prevents conditions from worsening significantly in the most vulnerable places—or unintentionally spurs gentrification that may displace low-income and minority residents. Efforts to reform the most segregated urban schools likewise achieve mostly modest victories in a context offering long odds.

It is not enough to declare that both integration and group empowerment are important—that is, expanding housing choices across metropolitan areas for people of all backgrounds and ensuring that every neighborhood and every school, no matter how modest, can be a stepping-stone to opportunity. The larger task is leveraging the changes in metropolitan America to promote both aims—at once, at a meaningful scale. As Angela Glover Blackwell and Judith Bell explain in their chapter on innovations in practice and policymaking, attending to the inclusiveness and the long-term viability of a range of communities and their residents is the core wisdom of an agenda for equitable development (see chapter 13). Such dual attention is also at the heart of what David Rusk calls the "inside game/outside game" that can make both cities and suburbs work.[14] Any meaningful dual agenda will address the interests of the central cities that we typically associate with our deepest social ills and societal contradictions, as well as the less usual suspects—the older "at risk" suburbs struggling with city-like problems and limited resources to respond; the rapidly growing bedroom suburbs that are burdened by excessive, unplanned, growth; and the other types of communities that define metropolitan America.[15] Addressing this range of problems is crucial, since cities are not the only, and in some areas not the primary, gateways for new arrivals; suburban communities are increasingly

13. Rusk (1999).
14. Rusk (1999).
15. Orfield (2002).

important gateways for minority families, including many first- and second-generation immigrants. But moving from an agenda in principle to the civics of change requires a closer look at just how fast the local politics of social equity has changed in America in recent decades.

Addressing the Local Politics of Exclusion

Not only are exclusionary suburban communities fiercely protective of their autonomy on land use and fiscal matters, but thanks to steady suburbanization, cities have been losing ground for forty years in political representation at the state and federal levels. Chicago's share of Illinois' population dropped from 35 percent to 23 percent between 1960 and 2000, for example, and Detroit's from 21 percent to just under 10 percent of Michigan's.[16] In the same period, suburbanites and their interests came to the fore in Congress and by 1992 had come to represent the majority electorate nationally and the dominant focus of presidential campaigns.[17]

By far the most talked about political idea for addressing these realities is Myron Orfield's "winning coalition" strategy.[18] Drawing on his own leadership experience in the Minnesota state legislature, Orfield suggests that central cities and at-risk suburbs represent a natural coalition that can, if well organized, outvote the more affluent suburban interests that defend fiscal inequities and race and class exclusion. Orfield points to revenue sharing and other policy reforms as evidence of Minnesota's success at addressing enormous inequalities in the resources available to local communities. The key arena, says Orfield, is state legislatures, where the authority over local taxation, land use, transportation and infrastructure investments, and more are concentrated in America's system of federalism.

As political scientist Hal Wolman and his colleagues observe, though, very little careful analysis has been done of coalition formation in statehouses. In their four-state study of city and suburban governments' political strategies and state-level policy agendas, these researchers find that the potential for Orfield-esque coalitions is clear in varied state contexts but that it is mostly that—potential.[19] Cities and older suburbs, far from cooperating around fiscal equity interests, largely compete over infrastructure and other investments, defending their immediate interests in every-town-for-itself lobbying. Regionalism does not rank high for any jurisdiction, leaving a political vacuum. "Instead of conceiving a single regional fiscal interest," conclude the researchers, "coalitions should be built around different issue areas that have a regional dimension, such

16. Wolman and others (2002).
17. Dreier, Mollenkopf, and Swanstrom (2001).
18. Orfield (2002).
19. Wolman and others (2002).

as transportation, public education, and fair share housing."[20] These analysts acknowledge the role of leadership in mining the potential for new coalitions, and they underscore the fact that, because of their statewide constituency, governors, Republicans and Democrats alike, often have the strong "natural" interest in genuinely regional issues, such as economic competitiveness. Recent efforts by the Brookings Institution to provide research support for regional efforts to bring back distressed communities in Pennsylvania, Maine, and other states corroborate these initial conclusions by political observers: Common-stakes coalitions must be actively forged, often against the grain of short-term political horizons, well-established and narrow conceptions of what it takes to revive local economies (chasing after sports stadiums, for example), the perennial instinct to "build it new," and more. But once forged, coalitions can leverage important changes in state policy, reversing the common bias for new suburban or ex-urban growth and against older, built-up communities.

In *Place Matters*, a broader analysis of the political prospects for crossing the city-suburban divide, political scientists Peter Dreier, John Mollenkopf, and Todd Swanstrom emphasize, like Orfield, the ways in which demographic trends and voting patterns do not fit the stereotype through which political leaders play on the fears of a white, conservative suburban majority.[21] First, suburbs, as we have seen, are increasingly diverse in both race and class terms. Suburbs thus offer greater potential for novel issue framing—changing the way people think about important issues rather than talking about different issues entirely—to tap emergent interests, new coalitions among groups, and policy innovations than the ingrained image of the city-suburban divide suggests. Second, increased racial and ethnic diversity is creating new and varied patterns of conflict and cooperation among immigrant groups, native-born blacks, and whites—patterns that will be become more important as immigrants naturalize, register to vote, and mobilize around particular candidates and issues. In addition, redistricting could shift the balance of the congressional electorate in profound ways in the years to come. Finally, particular political figures—Bill Clinton, for example—show that elected officials can be quite successful by campaigning on common-purpose themes that appeal to a wide array of voters in city and suburbs alike.

Beyond electoral politics, note the researchers, important nongovernmental groups—business, labor, and civic organizations—are making use of the burgeoning supply of sophisticated regional analyses and commentary from opinion leaders in media and academia. These nongovernmental actors are crucial for overcoming the tendency of elected officials, in both cities and suburbs, to protect turf rather than engage in longer-run coalition building and serious

20. Wolman and others (2002, p. 31).
21. Dreier, Mollenkopf, and Swanstrom (2001).

change. Policy Link's work (chapter 13) is a standout example, and Mara Sidney's chapter examines political options available to nonprofit advocates in distinct political contexts, in particular to use issue framing and forge wider coalitions rather than hew to a narrower compliance orientation. One lesson of her careful case studies may be that we do need dedicated compliance agents (who support enforcement) but that some of these agents cannot effectively double as policy advocates (who build a broader political base and push for basic reform).

Edward Goetz, Karen Chapple, and Barbara Lukermann, in their chapter on how fair share politics and policy unraveled in the Twin Cities region, suggest a few key principles for the metropolitics of fair share housing strategies: First, policy tools that merely permit something controversial (affordable housing, say) will not deliver on it if local support has eroded or remains disorganized and if a shift in budget politics destroys needed development subsidies; and second, specific powers held by regional, state, or other supralocal levels of government indeed represent crucial levers for change. When regional authorities chose not to monitor and enforce fair share housing requirements, local communities in the Twin Cities region were free to ignore affordable housing, leaving fair share principles "on the books" but doing little to deliver on those principles. The Twin Cities experience does not suggest that fair share strategies are doomed to failure, only that their success hinges on political and fiscal support that endures beyond initial efforts by reformers to get progressive policy measures on the books.

Finally, as the infamous and long-litigated saga of exclusionary zoning in Mount Laurel, New Jersey, underscores, the courts remain an important arena for securing key public commitments when electoral and legislative politics fail to address them.[22] But as with fair share housing in the Twin Cities, what the New Jersey Supreme Court ruled as policy, and what families in search of wider housing opportunity actually realized in the way of benefits, were quite different. In its landmark 1975 ruling (*Mount Laurel I*) and a series of linked rulings in the decades that followed, the court found that exclusionary zoning violated the general welfare provision of the state constitution by failing to address regional housing needs. The court indicated that local governments throughout the state had an affirmative obligation to include low- and moderate-income housing in their development plans.[23] Data on the production of low- and

22. Haar (1996); Kirp (2001).

23. For an overview of the rulings and a comparison to Pennsylvania's distinct approach to exclusionary zoning over the same period, see Mitchell (2004). Assessments of the impact of inclusionary zoning (that is, over and above what would have happened in its absence) are rare. Using an innovative data set combining an aerial survey with the housing census for the 1970—90 period in the eight-county Philadelphia metropolitan area, which includes counties in both Pennsylvania and New Jersey, Mitchell finds that Pennsylvania's approach, which did not link the builder's remedy to inclusion of low- and moderate-income housing, has had a larger impact on the diversity of housing types produced over the long run. Mitchell suggests that New Jersey's Mount Laurel

moderate-income housing since *Mount Laurel I* suggest that about 26,000 affordable units have been produced around the state, most of them as a result of the policy, but that little racial integration—a secondary objective of the inclusionary ruling—has occurred. What is more, thanks to *Mount Laurel II,* the primary mechanism for overcoming exclusionary land use is a "builder's remedy," by which real estate developers can gain approvals in towns that fail to come up with an inclusionary plan. Once authorized by the court or a state administrative agency, developers must produce one housing unit affordable to low- and moderate-income families for every four new market-rate units.

By favoring new development, the Mount Laurel incentives are now clashing with a major push by state and local leaders to curb sprawl—both to preserve farmland and to protect wildlife habitat. As a land use attorney working for the New Jersey association of local governments told the *New York Times,* "It's not that people are opposed to affordable housing. They're just opposed to the sprawl that comes along with it."[24] Whether or not the first claim is valid, the second underscores the folly of ignoring competing objectives: Efforts to respond to economic and social diversity will struggle in new ways if diversity only comes with growth and growth itself is increasingly unpopular. Developing more varied policy tools to promote *inclusionary* growth, a theme discussed by Rolf Pendall, Arthur Nelson, Casey Dawkins, and Gerrit Knaap in their chapter on growth management and by Blackwell and Bell in their chapter on equitable development, will be crucial in the years ahead. So will efforts to build political support for the tools that offer results.

Summary

Strategies for expanding the geography of opportunity will, like it or not, reflect some resolution, however imperfect, of these four dilemmas—the necessary evolution of civil rights enforcement (recognizing the limits of antidiscrimination strategies for changing the geography of opportunity), a range of competing objectives that are not resolvable merely by invoking rights, the uneasy co-existence of integrationist and group empowerment aims, and local political

framework remained vulnerable to local opposition, which the Pennsylvania policy avoided by mandating a variety of housing types, including apartments and townhouses, without stipulating income levels of occupants. Cowan (2001), in a statistical analysis of inclusionary zoning in four states, finds credible evidence of positive impacts, most of all in communities with some preexisting racial and ethnic diversity. Supported by careful policy analysis, a multi-stakeholder task force in one of those states—Massachusetts—has developed new proposals to address the concerns of municipalities that oppose a diversity of housing types, including state funding formulas that would respond to increased enrollments in local public schools and thereby mitigate the exclusionary effects of fiscal zoning. See Carman, Bluestone, and White (2003).

24. Andrew Jacobs, "New Jersey's Housing Law Works Too Well, Some Say," *New York Times,* March 3, 2001. Some advocates argue that rural communities should be granted more flexibility to meet their obligations under Mount Laurel.

opposition—all in the context of shifting demographic sands in cities and suburbs. Before I outline a policy agenda that reflects these considerations, however, I consider next the odd character of housing as a public issue.

The Invisible, Contentious Public Issue

Given that housing is everywhere and is so basic a human need, it is curiously invisible as a public issue in America. Housing represents the single largest expense for most families, one-fifth of the nation's economy, far and away the primary source of wealth for most families who own their homes and, in the form of attaining homeownership, a key to asset building for the millions of renter families who have little or no wealth.[25] Housing was also a primary source of ballast in the recent economic downturn, as owners "cashed out" significant housing wealth—almost $100 billion in 2002 alone—to buy goods and services.[26] Over the past half-century, since the landmark Housing Act of 1949 declared "a decent home and a suitable living environment for all Americans" to be a national policy goal, America saw enormous change in its housing stock. The quality of our housing has increased dramatically—fifty to a hundred years ago, shacks and unhealthy tenement buildings constituted the most visible housing problem—and so, too, have the costs, as building codes became more stringent and as demand for bigger and better housing increased along with family incomes.

To be fair, certain things about housing require little ongoing public attention or policy response. Well-established tax and land use policies that reward homeowners and support the building, real estate, and financial services industries enjoy broad and deep political support. The federal income tax deduction for home mortgage interest and for local property tax payments represents a transfer of over $100 billion a year to homeowners, who are primarily middle and upper income; that is about five times the total spent on all housing programs for low- and moderate-income people.[27] Most Americans, whether they are owners or renters who wish to become owners, support pro-ownership tax policies, though, and the low mortgage rates that signal a healthy supply of credit and consumption in the economy as a whole.

It is particular housing problems, then, that are largely invisible to the body politic. They are not at all invisible, however, to the 28 million American households who live in unaffordable housing.[28] For a variety of reasons, housing costs

25. Bipartisan Millennial Housing Commission (2002).

26. Joint Center for Housing Studies (2003).

27. Dolbeare (2002).

28. "Affordable" housing is, by the federal government's definition, housing that does not cost its occupants more than 30 percent of household income. If Bill Gates's home meets this criterion, regardless of the dollar amount he spends, his home is "affordable" by this definition. "Subsidized"

and wages on the bottom of the economic ladder have diverged significantly over the past thirty years, particularly in high-demand regions of the country. This widening gap has created an affordability crisis in many metropolitan housing markets and is most acute for working families at low- and moderate-income levels and for the nonworking poor.[29] On average, a parent working full time must earn almost $15 an hour, about three times the federal minimum wage, in order to afford a "modest" two-bedroom home or apartment, by federal standards. This minimum "housing wage" is much higher in many of the nation's most vibrant metropolitan economies.[30] The evidence from leading economists is that land use regulation contributes mightily to the cost problem, particularly in the tightest housing markets, exacting a steep "zoning tax."[31]

Although careful investigations consistently find the scarcity of decent, affordable rental housing to be the biggest cost burden facing families on welfare or in the nation's large low-wage job market, attention to high housing costs, such as it is, is often not focused on the needs of these struggling low-income families.[32] Public attention to the gap between wages and housing costs often coincides with middle-class housing "crises"—when, for example, at the height of the dot.com boom in Austin, Boston, San Francisco, Seattle, and other hot local markets college-educated, middle-class professionals were lined up around the block to secure decent apartments at the same time that many urban neighborhoods began to gentrify under the new demand, displacing low- and moderate-income families and rendering some homeless.

---

housing is the generic term for housing units, whether in the private market or under government or nonprofit management, in which financial subsidies go to either the developer, the landlord, the tenant, or the owner—that is, subsidies to anyone with a financial stake in the housing. Technically, every homeowner who claims the mortgage interest and property tax deduction on his or her income tax return is living in subsidized housing. But "subsidized" has come to refer, more specifically, to subsidies aimed at low- and moderate-income households. Low- and moderate-income housing, meanwhile, refers specifically to housing developed and managed to be affordable to families of modest income, based on local household income levels: at or below 50 percent of area median income ("very low income"), between 50 and 80 percent ("low income"), or between 80 and 120 percent ("moderate income"). Some analysts and policy advocates have coined the term *workforce housing* to describe housing affordable to working families whose wages or incomes are below a given threshold.

29. This divergence holds even when housing size and other factors that vary over time are held constant. Quigley and Raphael (2004) find that a marked increase in the amount of housing consumed by the average American household, together with inflation and higher incomes, cannot explain the widening gap between wages and housing costs for low-income workers and their families. Unlike other government programs that provide health or income supplements to families based on means testing, housing programs do not make use of the single, nationally defined (federal) poverty threshold (see note above). Moreover, distinctions between housing cost burden in general and the scale of housing needs for families of modest incomes in particular have created labels that confuse public discussions about housing need and the rightful aims of housing policy.

30. National Low Income Housing Coalition (2003).

31. See Glaeser and Gyourko (2002, p. 24).

32. Edin and Lein (1997); Ehrenreich (2001).

Whatever the focus, America's first urgent housing problem is affordability, most of all for those with low and moderate incomes. Second is the problem of where housing affordable to those households is located. As I note in chapter 2, racial segregation patterns partly reflect the concentration of low- and moderate-income housing in particular neighborhoods of cities and older suburbs, a problem that careful observers have underscored since Charles Abrams wrote *Forbidden Neighbors*, a study of prejudice in housing, in 1955. Beyond the problem of cost, then, is an urgent need to expand the geography of affordable housing. This was a core element of many policy recommendations to enhance the viability of cities and also to improve race relations in the 1960s and 1970s. But in general, this aim, distinct from the aim of expanding the supply of affordable housing anywhere, has been a focus for a relatively small number of state and local governments plus a small, politically vulnerable constituency of housing advocates relegated to "playing defense" on the affordability problem. Focusing low-income housing assistance—for example, via public housing and the Section 8 rental subsidy program—on the poorest of the poor, a basic federal targeting decision that reflects a worthy commitment to the most vulnerable, has, sadly, only increased local opposition to dispersing low- and moderate-income housing.[33]

In *From the Puritans to the Projects*, an incisive history of "public housing and public neighbors," urban historian Lawrence Vale details the deep roots of our ambivalence toward the placement of the poor in our midst—and the mixed motives of policy efforts, since the New Deal, to house the economically marginal.[34] Beyond the cultural or attitudinal elements of this contention, there is the question of immediate economic and political calculus: When it comes to the forces that squeeze the housing supply or restrict it to certain geographic areas, the monetary interests of owners and renters are frequently in conflict. Most owners and other property investors become wealthier when land and housing prices increase, while renters benefit from lower prices. So those with an *investment* interest in housing do not naturally rally around the needs of those who merely *consume* housing.[35]

In this context, housing advocacy's important and largely defensive battle over affordability risks a number of hazards. One is trading away social inclusion as a public value: "Help them secure housing but not here in my community." A second hazard is increasing the concentration of affordable housing in inner-city areas or older at-risk suburbs, far away from quality schools, job growth, safer

33. Goetz (2003).

34. Vale (2000).

35. Students of local politics refer to this as a distinction between those who hold use values (only) and those who have exchange values in property. Logan and Molotch (1987) offer the classic analysis of this political economy of place, and Goetz and Sidney (1994) vividly demonstrate the conflicts between these two in a Minneapolis case they aptly title "Revenge of the Property Owners."

streets, and other keys to opportunity and upward mobility. That is, even if we manage to supply more affordable housing, if it is only across a sharply restricted geography our public policies will worsen the very geography of inequality that we need to overcome.

An earlier generation of housing assistance policies showed the folly of building low-cost housing wherever we could: Racially segregated ghettos grew up quickly around some of the largest high-rise public housing projects, especially when rules on eligibility and rent made it unattractive for working families to live in them.[36] Now, for better or worse, the winds of policy reform are blowing. Whereas "housing opportunity" had long been used as a mere synonym for housing assistance output (units added to the low-cost housing supply, tenant-based vouchers, and so on), in the 1990s a larger, richer concept of a housing opportunity bundle—including geographic access to key supports (better schools, areas of job growth, safer streets, perhaps richer social networks, and more)—became a staple of housing policy debates, at least at the federal level.[37] Beleaguered housing assistance programs swung back, belatedly perhaps, to the core axiom of all real estate practice: Location matters. As Sue Popkin and Mary Cunningham warn in chapter 8, the sea change in federal policy, felt most dramatically in the transformation of stigmatized public housing projects, brings new risks, such as reinforcing existing patterns of racial and economic segregation and leaving many vulnerable families at risk of losing shelter altogether.

Finally, if the availability and location of affordable housing for low- and moderate-income families garner little attention in today's political debates, a third housing policy aim, that of fighting discrimination by race, religious creed, disability, or other "protected classes," has been still more invisible and politically vulnerable. This is in spite of the fact that fair housing is, by nature, a universal policy that protects Americans of all backgrounds. Recall that most Americans think housing discrimination is wrong and know it is illegal but also believe that it is no longer much of a problem.

Housing Policy Redux

At least since the 1960s, government has faced dilemmas on all three fronts—housing cost, geographic concentration, and fair access. Most state governments spend little to help meet housing needs and largely defer land use decisions to

36. See Massey and Denton (1993). Under current provisions, federal rent vouchers—subsidies that follow families rather than physical developments—have largely failed, for more than two decades now, to deliver access to a wide range of quality neighborhoods, though they do much better than public housing (a fixed, place-based form of housing assistance). See Newman and Schnare (1997); Devine and others (2003). Several chapters in this volume assess the implications of expanding the geography of housing assistance (Rosenbaum, DeLuca, and Tuck, chapter 7; Goering, chapter 6).

37. Briggs (2003); Goetz (2003).

local governments. Local governments, in turn, behave according to their demographics, fiscal base, and organized constituencies: Central cities tend to have the best developed housing programs but weakest fiscal capacity, plus they can do little—at least, directly—to encourage suburbs to accept their fair share of low- and moderate-income housing.[38] Older suburbs fear becoming low-rise ghettos if a concentration of social need should "tip" their communities.[39]And affluent bedroom suburbs and suburban job centers tend to recognize no self-interest in accepting low- or moderate-income households from their less affluent neighboring communities. As Pendall and his colleagues explain in chapter 10, since local land use policy has long been linked to race and class exclusion, the new generation of efforts to rethink the management of local development will have to pursue inclusionary growth quite intentionally if inclusion is a goal.

As for federal action, the easiest way for the federal government to offer support is through financial subsidies—grants, loan guarantees, and tax credits—to nonprofits, businesses, and state and local governments. But political and fiscal pressure has steadily reduced these federal subsidies, both in real terms and as a share of domestic spending, over the last twenty-five years.[40] As Goetz, Chapple, and Lukermann show in chapter 11, the significant reduction in federal aid to local government housing programs was central to the unraveling of metropolitan fair share programs in the Twin Cities, a region often hailed for its progressive, interjurisdictional (metropolitan) approaches to urban problems. Along with a reduced fiscal commitment overall, the federal government stopped the expansion of public housing thirty years ago and has steadily increased the participation of businesses and nonprofit organizations in developing and managing low- and moderate-income housing.[41] Meanwhile, enforcing antidiscrimination protections is a federal obligation, but since bad behavior is so difficult to detect, effective fair housing enforcement depends on a host of local actions engaging government agencies, realtors, consumers, fair housing advocates and testing agents, and often prodiversity civic groups.[42] Here, too, federal funding has been modest—under $50 million in the 2004 fiscal year—and its effects limited.

In a prospective look at housing policy in the 1990s, Langley Keyes and Denise DiPasquale illustrate how major federal policy statements tend to reflect the prevailing political winds as well as these longer-run features of the housing policy landscape.[43] In 1968, for example, the report by President Johnson's

38. Haar (1996).

39. Orfield (2002).

40. Blank and Ellwood (2002); Bratt (2003).

41. Goetz (1993). Only about one-quarter of all eligible households actually receive federal rental assistance (Dolbeare 2002), a figure that did not increase even over the course of the nation's record-breaking economic expansion in the 1990s. At $15 billion to $20 billion in expenditure a year, this is the nation's largest single program to help low- and moderate-income families meet their housing costs.

42. Galster (1990); Turner and Ross, chapter 4; and Sidney, chapter 12, this volume.

43. Keyes and DiPasquale (1990).

Committee on Urban Housing assumed strong federal leadership and significant funding to expand and disperse affordable housing. Largely made up of distinguished private sector leaders, the committee believed that America's key housing problems were fixable and that public-private partnerships, while desirable, should not preclude federal activism where required.

In 1982 President Reagan's Commission on Housing struck a very different tone and articulated very different assumptions and policy priorities. It concluded that 1960s-era programs had largely compounded, not ameliorated, problems of urban deterioration and the isolation of low-income and minority families from economic opportunity. "The nation cannot afford yet another system of entitlements expanding endlessly out of effective control," said the report.[44] Dispersal and racial desegregation aims were nowhere on the agenda, but getting rid of costly regulations would, the commission assured, unleash "the genius of the market economy."

In 1988 the National Housing Task Force, which was formed by Congress and not the president, sounded a vital, if largely unheeded, warning: Most Americans had achieved the vision of the 1949 act, but "for millions of our families, we have not only fallen short, we are losing ground."[45] The task force noted that the nation's low-rent stock was eroding, making it crucial to both preserve existing affordable supply and to creatively expand that supply through partnerships with private and nonprofit actors.

The latest national policy group, the Bipartisan Millennial Housing Commission appointed by Congress, focuses its 2002 report on America's steadily growing affordability crisis, which generally reflects the trends highlighted by the task force some fourteen years earlier: a loss of affordable housing supply (low-rent units most of all) and growing demand from households that earn too little. The commission outlines a vision for the nation's housing that emphasizes wider access to opportunity: "To produce and preserve more sustainable, affordable housing *in healthy communities* to help American families progress up the ladder of economic opportunity."[46] The report's case for larger and wiser housing investments mentions the importance of neighborhood quality and geographic access to opportunity, and its outline of barriers to more affordable supply cites exclusionary zoning and costly fees imposed by local governments—the focus of the 1991 Advisory Commission on Regulatory Barriers to Affordable Housing, which had been appointed by HUD secretary Jack Kemp, and of a recent update on "barrier removal" published by HUD.[47]

44. Report of the President's Commission on Housing (1983, p. xxii).

45. Report of the National Housing Task Force (1988, p. 1).

46. Bipartisan Millennial Housing Commission (2002, p. 4), emphasis added.

47. Advisory Commission (1991); U.S. Department of Housing and Urban Development (2005). For a detailed critique of the Millennial Housing Commission's work by a long-time advocate of inclusionary and affordable housing, see Chester Hartman, "Millennial Misfire," *Shelterforce Online* (www.nhi.org/online [July 2002]).

But other than this indirect acknowledgment of how avidly most American communities exclude affordable housing, the Bipartisan Millennial Housing Commission sidesteps the question of segregation by race and class, and its policy recommendations do not include actions by the federal government to encourage states and localities to be more inclusionary as the nation's population grows and becomes more diverse. The commission echoes the importance of community quality as a key societal aim but—sadly—offers only tepid support for the fiscal or other changes that realizing this aim might require. It is unfortunate, given the demographic and spatial patterns so clearly reshaping the local landscape throughout America, that this bipartisan national policy statement offers so little recognition of segregation and virtually no support for a public response. More specifically, the commission fails to acknowledge the real risk: that we will succeed in expanding the supply of affordable housing but only in the well-contained geography that already hosts most such housing. Again, the risk is deepening the very inequalities of place that we need to undo as the nation becomes more diverse and the sharp inequality in incomes persists. Finally, it is unfortunate that the commission's report, such as it is, managed to attract so little attention, whether from policymakers, the media, or the general public. HUD, once the nation's ambitious agency for urban problem solving, did not even issue a statement acknowledging the release of this "millennial" report.

Conclusion

The public conversation in America has often ignored, and well-intended policy debates tend to muddle, a crucial distinction. Framed as a question of strategy, the distinction is this: Should we emphasize reducing *segregation* by race and class (through what I term "cure" strategies), or should we emphasize reducing its terrible *social costs* without trying to reduce the extent of segregation itself to any significant degree (via "mitigation" strategies)? Put differently, should we invest in changing where people are willing and able to live, or should we try to transform the mechanisms that link a person's place of residence to their opportunity set? These strategies respond to distinct definitions of the problem to be solved (see table 14-1).

For ethical and practical reasons, it is hard to imagine choosing one strategy, always and everywhere, instead of the other, and where mitigation strategies are concerned, in spite of the less satisfying label, proposals to offer car vouchers to low-income households (to address job sprawl) and to upgrade struggling neighborhoods and schools hint at urgent, and in some cases very immediate and practical, responses to inequality. These examples also hint at how widely policy proposals in this category range in terms of their do-ability, cost, potential leverage on the outcomes we care about (educational success, job attainment, health and well-being, and so on), and evident political support. Regardless, mitigation

Table 14-1. *Transforming the Geography of Opportunity: Which Strategies for Which Problems?*

Problem	*Strategy*
Problems leading to segregation	*Cures for problems leading to segregation (strategies for reducing rates of segregation)*
Exclusionary land use policies and limited supply of affordable housing	Create more choices through fair share housing policies, inclusionary zoning, review of local land use decisions for focal projects supported by higher governments, fiscal reforms to address "zoning for dollars," funding to expand supply and to subsidize demand by low- and moderate-income households, regional mobility programs for these households, and supportive housing for at-risk families.
Discrimination by sellers, lenders, brokers, and public housing agencies	Protect choices through fair housing testing, enforcement, and education (of sellers, consumers, real estate brokers, lenders).
Segregative residential choices of consumers (including "neighborhood avoidance") in cities and suburbs	Promote more informed choice and new choices through affirmative marketing (to all racial groups); through community development (area-based upgrading), including mixed-income and mixed-tenure housing development, to attract diverse in-movers; and through housing subsidies and counseling and choice incentives for low-income households.
Problems stemming from segregation	*Mitigation of problems stemming from segregation (strategies for reducing costs of segregation)*
Educational inequality across schools or school districts	Desegregate schools through voluntary choice and magnet programs, fiscal transfers to reduce funding inequalities or strengthen low-performing schools, and vouchers to encourage wider choice and competition, with racial equity safeguards.
Barriers to job access	Create transportation alternatives, such as car vouchers, reverse commute transit programs, regional workforce development alliances or networks (intermediation, matching of workers and jobs), equal employment opportunity (antidiscrimination) enforcement and education, and workforce development and "job readiness" programs
Spatially concentrated crime, lower quality housing and services, lack of amenities	Upgrade neighborhoods through reform of public services such as policing, health care, and human services
Neighborhood stigmas that discourage investment and hiring	Upgrade neighborhoods, use positive marketing

strategies could ensure that thousands of neighborhoods in central cities and at-risk suburbs act as stepping-stones, not isolating and damaging traps. Broadly, these strategies seek to improve places as *contexts* (valuable for what living in these places offers) and as *locations* (valuable for what one can access *from* these places). If we value competitive markets, local decisionmaking, and other features of society that generate some degree of economic inequality, then we should work to eliminate or substantially weaken the invidious link between where you can afford to live and what your life prospects, or those of your children, are.

Fair enough, but a society that venerates freedom of choice—with quasi-religious zeal, as the word *venerate* would imply—should also want to expand choices in ways that respond to the nation we are becoming, in demographic, economic, and other terms. Along with the other contributors to this volume, whose recommendations I examine below, I argue that expanding housing choice is a linchpin for any agenda to ensure equal opportunity and reduce inequality in a more and more diverse society. For this reason, and because the nature and quality of housing choices are also at the heart of the sustainable growth debate—the debate over sprawl and disinvestment in older places—I focus on cure strategies here.

In broad terms, expanding housing choices means three things: *creating* more valuable choices for a wider array of people, *protecting* those choices from discrimination and other barriers to choice, and *enabling* the choosers to make the best possible choices for themselves and their families. The narrowest reading of housing rights, for example, imagines a threshold protection of choice: access to the housing options one can afford, given the current rules of the development game. But as legal scholars and social critics Lani Guinier and Gerald Torres observe, the real questions for a changing society are: Who has a voice in setting those rules or changing them over time? And how can we set the rules in ways that deliver on the core of the American experiment—opportunity for all?[48] These questions underline the importance of creating more choices—of transforming what it means to have choices, not just protecting the limited choices that so many of us have.

Several chapters in this book suggest that tried-and-true policies to create more choices by expanding the geography, not just the supply, of affordable housing deserve more support. First, we need to significantly expand funding, and also lower regulatory barriers and development costs, for affordable housing overall. Federal, state, and local proposals to create or expand housing trust funds are especially promising, as are a new generation of efforts to understand which land regulations and building codes impose excessive costs relative to

48. Guinier and Torres (2002).

their benefits.[49] The flexibility of a trust fund—which typically originates with a guaranteed public revenue source but blends these with varied private dollars as well—is good politics, not just savvy finance, as the case of the highly successful Los Angeles housing campaign shows.[50] But new fund proposals at the state and federal levels should specifically consider financial incentives for localities or metropolitan regions that commit to lowering costly regulatory barriers and to dispersing housing for low- and moderate-income families.

Second, we should expand and diversify mixed-income housing policies and programs in particular. As Pendall and colleagues (chapter 10) and Blackwell and Bell (chapter 13) explain, mixed-income housing may represent our best hope for proactively integrating entire municipalities as well as neighborhoods. This is true both in exclusionary communities, which tend to offer high-performing schools and other special access to opportunity, and in revitalizing central cities, where many low-income families are being displaced by gentrification. But no one model works everywhere. For example, inclusionary zoning policies rely on significant new housing development to expand the supply and the geography of affordable housing, so inclusionary zoning best suits growing areas anticipating significant new housing development. Plus, most of these programs are race neutral, so promoting diversity, if that is a local aim, will hinge on social marketing or other supports to encourage racially and ethnically diverse occupancy.

Third, policymakers and advocates will need to negotiate a wiser second generation of fair share housing policies—learning from the 1970s and 1980s wave of reforms—as part of metropolitan planning, growth management, and investment. As Pendall and colleagues warn, local governments could decide to use the tools on the smart growth menu that protect open space and offer fewer public subsidies for private development but not the tools that would promote mixed-income housing and typically lead to greater racial diversity.[51] And as Goetz, Chapple, and Lukermann show in the rise and fall of fair share in the Twin Cities area, passive policy without political support and needed development incentives, including subsidies, will do little. Policies that merely "permit" inclusionary housing may not produce it.

Fourth, we need to dramatically scale up well-implemented, metropolitan-wide housing mobility programs for low- and moderate-income families. As Goering emphasizes in his chapter, the early lessons of the ongoing federal

49. Meck, Retzlaff, and Schwab (2003); U.S. Department of Housing and Urban Development (2005).

50. Dreier (2001).

51. Two major projects of the American Planning Association have produced useful guides; see Meck (2002), a study and public education effort that addresses growth management; and Meck, Retzlaff, and Schwab (2003), a study that offers a concise history of regional housing efforts as well as a host of strategies and state and local case studies.

Moving to Opportunity experiment are that low-income families do need special mobility encouragement and assistance but also that they can make successful, and potentially life-changing, moves to low-poverty areas. There are also signs that not all families adjust well, that there may be important challenges for particular members of mover families (such as boys, who seem to adapt differently from girls to new neighborhoods), and that housing assistance alone does not compensate for a lack of transportation to get around in more car-reliant areas (including suburbs) or for other barriers to social and economic success. Offering a new look at the Gautreaux mobility program in metropolitan Chicago, James Rosenbaum, Stefanie DeLuca, and Tammy Tuck (chapter 7) emphasize that new capabilities and preferences, while they may take years to develop for low-income minority families that move into new environments, can operate in powerful ways to help such families take advantage of a wider geography of opportunity, including access to advantaged school districts. But if we are serious about using housing policy to connect more families to economic opportunity, why not link housing vouchers to car vouchers (or other transportation assistance) and, at the same time, emphasize job and school connections for low-income movers?

Fifth, the large-scale transformation of public housing that began in the 1990s is probably the most important shift in America's low-income housing policy in a half century. But it will only be a positive shift if we find viable alternatives for many of the most vulnerable families who leave public housing. As Popkin and Cunningham show (chapter 8), without careful safeguards and programs to suit a range of family types—such as service-enriched "supportive housing"—the relocation of former public housing residents can reinforce existing patterns of racial segregation and leave many of the most vulnerable families at risk of losing shelter altogether.

Sixth, "doing less harm" ought to be a key tenet of the federal role in a new era of metropolitan opportunity and change. As Philip Tegeler indicates in chapter 9, we need to address the lingering, segregative effects of well-established federal housing and community development programs—including programs that now spur private and nonprofit developers, rather than public agencies, to produce almost all of the nation's affordable housing. A number of large-scale, very important programs skirt the federal "site and neighborhood standards" that are meant to further integration and access to communities of opportunity. Funding more community development on a metropolitan basis may address some of these trade-offs. But so would key changes to existing laws and regulations, which Tegeler outlines.

Seventh, and finally among the options for creating more choice, promoting fiscal equity would remove perverse local incentives to exclude affordable housing—and even family housing generally, in some instances. Local officials in some of the nation's fastest growing suburban towns use zoning to discourage family-scale housing development, such as condominium units with more than two bedrooms. Fearing that school and other service costs will exceed their property tax capacity, these officials in effect favor what the *Boston Globe* has labeled "child-proof" housing.[52] As I note in chapter 1, thanks in part to a high reliance on local property tax revenues to cover service costs, local governments in America have a perverse incentive to exclude (zone out) housing for low- and moderate-income working families in particular.[53] State-level and metropolitan agreements could change this.[54] Transfers from the federal level could help stimulate reforms, for example as part of broader metropolitan demonstration efforts to manage growth and strengthen connections to work for a wide range of families.

If creating new housing choices is the threshold strategy, however, *protecting* choice is equally important. As for discrimination in the search for housing, Turner and Ross, in chapter 4, outline stepped-up public education efforts (so an increasingly diverse consumer base knows its rights) along with updated testing and enforcement to detect and prosecute more violators, both for in-person and over-the-phone transactions. Meanwhile, William Apgar and Allegra Calder (chapter 5) emphasize the need to significantly improve the literacy of borrowers about credit schemes and financial risk, particularly in low-income and minority communities, and to strengthen laws against the most predatory lending, which has increased dramatically in just the past decade, proliferating new financial products but also stripping away hard-won assets from those who can least afford such losses. If one in six adult Americans is functionally illiterate, is it any wonder that so many millions are *financially* illiterate and thus prey to the worst abuses of deregulated capital markets? And finally, civil rights and community development advocacy are at last beginning to tackle the geography of opportunity beyond fair housing—through links to transportation equity and environmental justice, for example. Progress on these fronts would not only be advantageous and appropriate in and of itself but would also enhance the value of expanded housing choice.

In some instances, opportunities to create and protect housing choice are inextricably linked—one reason why making regional access to affordable housing should be a key agenda in more fair housing work. Mara Sidney shows in chapter 12 why reliance on narrowly defined federal fair housing policies may

52. Anthony Flint, "'Child-Proof' Housing Studied" (www.boston.com/dailyglobe2/261/metro [September 19, 2003]).

53. Compared to local counterparts in Europe and other affluent regions, local governments in the United States are extraordinarily reliant on local revenues. European rates of intergovernmental aid range from a low of 40 percent in France to 60 percent in Great Britain and 80 percent in Italy, excluding costs for education, firefighters, and police, which are often paid for entirely by national governments (Savitch 2002). By comparison, U.S. cities obtain only about 30–35 percent of their revenues from higher government (state and federal) sources. See also Nivola (1999) on the fiscal dimensions of land use decisions and development patterns in Europe and the United States.

54. Carman, Bluestone, and White (2003); Orfield (2002).

lead local fair housing advocates to marginalize themselves and miss out on key opportunities to build broader coalitions. On the other hand, supporting an expanded geography of affordable housing, in part by expanding the constituency for wider access, sometimes means choosing not to insist on racial set-asides or other guarantees of diversity. But as Sidney warns, "Continuing to avoid public discussion of race in order to win political support for housing measures does little to advance our political system's ability to address real racial injustices." Local context should determine the tactics that blend political confrontation and cooperation: going it alone versus acting in coalition, and "naming race" prominently versus addressing it more indirectly. A new generation of social marketing efforts could tap the interests of employers, schools and other public agencies, unions, and faith institutions in more proactively addressing racial and ethnic diversity in changing communities, especially in fast-growing ones. Rather than duck race (as an issue) in order to build broader coalitions, the practical politics of this will dictate the time and the place to make group-specific, including race-specific, claims. Clearly, not all efforts to promote racial justice and greater equity can be race-first or even race-based in their policy prescriptions. But just as clearly, they must be race-conscious in order to be credible as well as effective.

Finally, wider and better protected choices, while worthy in and of themselves, will not make the society less segregated if consumers make mostly segregative choices about where to live. In careful studies that encompass reported racial attitudes and preferences on one hand and actual housing choices (across several decades of census taking) on the other, researchers reaffirm the wisdom of an earlier generation of efforts, still going strong in a small number of neighborhoods and towns, to use affirmative, prodiversity marketing as well as community development (upgrading) strategies to attract a diversity of new residents.[55] Considering the tensions between integration and empowerment, the questions ahead are not only about "receiving" communities' willingness to be diversity friendly but about "sending" areas' willingness to make their residents aware of their exit options. One example is renter and homeowner counseling that highlights neighborhood and school quality in communities that are racially different from, and typically less poor than, the sender areas that families leave behind—the basis for the well-known Gautreaux housing experiment in Chicago that chapter 7 profiles in a new light.

Because the constituency for change remains narrow and fragmented, advocates for change, both inside and outside of government, will need to bring employers, unions, faith communities, and other stakeholders into this arena. It will take broad support and a host of tailored political messages—some about economic competitiveness and fiscal sanity, others about social justice

55. See Charles (chapter 3, this volume); Ellen (2000); Nyden, Maly, and Lukehart (1997).

and the practice of moral community—to make progress on these old divides (see table 14-2).

For employers, promoting housing that is affordable to working families is smart competitive strategy, as the companies that built up mill and mining towns (and subsidized worker housing) recognized in the nineteenth century. But the housing issue needs the *political* capital of business at least as much as enlightened financial investment. As the track record and commitment of the San Francisco Bay area's Silicon Valley Manufacturing Group shows, respected employers can make a big difference when advocating for well-designed affordable housing at local planning and zoning hearings, which do so much to determine the geography of housing opportunity in America. "Employer-assisted" housing programs, in which employers directly subsidize employees' mortgages or other housing costs but do not necessarily advocate for more affordable housing development in a wider array of communities, merely scratch the surface of engagement by business.

For faith institutions, housing and community development challenges offer special opportunities to practice religious community, in part because all of the major faiths define social inclusion as a core value, and because, as Habitat for Humanity has shown so well around the globe, housing can build communities—literally and figuratively. What is more, not every faith or faith-based institution need become a developer of housing or a direct service provider. There are many useful leadership roles to be played on housing and the economic opportunity issues to which housing is linked, including regionwide advocacy and financial investment.

For unions, housing affordability—more specifically, decent housing in communities of opportunity—is a bread-and-butter issue for the membership base, arguably as vital as, though much less understood than, good schools and good jobs.[56] Resurgent unions, mostly in the service sectors that represent the lion's share of economic growth now, are likely to be very important players in urban politics in the decade ahead. Unions of hotel and restaurant workers, janitors, and other occupations have already shown their muscle in state and local races in California, Nevada, and New York, and of course unions of teachers, police officers, correctional officers, and firefighters have long shaped state and local budget battles and electoral outcomes. It remains to be seen whether unions and their potential allies will develop savvy policy agendas and winning coalitions that leverage the role of housing as a linchpin of economic opportunity in America.

Given what I describe as housing's curious invisibility as a social policy issue, it is a shame that so much political analysis of the nation's changing cities and regions emphasizes formal theoretical modeling rather than developing lessons for practical politics. Even in the face of sharp conflicts or public apathy, change

56. Dreier (2001).

Table 14-2. *Interests and Priorities of Stakeholders in Affordable and Inclusionary Housing*

Stakeholders	*Interests*	*Priorities*
Employers	Recruiting and developing a more racially and ethnically diverse workforce; recruiting and retaining employees in high-cost markets; projecting a socially responsible public image; maintaining positive relations with city hall and other levels of government	Clear business purpose; public image
Unions	Recruiting and developing a more racially and ethnically diverse workforce; delivering "bread-and-butter" benefits to members (strong wages and benefits, good schools, affordable housing and healthcare); choosing socially responsible investments for union pension funds, such as affordable housing and community economic development	Increased membership; tangible benefits
Public school officials and advocates	Improving outcomes for disadvantaged students; reducing achievement gaps by race and income; heading off costly litigation; addressing increased racial diversity in enrollments (many suburban communities)	Achievement gaps; cost savings
Metropolitan transportation agencies	Creating access to jobs through flexible (multimodal) mobility strategies; reducing costs of new infrastructure; creating positive spillovers and more sustainable development, such as through transit-oriented housing and shopping hubs	Demonstrable public benefit; cost reduction
Faith institutions	Practicing religious community through collective action and ministry activities; developing faith-based nonprofits (where appropriate); promoting morality in public and private life, by message and example; choosing socially responsible investments, such as affordable housing and community economic development	For faith-based nonprofit service providers, operational capacity and social impact; for others, increase in membership, community morals, consistency with core ministry
Market-rate housing developers	Tapping new markets; innovating to reduce costs, apply new technology, and serve a more diverse customer base; streamlining the development process	Meet market needs; reduce development costs and delays
Affordable housing developers	Creating more product to house more families; creating positive spillover effects through housing and economic development projects; building resilient communities of choice, beyond "bricks and mortar" output	Funds to expand scale; operating capacity to manage complex projects, for example in transit-oriented development or other new areas; reduced development costs and delays

agents and other civic entrepreneurs often have more room for maneuver than they believe, as the evolving fields of negotiation, mediation, and consensus building illustrate. Efforts to map the interests of the range of stakeholders identified above should not only consider what key stakeholders actually value—as opposed to what an advocate may think they *should* value—but which issues or interests are most important to a given stakeholder. Where stakeholders value the same things equally, shared interests can lead to strong, natural coalitions. Where their priorities are very different, trades can often be negotiated, because one party can get more of what it wants at little cost to the other party.[57] Many coalition builders assume, wrongly, that only shared interests should be emphasized, forgoing opportunities to inventory differences that may be crucial to negotiated agreement. Powerful coalitions can be forged among unusual suspects with seemingly disparate priorities.

Broad political support will be especially crucial if advocates for wider housing choice manage to seize the opportunities created by the contentious politics of sprawl. While consensus building has its place, broad support need not aim for consensus measures. As Myron Orfield argues, the latter can lead to lowest-common-denominator, offend-no-one solutions that are not solutions at all.[58] And while an unfocused, everything-but-the-kitchen-sink approach should be avoided, housing advocates can work to recognize and make use of unexpected political opportunities. As Blackwell and Bell show in chapter 13, the growing public awareness of links among fair and affordable housing, access to jobs, school quality, and other regional opportunity priorities make for rich but challenging constituency organizing and political communication. Likewise, efforts by activist scholars, including those affiliated with the Brookings Institution's Metropolitan Policy Program, are supporting big-tent coalitions that emphasize common stakes and broad reinvestment agendas. Environmentalists, businesspeople and economic development professionals, racial justice advocates, faith communities, unions, and others have a huge, shared stake in revitalizing older communities and redeploying the billions of local, state, and federal dollars that currently—and quite effectively—underwrite sprawl. These efforts are much more promising, over the long run, than a community development agenda that limits itself to neighborhood improvement, one small place at a time.

Where the prospects for racial equity are concerned, we cannot ignore or hope to sidestep the tensions between an integrationist agenda and the agenda of community (group-specific) empowerment. While we emphasize the case for integration in this book, the real aim is expanding choices and improving access to opportunity wherever people live and whomever they choose to live among. The evidence of our nation's history is that we will never ensure equal opportunity in

57. Fisher and Ury (1991); Susskind and Cruikshank (1991).
58. Orfield (2002).

a state of high segregation. But integration and community empowerment strategies can both be part of more equitable development in our communities.

America's metropolitan dilemma is this: The promise and strains associated with rapid social change in our country—led by increased racial and ethnic diversity but reflecting growing economic inequality, an aging population, and other shifts as well—will register in the ways our communities choose to develop. There was nothing natural or inevitable about the current shape of things—the uneven geography of opportunity, the sprawl in housing and jobs, the sharp segregation by race and class. Nor are the alternatives to these patterns predetermined. But communities do have choices, and we should get on with the work of understanding and pursuing them.

References

Abravanel, Martin, and Mary Cunningham. 2002. *What Do We Know?* U.S. Department of Housing and Urban Development.

Advisory Commission on Regulatory Barriers to Affordable Housing. 1991. *"Not in My Backyard": Removing Barriers to Affordable Housing.* U.S. Department of Housing and Urban Development.

Bipartisan Millennial Housing Commission Appointed by the Congress of the United States. 2002. *Meeting Our Nation's Housing Challenges.* U.S. Government Printing Office.

Blank, Rebecca, and David Ellwood. 2002. "The Clinton Legacy for America's Poor." In *American Economic Policy in the 1990s*, edited by Jeffrey A. Frankel and Peter R. Orszag, pp. 749–800. MIT Press.

Bobo, Lawrence. 2001. "Racial Attitudes and Relations at the Close of the Twentieth Century." In *America Becoming: Racial Trends and Their Consequences,* vol. 1, edited by Neil J. Smelser, William Julius Wilson, and Faith Mitchell, pp. 264–301. Washington: National Academy Press.

Bratt, Rachel. 2003. "Housing for Very Low-Income Households: The Record of President Clinton, 1993–2000." *Housing Studies* 18, no. 4: 607–35.

Briggs, Xavier de Souza. 2003. "Housing Opportunity, Desegregation Strategy, and Policy Research." *Journal of Policy Analysis and Management* 22, no. 2: 201–06.

Carman, Edward C., Barry Bluestone, and Eleanor White. 2003. *Building on Our Heritage: A Strategy for Smart Growth and Economic Development.* Report and Recommendations for the Commonwealth Housing Task Force. Boston: Center for Urban and Regional Policy, Northeastern University.

Cashin, Sheryll. 2004. *The Failures of Integration: How Race and Class are Undermining the American Dream.* New York: Public Affairs.

Clotfelter, Charles T. 2004. *After Brown: The Ruse and Retreat of School Desegregation.* Princeton University Press.

Cooter, Robert, and Thomas Ulen. 2004. *Law and Economics.* Boston: Addison Wesley.

Cowan, Spencer. 2001. "Anti-Snob Land Use Laws and Suburban Exclusion." Paper prepared for Conference on Housing Opportunity, Civil Rights, and the Regional Agenda. Urban Institute, November 16.

Devine, Deborah J., and others. 2003. *Housing Choice Voucher Location Patterns: Implications for Participants and Neighborhood Welfare.* U.S. Department of Housing and Urban Development.

Dolbeare, Cushing N. 2002. *Changing Priorities: The Federal Budget and Housing Assistance, 1976–2007.* Washington: National Low Income Housing Coalition.

Downs, Anthony. 1973. *Opening up the Suburbs: An Urban Strategy for America.* Yale University Press.

Dreier, Peter. 2001. "Expanding the Political Constituency for Affordable Housing: Tentative Lessons from Los Angeles." Paper prepared for Conference on Housing Opportunity, Civil Rights, and the Regional Agenda. Urban Institute, November 16.

Dreier, Peter, John Mollenkopf, and Todd Swanstrom. 2001. *Place Matters: Metropolitics for the Twenty-First Century.* University Press of Kansas.

Edin, Kathy, and Laura Lein. 1997. *Making Ends Meet: How Single Mothers Survive Welfare and Low-Wage Work.* New York: Russell Sage.

Ehrenreich, Barbara. 2001. *Nickel and Dimed: On (Not) Getting by in America.* New York: Henry Holt.

Ellen, Ingrid Gould. 2000. *Sharing America's Neighborhoods: Prospects for Stable Racial Integration.* Harvard University Press.

Fisher, Roger, and William Ury. 1991. *Getting to Yes: Negotiating Agreement without Giving In.* 2d ed. New York: Penguin Books.

Galster, George C. 1990. "Federal Fair Housing Policy: The Great Misapprehension." In *Building Foundations: Housing and Federal Policy,* edited by Denise DiPasquale and Langley C. Keyes, pp. 137–56. University of Pennsylvania Press.

Galster, George C., and Erin Godfrey. 2003. "By Words and Deeds: Racial Steering by Real Estate Agents in the U.S. in 2000." Population Studies Center, University of Michigan. Paper prepared for the Urban Affairs Association annual meeting, Cleveland, March.

Glaeser, Edward L., and Joseph Gyourko. 2002. "Zoning's Steep Price." *Regulation* (Fall): 24–30.

Goetz, Edward. 1993. *Shelter Burden: Local Politics and Progressive Housing Policy.* Temple University Press.

———. 2003. *Clearing the Way: Deconcentrating the Poor in Urban America.* Washington: Urban Institute.

Goetz, Edward, and Mara Sidney. 1994. "Revenge of the Property Owners: Community Development and the Politics of Property." *Journal of Urban Affairs* 10, no. 4: 319–34.

Guinier, Lani, and Gerald Torres. 2002. *The Miner's Canary.* Harvard University Press.

Haar, Charles. 1996. *Suburbs under Siege: Race, Space, and Audacious Judges.* Princeton University Press.

Joint Center for Housing Studies. 2003. *State of the Nation's Housing.* Harvard University.

Keyes, Langley C., and Denise DiPasquale. 1990. "Housing Policy for the 1990s." In *Building Foundations: Housing and Federal Policy,* edited by Denise DiPasquale and Langley C. Keyes, pp. 1–24. University of Pennsylvania Press.

Kirp, David. 2001. *Almost Home: America's Love-Hate Relationship with Community.* Princeton University Press.

Logan, John, and Harvey Molotch. 1987. *Urban Fortunes: The Political Economy of Place.* University of California Press.

Massey, Douglas S., and Nancy A. Denton. 1993. *American Apartheid: Segregation and the Making of the Underclass.* Harvard University Press.

Meck, Stuart, ed. 2002. *Growing Smart Legislative Guidebook.* Chicago. American Planning Association.

Meck, Stuart, Rebecca Retzlaff, and James Schwab. 2003. *Regional Approaches to Affordable Housing.* Planning Advisory Service Report 513/514. Chicago: American Planning Association.

Mitchell, James L. 2004. "Will Empowering Developers to Challenge Exclusionary Zoning Increase Suburban Housing Choice?" *Journal of Policy Analysis and Management* 23, no. 1: 119–34.

National Low Income Housing Coalition. 2003. *Out of Reach: America's Housing Wage Climbs*. Washington.

Newman, Sandra J., and Ann B. Schnare. 1997. "'And a Suitable Living Environment': The Failure of Housing Programs to Deliver Neighborhood Quality." *Housing Policy Debate* 8, no. 4: 703–41.

Nivola, Pietro S. 1999. *Laws of the Landscape: How Policies Shape Cities in Europe and America*. Brookings.

Nyden, Philip, Michael Maly, and John Lukehart. 1997. "The Emergence of Stable, Racially and Ethnically Diverse Urban Communities: A Case Study of Nine U.S. Cities." *Housing Policy Debate* 8, no. 2: 491–534.

Orfield, Myron. 2002. *American Metropolitics: The New Suburban Reality.* Brookings.

Quigley, John M., and Steven Raphael. 2004. "Is Housing Unaffordable? Why Isn't It More Affordable?" *Journal of Economic Perspectives* 18, no. 1: 191–214.

Report of the National Housing Task Force. 1988. U.S. Government Printing Office.

Report of the President's Commission on Housing. 1983. U.S. Government Printing Office.

Rusk, David. 1999. *Inside Game/Outside Game: Winning Strategies for Saving Urban America.* Brookings.

Sampson, Robert J., Jeffrey D. Morenoff, and Stephen Raudenbush. 2005. "Social Anatomy of Racial and Ethnic Disparities in Violence." *American Journal of Public Health* 95, no. 2: 224–32.

Savitch, H. V. 2002. "Encourage then Cope: Washington and the Sprawl Machine." In *Urban Sprawl: Causes, Consequences, and Policy Responses,* edited by Gregory D. Squires, pp. 141–64. Washington: Urban Institute.

Schelling, Thomas C. 1971. "Dynamic Models of Segregation." *Journal of Mathematical Sociology* 1: 143–86.

Sparrow, Malcolm K. 2000. *The Regulatory Craft: Controlling Risks, Solving Problems, and Managing Compliance.* Brookings.

Susskind, Lawrence, and Jeffrey Cruikshank. 1991. "Breaking the Impasse: Negotiation to Consensus." In *Confronting Regional Challenges: Approaches to LULUs, Growth, and Other Vexing Governance Problems,* edited by Joseph DiMento and LeRoy Graymer, pp. 31–54. Cambridge, Mass.: Lincoln Institute of Land Policy.

U.S. Department of Housing and Urban Development. 2005. "Why Not in Our Community? Removing Barriers to Affordable Housing." An update to the Report of the Advisory Commission on Regulatory Barriers to Affordable Housing. Office of Policy Development and Research.

Vale, Lawrence J. 2000. *From the Puritans to the Projects: Public Housing and Public Neighbors.* Harvard University Press.

Wolman, Harold, and others. 2002. "Testing the Orfield Hypothesis: Cities, Coalitions, and Influence within State Legislatures." Paper prepared for the annual meeting of the Urban Affairs Association, Boston, March.

Contributors

William Apgar
Harvard University

Judith Bell
PolicyLink

Angela Glover Blackwell
PolicyLink

Xavier de Souza Briggs
Massachusetts Institute of Technology

Allegra Calder
Harvard University

Karen Chapple
University of California–Berkeley

Camille Zubrinsky Charles
University of Pennsylvania

Mary K. Cunningham
Urban Institute

Casey J. Dawkins
Virginia Polytechnic Institute and State University

Stefanie DeLuca
Johns Hopkins University

Edward G. Goetz
University of Minnesota

John Goering
City University of New York

Gerrit J. Knaap
University of Maryland

Barbara Lukermann
University of Minnesota

Arthur C. Nelson
Virginia Polytechnic Institute and State University

Rolf Pendall
Cornell University

Susan J. Popkin
Urban Institute

James Rosenbaum
Northwestern University

Stephen L. Ross
University of Connecticut

Mara S. Sidney
Rutgers University

Philip D.Tegeler
Poverty and Race Research Action Council

Tammy Tuck
Northwestern University

Margery Austin Turner
Urban Institute

William Julius Wilson
Harvard University

Index